Fidel Castro

★

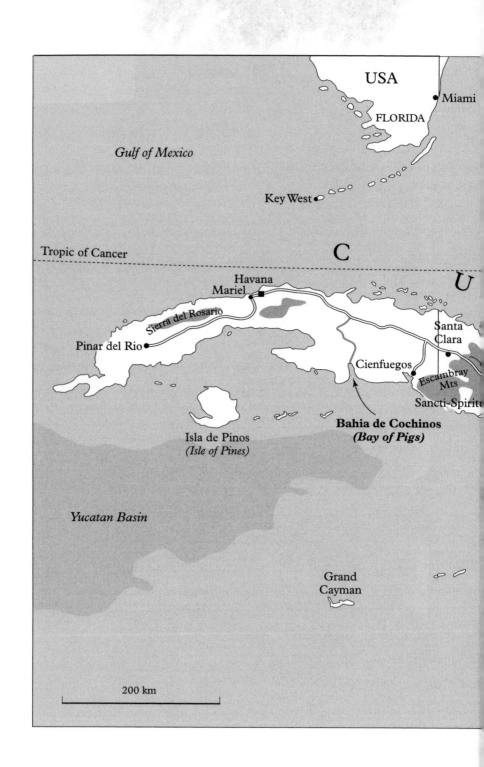

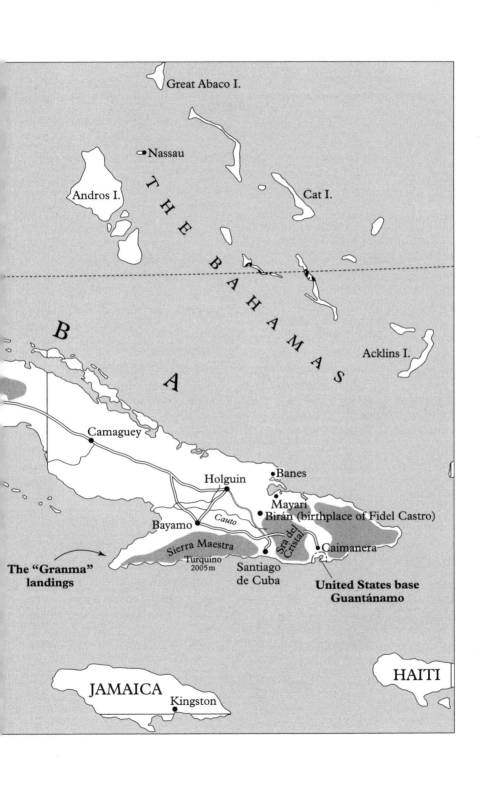

Great Abaco I.

Nassau

Andros I.

T H E B A H A M A S

Cat I.

Acklins I.

B

A

Camaguey

Holguin

Banes

Mayarí
Birán (birthplace of Fidel Castro)

Bayamo

Cauto

Sierra Maestra

Turquino
2005 m

Sra. del Cristal

Caimanera

**The "Granma"
landings**

Santiago
de Cuba

**United States base
Guantánamo**

JAMAICA

Kingston

HAITI

For Annette

Fidel Castro

★

A Biography

Volker Skierka

Translated by Patrick Camiller

polity

Copyright © this translation Polity Press 2004.
First published in Germany as *Fidel Castro: Eine Biographie*
© 2000 Kinder Verlag GmbH, Berlin.

First published in 2004 by Polity Press.
This edition published in 2006 by Polity Press.

Polity Press
65 Bridge Street
Cambridge CB2 1UR, UK

Polity Press
350 Main Street
Malden, MA 02148, USA

A catalogue record for this book is available from the British Library.

ISBN-10: 0745630065
ISBN-13: 9780745630069
ISBN-10: 0745640818 (pb)
ISBN-13: 9780745640815 (pb)

Typeset in 11 on 13 pt Plantin
by Servis Filmsetting Ltd, Manchester
Printed and bound in Great Britain by
MPG Books, Bodmin, Cornwall
For further information on Polity, visit our website: www.polity.co.uk

Contents

Contents

Plates

A Note of Thanks

★

My interest in Fidel Castro, one of the most fascinating of all twentieth-century personalities, was first awakened in 1990, when I traveled from Havana to Santiago de Cuba and visited his remote and idyllic birthplace near Birán in eastern Cuba, only to be cordially but firmly sent on my way by men in uniform. The idea of this book eventually began to emerge after another trip to Cuba, for the weekly *Die Zeit* and the Berlin Deutschlandradio station, in connection with the papal visit in early 1998. It occurred to me then that there was virtually a US monopoly on reference material concerning Fidel Castro and the Cuban Revolution. Since much of the existing literature betrayed all manner of prejudices, and since there was growing interest in the subject in Europe, I therefore thought that the time had come to investigate the character and life of Fidel Castro within a European perspective.

Uwe Naumann enthused himself and myself for what was initially conceived as quite a small volume. It has since grown larger, and this too is thanks to Uwe Naumann. In his role as editor, he proved a patient yet demanding adviser and companion, one I could scarcely value more highly.

Nina Grabe from Hamburg did me a great service with her competent work on the bibliography and index, as well as her copy-editing of the text. The librarian Brigitte Waldeck and the Latin American expert Wolfgang Grenz, both from the Institut für Iberoamerika–Kunde in Hamburg, generously helped me locate a large amount of reference material. I would also like to make special mention of the unbureaucratic support given me by Frau

A Note of Thanks

Kmezik from the Political Archive of the Foreign Office in Berlin, Frau Sylvia Gräfe from the Stiftung Archiv und Massenorganisationen der DDR at the German Federal Archives, and the specialists responsible for the papers of the former East German State Security. Numerous people with whom I had contact during my trips to Cuba were also of great assistance. Although I lacked support in official quarters, I was able to gain access in other ways to invaluable source material. I should also stress, however, that the Cuban embassy in Berlin made considerable efforts to supply me with up-to-date material and to help organize my trips to Cuba. Dr Georg Treffz and Dr Reinhold Huber, former ambassadors in Havana of the Federal Republic of Germany, gave me a great deal of advice and practical support at every level.

I am exceptionally grateful to Jürgen Meier-Beer, whose critical advice, as the first reader of the manuscript, helped me decisively in completing the final draft. I am glad that Susanne Gratius from the Institut für Iberoamerika–Kunde in Hamburg took the trouble to go through the galleys. I shall never forget the critical companionship and advice of numerous friends, and would like to thank them all in singling out Wilhelm Wiegreffe and Axel Schmidt-Gödelitz from our "Gödelitz Rambling Society."

My greatest thanks, however, are due to my family: to my wife Annette for her always intelligent, stimulating and encouraging companionship in the course of the project, and to our two daughters Antonia-Sophie and Isabel-Marie for their loving patience and forbearance.

Volker Skierka

Acknowledgments

The author and publisher would like to thank the following for permission to reproduce illustrations:

National Archives and Records Administration, College Park, Maryland: 1
Volker Skierka, Hamburg: 2
From Alina Fernández, *Ich, Alina. Mein Leben als Fidel Castros Tochter*, Reinbek 1999: 3, 4, 8
Ullstein Bilderdienst, Berlin: 5, 6, 10, 14, 15, 16, 21, 25
Deutsche Presse-Agentur, Hamburg, photo archive: 7, 9, 11, 12, 13, 17, 18, 19, 20, 23, 24, 26
Kristina Eriksson, Berlin: 22

The author and publishers would also like to thank the following for permission to reproduce copyright material:

Farrar, Straus and Giroux, LLC for Herberto Padilla, "Instructions for Joining a New Society," from *A Fountain, A House of Stone: Poems* by Herberto Padilla, translated by Alastair Reid and Alexander Coleman. Translation copyright © 1991 by Alastair Reid and Alexander Coleman.

Every effort has been made to trace the copyright holders, but if any have been inadvertently overlooked, the publishers will be pleased to make the necessary arrangements at the first opportunity.

Preface to the English Edition

★

It is not easy to write the biography of a still living figure from contemporary history, especially when, like Fidel Castro, he still guides the fate of his country with unbroken authority. No cooperation was received, nor indeed to be expected, from the Cuban revolutionary leader. But that also had its advantages, since it meant that he did not make the slightest attempt to influence the content or even express any wish to give it the kind of imprimatur that usually harms a book's credibility. My first close personal encounter with my subject occurred only in February 2002 in Havana, a year after publication of the first German edition. However, I received cooperation from the presidential offices during the filming of a documentary on Castro for German television when the film crew was supported by Castro's own cameraman, Roberto Chile, with excellent material. (A version of this documentary is available in English from Parthenon Entertainment Ltd., London/UK; www.pathenonentertainment.com).

Although Castro was in no way an open promoter of this development of a new Latin American left-wing populism and nationalism, he unexpectedly became the beneficiary of it. Thus in 2002, when an opposition group took the bold initiative of collecting signatures in favor of greater political openness, reforms, and free elections, he simply had the socialist form of state hammered into the Constitution as irreversible, at a time when three-quarters of the population of 11 million or more had been born since the victory of the revolution in 1959.

The highly individual, socialist-nationalist "*fidelista*" system, whose development was not at all to Moscow's liking, persisted into the new millennium as the most stable conception of anticapitalism since World War II – even though it showed some cracks and was crumbling at the edges, and even though it was increasingly doubtful whether Castro's charisma and historical authority would long survive him. As it happened, the aging Castro, who seemed more and more isolated in his Palacio de la Revolución, gained new popularity during the last decade of the old and the first decade of the new century, as shown in elections where the political pendulum in Latin America swung back to the political left, following failed neoliberal politics in the US backyard. Although Castro was in no way an open promoter, he unexpectedly he became the beneficiary of this development of a new Latin American left-wing populism and nationalism. Castro gained new respect as the world's longest-serving head of government against the will of Washington, and despite numerous assassination attempts he has outlasted nearly all his opponents, as well as their successors. This did not mean that all of Castro's new left or left-liberal colleagues would identify themselves with his "fidelista-system" in the way that Venezuela's Hugo Chávez does. But they demonstrated real respect for his lifetime struggle and survival.

For all its exemplary achievements in social and educational policy and in speaking up for the interests of the Third World, Cuba's political system did not appear in the eyes of the First World to meet the standards of a pluralist society. Yet the European countries, which had become indispensable economic partners for Cuba, made considerable efforts to reach a *modus vivendi* with the regime. Whereas the USA since the early sixties pursued an absurd embargo and thereby strengthened Castro's system – the opposite of its intended result – most countries of the Old World plus Canada wagered on "gradual change through rapprochement," especially after the collapse of Communism in Eastern Europe and the Soviet withdrawal from Cuba; this was supposed, even in a period of growing economic problems, to open a way out of the isolation inflicted on Cuba by itself and by others. The EU thereby showed a greater awareness of its responsibility to the Cuban people than did the successive governments in Washington.

In fact, after decades of fruitless debate, the United States still has no convincing idea for a post-Castro Cuba – except to follow the unwritten US doctrine that any policies, whether democratic or dictatorial, have to accord with the economic policies and interests of the United States. As a result, US policy on Cuba is hypocritical. The cry for democracy in Cuba (as elsewhere) is nothing more than an alibi for their efforts to dominate that island again, even though this would destroy the exemplary social achievements of the Castro era – achievements which could instead be transformed into a model for the Third World, where educational and social development are needed. This is clearly the situation as evidenced by other examples. The main interest underpinning Washington's Cuban policy is that of regaining economic dominance on this island over the interests of European and other competitors, such as Canada. The proof for this suspicion can be found in history and in the present US policy towards, for example, China, as well as towards the wider Middle East and the Caucasian region. There the fight for democracy quickly became a mission impossible, and seems to have moved from the top to the end of the political agenda, since it became clear that such a policy would harm huge US business interests in the fields of energy and trade. And there are more indications of hypocritical policy regarding Cuba: while the US officially continues its embargo policy, for years hundreds of US business people, and even Republican politicians, have been visiting the island to establish future contacts. Some results can already be seen in the delivery of food and medicine to Cuba from the US, worth around 500 million US dollars per year, requiring payment by cash in advance of delivery. No Helms-Barton law blocks this trade because it sails under the flag of humanitarian aid and is therefore exempt.

In May 2002 Nobel prizewinner Jimmy Carter finally attempted to break down the rigid US posture towards Cuba, becoming the first (former) US president since Calvin Coolidge in 1928 to make a trip of several days to the island. Hopes began to grow for an easing of internal and external tensions when Castro, as a kind of welcoming gift, ordered the release of prominent dissident Vladimiro Roca two months before the end of his five-year sentence. Moreover, like Pope John Paul II in 1998, Carter was able to criticize the lack of civil liberties and to argue for democratic reforms, in a Spanish-language speech at Havana University that was broadcast uncensored on Cuban state television. After the revolution of 1959, he complained, Cuba "adopted a socialist government where . . . people are not permitted to organize any opposition movements." Its "constitution recognizes freedom of speech and association, but other laws deny these freedoms to those who disagree with the government." While also criticizing the human rights situation in the United States, where the death penalty was applied much more harshly than in Cuba, Carter advised the Cuban government, as a gesture of good will, to accept the demand of the Geneva-based UN Commission on Human Rights for an observer to be allowed into the country.[1]

In a discussion afterwards, the visitor even referred to the "Varela Project" (named after a Catholic priest from the nineteenth-century independence struggle), a petition for greater civil liberties that had been submitted to the National Assembly together with a list of 11,000 signatures, about which the Cuban media had maintained almost total silence. Carter praised Osvaldo Payá's initiative in using a right granted to citizens under the Constitution to propose new legislation, which amounted to a demand for freedom of association, speech and publication, an amnesty for political prisoners, permission for private enterprise, free choice of occupation, and a new election law. In December 2002 Payá, a member of the oppositional Christian Liberation Movement, was awarded the EU Parliament's Andrei Sakharov Prize for Freedom of Thought at a ceremony in Strasbourg. The Cuban government naturally countered by organizing its own collection of signatures, in which 98.9 percent of people on the electoral register were officially reported to have declared that the country's economic, political, and social system was "inviolable." This laid the basis for a decision a few days later by the Cuban Parliament to make socialism an irreversible part of the Constitution. But, although this "neutralized" the main thrust of the "Varela Project" at the time of Carter's visit, the fact that the government had not prevented the collection of signatures raised hopes that greater tolerance would be shown towards critics of the regime. "When Cubans exercise this freedom to change laws peacefully by a direct vote," Carter suggested, "the world will see that Cubans, and not foreigners, will decide the future of this country."[2]

But there is a problem which makes this appear to be wishful thinking. Even with Castro passing his eighties, there is no opposition which can be taken as a serious alternative to the well-organized Communist government – not in Florida or Spain or in Cuba itself. There is no leader or utopian political alternative at hand to offer the Cuban people a better future than the one designed by Castro and his fellows. For half a century opposition in Cuba and from outside lamented every mistake of the past without offering an alternative. Even the poison of political hatred has failed to provide a viable alternative to Castro's policies, or any hope for a different future. No political alternative ahs been proposed by either Miami or Cuba itself.

Like the Pope before him, Carter also criticized US policy towards Cuba and called on Washington to abandon an attitude that had borne no fruit for more than 40 years. "It is time for us to change our relationship. . . . Because the United States is the most powerful nation, we should take the first step. First, my hope is that Congress will soon act to permit unrestricted travel . . . and to repeal the embargo."[3] But Carter's appeal was hardly likely to be taken up: the Bush family is traditionally linked to Castro's most violent opponents in the United States, and the president's brother, Florida Governor Jeb Bush, has long had the closest of contacts with militant Cuban exile circles such as those headed by old Bush cronies like Orlando Bosh and Luis Posada Carriles, who are held responsible for such incidents as the bombing of a Cuban jetliner during take-off at Barbados in 1976, which caused the death of all 76 mostly young Cuban athletes on board.

In a move designed not least to take the wind out of Carter's sails, the White House immediately announced that it intended to step up the economic pressure on Cuba and to increase its political isolation. Already, after the terrorist attacks of September 11, 2001, Cuba had been bracketed together with Taliban-style "rogue states" and Saddam Hussein's Iraq. And, before Carter left for Havana, a top State Department official had raised the stakes by spreading the rumor that Castro was developing biological weapons. No evidence, even fabricated or "sexed up," could be produced for such an allegation; Castro even invited Carter to have inspections carried out by experts on weapons for mass destruction. In the end, both Defense Secretary Donald Rumsfeld and Secretary of State Colin Powell could do nothing other than dissociate themselves from the claim.

But it is hard to imagine how even a fair-minded former president like Carter can be taken seriously if an administration like Bush's maintains a prison camp such as the one located on Cuban soil at the disputed US naval base in Guantánamo Bay in Eastern Cuba. Here the US Government has imprisoned for years hundreds of terror suspects, or so-called "enemy combatants," from Afghanistan with no chance of either a fair trial or the right to defense, even ignoring charges by international institutions concerning the use of torture to gain confessions or information. This has created a paradoxical situation, whereby Castro – always heavily criticized for his human rights record – grants his "prisoners" more rights and social contact with their families and lawyers than are permitted by the democracy fighters of Bush's war on terror.

The extent to which Castro, with his lifelong consistency, can be a bearer of hope for people in Latin America and the Third World was once more demonstrated during his 48-hour visit to Buenos Aires in May 2002 to attend the inauguration of Argentina's newly elected president, Néstor Kirchner. The trip to the homeland of his old comrade-in-arms, Che Guevara, turned into a triumphal march. The media vied with one another in reporting the visit, so that behind the scenes the generals began to murmur about the new president and had to be called to order by him. Kirchner seemed as surprised as Castro. Thus, when the news spread that the Máximo Líder intended to give a speech to 800 invited guests in the great hall of the law faculty, tens of thousands of people hurried to turn up there, bringing the city center to a halt and almost making it impossible for Castro himself to get through. In the end, the event had to take place several hours late and in the open air, spontaneously broadcast live on radio and television. Castro temporarily put in the shade not only President Kirchner but also two other guests present in Buenos Aires: Brazil's new and popular president, Lula da Silva, and the despotic Venezuelan leader and friend of Castro's, Hugo Chávez. After several decades, and in an age when ticker-tape welcomes are a thing of the past because the streets can no longer be lined with enough people, Castro alone can still attract a large enough crowd even on a trip abroad. All he has to do is let himself be seen – his long, tiring speeches notwithstanding. The trip to Argentina and later to Brazil and Caracas, combined with the visits of his new friends within the Latin American hemisphere to Havana, took place at a time when the world political situation and the battered international reputation of the Bush administration had to some extent made the climate in Latin America more friendly to Castro. At a time when security and familiar bearings were increasingly being taken away from people, especially in the Third World, Castro again suddenly came through as a man who had remained true to himself and whose astute analyses and criticisms somehow struck many as well-grounded – even if things were more complicated than he made them out to be. Has not the neoliberal economic policy ordered by the World Bank and the International Monetary Fund, which was supposed to bring Latin America higher growth and greater economic and political stability, ultimately had the effect of making the rich richer and the poor poorer? After the bacchanal of privatization, which often mainly enriched the privatizers and their cronies, are not Argentina and many other countries now left with empty coffers to pick up the pieces? Everywhere people are seething, because the clever prescriptions ordered by the First World are having no effect. For a long time there has been a new leftward tendency in these countries. The election of the left-wing workers' leader and friend of Castro's, Lula da Silva, to the Brazilian presidency is one expression of this trend, as was that of Hugo Chávez in Venezuela or of Evo Morales in Bolivia. Peru avoided a leftist president by only a narrow margin, while the majority in parliament was won by the left. In Chile a female socialist candidate won clearly against the right and the people of Mexico and Central America are switching to the left too. If conservatives win, they win only by luck.

The US-backed "Plan Colombia," with its large dollar resources to stem the drugs trade and the limitless violence in

Colombia, has all but broken down. Central America is facing complete economic bankruptcy. Many grand promises and hopes that Washington offered these countries through long years of civil war to keep them politically compliant have come to nothing. Even well-disposed Latin Americans therefore thought it simply grotesque when the government of Bush, Jr, asked for trouble by appointing as top officials on Latin American policy 'old school' militants who were anything but-diplomatic, many of them well-known in connection with the US-funded contra mercenaries in Central America. Sure enough, these premonitions were confirmed when it became clear that the US embassy in Caracas had been mixed up in an attempted putsch by pro-US economic circles against the undoubtedly autocratic and, even inside Venezuela, rather unappealing President Chávez – an adventure that failed because of the amateurish way in which the *coup d'état* had been prepared. And the only result had been an even closer cooperation between Cuba and Venezuela. By 2006 Cuba had already stationed around 45,000 teachers, doctors, military and policial advisers in Venezuela in exchange for oil and other products to guarantee the survival of the Cuban economy. Even Chávez' bodyguards have been sent from the Cuban secret service to guarantee the survival of Castro's friend in Caracas, who appears as the heir of Simon Bolivar from Caracas, the Liberator of South America.

Relations with the European Union, culminating after long negotiations in the opening of an EU mission in Havana in 2003, could not have worked out better. But perhaps everything went too well, perhaps everything was too friendly and free of conflict. In a pattern familiar from Moscow, any political spring in Cuba has been followed in the past by a sudden return of the ice – in order to maintain an ideological distance and to prevent a flagging of principles. And, this time too, there was a startling change of direction, at once disturbing and difficult to understand. In March 2003, no sooner had the world's attention been diverted by the first American air raids on Baghdad than it was reported in the press that 75 oppositional journalists, writers, librarians, and other intellectuals had been arrested in Cuba. Within little more than two weeks, they were convicted as "mercenaries in the service of the

Empire" (that is, the United States) and sentenced to terms of 10 to 26 years in prison, which were immediately confirmed by the relevant courts of appeal. A total of 1,454 years imprisonment, as the *Neue Zürcher Zeitung* pointed out. A few days later, death sentences were carried out on three men who, in another brief trial, had been convicted of attempting to divert a ferry with 50 passengers from Havana to Miami. (A unit of Cuban special forces had intervened to end the hijacking.) The execution of these draconian sentences was a source of consternation, especially for those in the international community and human rights organizations, who for some time had thought that the Cuban state was willing to deal more leniently with critics and to forego applying the death penalty. Recent condemnations of Cuba by these institutions have turned out to be correspondingly moderate. The European Union, in particular, was largely agreed that Havana did not actually need to resort to such measures, because the people in question did not pose any real danger to the system and the government. Criticism poured in from all sides, including from people friendly or generally well-disposed to the regime. Many deplored what had been done, seeing it as an expression not of strength but of weakness and lack of confidence. Those who, against strong resistance, had managed to break down aversions abroad and to promote a rapprochement with Cuba now saw themselves as having been duped and robbed of the fruits of their patient, well-meaning labor.

Castro could not have given the United States a better present. The Bush administration immediately announced a further intensification of sanctions, and the EU scarcely had any choice but to react accordingly. But economic sanctions, on the other hand, were explicitly ruled out. These altogether moderate reactions, necessary for the EU to save face, sparked a furious reaction in Havana. A crowd of hundreds of thousands, headed by Castro himself, marched to protest against the measures in front of the embassies of EU countries (most notably, Spain and Italy). The EU's decision to include dissidents on embassy guest lists so infuriated the Cuban leadership that it announced for its part that it would not send government representatives to any official event to which critics of the regime had also been invited. The disproportionate Cuban response during this period, against internal opponents as well as criticism from outside, started a guessing-game as to whether something more might lie behind it. There was even hushed speculation that dramatic events might be in the offing, and that the Cuban leadership was trying to intimidate or lock away critics of the regime as a precautionary measure. Again and again there have been rumors of this kind, including the whispers of crystal-ball gazers that Castro might soon hand over his official duties to a successor before retiring into old age as the superintendent father of the revolution.

It is possible that more was involved than one was initially prepared to believe. After all, Cuba could not afford the conflict with the European Union, either politically or economically; and closure of the EU mission in Havana, which was also within the realm of possibility, would have caused almost irreparable longterm damage. Or was the Cuban behavior simply provoked by covert action on the part of the "arch-enemy," going beyond the bounds of the acceptable? There was much evidence of such activity: diplomatic and journalistic circles were increasingly speaking of provocations by the US mission in Havana, which had gone far beyond what was customary in international diplomacy, with the intention of sooner or later forcing the Cubans to respond. Wayne Smith, a Cuba expert who had himself been head of the Interests Section in Havana during the Carter era, seemed to share this view. Although he too deplored the Cuban reaction and evidently considered it overdone, he wrote in an article that appeared in *The Nation* on May 12, 2003:

Why the crackdown? In part, it was a reaction to growing provocations on the part of the Bush Administration, which had ordered the new chief of the US Interests Section, James Cason, to hold a series of high-profile meetings with dissidents, even including seminars in his own residence in Havana. Given that Cason's announced purpose was to promote "transition to a participatory form of government," the Cubans came to see the meetings as subversive in nature and as highly provocative. And, in fairness, let us imagine the reaction of the Attorney General and the Director of Homeland Security if the chief of the Cuban Interests Section in Washington was holding meetings with disgruntled Americans and announcing

that the purpose was to bring about a form of government – a socialist government – in the United States. He would have been asked to
leave the country.

Smith also referred to the character of US propaganda over the
previous months, in which Cuba, without any supporting evidence, had been labeled part of the "axis of evil."

Nevertheless, Cuba's harsh response landed it in the same
dead-end as in previous decades and the diplomatic and political
consequences lasted for years and years. Familiar low-level provocations were met with knee-jerk reactions that betrayed a lack of
self-confidence and command of the situation, as well as threatening to forfeit the sympathy of well-wishers. In any event, it would
harm the cause of dissidents to allow oneself unthinkingly to be
used for the aims of a US government which, not for the first time,
has played a cynical game with innocently trusting critics of the
regime and, together with the Cuban state apparatus, turned them
into martyrs. In this connection Osvaldo Payá, who has been left
untouched by the Cuban authorities, stressed in his criticism of the
arrests and jail sentences that he rejected any US financial support
for Cuban dissidents. And so, the wheel turned full circle insofar
as things were the same as before. David against Goliath. While the
Europeans to a large extent (including on the issue of dissidents)
hoped for "change through rapprochement," and while the
Americans fine-tuned an embargo that could hardly be tuned any
further, Castro soldiered on largely unimpressed by all the hostility shown towards him, in the hope that posterity would reward
him for an ascetic life devoted to the revolution. And, as he had
repeatedly demonstrated with success before, so too in his anniversary year he gave proof of his continuing power and understanding of the right course to be maintained by the Cuban revolution.
His reshuffling of the polit bureau involved criticizing and firing
key political figures, including ministers and old friends, all under
suspicion of corruption, arrogance, and abuse of power. One of
them was Juan Carlos Robinson Agramonte, the party chief of
Castro's home province of Santiago de Cuba and Guantánamo, a
young man in his forties and representative of the black Cuban
population. In a special session of the polit bureau Castro person-

ally stripped him of his powers and duties. In June a court sentenced the man to a 12-year imprisonment, without announcing details of the charges. This act was aimed at demonstrating once more the unchallenged power of the Máximo Líder and his unbroken will to continue until his last gasp.

And what happens next? Nobody really knows. There is lot of speculation. Castro himself has confirmed repeatedly that his brother Raúl will follow him. Interestingly, sanctioned by Fidel, some years ago Raúl set up some secret meetings between retired American Generals – members of the Center for Defense Information, a military think-tank – and Cuban military counterparts in Havana to discuss future relations. As Frank O. Mora, a specialist on Cuban affairs from Memphis, Tennessee, wrote in an article puvblished in 2002, on the American side their meetings were aimed at calming down Cuban apprehensions of an American invasion after Fidel Castro's death, while the interest of the Cubans lay in checking out possibilities for a rapprochement.

Even in the event of Raúl Castro being too old for takeover, the succession is arranged within the party's ranks, Castro told the French journalist Ignacio Ramonet in 2006. As in the nineties, so too during the first decade of the new millennium the obvious candidates for the takeover of power after Castro's departure appear to be Carlos Lage, the Vice-Prime Minister and creator of the independent new socialist Cuban economy after the breakdown of the Soviet imperium, Felipe Pérez Roque, the foreign ministers, Ricardo Alarcón, the long-time president of the national assembly, and other long-serving ministers. The problem might not be how the Cubans handle the transition of power to a succeeding generation, but rather how the European Union, with its large investment in Cuba, and the United States, wanting to regain its old investment and expand its influence by creating new investment in post-Castro Cuba, will react. There appears to be no blueprint or guideline held by either Washington or Brussels for the actual event. But one thing seems to be clear: all dealings will still be with the Communist Party. The only "reform" to be expected in future could be the development of a Chinese-style economic model. Every alternative based on force and violence bears the risk of a total breakdown, with the consequent total loss of assets, bloodshed, and revenge. Reason has to be promoted as the only alternative to gain survival, peace, and freedom.

And Castro? How will future generations judge his time? "History will absolve me," he confidently asserted in October 1953, when he was sentenced for the attack on the Moncada Barracks. It remains to be seen whether it will absolve him. But, with or without absolution, one thing is certain: he will go down in history as one of the few revolutionaries who remained true to his principles.

Volker Skierka

1

The Heroic Myth

"One thing is certain: wherever he may be, however and with whomever, Fidel Castro is there to win. I do not think anyone in this world could be a worse loser. His attitude in the face of defeat, even in the slightest events of daily life, seems to obey a private logic: he will not even admit it, and he does not have a moment's peace until he manages to invert the terms and turn it into a victory."[1] The man who wrote these words is the writer Gabriel García Márquez, a longstanding friend of the Máximo Líder. They give us some idea of what may have driven Fidel Castro for more than half a century to outlast his various enemies, opponents and critical friends: namely, a wish to be proved right, to be morally as well as politically victorious. No self-doubt: "his" Cuba for the Cubans! The final verdict on his "mission" would rest with history alone – although Castro also tried from the beginning to keep the last word for himself and to anticipate the verdict of history. In 1953, at his trial for the abortive attack on the Moncada Barracks in Santiago de Cuba which launched his career as a professional revolutionary, he concluded his famous defense plea with the certainty: "History will absolve me!" For García Márquez, "he is one of the great idealists of our time, and perhaps this may be his greatest virtue, although it has also been his greatest danger."[2] Yet an even greater danger has always been lurking in the background: the danger of isolation. For only in isolation is there no possibility of contradiction.

With an iron will Castro has survived generations of American presidents, Soviet general secretaries, international leaders of states and governments, democrats and potentates, until he has become by far the longest-ruling "number one" of the twentieth century and one of the most interesting figures of contemporary history. Bearded, always dressed in his green uniform, a hero and object of hate in one: this is how the world knows him. Against no one else are so many murder plots supposed to have been hatched. Leaders who are so unyielding, so "unpolitical" in their refusal to compromise, do not usually survive for long in that part of the world; they tend to be overthrown or killed. The fact that Castro is still alive is little short of a miracle. It is due to the alliance of his own well-trained instinct with a ubiquitous security apparatus that is considered among the most efficient in the world. From soon after his twentieth birthday Castro had assassins and con-spirators on his trail: political gangsters at Havana University in the late 1940s, henchmen of the dictator Fulgencio Batista, traitors in his own ranks, big landowners evicted during the Castroite revolution in 1959, Cuban exiles in Florida working hand in hand with the CIA and the Mafia. Their bosses, most notably the legendary Meyer Lansky, lost a fortune estimated at more than US$100 million in hotels, clubs, casinos, brothels and other such establishments – a good tenth of the value of US assets taken over by the Cuban state. That a stubborn farmer's son from the underdeveloped east of the island simply came and took away this lucrative paradise and sink of iniquity from the fine, upstanding United States; that he went on to humiliate the "Yankees" and President Kennedy in the eyes of the world when they attempted an invasion with exiled Cuban mercenaries in 1961 at the Bay of Pigs; that Soviet nuclear missiles installed for his sake in Cuba nearly led in 1962 to a third world war – these deep narcissistic wounds will never be forgiven, even after his death, by the great power to the north.

There are scarcely any photos that show Castro laughing. Yet the Cubans are a spirited people full of *joie de vivre*. Gabriel García Márquez described Castro as "one of the rare Cubans who neither sing nor dance."[3] He is said to have a good sense of humor – but it is as if he has forbidden himself any public display of laughter or pleasure. Such things are secret, and it is a state secret whether there is a private Castro behind the political Castro.

Information about himself and his family is filtered for public consumption, becoming partly contradictory or inaccurate. On the whole, then, not much can be gleaned about his personal life. We know that his marriage came to an early end, that he had a few passionate affairs such as those with Natalia Revuelta (once the most captivating woman in Havana) and Marita Lorenz (a German captain's beautiful daughter who was later contracted by the CIA to assassinate him). He has one son from his marriage, Fidelito, a nuclear scientist with a doctorate, as well as several children born out of wedlock and a host of grandchildren. In each case, so it is said, he is a kind yet strict father or grandfather – yet Alina, his daughter by Natalia Revuelta, keeps tormenting him with her hatred. It is well known that Castro likes to go swimming and diving; that he enjoys baseball, sleeps little and has a mania for working at night; that he had to give up smoking cigars for health reasons; that he lives an ascetic existence with few material demands, but is fond of ice cream and likes to cook spaghetti for himself. When García Márquez once found him in a melancholic mood and asked what he would most like to do at that moment, Castro astonished his friend with the answer: "Just hang around on some street corner."[4] Did he ever think that perhaps he ought to have become a baseball player? He certainly had the opportunity. For in his student days, he was such a good pitcher that the New York Giants offered him a professional contract. Had he accepted, part of world history would have taken a different course.

Instead, this son of a big landowner from eastern Cuba felt called to lead a handful of comrades – including the Argentinean Che Guevara, later deified as a pop icon of the sixties generation – in a movement to bring down the dictator Batista. Since 1959 Castro has ruled his people like a large family, with the stern hand of a patriarch. The whole island is his "latifundium." He wants to be seen not as its owner, however, but as its trustee. Under his rule, sweeping reforms have made Cuba's health and education systems unparalleled in Latin America and beyond; and for the first time Cubans have been able to develop a national identity, even maintaining it through a period of political and economic dependence upon the Soviet Union. These achievements, and not just the ever-present straitjacket of state security, may be one of the reasons why Castro's system has been able to last so long despite its lack of democratic and material freedoms. For decades now the majority of Cubans have lived with a split mentality: on the one hand, a love–hate relationship with the United States and a longing for the life conjured up by the glitter of Western globalization; on the other hand, admiration and respect for Fidel as their patron even in times of greatest hardship.

Although Fidel Castro seems to have taken more after his father, we should not underestimate the influence that his mother's strict Catholicism and his long years at a Jesuit boarding school had upon his essential character. It is no accident that he has repeatedly drawn parallels between early Christianity and his understanding of socialism, even if he has long been in conflict with the official Church. In this way, he has over the years developed an "ideology" of his own that involves more than just the adoption of Soviet-style Communism. His Caribbean model of socialism is "Castroism," or, as Cubans say, "Fidelism" – a pragmatic mixture of a little Marx, Engels and Lenin, slightly more Che Guevara, a lot of José Martí, and a great deal indeed of Fidel Castro. Martí was the Cuban fighter who, in the late nineteenth century, launched the decisive struggle for the country's independence from Spain; Castro identified with him from early youth and always saw himself in the role of his heir and descendant. "He knows the 28 volumes of Martí's work thoroughly," writes García Márquez, "and has had the talent to incorporate his ideas into the bloodstream of a Marxist revolution."[5] Martí, who was killed in the early months of war in 1895, was spared from seeing how the United States eventually intervened and, after the Spanish defeat in 1898, established its own dominance over the island. But on the day he died, he wrote with great concern to a friend: "Belittlement by a mighty neighbor who does not really know us is the worst danger for our American continent."[6] Precisely this is the deeper cause of the Cuban–American and indeed the Latin American dilemma, and it will remain such after Castro himself has departed from the scene.

2

The Young Fidel

★

Among Jesuits

The name of the Cuban citizen Fidel Castro first entered the White House files in 1940. On November 6 of that year the young boarder at the Jesuit Dolores College in Santiago de Cuba sent a three-page letter to US President Franklin D. Roosevelt congratulating him on his re-election. Before signing off with a bold flourish, "Goodby Your friend," he added a personal request: "If you like, give me a ten dollars bill american, because I have not seen a ten dollars bill american and I would like to have one of them."[1] In the letter Castro stated that he was 12 years old – a claim which, if true, would have meant that he was two years younger than he is officially reported to be.[2] He received no reply from the president, only a letter of thanks from the State Department. Nor did it contain a ten-dollar bill. No one could then suspect that the boy would grow up and confiscate everything that the North Americans owned in Cuba.

At the very time when Fidel Castro was penning his lines to Roosevelt, the man who 12 years later would embody his enemy-image of an American lackey was making his debut as Cuban president: Fulgencio Batista y Zaldívar, the son of a mulatto worker from Banes, not far from Castro's own birthplace in Oriente province. Born in 1901, Batista had a reputation for being shifty, ruthless, and open to bribery. In 1933, after the fall of the dictator General Gerardo Machado, this former military stenographer had organized a revolt in a political arena already dominated by corruption and violence. At first he kept in the background, but as the American man he controlled the country's direction and advanced to become chief of the general staff. His path crossed with that of the Mafioso Meyer Lansky, and their friendship would later mark the political landscape.

In the space of seven years Batista got through seven puppet presidents, until no real alternative remained but to have himself elected to the highest state office. During the four years from 1940, he was Roosevelt's right-hand man on the sugar island, whose economy was completely dependent on the trickle from the United States. One of the members of the government coalition was the pro-Moscow Partido Socialista Popular (PSP) – a situation accepted by Washington in the context of wartime alliances. At that time Cuba had the most progressive Constitution in Latin America, even if important parts of it (such as the redistribution of land owned by US corporations) were not implemented. After a time-out lasting eight years, when the presidency was assumed by the equally corrupt Ramón Grau San Martín (1944–8) and Carlos Prío Socarrás (1948–52), Batista seized power on March 10, 1952, just before presidential elections were due to be held, and established a dictatorship that played into the hands both of his friends around Meyer Lansky and of the government in Washington. On January 1, 1959, he was finally overthrown and chased from the country by a young revolutionary called Fidel Castro.

Castro's origins had pointed to anything but a revolutionary career. "I was born into a family of landowners in comfortable circumstances. We were considered rich and treated as such. I was brought up with all the privileges attendant to a son in such a family. Everyone lavished attention on me, flattered, and treated me differently from the other boys we played with when we were children. These other children went barefoot while we wore shoes; they were often hungry; at our house, there was always a squabble at table to get us to eat."[3]

Information issued by the Cuban Council of State declares that the future revolutionary and head of state was born on August 13, 1926; he saw the light of day around two in the morning, weighing just under ten pounds.[4] According to his siblings,

Ángela and Ramón, he was already the third natural child of the 50-year-old landowner, Ángel Castro y Argiz, and his housekeeper and cook, Lina Ruz González (who was roughly half his age). Like his brother and sister, he was given the name of a saint, Fidel, and a middle name Alejandro. In fact, Fidel is derived from *fidelidad*, the Spanish word denoting faith or fidelity, loyalty and dependability. "In that case," he once said, "I'm completely in agreement with my name, in terms of fidelity and faith. Some have religious faith, and others have another kind. I've always been a man of faith, confidence and optimism."[5] In fact, "the origin of the name [wasn't] so idyllic. . . . I was called Fidel because of somebody who was going to be my godfather." This was Fidel Pino Santos, a friend of his father's, "something like the family banker. He was very rich, much richer than my father. People said he was a millionaire. . . . To be a millionaire in those days was something really tremendous. . . . That was a time when people used to earn a dollar or a peso a day."[6]

Relations in the family were pretty disastrous. María Luisa Argote, the wife with whom Fidel's father had two other children (Pedro Emilio and Lidia), seems to have left the home after Fidel was born, and the marriage was later dissolved. Ángel Castro eventually married his servant, who bore him four more children: Juana, Raúl, Emma, and Augustina. Their wedding ceremony – the year of which remains unclear – was performed by Enrique Pérez Serantes from Santiago de Cuba, a priest and friend who, like Ángel Castro and the parents of Lina Ruz, had originally come from Galicia in Spain. It was also he who baptized Fidel – but only when he was sent "at the age of five or six" to stay with a family in Santiago, where he received private lessons. Evidently the lack of a clear family relationship in connection with Fidel's birth was the real reason why the godfather became unavailable, and why the young boy had to wait so long for the Church's seal. Meanwhile, Fidel later recalled, "people called me a Jew. They used to say, 'He's a Jew.' I was four or five and was already being criticized. . . . I didn't know the meaning of the word *Jew*, but there was no doubt that it had a negative connotation, that it was something disgraceful. It was all because I hadn't been baptized, and I wasn't really to blame for that."[7] Since "my wealthy godfather hadn't materialized and the baptism hadn't been performed – I was around five years old and, as they said, a 'Jew' . . . – a solution had to be found for the problem. . . . One afternoon, they took me to the cathedral in Santiago de Cuba, [where] they sprinkled me with holy water and baptized me, and I became a normal citizen, the same as the rest."[8] Thus, religious prejudice exposed him to discrimination from which he continued to smart in later life, without at first really being able to pinpoint the circumstances that lay behind it. And in the end this helped to ensure that it was his foster-father – his teacher's sister's husband and Haitian Consul in Santiago – who agreed to take on the role of his godfather. It is not clear whether Fidel's real parents were even present at the baptism. Many years later the priest who performed the ceremony, by then Archbishop Pérez Serantes, is said to have saved Fidel's life when Batista's troops captured him soon after the abortive attack on the Moncada Barracks and wanted to make short work of him.[9] The man in the cassock also became an important link-man for Castro's revolutionary movement, but one day he grew disillusioned with the revolution and was even placed under arrest for a short period.

Castro's home, the "Finca Mañacas" (Palm Farm), nestles in the idyllic Nipe foothills of the Cristal mountains between Santiago de Cuba (the country's second-largest city) and the town of Mayarí, some 12 miles south of the Bay of Nipe. The old "royal road" passes nearby, on its 600-mile way to Havana at the other end of the island. The area, one of the most beautiful in Cuba, had in those days the reputation of a Wild West, where bandits and the armed "sheriffs" of the United Fruit Company imposed the rule of force. The old men from the Buena Vista Social Club made it known all over the world through their song "Chan Chan," which sold millions of CDs in the late 1990s. "Few places in Cuba," writes Hugh Thomas, "were quite so dominated by the North American presence."[10]

There, near the village of Birán, lay the Finca Mañacas sugarcane plantation, with its 800 hectares of freehold and another 10,000 hectares on leasehold, whose other main sources of income were livestock and timber, as well as a small nickel mine. On the shores of a small lake, half-surrounded by a palm grove, single-

and double-storey houses had been built on stilts in the Spanish Galician style; they are still preserved today as a kind of museum. The farm had its own post and telegraph office, a dairy, a general store, a baker's and butcher's shop, a workshop, a school, and a cock-fighting pit. Some "two hundred, perhaps three hundred" families, or "roughly a thousand people," most of them black Haitian laborers and their families working in the cane fields and woods, lived here under the sway of Fidel's father, in simple palm huts with bare clay floors.[11] "There wasn't a single church, not even a small chapel," although most of the people were Christian. "At that time, the farmers had all kinds of beliefs. They believed in God, in the saints . . . , in the Virgin. . . . They believed in Our Lady of Charity, Cuba's patron saint. . . . Many people also believed in spirits and ghosts."[12]

The area around Santiago de Cuba has always been a bastion of the Afro-Cuban religions and cults which African slaves brought with them in the form of their own gods and voodoo ceremonies, and they have reacted imaginatively to the constant attempts by the official Catholic Church to suppress the obscure mysticism of their so-called *santería*. Often they have simply mixed their African rituals together with Catholic doctrine and liturgy, taking over Christian saints and attaching them to their own gods or *orishas*, so that Changó, for example, has become Saint Barbara, or Saint Lazarus "Babalu Ayé." "I remember," Castro told Betto, "that, as a child, I heard stories about spirits, ghosts and apparitions. People believed in superstitions too. . . . For example, if a rooster crowed three times without getting an answer, that meant some tragedy might occur. If an owl flew over at night and you could hear the sound of his wings and his screech – I think they called it 'the owl's song' – that too was a harbinger of tragedy. . . . In that sense, the world I was born into was quite primitive, because there were all kind of beliefs and superstitions."[13]

Surrounded by nature and animals, the young Fidel Castro went hunting on horseback in the woods, swimming in the River Birán or skin-diving in the Bay of Nipe; his playmates were the workers' children. It was thus at an early age that he first came into contact with agriculture and social hardship, with the privation that ordinary people experienced during the periods between harvests. His own parents learned to read and write only late in life, and the family lifestyle was in keeping with their origins and the harsh environment.

> There, we lived among the people, the workers, . . . we even had animals under the house – the cows, pigs, chickens and all. I wasn't the grandson or great-grandson of a landowner. Sometimes the great-grandson of a landowner didn't have money anymore, but he kept the culture of the aristocratic or rich oligarchic class. Since my mother and father had been very poor farmers who managed to acquire some money and accumulate some wealth, my family didn't have the rich people's landowners' culture as yet. They were people who worked every day in harsh conditions. They had no social life and hardly any relations with people like themselves.[14]

Fidel's father was a tight-lipped, hard-working man, coarse and quick-tempered, quarrelsome and intolerant of contradiction – the very picture of a patriarch. Well-built and over 6 feet tall, always with a wide hat covering a bald head that his wife and daughters had to keep shaved and polished, he ruled the home and farm with a strict hand. Ángel Castro had been born on December 8, 1875, the son of a miner in the small village of San Pedro Láncara near Lugo in the bleak province of Galicia in North-West Spain, not far from the pilgrims' route to Santiago de Compostela. He first came to know the east of Cuba between 1895 and 1898, where he served as a cavalry quartermaster in the Spanish army during the Cuban war of independence. Since his only prospects back home were those of a day laborer, he returned to the island as an immigrant in 1905, at the age of 30, and worked first in the nickel mines near Santiago and then for the United Fruit Company. Later, he struck out independently (providing transport services for the Company, among other things) and eventually bought some land of his own, so that by 1920 he was already quite well-off. Hugh Thomas thinks that Ángel Castro must have worked very hard, but that "he hacked his farm out of forest, perhaps sometimes on moonless nights, perhaps by stealing title deeds."[15] According to Fidel, he was "a very active, enterprising person, and he had an instinctive sense of organization."[16] In 1950 his assets were estimated at half a million US dollars.

The mother was the balancing character in the family: she gave her children the closeness lacking in the father, and ensured that, from the early age of probably five, Fidel attended the village school at Maracané near Mayarí. His exceptionally good results soon persuaded the parents to send him to the provincial capital, Santiago de Cuba, where he was given private tuition by a black female teacher. "Those classes consisted of having me study the addition, subtraction, multiplication and division tables that were printed on the cover of my notebook. . . . I believe I learned them so well I've never forgotten them. Sometimes I calculate almost as quickly as a computer."[17] Castro later looked back: "Of all the people I knew, she was the first who was able to motivate me; she gave me a goal and aroused my ambition."[18]

When he was six-and-a-half or seven, he was sent to the "La Salle College" run by the Franciscan order of Marianist brothers in Santiago de Cuba. "I was away from my family, my home, the place I loved, where I used to play, run around and enjoy freedom. . . . [S]uddenly, I was sent to a city where I had a difficult time, faced with material problems."[19] Above all, he seems to have missed his mother. Clearly, ever since he was a small child he felt closer to her than to his father – perhaps the two males were just too alike, as Fidel seems to have taken after his father in many ways. He too showed an early strength of will, and a similar self-assertiveness and refusal to compromise.

Once, Fidel's father heard reports that he and his brother Ramón had been behaving like rowdies at the La Salle school – Fidel was even supposed to have returned a teacher's box on the ears – and was on the point of bringing them back to the farm. It was only their mother's intervention which prevented things from going so far. "It was a decisive moment in my life, . . . although a boy wasn't supposed to like studying at that age, I felt that taking me away from school was a punishment I didn't deserve and I was being hurt, unfairly hurt. . . . I remember going to my mother and explaining that I wanted to go on studying. . . . I told her . . . that if I wasn't sent back, I'd set fire to the house. . . . I really threatened to set the whole place on fire."[20]

11

By the time he was 13 he was trying out his first insurrection. Accusing his father of exploiting the sugarcane workers on the farm, he stoked them up and tried to organize a strike. This sudden assault was bad enough in itself, given the taboo surrounding the boss's authority in Spanish American countries, but the fact that the son conducted it against his father in front of everybody led to a deep rift between the two. When looking back at the past, Castro has never done more than make brief mention of his father, whereas he has always expressed himself with great warmth and affection about his mother.

> His education in Catholicism played an important role from earliest childhood on. One of the first things we were taught to believe in were the Three Wise Men. I must have been three or four the first time the Wise Men came. I can even remember the things they brought me: some apples, a toy car – things like that – and some candy.... We were told that the Three Wise Men, who'd traveled to pay homage to Christ when He was born, came every year to bring children presents.

Santa Claus has never been popular in Cuba, and so instead "children wrote letters to the Three Wise Men: Caspar, Melchior and Balthazar."[21]

Curiously, the young Fidel spent three successive feasts of the Epiphany not on the family farm at Birán but with the apparently childless foster-parents in Santiago de Cuba, even though his relations with them became increasingly difficult. It was there that he wrote his first letters to the Three Wise Men.

> I wrote when I was five and asked them for everything – cars, trains, movie cameras, the works. I wrote long letters to the Three Wise Men on January 5.... The disappointments came later.... I remember that my first present was a small cardboard trumpet; just the tip was made out of metal, something like aluminum. My first present was a small trumpet the size of a pencil.... For three consecutive years, three times, I was given a trumpet; I should have become a musician.... The second year, the Three Wise Men brought me a trumpet that was half aluminum and half cardboard. The third time, it was a trumpet with three small keys, made completely of aluminum.[22]

It remains a mystery why Fidel was so often away from home during the Christmas period and the most important feast in the year. Was it because of domestic tensions on the family farm? The young boy must anyway have suffered for a long time as a result. How much he missed home can be felt in later recollections.

> The countryside was freedom. For example, Christmas Eve was a wonderful thing, because it meant fifteen days of vacation – and not just fifteen days of vacation, but fifteen days of a festive atmosphere and treats: cookies, candy and nougats. We had a lot of them at my house. . . . When that time came, you were always excited, from the time you took the train and then continued on horseback until you finally arrived. . . . The roads were nothing but huge mudholes. During the first few years in my house, there weren't any cars or even electricity. . . . Christmas vacations were happy times. Holy Week was another wonderful time, because we had another week of vacation at home. . . . Holy Week in the countryside – I remember from when I was very young – were days of solemnity. What was said? That Christ died on Good Friday. You couldn't talk or joke or be happy.[23]

Unlike his father, Fidel's mother was very religious – "she prayed every day. She always lighted candles to the Virgin and the saints. She requested things from them and prayed to them in all kinds of circumstances. She made vows on behalf of any family member who became ill or who was in a difficult situation." Later, through all the risks of the revolutionary struggle, his mother and maternal grandmother "made all kinds of vows on behalf of our lives and safety. The fact that we came out of the struggle alive must have greatly increased their faith. . . . I could see the strength, courage and comfort they got from their religious feelings and beliefs."[24]

Such things leave their mark – especially in a Latin American country, where the mother is often revered as a saintly figure. In the early sixties, after Castro's profession of faith in communism, the Roman Church and the Cuban clergy, still feeling tied to the old oligarchy, came out in opposition to the new regime, while for a long time the only faith he allowed on the island was faith in the revolution. Anyone who declared for the Church was subject to discrimination. Subsequently, in the spirit of his own *fidelista* dialectic, Castro has never tired of pointing up a close affinity between early Christianity and socialism,[25] and has placed the heroes and martyrs of his revolution on a level with the martyrs in the history of Christianity. Yet the things that fill the clergy with indignation do not disturb him; in the end, the Church is not God.

It was not easy for him early in life. But although he was looked down upon because of his rural origins, his birth out of wedlock and his late baptism, he managed to pull through. His brother Raúl, who experienced school as a "prison," with endless "prayer and fear of God," recalled: "But Fidel was different. He dominated situations. . . . And, every day, he would fight. He had a very explosive character. He challenged the biggest and the strongest ones, and when he was beaten, he started it all over again the next day. He would never quit."[26] He also stood out by his intelligence and dazzling memory. In the end, the brothers at La Salle advised his parents to send him to the Jesuits' strict and respected Dolores College.

"I never had good marks in maths, grammar and other subjects – except for history, a subject I like a lot, and in geography."[27] At first he was a day boy, but as he wanted to be a boarder he provoked a breakdown in relations with the family where he had lodgings.

> I had had enough of that place, and one day I . . . told them all to go to the devil, and entered school as a boarder that very after-noon. This was the second time, or the third, fourth, fifth, I don't remember which, that I had to take it upon myself to get out of what I considered an unpleasant situation. . . . From then on I definitely became my own master and took charge of all my own problems without advice from anyone.[28]

Fidel concentrated his physical energies mainly on long hikes in the Sierra Maestra, the range of mountains rising to almost 2,000 meters at the gates of the city, with their humid forest that was often so difficult to penetrate. It was here, nearly 20 years later, that his revolution would begin its triumphal march across the 1,000 kilometers to Havana. "Of the whole group, I was the enthusiast, the mountain climber par excellence. I did not imagine that mountains would one day play such an important role in my life."[29]

In his last year at the Colegio Dolores, Castro recorded, "I was one of the best in my class."[30] This encouraged his parents to send him to the top school in the country, the Jesuit college of Belén (Bethlehem) in Havana, where he eventually obtained his school-leaving certificate. It was the elite school of the Cuban aristocracy and bourgeoisie, a training ground for the rising generation of conservative politicians. Fidel passed the entrance examination in October 1941 and left behind the "Wild West" of the island. In fact, the examination also involved a kind of preliminary test of political talent, at which candidates had to speak freely for ten minutes. Fidel obviously made a lasting impression, and right from the start – as classmates later recalled – the Jesuits detected in him an exceptional gift for political leadership. In the eyes of his examiner, the head of the oratory academy and college "ideologue" Father José Rubinos, he soon developed into the most capable pupil and the best athlete among the boarders.[31]

The fathers were convinced supporters of the Spanish fascist dictator Francisco Franco – anti-Communist but also, for historical reasons, inclined to anti-Americanism. They dreamed of countering US economic imperialism and the influence of Anglo-Saxon culture in Latin America with a renewal of *hispanidad*, and of reviving the traditional ties with Europe in the shape of Franco's "New Spain." They brought to life for their pupils such historical figures as Julius Caesar, Simon Bolívar, Benito Mussolini and Francisco Franco, as well as Antonio Primo de Rivera, the founder and spiritual father of the Spanish Falange, whose writings Fidel had to study. But the personality he discovered for himself at Belén, and with whom he would identify for the rest of his life, was the freedom-fighter José Martí, in a sense the George Washington of Cuba. In his writings, Fidel found the roots for his own later development. For what that multilingual writer and staunch republican had championed in the second half of the nineteenth century had been the view that a new political leadership must associate the independence struggle against Spain with a far-reaching revolution in colonial society, a revolution that would abolish slavery and bring land reform, racial equality, and social justice.

Born in Havana on January 28, 1853, Martí died on May 19, 1895, at the beginning of the final war of independence, near Dos Ríos in Oriente Province, just 25 miles from the Finca Mañacas. He was only 15 when he rebelled against Spanish rule and founded the paper *La Patria Libre* (Free Fatherland); he was imprisoned for six months for his part in an insurrection and then deported to Spain in 1871 because of his seditious writing. He lived as an exile in France, Mexico, and Guatemala, but eventually wended his way back to Cuba. In 1892 he was elected chairman of the Partido Revolucionario Cubano (Cuban Revolutionary Party) and again banished from the island. He set up his headquarters in New York, using it as a base to plan another rising against Spanish rule in Cuba.

Castro found many parallels with his own life, and over the years these evidently fostered a belief that he was called upon to be Martí's successor. Both their fathers had come to Cuba as Spanish army sergeants during the wars of independence that persisted with long interruptions from 1868 to 1898. José Martí, like Fidel Castro – and also for political reasons – had had a very difficult relationship with his father; both men sacrificed their marriage to politics; both had one son; both were imprisoned on the Isla de Pinos as leaders of an uprising, released soon afterwards and sent into exile; both first collected funds for the freedom struggle in the land of the American arch-enemy. And one day Castro, like Martí, would land with a little group of followers on the lonely southern coast of Oriente Province to launch the armed struggle. They proved similarly mistaken in thinking that the country would immediately rise up and support the revolutionaries. Like Martí, Castro then led a minuscule struggle against a powerful army, and finally brought down a regime that knew how to impose its will only by terrorizing the population. Unlike Martí, however, Castro both survived the struggle and escaped the disillusionment that had set in after the victory of the war of independence in 1898.

Three years after Martí's death, as the hour of Spain's defeat approached, the United States joined in for the last round without being asked, so that it could then exclude the independence movement from the peace agreement that was concluded in Paris on December 10, 1898. Moreover, the freedom fighters in Washington accepted only to a limited degree Cuba's longed-for right to self-determination.[32] The pretext for US intervention had been an explosion on the battleship *Maine* on February 15, 1898, in Havana Harbor, when 266 members of the crew had lost their lives. The ship had been lying at anchor to evacuate American citizens during the final phase of the war on the island. But although a fire spreading from the ship's coal bunker to its ammunition store had obviously been the cause of the disaster, Washington promptly accused Spain of a warlike attack and, stoked up by the Hearst press, declared hostilities under the banner "Remember the Maine." The 39-year-old deputy navy minister and future president, Theodore Roosevelt, a former cowboy, deputy sheriff, and buffalo hunter, rode through a hail of bullets to mount furious attacks on the Spanish, at the head of a bunch of so-called "Rough Riders" made up of hunters, trappers, Indians, adventurers, Harvard students from the New York upper classes, and accompanying newspaper reporters.[33]

The right to self-determination mentioned in the peace agreement was not worth the paper on which it was written. The United States, which had long been seeking to get its hands on the island, now treated it as war booty. American troops pulled out only in 1902, after Congress had forced Cuban politicians the year before to introduce into the new Constitution a clause highly dubious under international law that virtually made the island a US protectorate. This Platt Amendment, named after Senator Orville H. Platt who thought it up, gave Washington the right to intervene militarily in Cuba whenever it perceived a threat to American interests there. From that time, Cuba was unable to enter into agreements with another state unless they had the approval of the United States, and it was required to make land available for the building of US Marine bases (the last one, now highly contentious, being in the bay of Guantánamo).[34] The Platt Amendment implied an expansion of the notorious Monroe Doctrine to the islands of the Antilles that had remained in the Spanish or British sphere of influence.[35] And there would be more than one occasion when Washington exercised its "right" to military intervention in Cuba: in 1906, 1912, and 1917.

This aggressive involvement of the United States may be explained, right up to the present day, by the huge stake it had in Cuba. Already in the nineteenth century there was a strong economic lobby that threw its weight behind calls for annexation of the sugar island. The Spanish turned down an American offer to purchase it for the sum of 130 million dollars, but in the end it went indirectly for much less than that, after the war of independence had so devastated the sugar and tobacco plantations that the economy fell an easy prey to speculators. The US military governor of Cuba, General Leonard Wood, himself complained in 1902:

> One of the hardest features of my work was to prevent the looting of Cuba by men who were presumed respectable. Men came down there apparently with the best recommendations and wanted me to further the most infamous of schemes. They expected to profit by sharp business practices at the expense of the people of the island.[36]

In the same year, US investments were already valued at 100 million dollars. And by the time that Fidel Castro was born, two-thirds of agriculture was in North American ownership.

A recent study of the situation in Cuba after independence has highlighted the early causes of the political aberrations that would give rise to Castro's revolution.

> When Cuba became independent on 20 May 1902, . . . the Cuban economy was dominated by the interests of US capital, which, in alliance with the Cuban upper classes, blocked any recasting of colonial property relations. Until the revolution in 1959, the gearing of the Cuban economy to sugar monoculture cemented its external dependence on the world market and the United States (as the main buyer of the product), as well as the dominance of the large sugar producers inside the country. Broad layers of the population who had made great sacrifices for the cause of independence – especially members of the liberation army itself – found themselves robbed of its fruits, and this led to a widespread sense of frustration even as the republic was coming into being.[37]

In 1934, as part of a "good neighbors" policy, the Platt Amendment was revoked under President Franklin D. Roosevelt (whose father was a cousin of Theodore Roosevelt), but this did not prevent Washington from continuing to pursue a self-interested policy in Latin America, through the cultivation of a tightly knit web of military and political forces.

For Castro, daily life in the Jesuit college of Belén mirrored the results of that historical tragedy. The "farmer's son" from the far east of the island was treated more condescendingly than the boarding-school boy had been in Santiago, by that section of the old Cuban oligarchy which had been able to keep its prosperity through the struggle for independence and to forge in time close links with the new masters. Castro again dealt with such slights by redoubling his efforts at school, especially in the field of sport, and this earned him a degree of popularity as well as some superficial friendships. Soon after he started there, he even won a dubious respect when he bet with some schoolmates that he was capable of extreme deeds and, looking straight ahead, rode a bicycle with full force into a stone wall; he fell down unconscious and had to spend several days recovering from concussion. The memory of such uncompromising audacity, such wild and literally hard-headed determination, remains alive at the school today. In the year 1943–4, the young Fidel was even awarded the prize for the best sports all-rounder in Cuba. One former schoolmate recalls that the Belén baseball team was much feared because he scored a point with every ball he hit, and that his efforts helped the school to win numerous competitions, championships, and medals. The other side of this was that he was seen more as a solo runner than a team player. Teachers and pupils alike kept a strong impression of his huge powers of concentration and his outstanding memory. He learned faster than others, and sometimes astounded everyone by rattling off a page of text that he had previously read.[38]

An ideological gulf later separated Castro from the world of his former teachers, and he looked back on the daily mass and sermons as "a form of mental terrorism."[39] All his life, however, he has been full of respect for his teachers and the school: "The Jesuits . . . valued character, rectitude, honesty, courage and the

19

ability to make sacrifices. Teachers definitely have an influence. The Jesuits clearly influenced me with their strict organization, their discipline and their values. They contributed to my development and influenced my sense of justice."[40] Belén thus became a training for life:

> I met . . . teachers and other men who were interested in molding the students' character. . . . I acquired ethics and norms that weren't just religious. I got a human influence from the teachers' authority and the values they attached to things. They encouraged sports and trips to the mountains. . . . Nor did I dream I was preparing to be a guerrilla, but every time I saw a mountain, it was a challenge to me.[41]

At the end of his school years, Father Francisco Barbeito noted in the college yearbook: "Always Fidel distinguished himself in all the subjects related to letters. He was *excelencia* [in the top ten of the graduating class] and *congregante* [a student who regularly attended prayers and religious activities]. . . . He will make law his career, and we do not doubt that he will fill with brilliant pages the book of his life."[42]

Among gangsters

In 1945 the 18-year-old Fidel returned with a brilliant leaving certificate from the Jesuits in Belén to his proud parents in Birán. His father rewarded him with a Ford Cabrio. Then, after a long carefree summer in the country, he enrolled in October 1945 to study at the law faculty of Havana University. "I myself wonder why I studied law. I don't know the answer. I partly associate it with those who said: 'He talks so much he should become a lawyer.' Since I was in the habit of debating and discussing, I was sure I had what it took for the legal profession."[43]

No sooner had he outgrown the well-guarded elite school than a real struggle for survival began. The campus was ruled by the *gangsterismo* of two rival groups, which used violence and money to influence political life in the capital. One was the Movimiento Socialista Revolucionario (MSR – Revolutionary Socialist Movement), led by former Communist Rolando Masferrer; the other the Unión Insurreccional Revolucionaria (UIR – Revolutionary Insurrectional Union), led by the one-time anarchist Emilio Tro. The names were little more than a joke: neither the "socialism" nor the "revolutionary" meant anything at all. For people in general, their members were simply a bunch of *pistoleros*. They controlled the students' union, the Federación Estudiantil Universitaria (FEU). And the government of President Ramón Grau San Martín (1944–8) was highly dependent upon them, as was that of his successor, the much-derided cocaine addict Carlos Prío Socarrás (1948–52). During Grau's term alone, more than 120 mob-style murders were attributed to them, either in the service of politicians or to settle accounts with each other. In the spring of 1947, Grau even appointed as head of the criminal investigation department an MSR leader, Mario Salabarría, a notorious killer who later targeted Fidel Castro. Tro, the UIR boss, made it as far as head of the national police school (but was then himself murdered), and the long-serving FEU chairman, MSR leader Manolo Castro, got the job of national sports manager. After 1948 President Prío surpassed even Grau, entering into a secret pact whereby gang members would obtain jobs in the police and draw a kind of basic income from the state coffers.

Such crude provisions were no longer needed by the US-based Mafia, which saw Cuba as especially fertile terrain for its operations. In the late thirties Meyer Lansky's friend and "business partner" Batista had given it exclusive "grazing rights," and both Grau and Prío ensured that these were not infringed. The Mafia purposefully set about turning the Caribbean island into one big gambling casino and brothel, where for hard dollars prudish America could act out its secret desires and fantasies beneath the king palms.

Cuba's importance at that time for organized crime may be seen in the quite special society that Havana's exclusive Hotel Nacional hosted in February 1947, when the Who's Who of the American underworld gathered there for one of the largest meetings in its history. A group of 36 godfathers plus entourage, making a total of some 500 persons, answered Meyer Lansky's invitation to join the party and to discuss the scope for business expansion. Among them were Albert "Butcher" Anastasia, Frank Costello, Carlo Gambino, Willie Moretti, Mike Miranda, Vito Genovese, "Fat Man" Joe Maglocco, Carlos Marcello, Al Capone's heirs Charlie and Rocco Fischetti, Joe Bonanno, Santos Trafficante and Tommy "Three Finger Brown" Lucchese. The boss of bosses, however, *il capo di tutti capi*, was Charles "Lucky" Luciano, who had found refuge from criminal prosecution in a thirties suite in the Catalan-Moorish neoclassical hotchpotch of the Hotel Nacional. The others duly paid homage, presenting him with dollar-stuffed envelopes to help cover his living costs. Frank Sinatra flew down specially for the informal side of things. According to Joseph "Doc" Stacher, Meyer Lansky's link to Batista, "the Italians among us were very proud of Frank. . . . They had spent a lot of money helping him in his career."[44]

Fidel Castro soon realized that the rules at the 200-year-old university were different from those at Belén College. He recalled:

> When I was 18, I was, politically speaking, illiterate. Since I didn't come from a family of politicians or grow up in a political atmosphere, it would have been impossible for me to carry out a revolutionary role . . . , in a relatively brief time, had I not had a special calling. . . . I had the feeling that a new field was opening up for me. I started thinking about my country's political problems. . . . I spontaneously started to feel a certain concern, an interest in social and political questions.[45]

At first his fellow-students did not know what to make of him. "I was in a panic," recalled Alfredo Guevara (no relative of "Che") of their first encounter in autumn 1945. "Here was this Castro dressed up fit to kill in his black party suit, handsome, self-assured, aggressive, and obviously a leader. . . . I saw him as a political threat." Guevara, already then a Communist activist and still today reputedly a close follower of Castro's, was convinced that the very "spectre of clericalism" had come to clean up the campus.[46] But he was mistaken: Castro was no one's instrument. His goals were his own.

22

It quickly became clear that Castro was not interested only in studying; he also wanted to get involved in university politics. His aim was to become president of the FEU. The groups running the organization courted him as a student with leadership abilities and a gift for public speaking, and the then-president Manolo Castro would have been quite happy to see his namesake succeed him. Evidently some of them trusted the farmer's son from Oriente to show a firm hand in conducting the union's crooked practices. Although Fidel realized he could do nothing politically without the UIR or the MSR, he tried various juggling acts. For if he was to be president of the FEU, he did not want to be at the mercy of those responsible for the deplorable state of affairs; he needed to have his own power base. This took time to achieve, and it was only in his third semester that he managed to become vice-president of the students' union in the faculty of law. For a year or so, he tried to raise his profile as an independent figure.

The MSR was not prepared to accept that and eventually put him on its blacklist. Masferrer's henchman Salabarría, whom Fidel described as "master of the capital,"[47] issued him with an ultimatum: shut up or quit the university. Fidel reminisced:

This was a great moment of decision. The conflict struck my personality like a cyclone. Alone, on the beach, facing the sea, I examined the situation. Personal danger . . . made my return to the University an act of unheard-of temerity. But not to return would be to give in to threats, to give in before bullies. . . . I decided to go back and I went back – *with arms in my hand.*[48]

Clearly, for a time Castro would draw closer to the UIR and seek its protection.

Back at the university, defying threats with a kind of bodyguard of friends, he began to settle into the role of spiritual grandson of the martyred apostle José Martí and to make the unfinished Cuban Revolution his personal cause. Theory and practice gradually became welded together. From Martí's voluminous work, "whom [he] never tired of reading in those days,"[49] he stored a treasure of quotes in his memory to embellish his carefully rehearsed speeches. He started to make ever more frequent appearances outside the university, acting as main speaker and agitator in demonstrations against the government. The newspapers published reports about him, sometimes splashing them across their pages. Charming and agile with words, tall, youthful and sporting, decked out in double-breasted suit and tie, with dark back-combed hair and a classical Greek profile, the young man just turned 21 cut an impressive figure and answered the dreams of many a potential mother-in-law. According to the later testimony of fellow-students, he was very shy and reserved with women, though anything but chaste. Slightly tending to corpulence, he nevertheless managed to keep fit through his favorite sport, baseball, which he played for the university in spite of the political demands on his time. As we have seen, he performed remarkable feats on the field, and his success in matches against US teams eventually brought him to the attention of American talent scouts. In 1949 the New York Giants offered him a professional contract, with a bonus of 5,000 dollars on signature. "We couldn't believe he turned us down," their negotiator later recalled. "Nobody from Latin America had said 'no' before."[50]

His temperament was beginning to get the better of him. Shortly after a police truncheon had found his head at a demonstration against higher bus fares and left him sporting a thick bandage, he attended a meeting between students and President Grau. When the latter left the room for a brief moment, Castro whispered to his friends: "I have the formula to take power and once and for all get rid of this son-of-a-bitch . . . when the old guy [Grau] returns, let's pick him up, the four of us, and throw him off the balcony. Once the president is dead, we'll proclaim the triumph of the student revolution and speak to the people from the radio." His companion, Alfred "Chino" Esquivel, immediately squashed the idea: "Listen, dope, you're off your head." The president remained alive.[51]

On three occasions Castro was accused of involvement in an assassination attempt, but the claims were never substantiated and turned out to have been at least partly invented for ulterior motives.[52] In the first case, he is supposed to have shot a UIR fellow-student in the lung in December 1946;[53] other sources suggest that he missed his intended victim when the bullet hit an uninvolved student in the leg.[54] On February 22, 1948, the national sports manager Manolo Castro (no relative of Fidel's) was gunned down outside a Havana cinema. Although a UIR member was arrested pistol in hand as the presumed assassin, a nephew of MSR boss Masferrer publicly accused Fidel of the deed. Apparently, the murder was an act of revenge for the spectacular slaying of UIR leader Tro by Salabarría's *pistoleros*, in the course of a gun battle that raged for hours. Many years later, Manolo Castro's comrade and successor as FEU president, Enrique Ovares, said at his home in Miami to Fidel's American biographer Tad Szulc: "Fidel had absolutely nothing to do with the Manolo Castro thing."[55] Hugh Thomas, for his part, concludes that Fidel probably took part in a meeting which agreed on the assassination.[56] In the third case, a little under four months later, Fidel was accused of shooting a police officer, Óscar Fernández Caral, outside his home on June 6, 1948. Allegedly Caral identified Fidel as the assassin with his dying breath, but after he publicly protested the witness admitted that the police had bribed him to say this.[57] In the days following the victory of the revolution, Fidel himself looked back on the period: "I was the Don Quixote of the university, always under the guns and bullets. What I suffered at the university has more merit than the Sierra Maestra."[58] He certainly seems to have been involved in tough battles. "I lived through difficult moments in this university, very difficult, so much so that it is purely by chance that I survived those university years."[59]

As in his school years, he trusted very few people sufficiently to take their advice. One of these few was Eduardo Chibás, then a 40-year-old senator, who in spring 1947 left his original political home as an *auténtico* (a member of the Authentic Revolutionary Party of Cuba, from which Grau and Prío also came) and founded the Partido Popular Cubano (PPC – Cuban People's Party). The PPC, which soon became known as the "Orthodox" party, won support as the first serious opposition to the government and embraced the values and principles of the heroic freedom-fighter Martí: that is to say, "nationalism, anti-imperialism, socialism, economic independence, political liberty and social justice."[60]

Castro immediately joined the party and remained a member until it broke up eight years later. For the first time he too had something like a political home. Chibás, nearly twice the age of the 21-year-old Castro, became his mentor and model. His unyielding and honest political behavior, expressed in frequent radio broadcasts exposing cases of political corruption, made a great impact on Castro and eventually encouraged him to stand for Congress in the parliamentary and presidential elections of 1952.

Meanwhile, however, Castro seems to have agreed a kind of truce with his enemies. In the summer of 1947, he was in on the action when the Dominican writer and future president Juan Bosch, together with a group of wealthy exiles, assembled a motley force of 1,200 men to overthrow the bloody US-backed dictator Rafael Trujillo in the Dominican Republic. Castro thus found himself in the company of all manner of idealists, as well as adventurers and university gang members hired as mercenaries. They carried out two months of guerrilla training, not far from his own birthplace, but the bizarre enterprise failed as a result of treachery. The Cuban navy, apparently under pressure from Washington, boarded their little ship the *Fantasma* off Cuba's north-east coast. Profiting from a moment when no one was watching, the chairman of the Cuban University Committee for Democracy in the Dominican Republic – none other than Fidel Castro – jumped overboard and swam nearly 10 nautical miles, through supposedly shark-infested waters, to Saetía in the familiar Bay of Nipe, and then made his way to his parents' home in Birán. An almighty row ensued with his father – not least because Fidel had wasted the whole semester on his first revolutionary activities.

Castro took a growing interest in Latin American politics. Again like Martí before him, he even became active in the movement for Puerto Rican independence, as well as showing solidarity with the student movements in Argentina, Venezuela, Colombia, and Panama, which were demanding an end to colonialist policies (especially of the United States) in the region. In April 1948 he helped organize a congress of Latin American student organizations in the Colombian capital Bogotá – to be held in parallel with the Ninth Interamerican Meeting of Foreign Ministers, which was supposed to prepare the founding of the Organization of American States. Castro traveled with his friend, the FEU general secretary Alfredo Guevara, to a country which for two years had been wracked by a bloody civil war between supporters of the Conservative and the Liberal Party.

On April 7 in Bogotá, Castro met the popular leader of the Liberal opposition, the lawyer Eliécer Gaitán, who struck him as in many ways similar to "Eddy" Chibás. Two days later, an hour or so before they were due to meet a second time, Gaitán was gunned down in the street in front of his office. The presumed assassin, the mentally deranged Juan Roa Sierra, was lynched on the spot by an angry crowd. Gaitán's death triggered a day-long orgy of violence, during which Fidel allowed himself to get carried away with gun in hand amid the streetfighting. "I realized that it was a revolution. . . . Gaitán's death was a terrible crime. So I took sides. . . . There was tremendous disorder, almost no discipline and no organization. . . . I was filled with revolutionary fervor, trying to get as many people as possible to join the revolutionary movement."[61] More than 3,500 people were killed during the disturbances, which have gone down in the history of Latin America as the *bogotazo*. Subsequently, the security forces blamed "communists from Cuba" (that is, Castro and his comrades) for the acts of violence. But "the truth is," he said later, "that we had nothing to do with it. As young, idealistic, Don Quixote-like students, we simply joined in the people's rebellion."[62] They only barely escaped with their lives. "It's incredible, truly incredible, that we weren't all killed."[63] Was Castro a Communist by that time? "I had already studied the basics of Marxism-Leninism," he tells us, "but I could not say that I was a Marxist-Leninist at that time, much less a member of the Communist Party or even of the Communist Youth."[64]

On October 12, 1948, two days after the inauguration of Grau's successor Prío as Cuban president, the 22-year-old Fidel Castro married a philosophy student of the same age, Mirta Díaz-Balart, the sister of his fellow-student and friend Rafael Díaz-Balart. The ceremony took place in the Catholic church in the bride's home town of Banes, in Oriente Province, not far from Fidel's own birthplace. As it happened, Fulgencio Batista also originated from Banes, a town that owed its very existence to the United Fruit Company. Mirta's father was its mayor and public prosecutor, and apparently also worked for Batista, so that Fidel was marrying into a family with the best political connections. Admittedly he seemed to belong in the opposition, but there was a secret hope that the family bond might recoup his evident political talents for the other camp. The bride's father came up with 10,000 dollars for their three-month honeymoon, and Batista himself is said to have contributed 1,000. The couple traveled to Florida, and then by train to New York, where Fidel apparently bought a copy of Marx's *Das Kapital*.

The following year saw the birth of their son, on September 1, 1949. In keeping with Cuban tradition, he was given his father's name – only in the diminutive form of Fidelito ("Little Fidel"). Soon Castro was finding less and less time for the family. It was his wish that, despite having affluent parents, they should live in the most modest circumstances, which meant at first a hotel room in Havana and later a sparsely furnished two-room flat. From his own father he received 80 pesos a month. But for a while they had so little to eat that their child fell seriously ill with deficiency symptoms. When his car was taken away because he could not keep up payments, Castro temporarily sank into depression and kept to his bed. He kept his wife out of his political activities, perhaps because he felt suspicious of her family.

Soon after the founding of the Orthodox Party, Castro started to build a power base of his own in the shape of a youth organization, the Acción Radical Ortodoxo (ARO). But in 1949, when the ARO and the youth organization of the Communist Party set up a "30th of September Committee" to combat the spread of political gangsterism, his unexplained associations with the gangs meant that he initially had to remain outside. Feeling compelled to make a spectacular gesture that would clear him of all suspicion, he publicly distanced himself from both the UIR and MSR in late November 1949 before a meeting of heads of faculties and some 500 students; he astounded his audience and delighted the newspapers by naming all the gang members, politicians, and student leaders who had been profiting from the "pact" with

President Prío. "The problem then was to get Fidel out of there alive," remarked Max Lesnick, leader at that time of the Orthodox Youth Association. He placed Castro in the passenger seat of his Cabriolet and, using the element of surprise, simply roared off in full view of everyone. He then hid Castro for a fortnight in his apartment, because those he had accused were in such a rage that "he would [have been] killed if he went out in the street."[65] Friends persuaded Castro to make himself scarce for a while, and he spent a period of four months "in exile" in New York – again like his model Martí. Not even his wife, left at home with the three-month-old Fidelito, knew where he was staying.

When Castro returned to Havana early in 1950, half a year was enough for him to catch up with two missed years of study. "No, I was not a good student. . . . I became a last-minute crammer, . . . a good finalist."[66] In any event, his quickness of comprehension and his exceptional memory ensured that in September 1950, at the age of 24, he passed his exams and became a doctor three times over: in law, social science, and international law. His marriage to Mirta Díaz-Balart had opened doors to the Cuban oligarchy and well-paid legal work, as well as bringing such advantages as membership of the exclusive Havana Yacht Club (to which not even Batista was admitted, because of his half-caste origins). Castro's brother-in-law Rafael Díaz-Balart, who at that time was leader of the youth wing of Batista's Unitary Action Party, set up a meeting between Batista and Castro in the former's luxurious estate near Havana, even though Castro was already considered a political opponent.[67] But the future dictator did not manage to win the young man's support for his interests. Instead, Castro and two ex-student friends opened a legal advice center for poor people in a rundown office block in the Old Town; he continued to live from hand to mouth and moved back into politics.

A mysterious event occurred on the evening of August 5, 1951, when Eduardo Chibás, who had excellent prospects of becoming president after the 1952 elections, shot himself in the belly with a .38 Colt during his weekly radio broadcast. Castro rushed over and took him to hospital, but he died there 11 days later. As the reason given for Chibás's act of despair was his inability to prove

29

the charges of corruption he had made against one of Prío's ministers, Castro now felt compelled to furnish the proof posthumously for his former patron. He came up with the goods four months later, and their publication unleashed a major political scandal.

Many already thought that Castro was not just a promising contender for Congress but a president in the making.[68] They were right, of course, although Fulgencio Batista, the friend of his parents-in-law, made sure that he did not take the customary route to that office. At daybreak on March 10, 1952, the presidential candidate with the least chance of success staged a military coup that put an end to the election campaign and Cuba's corrupt democracy. Proclaiming himself head of state, Batista went on to build a thoroughly corrupt dictatorship. It would not be long before the mafioso Meyer Lansky became his official adviser for casino reform, and not much longer than that before both men were raking in the millions.[69]

3

The Young Revolutionary

✭

Storm and stress: Moncada

Chibás, Castro's first political teacher, mentor and model, the catalyzer of his radical energies, was dead. President Prío had pocketed some 90 million dollars from the state coffers and gone into exile in the United States.[1] Cuba was again in the hands of gangsters' pal Batista, whose coup had received Washington's seal of zealous diplomacy as well as the ecclesiastical seal of absolution from the Archbishop of Havana, Manuel Arteaga y Betancourt,[2] and on that date of March 10, a hastily organized parade of the oligarchy in front of the presidential palace rendered due homage to the new ruler and distributor of sinecures.[3] All that remained to Fidel Castro were the ideas bequeathed by Martí and Chibás and a mysterious doorkey that was delivered to him on the very day of the coup. It fitted the lock of a luxury flat, so that he could use it as a hiding-place in an emergency.

The flat belonged to one of the most beautiful women in Havana: Natalia Revuelta. She was tall, fair, prosperous and well-educated, having been brought up in the United States and France and married to the well-known Cuban heart surgeon Orlando Fernández-Ferrer. For a long time she had been a secret admirer of the attractive rising star of politics; now they got to know each other better and fell in love. "Naty" Revuelta, with her upper-class façade, also played an important role in Castro's early plans for underground opposition to the dictatorship. She gave him money, even selling some of her jewelry and books, and she allowed a secret store of weapons to be kept in her house.

A few days after the coup, at a gathering of the Ortodoxos at the grave of party founder Chibás, Castro furiously declared war on the dictator: "If Batista grabbed power by force, he must be thrown out by force!"[4] Before the Supreme Court, he instituted proceedings against the coup that Batista was shamelessly calling a revolution. He accused the dictator of violating the very Constitution that he had issued in 1940 together with Communist members of his government, and which was now the first item he had revoked. Although for 12 years it had been more abused than really applied, it was still considered the most progressive Constitution in the continent.

It is worth noting the arguments Castro used to challenge Batista's legal justification for his takeover. Batista and his men claimed that, because their coup d'état was a revolution, it automatically canceled the previous system of laws and instituted a new legality; the "revolution" could not therefore be condemned as illegal. Castro retorted: "Instead of revolution, there is restoration; instead of progress and order, there is barbarism and brute force. . . . Without a new conception of the state, of society, of the judicial order based on profound historical and philosophical principles, there will be no revolution that generates laws."[5] This line of argument – which would later play an important role in establishing his own moral credentials – implied that, in circumstances when it served social progress, enjoyed popular support and was more than just a military seizure of power, a revolution might be thoroughly justified. The theoretical basis for the legitimacy of a revolution had been provided by the Enlightenment thinkers of the seventeenth and eighteenth centuries, as well as by Marxism and the writings of Martí.

Castro immediately got down to the job of building his revolutionary movement.

I began to organize the first combatants, the first fighters – the first cells – within a few weeks. First, I tried to set up a small, mimeographed newspaper and some underground radio stations. . . . We became true conspirators. . . . At the beginning, that movement had one professional cadre: me. . . . We organized that movement in just 14 months, and it came to have 1,200 men. . . . All that effort was devoted to the organization, training and equipping of the Movement. How many times I met with the future fighters, shared my ideas with them and gave them instructions![6]

The core recruits came from the radical wing of the Orthodox Party. As to the Communists, then operating under the name of the Partido Socialista Popular (PSP), Castro showed that his attitude had not changed since the days of the *bogotazo* in Colombia.

It wasn't that I had any prejudices against the Communist Party; rather, I realized that the Communist Party was very isolated and that it would be very difficult to carry out my revolutionary plan from within its ranks. That's why I had to choose: to become a disciplined member of the Communist Party or to create a revolutionary organization that could act under Cuban conditions.[7]

He was also distrustful of them, since the period between 1940 and 1944 when they had had two ministers in Batista's government.

The Communists were no less distrustful: Castro was, in their view, a hothead and adventurer who did not fit their strict cadre system; he treated the pure doctrine of Marxism-Leninism not as an absolute, but only as a building block for his own *fidelista* conception of social revolution. For the Communists, then, there was no future in Castro and his plans. Nevertheless, some of the closest comrades in his movement were either young Communists or people influenced by Communism; indeed, his own brother Raúl became a member of the Communist Youth in 1953. Melba Hernández, who in those days had been part of Castro's inner circle, later told Tad Szulc:

In our ranks in that period there was never talk about Communism, socialism or Marxism-Leninism as an ideology, but we did speak of the day when the revolution would come to power, that all the estates of the aristocracy must then be handed over to the people and must be used by the children for whom we are fighting.[8]

33

With a group of handpicked comrades, Castro spent months carefully preparing his action against Batista; they also eventually composed a victory anthem and drew up a manifesto. His plan was to capture the massive Moncada fortress in Santiago de Cuba, to break open its arsenal of weapons, and to spark a popular uprising in the east of Cuba that would spread to the whole country and bring the regime crashing down. Only his closest associates were in the know – one of these being Naty Revuelta, who, in the event of success at Moncada, had the task of broadcasting the news over the radio.

On July 24, 1953, the 162 people selected for the attack were sent in small groups from Havana to the rented "El Siboney" chicken farm a couple of miles east of Santiago. When Castro disclosed the plan there, some of them recoiled in horror: 10 wanted to pull out and were placed in detention. The weapons at their disposal for the dangerous undertaking were relatively modest. Juan Almeida – a mulatto bricklayer from Oriente Province who, half a century later, was still said to be Castro's most loyal and influential follower – recalled: "I waited for my rifle like the Messiah. When I saw that the one they gave me was a .22-calibre [hunting rifle] I froze up."[9]

In histories of Cuba published under Castro, Sunday, July 26, 1953, marks the official beginning of his revolution. At 5:15 a.m., 111 men and two women (Melba Hernández and Haydée Santamaría) in ill-fitting uniforms set off in 26 American limousines on the road to the Moncada Barracks, which on that day were occupied by some 700 troops. At the same time, a second group of 27 men were preparing an attack on the Bayamó Barracks further to the west, in order to close there the narrow road that carried military supplies between the west and east of the island. As it was carnival time, Castro reckoned that many soldiers would either be on leave or be lying drunk in bed.

Although an advance guard managed to penetrate the barracks and briefly to pin down a dormitory full of dazed, scantily clad soldiers, both attacks soon broke down under withering fire from the defenders. Castro recalled:

By a terrible mistake, the best-armed half of our troops was delayed at the city gates and so was not present at the vital moment. . . . My car ran into a military patrol armed with machine guns, and the struggle began. Our reserve division, which had almost all our heavy weapons, . . . made a wrong turn, and completely lost its way in a city that was unfamiliar to them.[10]

Fidel himself, in the front rank, tried to cover his comrades by shooting wildly at the soldiers but miraculously came through unscathed, whereas some other men fell around him. Finally, he accepted failure and ordered a retreat. There was no greater success at Bayamó, where shying horses and a barking guard-dog sounded the alarm and roused the troops in the barracks to reach for their weapons. The rebels made a mad dash to escape their pursuers, but many of them were captured shortly afterwards. Castro, together with Juan Almeida and a few others, managed to flee to the Sierra Maestra. "Naty" Revuelta, with a group of fellow-conspirators, seized a radio station in Havana, read out a revolutionary manifesto invoking the name of Martí, played Beethoven's *Eroica* symphony in celebration of the day, and then just had time to go underground and escape detection.

During the attacks on the barracks, 19 soldiers were killed and 27 wounded – against eight killed on Castro's side. But 61 more rebels were horrifically tortured and murdered after their capture, eyes gouged out and genitals or other body parts ripped off. Haydée Santamaría lost her fiancé as well as her brother Abel, who had been Castro's deputy during the action. The order to kill the detainees had come down indirectly from Batista and his chief of staff Francisco Tabernilla, who had thereby disregarded all the provisions of the law that held jailers responsible for the physical integrity of their prisoners. Secret photographs of the corpses, published in the magazine *Bohemia*, shocked the whole country and unleashed a wave of sympathy for the rebels.

Five days after the failed attacks, a 12-man army patrol surprised Castro's own little band as they were sleeping. Once again, Castro was within a hair's breadth of death, but the black officer in charge of the patrol, Lieutenant Pedro Manuel Sarría, stopped his men from executing the revolutionary on the spot. "We were convinced they were really going to kill us. . . . [But Sarría] put pressure on the soldiers, and then, more quietly, he repeated, 'Don't shoot. You can't kill ideas; you can't kill ideas.' . . . He repeated this around three times: 'You can't kill ideas.'"[11] Together with Archbishop Enrique Pérez Serantes, the officer ensured that Castro and his companions escaped the blood lust of Moncada commander Alberto del Río Chaviano and reached prison in one piece.[12]

A total of 29 rebels came up for trial in Santiago between September 21 and October 16, 1953: four (including Fidel's brother Raúl) were sentenced to 13 years in prison, 20 to 10 years, three to three years, and the two women to seven months. Fidel Castro received a term of 15 years, following an extempore speech lasting four hours, "History Will Absolve Me," which he wrote up in prison and smuggled out in matchboxes for publication. It soon became famous as the authoritative political manifesto of "Castroism."

The main points in this reformist rather than revolutionary program call for redistribution of land to small farmers, workers' participation in company profits, confiscation of illicit gains, economic conversion of Cuba from a supplier of raw materials to a producer of industrial goods, and reintroduction of the 1940 Constitution revoked by Batista. Castro ended his speech on October 16 with the words: "Condemn me, it does not matter. History will absolve me!"[13]

The next day, Castro was flown to the prison island of Isla de Pinos, where he joined his 24 comrades as Prisoner No. 3859. They made him their leader, and he immediately began preparations to rebuild his revolutionary movement. "I would honestly love to revolutionize this country from one end to the other!" he wrote on April 15, 1954. "I would not be stopped by the hatred and ill will of a few thousand people, including some of my relatives, half the people I know, two-thirds of my fellow professionals, and four-fifths of my ex-schoolmates."[14] Fidel sent long letters to his friends – especially the radio journalist Luís Conte Agüero, his most important contact in Havana, and his half-sister Lidia. His sure sense that public relations are often as important as the operation itself was immediately apparent. On April 17, 1954, he wrote to Melba Hernández, after her early release: "Our propaganda must not let up for one minute, because it is the heart of the struggle."[15]

Quite a different Castro is revealed in a series of letters to "Beloved Naty," which were published only four decades later.[16] "If you have suffered in many ways on account of me, think that I would gladly lay down my life for your honor and your happiness. . . . Despite the wretchedness of this existence, there are certain enduring things, eternal things, such as my feelings for you, which will accompany me indelibly into the grave," he wrote on November 7, 1953. And on January 5, 1954, he confessed: "Whenever I read your letters, they confirm my belief that nature has been extraordinarily generous with you in terms of your soul and your intelligence – which is not to forget for a moment other, non-mental forms." On January 31 he again went into raptures:

> All your letters have a good effect on me and hold my interest; they are a pleasure that never subsides. The forms are as diverse as the stars. . . . What distinguishes one ray of light from another ray of light? Nothing. And yet, there is always a different color shining in them. One kiss is like another, but lovers never grow weary. There is a honey that never hardens. That is the secret of your letters. . . . It matters not that it will be a little longer before I can hold you tight in my arms, so tight that I will squeeze you like a flower between my hands. Nor did I have to see you to love you even more than months ago, just because of the fine charm of your letters and the ardent affection that speaks in them.

By no means, however, did they exchange only whispers of love. Castro's epistolary discourses on philosophical and historical themes testify to very wide reading on his part.

Only one letter from Natalia Revuelta to Castro has so far been published – in the bitter memoirs of the daughter they later had together, Alina. But this is enough to show how captivated she was by him.

37

I feel so tiny beside your immeasurable knowledge, your philosophy and your tenderness. You know so much, but what impresses me even more is the flattering and generous way in which you let me share in everything you achieve so naturally. You take me by the hand and lead me through the history of mankind, philosophy and literature; . . . you open up to me new, unexplored and surprising horizons. . . . No, Fidel, all this wealth is inside you . . . ; you were born with it, and it will die with you. . . . It would be very dishonest of me not to say that it makes me very happy that you are the way you are, and that it would fill me with pride if you never changed. As always, your Naty.[17]

A radio broadcast that Castro heard in his cell on the morning of July 5, 1953, started a process that would soon result in the end of his marriage. The report stated that the ministry of internal affairs had "sacked" Mrs Mirta Díaz-Balart. He was stunned: he had no idea that his wife was supposed to have worked behind his back for the Batista regime, along with her brother, Castro's student friend Rafael Díaz-Balart, who had risen to become deputy to Interior Minister Ramón Hermida. At first Castro explained the whole thing as one of Hermida's little intrigues, and in a letter to Luís Conte Agüero he attacked the interior minister for his homosexuality. In the end, Hermida had a private meeting with Castro in prison and claimed that his brother-in-law "Rafaelito," who was "always acting like a spoiled brat," was the only one behind it.[18] Rafael took his revenge by publicly disclosing his superior's visit to the prisoner, but all this meant was that both minister and deputy minister lost their jobs.

The marriage ended in divorce in the spring of 1955, and a year later Mirta married a politician in the Orthodox Party.[19] The struggle for custody of their son Fidelito – temporarily "kidnapped" by one side or the other to the United States, Mexico, or elsewhere – would last for many years before Fidel came out on top.

On May 15, 1955, after one year and seven months in jail, public pressure and the mediation of Archbishop Pérez Serantes (who apparently argued that they no longer posed any danger) secured the release of Castro and his associates as part of a wider amnesty.[20] Already at the prison gates, Castro declared that he intended to remain in Cuba and to continue his struggle there. Condemning the bomb attacks that had been shaking Havana for some time, he expressed a suspicion that the government itself was mounting them in order to justify further repression. For: "No one with any sense can think that setting off a bomb in any old doorway can cause the fall of a government."[21]

First, as he had promised, Castro took "Naty" in his arms; they met in a secretly rented apartment, and their daughter Alina was born the following year, on March 19, 1956.[22] Natalia's husband was bitter about the liaison, but to keep up the bourgeois façade he initially accepted the child and agreed that it should bear the family name. Anyway, by then Castro had long been living abroad.

On June 12, 1955, Fidel Castro, still a member of the Orthodox Party, founded his own political organization in the shape of the 26th of July Movement. The chairman: Fidel Castro. It was done without any public announcement, but he and his friends must have realized that they were no longer safe in Cuba, as Batista had openly threatened violence: "The governing parties have brains, ears, and also hands."[23] By chance Castro heard that a car had already been riddled with bullets, so that his corpse could be placed there to make it look as if he had been killed in a shoot-out with the police. He decided to go into exile.[24] On July 7, the day he left Havana to join Raúl in Mexico, he wrote a letter to his comrade Carlos Franqui which the latter published in the popular magazine *Bohemia*:

I am packing for my departure from Cuba, but I have had to borrow money even to pay for my passport. . . . All doors to a peaceful political struggle have been closed to me. Like Martí, I think the time has come to seize our rights instead of asking for them, to grab instead of beg for them. Cuban patience has its limits. I will live somewhere in the Caribbean. There is no going back possible on this kind of journey, and if I return, it will be with tyranny beheaded at my feet.[25]

"Che," the Argentinean

Soon after his arrival in Mexico, Castro met a well-known fellow-Cuban, the one-eyed Alberto Bayo Giroud. This 65-year-old, famous (or notorious) as an old warhorse and expert in guerrilla warfare, had fought in the Spanish Civil War against Franco's armies and in Nicaragua against Anastasio Somoza. Bayo later recalled of Castro:

> The young man was telling me that he expected to defeat Batista in some future landing that he planned to carry out with men "when I have them," and with vessels "when I have the money to buy them." At that moment, however, he had not a single man or a single dollar. . . . Wasn't it amusing? He was asking me whether I would commit myself to teach guerrilla tactics to his future soldiers. . . . But what did it cost me to please him? "Yes," I said. "Yes, Fidel, I promise to instruct these boys the moment it is necessary."[26]

Castro, just turned 29, had already won the first three members of his expeditionary force: his brother Raúl, five years younger than himself; his old comrade Antonio "Nico" López; and a 27-year-old Argentinean asthmatic with wheezing lungs, Ernesto Guevara, whom his friends called by the Argentinean slang word for buddy, "Che."

"Che" was a doctor and a convinced Marxist, who had already been in Mexico City for three-quarters of a year, since September 1954. On his way there from Buenos Aires, he had spent some time in Guatemala and seen how, in response to a law on agrarian reform, the United States government, the United Fruit Company and CIA-funded mercenaries, together with disloyal officers in the Guatemalan army, had overthrown the democratically elected government of Jacobo Arbenz Guzmán. After fruitless attempts to help build a kind of revolutionary resistance in Guatemala, Guevara had had to leave for Mexico – which at that time, with its revolutionary history, was a gathering point for left-wing Latin

American exiles. Being short of money, he struggled along as street photographer and seller of books and toys, before finding work as a specialist in allergic diseases in Mexico City's central hospital. One day Nico López showed up there, with the ailing Raúl Castro in tow. López, who had commanded the attack on Bayamó during the Moncada episode and managed to escape capture, had already met and befriended Guevara in 1954 in Guatemala. López and Raúl now invited Che to meet Fidel – something he himself had had in mind since 1953, when he had listened in Central American cafés to the story of his epic challenge to Batista.

On the evening of July 8, 1955, the day after Fidel Castro's arrival in Mexico City, the two men met in Calle Empéran at the house of María Antonia González, a friend of Fidel's and Raúl's from Cuba.[27] It was to be a historic encounter: Fidel Castro, the daring figure with a natural talent for politics and the aura of a battle-tried revolutionary, always at the center of things, determined, energetic and confident of victory; and the quieter Che Guevara, more reserved and physically less robust, but equally self-assured and resolute.

They immediately felt a great sympathy with each other – even if they were not yet on the same wavelength ideologically. Years later Castro noted that at that time Che's "revolutionary development was more advanced than mine, ideologically speaking. From a theoretical point of view, he had a better background, he was more advanced as a revolutionary."[28] Their encounter in the Old Town of the Mexican capital was the beginning of a close friendship and a common political fate, in which Che, as chief ideologue, became the powerful number two in Cuba and decisively influenced the orientation of the revolution.

In his travel diary, Che observed: "I met Fidel Castro, the Cuban revolutionary. He is a young, intelligent guy, very sure of himself and extraordinarily audacious. We hit it off well."[29] The meeting finally offered him the perspective in life for which he had been searching: "After a few hours – by dawn – I had already embarked on the future expedition. . . . Fidel impressed me as an extraordinary man. He faced and resolved the most impossible things. . . . I shared in his optimism."[30]

The Calle Empéran apartment was rapidly built up into a kind of headquarters and information center for the *fidelistas*. On August 2, Castro wrote to his half-sister that his life in exile was "sad, lonely and hard." He also had a bout of 'flu: "My whole body aches. I have no Cuban cigars, and I really miss them."[31] To build and arm a guerrilla force required money – and he was virtually penniless. And on July 24 he wrote to Melba Hernández: "I had to pawn my coat to be able to bring out the first manifesto" [of the 26th of July Movement] by August 8.[32] In the end, he decided to turn to where Martí had found the means for his landing in the struggle for independence: to the Cuban exiles in the United States.

He even had to borrow the money for a train ticket, but on October 12 he set off through Texas and stayed for two months. After stops in Philadelphia, Union City (New Jersey), and Bridgeport (Connecticut), he arrived on October 23 in New York and then moved on to Miami, Tampa, and Key West. He addressed fund-raising rallies in each place, and set up a chain of "patriotic clubs" and "M-26-7 clubs" to support the movement. His most spectacular performances were on October 30, before an audience of 800 at the Palm Garden Hall, New York, and on November 20 before 1,000 invited guests at the Flagler Theater in Miami. Always elegantly dressed, in a grey three-piece suit and a striped tie, he presented himself as "following in Martí's footsteps" and promised: "I can inform you with complete certainty that in 1956 we will be free or we will be martyrs!"[33] After all expenses had been paid, he came away with 9,000 dollars; the clubs of sympathizers would later play a major role in funding and supplying the guerrilla war in the Sierra Maestra, and he also received money and weapons from Puerto Rico, Costa Rica, and Venezuela. But there were limits to what could be raised outside the country. Back in Cuba, many businessmen paid "revolutionary taxes," as a precaution in case the guerrillas were triumphant. The chairman of the Bacardi Rum Company, José M. Pepin Bosch y Lamarque, is said to have alone disbursed a million dollars into the coffers of the revolution.[34] That was still some way off, however. After his return to Mexico on December

10, the FBI opened a file on his activities in the United States and began to infiltrate the solidarity clubs.[35]

Stormy crossing on the *Granma*

In a manifesto published in *Bohemia* on March 19, 1956, Castro declared that his "26th of July Movement" was the only "revolutionary opposition of ordinary people, by ordinary people and for ordinary people," and the true heir of Eddy Chibás, the founder of the Orthodox Party.[36] Fresh support came from the Directorio Revolucionario (DR) led by the 24-year-old president of the FEU student federation, José Antonio Echeverría. On August 30, 1956, he and Castro signed a joint declaration in Mexico, undertaking to organize sabotage and other armed operations in Cuba that would create the revolutionary climate for an invasion and to coordinate all their further actions. Castro thought that this would keep a potential rival on a tight rein, but he was mistaken. For Echevarría soon tried to improve his position by organizing operations on his own initiative, and the following spring, when he staged a spectacular action to precipitate the downfall of Batista, he paid for his rashness with his life.

Other forces were at work in Cuba while Castro's people in Mexico practiced shooting and his supporters stirred up the island with attacks and protest actions. Early in April 1956, a small group of young army officers banded together in an anti-Batista conspiracy around Colonel Ramón Barquín; these *puros*, as they called themselves, were part of the establishment and stood close to the Orthodox Party. But their plans were betrayed, and Barquín was imprisoned on the Isle of Pines until the fall of Batista.

As Castro made no secret of his goals, the dictator did his best to forestall him. An agent of his army secret service, the SIM, traveled to Mexico and offered a reward of US$20,000 for some killers to dress in police uniform, arrest Castro and make him disappear. But Castro was tipped off, and the operation was eventually cancelled.

On June 20, 1956, however, the Mexican police suddenly detained Castro and his bodyguards, Universo Sánchez and Ramiro Valdés (later to be security chief after the revolution), after a spy had betrayed the whole logistical side of the organization, including its hideout and training camp on a farm outside Mexico City. On June 24, 28 rebels landed in jail, and Castro found himself accused of organizing a Communist conspiracy. Immediately he fired off an article from his prison cell, which was published in *Bohemia* in mid-July:

> Naturally the accusation of my being a Communist was absurd in the eyes of all who knew my public path in Cuba, without any kind of ties with the Communist Party. . . . What moral authority, on the other hand, does Mr Batista have to speak of communism when he was the Communist Party presidential candidate in the elections of 1940, if his electoral posters took shelter under the hammer and sickle, . . . if half a dozen of his present ministers and trusted collaborators were well-known members of the Communist Party?[37]

Thanks to great efforts on the part of Mexican and Cuban friends, and the support of sympathetic lawyers and Mexico's liberal former president, Lázaro Cárdenas, members of Castro's group were released in batches towards the end of July. But with Mexico no longer safe, time was pressing. Not only his widely known promise (to land in Cuba by the end of the year), but also the political acrimony of Echeverría and others inside the country, were impelling him to force the pace.

Then something unforeseeable distracted him: a woman threw his revolutionary plans into confusion. While he and his friends were in jail, Teresa "Teté" Casuso, a well-educated, attractive Cuban blonde and widow of the writer Pablo de la Torriente Brau who had been killed in the Spanish Civil War, read about them in a newspaper and showed up to ask for their help. She was accompanied by another Cuban, Isabel Custodio, a tall, exceptionally beautiful girl of about 18 who was staying with her at the time. In Teresa Casuso's words, the young woman "looked like an elegant model, with the rims of her enormous, innocent, greenish-brown eyes darkly accented in what she called the Italian fashion. On that day, her hair was its natural color of dark gold."[38]

Teresa Casuso remembers first seeing the crowd of men in the prison courtyard.

> In the middle, tall and clean-shaven with close-cropped chestnut hair, dressed soberly and correctly in a brown suit, standing out from the rest by his look and his bearing, was their chief, Fidel Castro. He gave one the impression of being noble, sure, deliberate – like a big Newfoundland dog. . . . He looked eminently serene, and inspired confidence and a sense of security.[39]

Continually glancing at Isabel Custodio out of the corner of his eye, he let Teresa Casuso know how honored he was by their visit. At the end, he and his men sang the Cuban national anthem for the two women.

After their release, Castro's attention turned in more senses than one to "Teté" Casuso's apartment, where he went not only to stash away weapons but always also to meet the young Isabel. His comrades now got to know a completely new side of their 29-year-old leader, who had fallen head over heels in love. Soon a passionate affair was developing between them: they seemed inseparable; he bought her little presents, new clothes, shoes, a large bottle of French perfume, and – because he disliked her all-too-revealing bikini – an old-fashioned bathing costume. Although he would have known that he was making himself "vulnerable" – since a "true revolutionary" had to give himself body and soul to the revolution – he treated her "like a princess," with tenderness and sensitivity, "just as a man should" (to quote her own words).[40]

After two months, he finally proposed to her and tried to obtain her parents' consent. But although at first she was willing enough, the relationship broke down soon afterwards, apparently because he wanted to make her a revolutionary and take her with him to Cuba. "The idea of going on the boat with him," she recalled, "was a subject of dispute because I would be the only woman. . . . It was a very difficult break. I left. I can't say why."[41]

45

She immediately went on to marry a Mexican businessman and former boyfriend. Castro was visibly disappointed, and one day when Teresa Casuso came across him assembling a machine pistol, he said to her that the revolution was also a "beautiful fiancée."[42] Teresa Casuso, for her part, long remained close to Castro and later worked for the Cuban diplomatic service.

In the second half of October, just a few days after another meeting between Castro and Echeverría, two of the latter's close comrades from the Directorio Revolucionario shot the head of Cuban military intelligence, Colonel Manuel Blanco Río, as he was leaving a night club in Havana. One of the two assassins was Rolando Cubela, a man who in the sixties would be hired by the CIA to murder Fidel Castro.

Since the revolutionaries were still without a ship, or money to buy one, Castro at last seemed disposed to make a pact with the devil. In late September, having swum the Río Grande unnoticed, he met in the small Texan town of McAllen none other than Cuban ex-President Prío, who placed the sum of 100,000 dollars at Castro's disposal in the hope of regaining power.[43] In October, Castro finally got his hands on a boat, using the services of his Mexican arms supplier. It was the *Granma* ("Grandmother"), then lying in a harbor near Tuxpán, whose external appearance was thoroughly in keeping with its name. He paid US$17,000 for the ramshackle wooden yacht, which had belonged to Robert B. Erickson (an American living in Mexico) and was badly in need of repair, plus another $2,000 for the use of a shed in which the rebels could prepare their sea journey.

On November 21, the Mexican authorities gave Castro and his men three days to leave the country, while the police seized the store of weapons in Teresa Casuso's house and placed her under temporary arrest. Castro lost no time before he gave his marching orders. The men moved at once from their hiding places to the perfunctorily repaired "landing craft," and loaded it with food, water, and matériel: that is, 35 rifles with telescopic sights, 55 Mexican rifles, three Thompson submachine guns and 40 light machine pistols, as well as two attack guns and boxes of ammunition.[44] On November 25, 1956, at 1.30 in the morning, the 21 by 5 meter *Granma* finally slipped, with navigation lights dimmed, out of the little port of Poza Rica near Tuxpán de Pantepéc. On board the former leisure boat, built way back in 1938 for a maximum of 25 persons, 82 guerrillas (50 having been left behind for lack of space[45]) now pitched and tossed in a stormy, rainy night as the two six-cylinder 250-PS diesel engines carried them the 1,235 nautical miles to their uncertain goal: the Cuban Revolution. As they entered the Gulf of Mexico, the men struck up the Cuban national anthem in defiance of the lashing waves, before sinking, like sardines squashed together in a tin, into long days and nights of sea-sickness.[46]

It was little short of a miracle, down more to luck than seamanship, that the *Granma* reached anywhere at all. For seven days (two more than planned), riding only just above the waterline, the overloaded boat had to contend with unrelenting bad weather and stormy seas. One engine broke down, the men had to bale out water, and after five days there was nothing left to eat or drink. The landing itself was considerably less smooth than Martí's 60 years before, as the *Granma* ran out of fuel around four o'clock on the morning of December 2. The boat eventually ran aground before the mangrove swamps of Los Cayuelos on the south coast of Oriente Province, some 60 yards from shore and $1\frac{1}{4}$ miles short of the target beach at Las Coloradas. "It wasn't a landing, it was a shipwreck," said Juan Manuel Márquez (Castro's deputy, soon to be captured and killed by Batista's troops).[47]

In the end, most of the equipment had to be left behind. Hungry, thirsty and weak, completely exhausted, the men had to make incredible efforts, often up to their chins in marshy water, to struggle through the mangrove tangle to reach dry land. Then, as daybreak came, spotter planes flew overhead. In an interview a fortnight earlier with the pro-government paper *Alerta*, Castro had sent a message to Batista: "We strongly reaffirm the promise we made for the year 1956: We will be free men or martyrs."[48] And so, they found a large military force awaiting them. No sooner did they have solid ground beneath their feet than days of hide-and-seek began.

Only when they had reached the 90-mile long by 30-mile wide chain of the Sierra Maestra, with its thick, almost impenetrable rainforest, did Castro and his men feel some degree of safety.

After three days, at noon on December 5, an army patrol surprised them near Alegría del Pío and opened fire. A peasant met en route, as well as some carelessly discarded scraps of sugarcane, had given them away. It was nearly the end: some of Castro's people fell; Che Guevara was badly wounded in the shoulder and lost a lot of blood. For days the army kept up the chase, pursuing them with incendiary bombs through the sugar plantations.

"Our group was completely dispersed," Castro later said. "I had two men and two rifles with me."[49] He did not know where the others were, or even whether any of them had survived. The 30-year-old leader, together with his bodyguard Universo Sánchez and doctor Faustino Pérez, both aged 36, lay for five days in a cane field without stirring. There was only one thing Castro could not refrain from doing: he talked and talked – in whispers. Despite their seemingly hopeless situation, Faustino Pérez recalled, "speaking with the enthusiasm that characterizes him, Fidel told us his future plans. But not only plans for the future . . . about organizing the country, about the people of Cuba, the history of Cuba, the future of Cuba. And about the necessity of launching a revolution, a real revolution." Sánchez, a simple farmer, said to himself at one point: "Shit, he's gone crazy."[50] He could not believe they would be alive for much longer.

A guerrillero in the Sierra Maestra

During the days of pursuit, Castro lost three-quarters of his guerrilla force: 61 men. On December 16, he and his two companions finally reached the rendezvous at the farm of Ramón "Mongo" Pérez, in a hard-to-reach area on the western slopes of the Sierra Maestra. When Raúl and four more men showed up a couple of days later, Fidel Castro amazed everyone with the assurance: "We'll win this war. We are just beginning to fight."[51] Next to arrive was a group of eight, including Che Guevara, Camilo Cienfuegos and Juan Almeida, so that for Christmas 1956 there were 16 of them. Over the next few days, another five found their way back. Around New Year, when they entered the mountains, 21 of the original 82 had made it – to which eight farmers from the surrounding area added themselves. Their meager weaponry seemed better suited for a hunting party than a revolution.

The outside world thought they were long since dead, as the American UPI news agency had reported on December 4.[52] The press and radio also quoted government sources to the effect that the invading force had been wiped out, and that Fidel and Raúl Castro had lost their lives.

Some knew better, though – one of them being the dictator Batista. More and more often his soldiers were having to deal with the "dead men," who would suddenly appear from the forest, launch an attack, and again melt away into the trees. Mountain farmers also knew that the guerrillas were there, for they helped them and were often pillaged, tortured or killed by the army for that reason. And members of the National Directorate of the 26th of July Movement knew from messengers that Castro was alive.

Once he had moved into the mountains and established a supply link with Santiago de Cuba and Manzanillo, Castro arranged a meeting for February 16 with the core of the 11-person National Directorate, in the Los Chorros farmhouse on the northern side of the Sierra. Apart from the Castro brothers, Che Guevara, and Faustino Pérez, the other participants were the 21-year-old Frank País (head of the movement in Oriente), the 36-year-old Celia Sánchez from Manzanillo (who helped País coordinate resistance activity in Oriente), Haydée Santamaría (Castro's comrade from the Moncada attack) and her new fiancé, founder member Armando Hart, and País's close colleague, the 27-year-old Vilma Espín, a rum producer's daughter with a chemistry degree from the Massachusetts Institute of Technology. Just as Celia Sánchez would now be Fidel's closest friend and partner and live mainly with him in the Sierra from the end of 1957, so Vilma Espín moved up to become Raúl's companion. After the revolution, she became his wife.

The purpose of the meeting was to take the struggle out of the mountains into the towns and villages, and to formulate a country-wide strategy of underground resistance to the dictatorship. The outcome was Castro's "First Manifesto from the Sierra Maestra," dated February 20, 1957, which sympathizers of the 26th of July Movement soon began to distribute among the Cuban public. The tone was as exaggerated as it was confident of victory.

> Unable to defeat the Revolution with arms, the regime started spreading the most cowardly lie that our expeditionary force and I had been exterminated. After almost three months of sacrifice and effort, we can tell the country that the "exterminated" force smashed a siege of more than a thousand soldiers between Niquero and Pilón; . . . that the "exterminated" force, whose ranks were steadily reinforced by the peasants of the Sierra Maestra, bravely resisted the attacks of the air force and the mountain artillery; and it fought successfully almost every day against more than 3,000 men equipped with all kinds of modern weapons: bazookas, mortars, and several types of machine guns. Their desperate but powerless efforts have converted the Sierra Maestra into a hell, where falling bombs, the rattle of machine guns, and bursts of rifle fire are heard incessantly.[53]

The manifesto summoned the whole country to civil disobedience and violent, paramilitary actions against the Batista regime – including, where necessary, assassination of "lackeys who torture and kill revolutionaries . . . , and all those who stand in the way of the Movement's success."[54] Particular aims were to be the building of resistance organizations up and down the country and the raising of sufficient funds. Revolutionary groups in the towns and villages were to mount sabotage operations against state institutions and to destroy the country's main source of income, sugarcane. To set a good example, Castro ensured that the first cane fields to go up in flames were those of his own family in Birán. His father did not have to witness it, however, as he had died there at the age of 80 on October 21, 1956, a few weeks before the *Granma* landing. From that time, the property was managed by Fidel's elder brother, Ramón. According to their sister Juana, who in 1963 fled via Mexico to exile in the United States, the devastation of the family's own plantations permanently damaged the relationship between Fidel and his mother.[55]

50

Castro scored a major coup when the experienced war correspondent of the *New York Times*, Herbert L. Matthews, visited him in the Sierra Maestra and instantly placed his revolutionary struggle in the international limelight. After a difficult climb, during which he had to be continually on the alert for Batista's soldiers, the 57-year-old journalist reached Castro's headquarters on the morning of February 17, 1957. "He knew he needed publicity," Matthews explained; "he always had a keen eye for that."[56] Celia Sánchez later recalled that, since "at that time there were only eighteen partisans in the Sierra Maestra,"[57] they decided to put on a show for their guest. While the interview was taking place, Raúl Castro directed the little band as in a revolving-door farce, moving it noisily around to perform various activities on all sides. At one point, a messenger ran up bathed in sweat to deliver an important report from a "Second Column" that still existed only in the realm of the imagination.

When the interview appeared on the front page of the *New York Times* on February 24, 1957, "with a photograph of Fidel holding his precious telescopic rifle, it created a tremendous sensation in Cuba and throughout Latin America. The story had come at the ebb tide of Fidel's fortunes, and . . . made him a hero and symbol for the resistance."[58] At first, Batista's defense minister flatly denied that the interview had taken place at all. But, Matthews notes, "my newspaper thereupon published a photograph of Fidel and myself together in the Sierra."[59] The accompanying article characterized Castro as follows: "The personality of the man is overpowering. It was easy to see that his men adored him and also to see why he has caught the imagination of the youth of Cuba all over the island. Here was an educated, dedicated fanatic, a man of ideals, of courage and of remarkable qualities of leadership."[60] Castro's adversary, Batista, admitted after his own flight from Cuba: "The interview . . . was of considerable propaganda value to the rebels. Castro was to begin his era as a legendary figure."[61]

The confirmation that Castro was alive did not cause rejoicing among all Batista's opponents. Rivals felt under pressure to take some action to counter his fast-growing popularity, and in the course of 1957 many attempts were made to forestall and sideline the man supposedly stuck in his Sierra Maestra stronghold.

On March 13 Castro's ally from the Directorio Revolucionario, José Antonio Echeverría, seemed to show that the ends could just as well be served without a detour via Mexico and the mountains. With a little over 150 young men, far more than the number of fighters available to Castro at that time, he stormed into the presidential palace in Havana with the aim of killing Batista. He also occupied a radio station and personally announced that the dictator had been executed, but in reality Batista had been able to climb a short flight of steps to safety in the top part of the building. The crazy putsch attempt ended shortly afterwards in a hail of bullets, and Echeverría found his "hero's death" on the pavement in front of the university steps. Altogether, 40 people were killed – not including the oppositionists and innocent people who were tortured and killed in the ensuing round up.

Ex-President Prío, who had put up the funds for *Granma*, also wanted to block Castro's path to power and organized a landing of his own. In late May the yacht *Corinthia* completed the crossing from Miami and reached the north coast of Oriente Province with 27 rebels on board, but four days later, on May 28, they were betrayed by a farmer and 23 of them were hunted down and shot without hesitation.

Four months after that, on September 5, a revolt by liberal-minded naval officers from the Cuban aristocracy broke out in Cienfuegos, and air force Colonel Carlos Tabernilla, the son of Batista's notorious chief of staff, had the city unceremoniously bombed. Hundreds of innocent people were killed. The operations were carried out by US-supplied B-26 bombers, even though the Cuban–American military cooperation pact expressly forbade their use in internal crises. The dictator's troops then broke back into the city, torturing captured rebels and shooting 33 officers. Whereas top US generals acclaimed Batista as a "great president" and "outstanding soldier," and bestowed a decoration of the US Legion of Merit on Colonel Tabernilla, liberal forces in the State Department were appalled at what had happened.[62] They thought it better for Batista to be removed, so that the wind could be taken in good time out of Castro's sails.

On the very day when the *Corinthia* rebels were being mopped up, Castro further strengthened his own position by capturing El Uvero, a strategically important garrison of 57 soldiers on the edge of the Sierra Maestra. He used for the attack 80 of a force now numbering 127 men; six were killed in that dawn of May 28, 1957, two received life-threatening injuries, and seven more were wounded, while on the other side 14 soldiers were killed and 19 wounded. Che Guevara noted in his diary: "It was an assault by men who had advanced bare-chested against an enemy protected by very poor defences. . . . For us this was the victory that marked our coming of age. From this battle on, our morale grew tremendously; our decisiveness and our hopes for triumph increased also."[63]

Che, who had long been part of Castro's leadership, proved himself as one of the most daring and canny fighters, despite the severe asthma that often forced his comrades to carry him through the mountains. Soon after the skirmish at El Uvero, Fidel Castro promoted his "field doctor" – with whom he had developed a brotherly relationship – to the rank of *comandante*, the highest in his guerrilla hierarchy. Until then there had been only one: Castro himself. "It made me feel the proudest man on earth that day," wrote Guevara.[64]

The guerrillas won the sympathy of the poor, and not only by paying whenever possible for the food they took or were given along the way. As they advanced into new land, they declared it a "liberated area" – liberating the rural population from the landowners and their bailiffs, and providing them with means of subsistence through, as it were, an advance land reform. They executed one notorious overseer who had murdered landless peasants and rebel sympathizers; and they distributed captured livestock to the *campesinos*, thereby also ensuring their own supplies. Batista's army, by contrast, spread only fear and terror among the rural masses, wreaked only murder and destruction as they combed the land for the insurgents.

Castro and his comrades showed no mercy, however, towards farmers who acted as spies for the Batista regime. In one case, which served as a warning to others, they were able to prove that a scout of theirs, Eutimio Guerra, had accepted 10,000 dollars from the army to lead the guerrillas into a deadly ambush and to murder Castro with his own hands. Castro sentenced him to death. "Precisely what happened next has remained a carefully guarded Cuban state secret for four decades," wrote Guevara's biographer, John Lee Anderson, in 1997.[65] According to "Cuban sources," Che Guevara personally killed Eutimio and, from then on, had a reputation for ruthlessly dealing with any breaches of revolutionary norms. In Guevara's original diary, we read: "The situation was uncomfortable for the people and for [Eutimio], so I ended the problem giving him a shot with a .32 pistol in the right side of the brain, with exit orifice in the right temporal. He gasped a little while and was dead."[66] Anderson shows that this version differs considerably from Che's official report, and that these sentences do not appear in any of Guevara's *Selected Works* published up to now.

Castro's skirmishes, his growing number of fighters and his territorial gains in the mountains could not obscure the fact that the movement was making no headway elsewhere in Cuba. In the view of the young and self-confident Frank País, whom Castro had made national coordinator of its operations, the 26th of July Movement suffered from a "caudillo problem."[67] Castro was seen as crude and intemperate, and people were especially afraid of his outbursts of rage against such close comrades as Celia Sánchez; the only one spared them seemed to be Che Guevara. País complained to Raúl Chibás, brother of the founder of the Orthodox Party, that Castro took decisions without regard for the directorate of the Movement; and that, with his "All weapons for the Sierra!" position, he attached too little importance to the fighters in the lowlands, who, at great risk to themselves, were conducting countrywide operations to destabilize the regime as well as organizing the chain of supplies to the mountains.[68]

In a series of spirited letters to Castro, País tried to convince him that it was necessary to have a number of bourgeois-liberal reformist politicians on his general staff: "You must have heard the tendentious statements that attempt to portray you as an ambitious man, surrounded by immature boys . . . but without . . . support from serious and responsible elements. . . . In a revolution one cannot always hold meetings, nor can everything be centralized in one person."[69] País did emphasize that Castro would naturally have the final say, but the challenge to his authority was clear, and it was only with difficulty that Castro held back his anger. He wrote to País:

> I'm very happy, and I congratulate you, that you so clearly saw the necessity of formulating plans on a national and systematic scale. We'll keep fighting here as long as it is necessary. And we'll finish this battle with either the death or triumph of the real Revolution. . . . What is referred to as our little world, the Sierra, . . . is really our big world. . . . Your letters speak for themselves.[70]

Tactician that he was, however, Castro followed some of País's advice in a further "Sierra Maestra manifesto." This promised free elections, on the basis of the 1940 Constitution, after a period of transition from the Batista dictatorship; social and economic reforms; an agrarian reform, with appropriate compensation for big landowners; and a mass literacy campaign. It also warned other countries against intervention in Cuba.

When it was published in *Bohemia* on July 28, 1957, the manifesto had precisely the desired effect and won Castro the broader support for which País had been looking. But País was no longer able to rejoice at the success of the initiative: on July 30, just two days after its publication, he and another comrade fell into the hands of Santiago police chief José María Salas and a particularly notorious policeman, the "Black Hand," who killed them with a bullet in the base of the skull. Apparently, a tapped telephone conversation with Vilma Espín had set them on his trail. País's death provoked huge protests and a three-day general strike in Santiago. Remarkably, however, the man whom local cadres appointed to succeed him was not Castro's choice, Faustino Pérez, but País's own close collaborator René Ramos Latour, who would himself fall in battle exactly a year after País's death.

Representatives of seven Cuban opposition groups (including the Auténticos, the FEU, and the Directorio Revolucionario), which all seem to have received financial support from ex-President Prío, took the July manifesto as the occasion for a meeting in October 1957 in Miami. Two people from Castro's

26th of July Movement were also there – without his authorization. The meeting resulted in the adoption of the so-called Miami Pact, published in the US press on November 1, which envisaged the formation of a Junta de Liberación Cubana (Cuban Liberation Council) and a request for recognition by the United States.

In the Sierra Maestra, the pact was immediately seen as part of the intrigues of old power groups and freeriders, through which Prío in particular, already linked to the CIA, sought to advance himself as an alternative to Castro. After nearly six weeks of silence, Castro's eventual refusal to support the pact ensured that it would never be more than a scrap of paper. What incensed him most was that it did not even categorically reject the prospect of a military junta for Cuba. And he regarded as a provocation the idea that, after the fall of Batista, his rebel army should integrate into the regular (that is, "Batistan") armed forces. "The leadership of the struggle against tyranny," he wrote, "is and will continue to be in Cuba and in the hands of the revolutionary fighters. . . . The exiles must cooperate in this struggle. . . . If our conditions are rejected, . . . we will continue the struggle alone, as we have up to now."[71] One of these conditions was that his candidate for provisional president of the Republic should be accepted. He had already chosen the respected judge Manuel Urrutia Lleó for that post, a man who had shown great civil courage at a trial of eight rebels in May 1957, when he had (unsuccessfully) opposed their imprisonment for eight years, on the grounds that they were "models of dignity and patriotism."

The next attempt to involve Castro in a political alliance and to end the civil war came on March 1, 1958, from the bishops of the Catholic Church, under Cardinal Arteaga, who proposed the establishment of a "commission of reconciliation" and a government of national unity. But the majority could not bring themselves actually to demand the resignation of Batista as a prerequisite for such a peaceful compromise. This gave Castro the opportunity to reject this initially popular initiative, with the argument that the Church was placing itself on the dictator's side.

At the beginning of 1958, after numerous battles and skirmishes in eastern Cuba, the rebels controlled nearly 2,000 square miles of territory[72] and were constantly expanding their radius of operations, although they still had fewer than 300 men under arms. Raúl Castro, now also a *comandante* along with Juan Almeida and Camilo Cienfuegos, opened a second front in March in the Sierra del Cristal and Sierra Nipe, to the east and north of the Sierra Maestra, more or less encircling the brothers' parental home. Meanwhile the rebels did what they could to put together an infrastructure in the "liberated territory." On Che Guevara's instructions, they built hospitals, clinics and schools and brought out a hectographed newspaper; they created workshops, a small cigar factory and even an ammunition factory, as well as a training center for new recruits. From February 24, 1958, the Radio Rebelde transmitter broadcast pro-Castro propaganda and announcements, under the direction of the journalist Carlos Franqui. The confiscation of 10,000 cattle and other livestock from big landowners, and their distribution mostly to peasants without any property, ensured provisions for both the local population and the rebel forces. The lawyer Humberto Sorí-Marín drew up the legal basis for these actions in October 1958, in the shape of a revolutionary agrarian reform.

321 against 10,000

When Batista, on March 12, 1958, again suspended basic rights, the rebels issued a 22-page manifesto calling for a general strike early the following month. Castro was skeptical about its chances of success, as the rebels could count neither upon the Batista-controlled trade union federation (the Confederación de Trabajadores de Cuba) nor upon the Communists. He was right: the strike call was not widely heeded, especially in western Cuba. This brought such a loss of face that Batista thought he could turn the episode to his advantage. Inside the movement, however, the setback actually strengthened the position of Castro, who in a circular letter blamed it on poor organization by the lowland-dominated National Directorate. In a letter to Celia Sánchez, the fury that had been building up for months finally burst forth:

I am the supposed leader of this Movement, and in the eyes of history I must take responsibility for the stupidity of others, and I am a shit who can decide on nothing at all. With the excuse of opposing caudillism, each one attempts more and more to do what he feels like doing. I am not such a fool that I don't realize this. . . . I will not give up my critical spirit and intuition which have helped me so much to understand situations before.[73]

Batista, sensing his chance, now mobilized more than 14 battalions or a total of 10,000 soldiers for a general offensive (codenamed *Fin de Fidel,* "End of Fidel"), which began on May 20, 1958. Three combat forces assailed the Sierra Maestra fortress, one landing on the coast to the south, the other two advancing from the north and north-west, with the support of heavy artillery, armored vehicles, helicopters, aircraft, and navy frigates. The objective was to surround and "exterminate" the enemy.

At this time, Castro had 321 men at his disposal,[74] inadequately armed and especially short of ammunition. His brother Raúl had another 150 on the second front, but now he needed them himself. On the other hand, the guerrillas could draw "reinforcement" from the now-familiar mountains, forests, gorges, and valleys, in a Sierra Maestra that was still uncharted territory on the Cuban army's maps.

The government troops were under the command of General Eulogio Cantillo and Fidel's arch-enemy from Moncada days, General Alberto del Río Chaviano, the son-in-law of Batista's chief of staff Francisco Tabernilla. The two generals, who had a deep aversion to each other, were later blamed for a number of serious mistakes. It even seems that Cantillo had a certain sympathy for the rebels – or at least one imagines so from Castro's emotional letter to him in which he tried to drive a wedge deeper among the top ranks of the army. He wrote:

I realize that you are today the most prestigious and influential officer in the inner councils of the army, whose fate you can influence decisively for the good of the country, and it is to the country alone that the soldiers owe their allegiance. Perhaps when the offensive is over, if we are still alive, I will write you again to clarify my thinking and to tell you what I think that you, the army, and we can do for the benefit of Cuba, on which the eyes of all America are focused at this moment.[75]

The start of the offensive seemed to go well for the military. Troops pushed on through the foothills, while aircraft bombed what were suspected to be rebel positions. Only a few minor exchanges took place with the invisible enemy, who was trying to entice them into the forest. But the army's numerical superiority allowed it to draw dangerously close to the key rebel positions.

The threat was especially acute in the River Plate area on the south coast, where the insurgents had overrun their first army post in January 1957, and where they had since located part of their infrastructure, including a secret landing strip. Castro's own headquarters lay near the river's source, sheltering in the proximity of the 2,000-meter Pico Turquino, the highest in the Sierra. From a captured plan of battle, the guerrilla leader knew that the military would concentrate its main strike force in this area – and he was becoming nervous. On June 19 he reported from headquarters to Guevara: "The situation at the beach is extraordinarily dangerous. . . . We're running the risk of losing not only the territory but the hospital too, the radio station, the bullets, mines, food, etc. I have nothing but my rifle here to confront this new situation."[76] That day, June 19, 1958, marked the most critical phase for Castro. One month after the start of Batista's big push, the rebels were running short of food and ammunition; they had only a few square miles still under their control.

Yet the Batista army, despite its superior numbers and its air support, does not appear to have grasped the reality on the ground. "For two hours the fucking planes have been at us," he reported to Guevara. "The bombs they are dropping are napalm."[77] Numerous civilians fell victim to this hellish force, but in the end it was not capable of wiping out Castro's units. Since he could not afford a pitched battle, he relied on flexible guerrilla tactics: his men drew the soldiers into ambushes, laid high-explosive mines, occupied narrow gaps, turned the jungle-clad sierra into a deadly trap for individual soldiers. By implanting the idea that they were lurking everywhere, the rebels sowed terror among the government forces (two-thirds of whom were raw recruits) and continually eroded their morale. Not only did the rebels' real strength remain a mystery, but loyalty was crumbling in the ranks of the army. The ferment had been growing especially since the spring, when the US Congress had suspended military aid to Batista.

Soon there were signs that the tide had turned in Castro's favor. On June 29, 1958, he gave the order for an all-out attack on a key position and gleefully predicted: "That will be the end of the offensive and of Batista."[78] The day before, on the Yara River near Santo Domingo, the rebels had ambushed and wiped out three companies of the 22nd Battalion. Castro described the battle as follows:

> The 22nd Battalion . . . advanced in order toward the Sierra, but a powerful mine with more than 65 lbs of TNT exploded. . . . The first company was totally decimated by the rebel forces. . . . When Major Villavicencio ordered the retreat, Batista's soldiers fled in complete disarray, abandoning large numbers of dead and wounded, as well as quantities of equipment, on the field of battle. . . . Lieutenant Colonel [Ángel] Sánchez Mosquera sent a new company. . . . But the rebels . . . prepared a new ambush, with a new TNT mine, which exploded in the middle of the advancing new company.[79]

Out of a total of nearly a thousand soldiers, only a third or so came out of it alive.

On July 28, 1958, in the Venezuelan capital Caracas, the eight major Cuban opposition parties and anti-Batista groups signed a "Manifesto of the Civil-Revolutionary Opposition Front" and proclaimed Fidel Castro sole leader of the revolution. The agreement, which was read out over Castro's Radio Rebelde, called for "a broad civil–revolutionary coalition" to overthrow the "criminal dictatorship" and, following the establishment of a transition government, the reintroduction of "constitutional democratic norms."

The signature of the Communist PSP was missing from the appeal, which had been composed by Castro and the head of

Radio Rebelde, Carlos Franqui. But in late July, to avoid being left on the shelf, PSP leader Carlos Rafael Rodríguez – the Party's most experienced politician, who had been part of Batista's cabinet in the early 1940s – struggled off to the Sierra to eat humble pie. He stayed there until August 10, and it seemed that the PSP was willing to accept Castro's claim to be supreme leader of the opposition to Batista. For a time after the victory of the revolution, Rodríguez would be one of the most important figures in Castro's team – and he remained part of it until his death in December 1997. For, indeed, since the abortive general strike, it had been clear to Castro that he would not be able to build a new state with only amateurs, and that he needed reliable people with organizational experience who were prepared to work under tight discipline. This apparent readiness of Castro to work with the Communists on an ad hoc basis brought him closer to the positions of his brother and Che Guevara.

The top command of Batista's task force never recovered from the crushing defeat of three battalions; the troops' morale hit rock bottom, with thoughts of escape uppermost in their minds. Thus, when bad weather further hindered military activity, the big push against Castro fell apart – as in a bad dream, the soldiers suddenly vanished. On August 20, 1958, Castro triumphantly broadcast over Radio Rebelde:

> After 76 days of unceasing fighting on the First front of the Sierra Maestra, the Rebel Army has clearly repulsed and virtually destroyed the cream of the forces of the tyranny. . . . More than thirty clashes and six large-scale battles have taken place. . . . The rebel columns will advance in every direction toward the rest of the territory of the nation and nothing or no one will be able to stop them.[80]

It has been estimated that 1,000 of Batista's soldiers were killed or seriously wounded in the fighting.[81] The guerrillas put their own losses at just 27 dead and approximately 50 wounded. A total of 433 Batista troops were captured, along with large quantities of weapons and ammunition.[82] There are no figures concerning the evidently high number of civilian casualties in Oriente Province.

While Castro and his men remained in the east and, together with Raúl and Almeida, continued harassing the government forces, Che Guevara and Camilo Cienfuegos took the war to the center of the island with a force of some 600 guerrillas. But although they won every skirmish with Batista's army, they lost all their vehicles to air attacks or fuel shortages and had to travel hundreds of miles on foot, often across swamps or raging torrents. By the autumn, when they finally reached their goal in central Cuba, they were starving and their clothes were in tatters. First, they managed to cut the only west–east road from Havana to Santiago and to put the railway out of operation, spreading chaos and disintegration throughout the country. But the real turning-point came between December 29 and 31, 1958, when Che Guevara and 300 rebels besieged and finally took Santa Clara, a strategically important city with 150,000 inhabitants. During the action, they captured a whole garrison of 2,500 soldiers, who were thoroughly demoralized despite the 10 tanks at their disposal, and (by surrounding and threatening to blow it up) the last armored train, whose 19 wagons held 400 soldiers and a number of heavy weapons.

Military successes in mountainous terrain were not the only decisive element in the collapse of the regime. The island was also progressively shaken by an estimated 30,000 acts of sabotage[83] against public companies and institutions in the cities, sugar-processing plants or large estates in the country, and key public or private-sector economic installations. State terror and corruption, bestial torture, and murder of political opponents as well as non-participants, meant that more and more people came to see the rebels as liberators. The agency with the greatest responsibility for the bloodshed was the SIM, the Military Intelligence Service set up with the help of the FBI, which, as the US consul in Santiago was aware, took "no prisoners."[84] Similar in style was the much-feared BRAC (Bureau for the Suppression of Communist Subversion), whose "father" was rumored to be former CIA boss Allen Dulles, brother of Secretary of State John Foster Dulles.[85] Anger at the activity of these repressive forces had been rising also among American liberal opinion and political circles, especially since the Congressional elections of 1956 had resulted in a Democratic Party majority and put pressure on the pro-Batista policies long pursued by conservative Republicans.

Cuba was more dependent than ever upon the United States. Between 1953 and 1958, direct US investment had increased by more than a third from $686 million to one billion dollars. Roughly 40 percent of Cuban sugar was produced in US-owned refineries; 90 percent of telephone and electricity services were controlled by US corporations; the island's railways, oil industry, and nickel mines were in US hands, as were large parts of its banking system. The American Mafia ran gambling, prostitution, and whole sections of the tourist industry. The United States bought at subsidized prices 58 percent of Cuba's annual sugar production, covering a third of its total requirement. Sugar represented 80 percent of all Cuban exports, but whereas two-thirds of that total went to the United States, three-quarters of all Cuban imports originated there. The sugarcane monoculture dictated by the mighty "sugar barons" and the US market meant that Cuba was forced to spend good money on grain, flour, and rice from its neighbor to the north – so much on rice, in fact, that it took a third of all US exports of the commodity.[86] The American Way of Life, which 150,000 relatively well-paid Cuban employees of US firms were among the most conspicuous to enjoy, marked large parts of the country's social landscape.

The CIA appears to have been the only institution which finally recognized, in late summer 1958, that the days of the Batista regime were numbered. In fact, not only did it try to keep an eye on the rebels, it also built up contacts with them at an early stage, for any future eventuality. The US vice-consul in Santiago, Robert D. Wiecha, was reputed to be the CIA's link with the rebels in the mountains, who supplied them with important equipment so that contact could be made with them as and when it was necessary. But claims that as much as 50,000 dollars passed through Wiecha to Castro's forces, or that weapons from Castro support groups in the United States were delivered to them via the CIA front company Interarms, have never been confirmed.[87] Referring to credible sources, Tad Szulc concludes that the CIA organized arms flights to Raúl Castro's second front.[88] And Castro did indeed receive weapons from Cuban exiles in the United States who were well disposed towards him.

It has also been persistently claimed that the Mafia, through its leading member on the spot, Santos Trafficante, did the rebels many a favor in this respect; it had a lot to lose and thought well ahead. Although Castro at first announced: "We are not only disposed to deport the gangsters, but to shoot them,"[89] after the victory of the revolution he bowed to pressure from the tourist industry and allowed them to continue operating for several months. But Trafficante was arrested in April 1959 and packed off to the United States in July, it being rumored that the time he had spent behind bars had been pleasant enough. The powerful Meyer Lansky did not remain that long: he followed his own instincts and headed off early in January.

As Castro had feared, the Cuban general staff worked with the United States to cheat him of victory at the last moment. Eisenhower's people in Washington desperately tried to neutralize Castro and, when they finally gave up on the Batista regime, stumbled from one political dead-end to the next in their search for an alternative. Elections held under their pressure on November 3, 1958, proved to be a complete farce, as the opposition boycotted them and Batista's cronies capped it all by crudely falsifying the results. The "victory" of a pro-Batista nonentity, Andrés Rivero Agüero, was lost from view amid the public ridicule. Nor did he ever manage to assume office, since the capture of Santa Clara by Che Guevara and Camilo Cienfuegos had practically decided the outcome of the civil war. All around the country, the army was laying down arms; the leaders of the repression thought only of saving their skins and their money. Fidel and Raúl Castro, with a force now numbering 3,000 men, scarcely fired a shot in capturing a Santiago occupied by 5,000 of Batista's troops. Nor did they meet any resistance on their way into Havana.

After the collapse of Batista's offensive, Castro used secret contacts in an effort to win over vacillating officers as well as his former adversary in the Sierra Maestra, General Cantillo, whom he eventually met on December 28 in Oriente Province. The two men agreed that the armed forces would surrender unconditionally on December 31. But it turned out that the general was playing a double game. Having immediately taken Batista into his confidence, he shortly afterwards asked Castro for a week's delay – with the aim of taking over himself and leaving Castro empty-handed.

On January 1, 1959, Batista signed his resignation statement, transferred command of the armed forces to General Cantillo, and handed over his presidential powers to the aged head of the Supreme Court, Carlos Manuel Piedra. Around two o'clock in the morning, he climbed aboard a waiting DC-4 together with 40 or so relatives and friends, wished "good health" to those for whom there was no room, and flew away to exile in the Dominican Republic. In the course of the night, two more aircraft took off with Batista's henchmen and their families.

So that he would not have to pinch and scrape, the dictator had meanwhile plundered the national currency reserves. Thus, when the first Cuban president of the National Bank, Felipe Pazos, gave his report five weeks later, it was revealed "that the previous regime had embezzled or appropriated $424 million of the gold and dollar reserves covering the Cuban peso."[90] Batista's own "personal" fortune was then estimated as high as US$300 million, leaving the victorious rebels just $20 million that he had forgotten in his haste to take with him. Also left behind were mountains of documents that testified to the corruption and crimes of the Batista regime, so that the *barbudos* [that is, the "bearded men," as they were popularly known] would have an easy job demonstrating the necessity and legitimacy of their revolution, as well as proving the guilt of thieves and murderers from the old regime, who were apprehended and brought before a revolutionary court. The documents also revealed the extent of cooperation between the United States government and Batista's criminal regime.[91]

Castro celebrated the New Year in his headquarters at Palma Soriano near Santiago de Cuba, in the illustrious company of Celia Sánchez, PSP leader Carlos Rafael Rodríguez, the popular American actor Errol Flynn, and many of his close comrades in the rebel army. It was here that Castro learned over Radio Rebelde that Batista had fled and that Cantillo and Piedra had been installed as his successors. Castro was beside himself. "General Cantillo betrayed us," he declared in a statement the next day.

"All the positions and ranks conferred by the military junta . . . are null and void, and whoever accepts a position designated by the military junta will be guilty of treason, and it will be considered a sign of a counterrevolutionary attitude."[92] Over Radio Rebelde he called a general strike for January 2 and, as a precaution, declared Santiago de Cuba provisional capital of the country. Once it became clear that Cantillo had no authority, no power base and no support, the Americans desperately forced him to play the last card of releasing Colonel Barquín (the jailed leader of a naval mutiny at Cienfuegos) and positioning him at his side. Barquín, however, realizing that there was nothing more to be gained, went over to the other side and immediately had Cantillo arrested. Then he made contact with Castro and asked his nominee, Urrutia, to take over the functions of president and to form a government. On January 3 the 26th of July Movement finally assumed power.

The path to victory had been made easier by the political vacuum that had enveloped all the institutions. After Batista's coup in 1952, many Cubans had been prepared to put up with him, so long as he offered an end to political and criminal violence on the streets. But things only grew worse: the corruption and mob rule reached new peaks, while the people's living standards, previously among the highest in Latin America, went into decline. Windfall profits due to a rise in world sugar prices provided some relief, but then unemployment rose in the course of 1958 from 8.9 to 18 percent; the poor became poorer, and the relative prosperity of the middle layers was eroded by inflation and falling sugar prices. Already in the first two years following Batista's coup, income per head of the population had fallen 18 percent; in 1958 it fell back to the level of 1947, and just between 1956 and 1957 prices for staple foods shot up 40 percent. The US economy, dominating Cuba in the same old free-and-easy manner, made even sections of the middle and upper classes susceptible to Castro's struggle for national independence.[93] Soon the "voluntary" payment of taxes to the revolution was running so high that the rebels often had more money than ammunition, and Castro could even instruct his Comandante Almeida to pay, if necessary, one dollar for a single rifle bullet.[94]

Batista, the mulatto son of a construction worker from Oriente, had not seized power as the representative of a particular social layer, but had supported himself on army officers who had risen alongside him in the 1930s; socially and politically he had no fatherland. The officer elite recruited from the middle and upper classes – the elite to which the Cienfuegos naval mutineers belonged - had many reservations vis-à-vis this power cartel.[95] Lacking stable roots, Batista could survive only so long as he maintained a social balance, if necessary through terror, and used his authority to safeguard the interests of economically powerful groups in Cuba and the United States. Besides, there was no civilian political alternative. The parties or political groupings, internally divided, discredited by corruption and gangsterism, were incapable of renewing themselves. Admittedly, after the bloody crushing of the revolt at Cienfuegos, there were officers with links to the Americans who considered the possibility of another military putsch. But the indulgence of Batista by conservative Washington, and by the US ambassador in Havana, Earl T. Smith, frustrated such plans until it was too late. In the end there was no real alternative to Castro, especially as he had let every other player know that he would simply go on fighting if an attempt was made to deny the revolution its victory.

67

4

The Young Victor

Communists and "barbudos"

"Night falls as we, the barbudos, come down from the mountains looking like the saints of old," writes Carlos Franqui in his reminiscences. "People rush out to meet us. They are wild; they touch us, kiss our filthy beards."[1] Before them lay the glittering lights of Santiago de Cuba. Five years, five months and five days after the abortive attack on the Moncada Barracks, they had attained their goal. "This was a real New Year's party, and a charge of collective joy ran through the rebels. One of them, though, felt nostalgic, as if he had left the one thing that mattered most to him back in the Sierra: Fidel Castro. It may be that peace is more frightening to a fighting man than war." For Castro, the revolution had by no means ended when the guns fell silent. On that night of January 2, just as Che Guevara and Camilo Cienfuegos were entering Havana, he made a speech before a crowd of 200,000 in Santiago. Flanked by the new president, Urrutia, and Archbishop Enrique Pérez Serantes, the man who had baptized him and once saved his life, he declared:

> The Revolution begins now. . . . This time, luckily for Cuba, the Revolution will truly come into power. It will not be like 1898, when the North Americans came and made themselves masters of our country. . . . Neither thieves nor traitors, nor meddlers; this time, it will really be the Revolution. . . . I am sure . . . that for the first time the republic will really be entirely free.[2]

If Castro stressed that "this war has been won by the people," it was by no means a rhetorical device to ingratiate himself with his audience. Without the determination of the majority of the population, his revolution could scarcely have emerged from the forests of the Sierra Maestra. Numerically and in terms of weapons, the rebel forces had always been inferior to the US-armed troops of Batista, although by December 1959, towards the end of the war, they had grown to a total of 7,250 fighters.[3]

The number of casualties is even today uncertain. According to Castro 6,000 people lost their lives during seven years of Batista's dictatorship up to August 1958, while the paper *Revolución* referred on January 2, 1959, to 10,000 dead, and a special edition of *Bohemia* even spoke on January 11, 1959, of a total of 20,000.[4]

On January 3 Castro started out on his 600-mile victory parade across the island, by open jeep, helicopter, or on top of a captured tank. Surrounded by fellow-combatants, in an olive-green uniform with an amulet of Our Lady of Mercy around his neck, he always seemed to have a cigar between his teeth and his American semi-automatic M-2 rifle with telescopic sights slung casually on his shoulder. For the last part of the journey, his nine-year-old son Fidelito was able to join him from New York; then, on January 8, 1959, the column finally entered Havana to the sound of church bells and factory and ship sirens. When Castro saw his old *Granma* lying in the harbor, he stopped for a moment lost in emotional recollection.

Enthusiastic crowds filled the streets and greeted him as a savior. His suggestive capacity was on display as never before, as he captivated hundreds of thousands for the several hours of a speech freely delivered from the balcony of the presidential palace. For the British Ambassador of the time, he was "a mixture of José Martí, Robin Hood, Garibaldi and Jesus Christ."[5] *New York Times* correspondent Ruby Hart Philips noted: "As I watched Castro I realized the magic of his personality. . . . He seemed to weave a hypnotic net over his listeners, making them believe in his own concept of the functions of government and the destiny of Cuba."[6]

The taking of the capital had gone quite smoothly, with no orgy of bloodletting. For just a few hours before Che Guevara and Camilo Cienfuegos entered with their men, there was some shooting and looting, as well as attacks on unknown torturers who had served Batista; a residual group from the Directorio Revolucionario briefly occupied the presidential palace and the university. What were objects of blind violence, however, were the parking meters and casinos, whose receipts had gone straight into the pockets of Batista and his friends. The British journalist Edwin Tetlow reported that Castro's soldiers were "one of the best behaved armies you could imagine. . . . To a man they behaved impeccably."[7] "So that no one will one day be able to make dishonorable accusations against our revolution," Castro had already warned his people in November to observe the strictest discipline during the transfer of power. No doubt he had the street disorders of 1948 in Bogotá still before him. There was to be no "looting, destruction of property, unnecessary bloodshed. No one should take revenge on anyone else. The spies and the elements known for their inhuman acts against the people should be arrested and interned in prisons to be later judged by revolutionary tribunals."[8]

Tad Szulc, the former *New York Times* reporter who personally knew Castro and had the privilege of observing him closely over a long period, wrote in his biography:

> In peace, as in war, Castro was a master both of strategy and of timing. . . . He knew exactly what he was doing, . . . his apparent improvisations had been carefully thought out, . . . nothing was left to chance. . . . Castro understood above all else that his own personality was, as a purely practical proposition, the key to the success of his entire enterprise. Having always insisted that propaganda was vital in mobilizing the masses for a revolution, Castro immediately seized on television, which was already quite well-developed in Cuba in 1959 [there were some 400,000 sets on the island]. . . . He was a natural television personality and, literally, he sold the revolution on TV.[9]

Hugh Thomas agrees: "The Cuban civil war had been really a political campaign in a tyranny, with the campaigner being defended by armed men."[10]

70

For Cuba, January 1, 1959 represented the first real turning point of the century. Under Batista the rule of law had finally broken down: the corrupt system had been able to maintain itself only with the backing of a "clean-handed" United States, which had refused to acknowledge that the state system there was dissolving before its eyes. Now, 90 years after the beginning of the struggle for independence, 64 years after the death of Martí, Cubans had their goal in sight.

The young Castro stood for a radical Cuban nationalism interspersed with elements of utopian socialism – what Hugh Thomas called "Garibaldian romanticism." The primary goals of the revolution included a drive to achieve literacy for the whole population, a solid and free public health service, and an immediate land reform. Castro's admiration for Franklin D. Roosevelt had lasted beyond his school years. Indeed, while he was imprisoned on the Isle of Pines, he declared himself to be a supporter of the New Deal of the thirties, and in the Sierra Maestra he is even said to have carried with him a photograph of the former American president. "I want to find out as much as I can about Roosevelt and his policies: in the agricultural sector . . . , in the area of social programs . . . , restructuring industry . . . , and the general economy," he wrote from prison to friends on April 15, 1954. "The US economy was stagnant and on the brink of collapse when Roosevelt gave it a shot in the arm . . . , reducing certain privileges and attacking powerful interests. . . . Roosevelt actually did some wonderful things, and some of his countrymen have never forgiven him for doing them."[11] If Castro had been dealing with a similar-minded president to the north, before and after January 1959, the history of relations between Cuba and the United States might have been in many respects different. But no "new deal" was possible with Eisenhower's Republican administration, still marked by the witch-hunting of the McCarthy years, or with an economic elite still trapped in a colonial mindset.

Even so, a Communist regime did not yet appear to be on the cards in Cuba. In *Bohemia*, whose special edition of a million copies was the most widely read paper of the times, an editorial of January 11 under the heading "Against Communism" acclaimed Castro not only for his statement that "the new government will decline any relations with dictatorial states," but also because in this connection he named "first of all the Soviet Union." The editorial went on:

> There cannot be the slightest agreement between those who have begun to emancipate their people and those who suppress the freedoms of a dozen European states, who shot down the unarmed Hungarian people [in the uprising of 1956] and who have built the worst example of despotism anywhere in the world. . . . As it marches surely on, the Revolution is Cuban and democratic in its core and in its conceptions.[12]

The first government under President Manuel Urrutia – the judge already selected by Castro in the Sierra Maestra – was made up almost entirely of representatives from the bourgeois-liberal camp. The prime minister was José Miró Cardona, the first chairman of the Havana-based Bar Association and Castro's former professor at university; while the foreign minister was Roberto Agramonte, successor to "Eddy" Chibás as chairman and presidential candidate of the Orthodox Party. In Rufo López-Fresquet as finance minister and Felipe Pazos (a signatory of the Miami Pact) as head of the national bank, the new government had two economic experts with a solid international reputation, especially in Washington. The 26th of July Movement was represented in the 15-man cabinet by no more than four members of its moderate wing: Education Minister Armando Hart, and three of Castro's comrades from the Sierra. Faustino Pérez, the doctor who had survived those days in the cane field by Castro's side, became minister for the recovery of misappropriated state property; Augustino Martínez Sánchez became defense minister; and Humberto Sorí-Marín, who had drafted the law on land reform for the "liberated territories" in the Sierra, took the post of agriculture minister. The only cabinet member whose past showed some Communist slant was Osvaldo Dorticós Torrado from Cienfuegos, who, like Miró Cardona, was a former chairman of the Bar Association and was now made the minister responsible for revolutionary legislation. The Communist PSP remained outside.

Fidel Castro himself remained without ministerial responsibilities, officially content with the position of supreme commander of the armed forces, and he also kept his three closest collaborators (Raúl, Che, and Camilo Cienfuegos) in the background. They had enough to do consolidating the victory of the revolution at both military and civil levels. Castro needed no government office, for in reality he was the government. This is how Franqui summed it up: "We all knew what Fidel was – the undisputed caudillo of the revolution. What Fidel was thinking no one knew. . . . As far as ideology was concerned, nothing was clear, and Fidel was the greatest enigma of all. . . . Now in Cuba power was concentrated in Fidel's hands. Urrutia was president of a government that didn't govern."[13]

Behind the scenes, the country's future direction was the object of intense battles – but not for long. According to Franqui, there were four main currents: "One was radically anti-imperialist, one was democratic-reformist, one was conservative and pro-United States, and one was Marxist and pro-Soviet Union." It was the fourth of these, including Raúl Castro, Che Guevara, Camilo Cienfuegos, and Ramiro Valdés, which emerged victorious. Valdés had been Raúl Castro's second-in-command on the second front in the Sierra Maestra and, like him, was a member of the still officially scorned PSP. "The *Granma* group . . . was the real new power in the nation."[14] And, under the name "Bureau for Revolutionary Planning and Coordination," it established a kind of parallel government for Castro, to which his friend from the *bogotazo* days in Colombia, Alfredo Guevara, as well as Vilma Espín (now Raúl's wife) also belonged. At first they used to meet regularly in Castro's penthouse suite on the twenty-third floor of the Habana Libre hotel (which had originally come into operation in 1958 as the Havana Hilton), but from March 1959 a former Orthodox Party politician also made available to Castro a more securely screened villa in the nearby fishing port of Cojímar, where Hemingway had once found the model for the hero of *The Old Man and the Sea*. Castro had another office in the Havana district of Miramar, close to the Chaplin Theater. But most important of all was the modest "office-apartment" he shared with

Celia Sánchez on 11th Street in Velado, which was also the location of his secret military command.

Castro's style of work and leadership was as chaotic as his living arrangements. "He never calls meetings to discuss what is to be done," Franqui observed. "He improvises and never shares power. . . . He never told us what he was thinking, but he didn't have to because he knew that he was the power and that any government was, therefore, meaningless."[15]

Celia, the doctor's daughter from Manzanillo, had been his closest companion and partner in the Sierra Maestra, and despite his numerous affairs she remained this until her death from cancer in 1980. He too evidently had many an amorous interest after the victory of the revolution. The relationship with Naty Revuelta, whose husband had meanwhile left her and who was living in Vedado with their daughter Alina, also warmed up again – although, watched suspiciously by Celia, he kept it on the back burner, and had only sporadic contact with the ever more unruly Alina.

Naturally there was another reason for the distance: the stunningly beautiful Marita Lorenz from Bremen, 19-year-old daughter of the captain of the *MS Berlin*. When the cruise ship put into Havana Harbor on February 23, 1959, one visit on board was enough for Castro to fall in love. Using all his powers of persuasion, he got her to move down from New York – officially as a translator – and to live close to him in the Habana Libre.

Marita Lorenz has written that, in the middle of October 1959, when she was six months pregnant, she was given a laced drink in her hotel suite, taken to an unknown place and subjected to an abortion – although she is not sure that this was on Castro's orders and does not exclude the possibility that it was a CIA operation, as the agency seems to have had her under observation for some time because of her proximity to the Cuban leader. In September 2000, shortly before his death, Castro's long-time assistant Jesús Yáñez Pelletier (who had since fallen out of favor) thought that Marita Lorenz had herself decided on the operation against Castro's wishes, and that it had been performed by a doctor friendly both to Castro and himself. In any event, the abortion brought the affair to an end after eight-and-a-half months; Marita Lorenz found herself stranded in Miami, where the CIA began to involve her in its plots against Castro.

Che Guevara, too, fell in love again – with Aleida March, a pretty 22-year-old teacher from an upper-class background, who had joined the guerrilla forces during their advance on Santa Clara. Guevara's first wife, the Peruvian Hilda Gadea, and their daughter had initially remained in Mexico and then returned to Peru, but in February she came to Havana, to be confronted with the end of the relationship. Guevara and Aleida March, who were later to marry, had moved into a house by the sea in Tarará, $12^1/_2$ miles west of Havana, where the family of Castro's ex-wife Mirta had its summer residence. Health factors (asthma attacks brought on by psychological stress) and a need for discretion during preparations for the new political course had led him to withdraw there for the time being. Meanwhile, a Council of Ministers decree had, with him in mind, retroactively conferred Cuban citizenship on all foreigners who had fought for the revolution during a period of at least two years – a provision which enabled him to continue speaking and acting for the revolution. It was thus under his direction that the "Granma group" prepared in Tarará many of the revolutionary laws that would be issued over the coming months, including the most important one on land reform.

One potentially explosive issue was the secret meetings which, within weeks of the entry into Havana, this circle had started to hold with leaders of the then 50,000-strong Socialist People's Party. While the foot-soldiers of the left-bourgeois 26th of July Movement and the PSP were publicly venting their aversion for each other, the leading group around Castro were deciding together with Carlos Rafael Rodríguez, Blas Roca (PSP general secretary since 1934), and Anibal Escalante from the Party's executive committee to work for a unification of all revolutionary groups. The way to the talks had been opened when the Communists showed themselves willing to recognize Castro as sole leader of the revolution, even though he was still not inclined to become one of the party faithful. Blas Roca later recalled how Castro once laughingly said to him: "Shit, we are the government now, and still we have to go on meeting illegally."[16] But the participants had every reason to maintain secrecy: the population at large would not find such an alliance acceptable, and at that time Castro himself was not interested in establishing a Moscow-style system on the island and falling into a new dependence. He pursued his own middle way, a Caribbean socialism that might be ideologically defined as "Castroism." The last thing he wanted was to give the United States a pretext for intervention.

At first Castro evidently just wanted to use the Communists; a tactical alliance with them would also allow him to neutralize and incorporate any opposition from the left. It was not necessarily a contradiction, then, but actually part of his power game, that he tried behind closed doors to link his revolutionary movement with the Communists, while in public he let others attack his future allies, or even did so himself, in order to ensure that they behaved in a disciplined manner. In late May, he was still stressing in a television interview that the revolution would be neither left nor right but "one step forward." Its color was "not red but olive green," like the uniforms of the rebel army.[17]

It was quite possible that, being without a discernible ideological commitment, Castro was at that time unsure where he would take Cuba. During a trip to the United States at the invitation of American newspaper editors, from April 15 to 26, he made much of this theme and declared with great realism: "I have said in a clear and definitive fashion that we are not Communists. . . . The doors are open to private investments that contribute to the industrial development of Cuba. . . . It is absolutely impossible for us to make progress if we do not come to an understanding with the United States."[18] Possibly, however, official Washington's curt rejection of his revolution was already leading him to the view that it would not tolerate a nationalist middle way between capitalism and Communism.

In the first weeks and months after the victory of the revolution, the people expected one thing above all else: a settling of accounts with Batista's paid torturers and murderers. The media were overflowing with reports about the victims of the former regime. Unimaginable instruments and practices of torture were described, together with tragedies of horrifying dimensions. Mothers and wives of the killed and missing marched through the streets demanding vengeance.

"*Parédon! Parédon! Parédon!*" – "Up against a wall!" – shouted several hundred thousand voices at a mass rally in Havana on January 22, 1959. Castro later told Frei Betto:

> Even before the triumph of the Revolution, in the Sierra Maestra, ... we drew up penal laws for punishing war crimes. ... When the Revolution triumphed, the country's courts accepted those laws as valid ... and many war criminals who couldn't escape were tried by the courts ... and given severe sentences: capital punishment in some cases and prison sentences in others.[19]

Huge rallies were one way to channel emotions and to prevent the kind of lynchings that occurred after the fall of the Machado dictatorship in 1933; another was a show trial in Havana sports stadium of three of Batista's worst officers. But this latter action – which, despite the evident guilt of the accused, had nothing in common with a regular trial – significantly damaged Castro's international reputation. For, however much foreign eyes and ears had been closed to the human rights violations of the Batista dictatorship, now that the murderers' lives were on the line the propaganda of the United States and its allies demanded humanity and mercy. One incident for which Raúl Castro was responsible had an especially powerful impact. On January 5, 1959, after summary death sentences in Santiago de Cuba, "some 70 prisoners were mowed down by rebel soldiers at the command of Raúl Castro and bulldozed under the ground without any semblance of a trial," the new US ambassador Philip W. Bonsal indignantly noted.[20]

In the early days, Fidel Castro himself made a few attacks on trial procedures when the verdicts did not go as he thought they should. But he was quick to respond to criticism, and subsequently allowed trials to take their course before orderly military tribunals or revolutionary courts. Most of the death sentences were carried out in La Cabaña fortress, on the orders of Che Guevara and Raúl Castro. "The Castro procedure of setting up special tribunals to try the cases of people who, on the basis of the Nuremberg principles, were accused of serious crimes, could have been an improvement over the earlier method," Bonsal finally conceded.[21]

Observers such as Tad Szulc were amazed at how little people took the law into their own hands, in comparison with the arbitrariness of human rights violations under Batista. Answering one US politician, he wrote:

> Cuban revolutionary trials ... bore no resemblance to the real bloodbaths that followed the Mexican, Russian and Chinese social revolutions in the twentieth century. ... By the same token the Cuban revolution refrained from institutionalized mass killings such as those perpetrated against hundreds of thousands of Chinese in Indonesia in the aftermath of the 1965 army anti-Communist coup, or those attributable to Chilean military authorities when they overthrew the Marxist president, Salvador Allende Gossens, in 1973. ... It is quite remarkable that violence-prone Cubans remained so unviolent.[22]

During his trip to the United States in April 1959, Castro is said to have admitted in private: "What we have to do is stop the executions."[23] At that time the US media were reporting a total of 521 since the victory of the revolution,[24] and a follower of Castro, later turned opponent, estimated that by the end of the year there had been roughly 1,900.[25] The leader of the revolution himself spoke of approximately 550 executed "criminals." Carlos Franqui points to the fact that, in a countrywide opinion survey, 93 percent of the population said that it supported the sentences and executions.[26] And Castro noted: "We have shot no child, we have shot no woman, we have shot no old people. ... We are shooting the assassins so that they will not kill our children tomorrow."[27]

1,500 revolutionary laws

The Máximo Líder, as he soon came to be known, could count on unconditional popular support for everything he did. "Right from the beginning," he told Betto, "the people realized that, at last, they had a government of their own. . . . Our basic ideas about how to do things . . . were correct. . . . The revolutionary laws made a tremendous contribution to our people's political awareness and political education."[28]

In the first nine months of 1959, an estimated 1,500 decrees, laws, and edicts were passed.[29] On February 7, the Urrutia government adopted a "Basic Law of the Republic," which partially restored the 1940 Constitution suspended by Batista. A law on housing reform provided for a 50 percent reduction of all rents below 100 pesos, and between 30 and 40 percent on anything higher, while obliging owners of waste building land either to sell up or to clear it for cheap housing. Electricity and telephone charges were also reduced, and the government took (initially provisional) control of the Cuban Telephone Corporation, a subsidiary of ITT. Between January and April, nearly all employment contracts were renegotiated and wages and salaries considerably increased; strong unions ensured that the rise was as much as 15 percent in the case of sugarcane workers. Confiscation measures were introduced on all property that had been acquired under dubious or simply illegal circumstances during the Batista years, especially by politicians and army officers. Private beaches had to be opened to the whole population, though a law ending racial discrimination was less popular at first, among the largely Creole population of Cuba. High customs duties restricted the importation of more than 200 luxury items, saving more than $70 million in foreign currency within the first year. Successive reforms followed in the areas of health and education, whereby all layers of the population gained an equal right of access to free medical care and appropriate education and training. Plans were laid for a huge literacy campaign, which began in 1961 and soon became a model for other countries in the Third World.

Towards the end of the Batista regime (when there was parity between the Cuban peso and the dollar), Cuba's annual per capita income stood at $335 – compared with $2,000 in the United States.[30] It counted among the most developed countries in the Third World, with one of the highest percentages of dollar millionaires per head of the population in Latin America and the Caribbean.

Long-term unemployment, on the other hand, affected a quarter to a third of the population fit to work – particularly blacks and mulattos, who made up a quarter of the population, living mainly in the east of the island. The rural population, nearly a half of the country's total, with an average annual income of just $91, was in every respect the most disadvantaged: only 4 percent could regularly afford meat, less than 2 percent eggs, 1 percent fish, 3 percent bread, and almost none fresh vegetables; only 11 percent drank fresh milk even occasionally; more than one in three suffered from deficiency diseases or parasitic infections; three-quarters of the rural housing consisted of palm huts, mostly without running water or electricity. Additionally, 27 percent of children in the towns and 61 percent in the countryside did not attend school, 43 percent of rural dwellers were illiterate, and only 50 percent of the total population could read and write with any degree of proficiency.[31]

The main, decisive goal was land reform; it was discreetly prepared by the "Bureau for Revolutionary Planning and Coordination," under Che Guevara's overall control in Tarará. Agriculture minister Humberto Sorí-Marín, who had drafted the first land reform in October 1958 for the "liberated territories," had no idea of what was going on. Indeed, he was still drawing up a plan of his own, on Castro's orders, when the publication of a new law on inheritance caught him by surprise on May 17, 1959. He at once bitterly broke with Castro's revolution and joined his opponents from the old oligarchy.

It seems that Castro himself would have preferred to omit some of the land reform measures, so that Washington would not come out too soon against the new regime. But Raúl and his Communist allies forced his hand, by encouraging Party supporters (for whom nothing could happen quickly enough) to occupy and expropriate land without the sanction of the law. The first clause of the new law, which came into effect on June 3, 1959, picked up where the old 1940 Constitution had left off, with a limit of 1,000 acres on land ownership. A higher limit of 3,333 acres was allowable for foreign companies, and for sugar or rice growers with yields more than 50 percent above the national average. But everything above that was nationalized, then either converted into a state cooperative, each one 27 hectares (67 acres) in size, or made over to the small private farmers who had been employed there or illegally farmed it on their own account. Although the law directly affected no more than 10 percent of agricultural holdings, these accounted for 40 percent of the land under cultivation.

Five US sugar producers, which together owned or controlled more than 2 million acres of land, were awarded compensation payable over 20 years at a annual rate of interest of 4.5 percent. (US industrial loans with a fixed rate of interest were averaging just 3.8 percent in 1958.) The basis of assessment for compensation, however, was the annual turnover posted with the finance authorities – and since landowners had systematically undervalued this to avoid paying taxes, their deceit over a period of years now turned against them.

This was the beginning of the first major dispute with the old oligarchy and landowners backed by the US government. As things heated up between Havana and Washington and made further negotiation impossible, the old American owners and Cubans now living in the United States found themselves left empty-handed. Other governments, such as that of Canada, refrained from a public quarrel and kept their citizens happy with compensatory payments of their own. (The relatively friendly political and economic relations between Canada and Cuba in later years can be largely traced back to this decision.) It is true that 82 percent of Cuba's land surface was suitable for agriculture, but at that time only 22 percent was actually in use, and 75 percent of that was controlled by US producers.[32] In the medium term, then, it was hoped that the new law would both diversify agriculture away from sugar and extend the area of land under cultivation, bringing improvements in diet and the general economic situation, including a fall in unemployment. At the same time, since fewer profits would be transferred to the United States, more money would remain in Cuba; income distribution would become fairer, and Cuba's external trade more balanced.

Some business sectors, and especially the Cuban middle class, initially welcomed the Mexican-style land reform as a move away from typical Third World disparities towards greater social equality, and experts in the United States – or at least those remote from big capitalist interests – took a similar position. Towards the end of 1959, a little over 2.5 million acres of land had already been taken over, but the implementation of the reform was slipping out of control as a disastrous combination of revolutionary zeal and low educational levels among the rural population undermined the rational beginnings. Franqui wrote:

> But it wasn't all sweetness and light. Production plummeted, and the rebel army began to seize farms, to imprison landowners, and to kill off breeding bulls just for fun. A class war had begun all through the countryside. On one side, the owners began to sabotage production, and on the other, the rebels disrupted what production there was. Every group hated every other group: it was as if a cyclone were picking everything up to blow it all away.[33]

Castro never wavered in his attitude, however. "That was the first law," he later told Betto, "which really established the break between the Revolution and the country's richest, most privileged sectors and the break with the United States and the transnational corporations. . . . This law affected the land owned by my own family."[34] After the expropriation of the Castros' farm, only the living quarters would remain for his mother until her death on August 6, 1963.

In May 1959, a National Agrarian Reform Institute (INRA) was established to implement the reform, with Castro himself as chairman. According to its director, Antonio Núñez Jiménez, the INRA took over from Castro's older "kitchen cabinet:" "Fidel turned the INRA into a duplicate of the most important functions of the revolutionary government,"[35] thereby further marginalizing the bourgeois-liberal cabinet that formally ran the country. This had anyway not been much in evidence since February 16, 1959, when Miró Cardona had resigned as prime minister because of his lack of power and influence, and Castro himself had taken over the office. Soon the INRA, rather than the government, was responsible for nearly all measures taken by the state in relation to the land: the building of roads, resettlement programs, training projects, health and tourism infrastructure, even the literacy campaign and the creation and funding of the Cuban Film Institute, the ICAIC. It was, in Núñez Jiménez's combative phrase, "the institution which dealt the death-blow to the bourgeoisie and imperialism."[36]

Under pressure from US agribusiness, the State Department in Washington issued a note on June 11, 1959, expressing "concern" about the measures and insisting on the immediate payment of adequate compensation. The Cubans saw this as an "affront to national feelings," and, in their reply of June 15, took the opportunity to state that – although the 1940 Constitution did provide for immediate cash compensation – Batista's emptying of the public purse had made it impossible to pay it in that form, and that it should be recovered instead from the assets he had hoarded away in the United States.[37]

Not only the big landowners and powerful sugar producers howled in protest. The middle layers, who, though initially optimistic, felt increasingly cheated of the fruits of their labor and their life prospects by a new law on real estate, also began to turn away from the revolution. "Instead of taking this into account and pursuing a wise and prudent policy towards those circles, the revolutionary government made a lot of mistakes," a GDR foreign ministry diplomat noted with irritation in a secret report, citing a conversation with PSP politician Carlos Rafael Rodríguez. "Many small shops and factories were even confiscated simply because their installation was needed for a state enterprise. A real panic then broke out among the middle layers and helped the counter-revolution."[38] The new friends were especially critical of Fidel Castro's role in the economic transformation: "Too often the prime minister himself has decided things in a 'partisan manner,' thereby causing harm to the development of the economy. It should also be said that his methods were adopted by others, leading to a complete mess." On this view of things, hardly anything would change in subsequent years.

The social and political reforms had a deceptive effect. Consumption figures shot up as unemployment fell away and people suddenly had more money in their pockets; the poor, in particular, could afford to eat better food and live in better accommodation. But it was an illusory boom, where the greater purchasing power was not covered by increased output and a higher GDP. Eventually, demand could no longer be met and no longer be financed by credit; indeed, productivity actually declined in all sectors of the economy, as a result of too little work and too little investment. More goods – especially food products – needed to be imported again, but for that too money was running short. Since the last thing Castro wanted was to go cap in hand to the United States, he traveled as early as January 21, 1959, to Venezuela to request a $300 million dollar loan from President Rómulo Betancourt. But it was in vain – as were other early attempts to borrow money abroad.

Castro's conservative opponents eventually picked up on the unease in his own 26th of July Movement at the infiltration of all public institutions by the Communists. Pointing to the leaders of the revolution, they charged that the olive-green uniforms were like water melons: green on the outside, red on the inside. The prototype was allegedly Raúl Castro, who was responsible for restructuring the old army and integrating it into the "Revolutionary Armed Forces."

Raúl, unlike his elder brother, did not enjoy enormous popularity: he was not a tribune of the people. Rather, he was seen as the "Stalinist" among the revolutionary leaders, narrow-minded and hence uncompromising and inflexible, nicknamed long ago *el casquito*, or the "little helmet." This was certainly a hasty judgment, however, as his unprepossessing exterior and often awkward manner concealed a personality with a great flair for organization and an iron discipline. Together with Che Guevara and Camilo Cienfuegos, he helped the Communists systematically to occupy key positions in the security apparatus, the government, the INRA, and the labor organizations. Partly with Fidel's approval, partly at his instigation, once-close friends and allies were relentlessly sidelined or removed from their posts on the grounds that they were too bourgeois – people like foreign minister Agramonte and four other cabinet ministers who were replaced in June 1959.

President Urrutia's turn came in July. After opposing and delaying more and more laws that broke the ostensible bourgeois-liberal consensus, he one day appeared on television to express his discontent over the growing influence of people from the PSP. This spelled the end of his presidency. In a televized speech, Castro angrily accused Urrutia of fabricating a "Communist legend" and of being "on the borderline of betrayal," and then, in a theatrical gesture on July 16, he announced that he was resigning as prime minister. This had the intended effect: countrywide protests and a mass rally in front of the presidential palace called for Castro's return and the removal of Urrutia. Dressed as a milkman, the humiliated president took refuge in the Venezuelan embassy and later went into exile. His successor was another cabinet member known for toeing the party line, Osvaldo Dorticós, who had previously been responsible for revolutionary legislation. (Dorticós kept the job until 1976, when Castro himself took over as Cuban president.) On July 26, in a speech commemorating the attack on the Moncada Barracks, Castro seemed content as he announced his return to the office of prime minister.

The signs of opposition continued, however, and eventually appeared in the ranks of the army. On October 19, two days after Raúl Castro was appointed head of the Revolutionary Armed Forces Ministry (MINFAR), the influential military commander of Camagüey Province, Huber Matos, a former comrade of Castro's in the Orthodox Party and a popular hero of the struggle in the Sierra Maestra, handed in an application to resign. This letter – which he significantly sent to Fidel, not to his immediate superior, Raúl – complained about Communist infiltration of the rebel army. It was an affront to Raúl's ideological orientation, and Fidel was quite beside himself. Suspecting a conspiracy, he sped down to Camagüey and ordered the arrest of Matos, together with 40 other officers who evidently shared his views. In a show trial, Matos was subsequently found guilty of "betraying the revolution" and sentenced to 20 years in prison. Raúl Castro even wanted to have him shot, despite his great services to the revolution, but Fidel refused this after Che Guevara quipped: "I guess we'll have to shoot the lot of them."[39]

By the autumn of 1959 Castro – together with his brother Raúl, Che Guevara, and the popular favorite Camilo Cienfuegos – had consolidated his position as sole ruler of the country. No longer dependent upon tactical alliances with wavering liberals, he had filled nearly all key posts in the state and the security apparatus with people trusted by himself or Raúl. On November 25, to the horror of the financial world, he appointed

Che Guevara, a man without any expert knowledge of economic policy, as director of the Cuban central bank, after the reputed former head, Felipe Pazos, had fallen out of favor for trying to help Matos after his arrest. One of Guevara's first actions was to sell the Cuban gold reserves in Fort Knox and send the money to various Swiss and Canadian banks, so that Washington would not be able to get its hands on it if relations took a turn for the worse.

Camilo Cienfuegos, the fourth man in the quartet, was not to remain there much longer. Having been entrusted by Castro to take over Matos's military command in Camagüey, he disappeared on the evening of October 28 as he was on his way to Havana for a meeting with the leader of the revolution; his Cessna 310 aircraft, said to have been flown by an inexperienced pilot, broke off radio contact shortly after take-off. A one-week search operation, even assisted by the US coastguard, came up with no trace. Speculation abounded that Cienfuegos had been assassinated by hostile officers and Matos supporters, or even that a Cuban fighter-pilot had shot him down after confusing his plane with one sent from Miami to drop fire bombs on cane fields.[40] As Cienfuegos's successor, Castro appointed Juan Almeida, a close comrade since the Moncada days.

Immediately after the victory of the revolution, Raúl Castro, Che Guevara, and Camilo Cienfuegos set about building their own security apparatus, and soldiers and officers from Batista's army who had a clean record were integrated into the new "Fuerzas Armadas Revolucionarias" (FAR). The highest rank, as in the guerrilla days, was that of Comandante (major). Military experts estimate that the FAR numbered approximately 100,000 in early 1960, and 300,000 by the year after.[41] Most of them, however, were poorly trained and armed, the weapons inherited from Batista's army having been for a force of roughly 25,000 men.

Ramiro Valdés, who took over as interior minister until the mid-eighties, built a new political police – the so-called G-2. Castro's secret service, the Dirección General de Inteligencia (DGI), was organized with help from the KGB and soon had a reputation as one of the best informed and most efficient. A connecting link to the army and police were the lightly armed militias, a 100,000-strong force recruited from the general population, which could be rapidly mobilized against counter-revolutionary operations such as acts of sabotage or raids from abroad. They would play a decisive role in repelling the Bay of Pigs invasion in 1961 (when their numbers were increased to 300,000), and they also served as a counterweight to the army in Castro's cleverly devised balance of power.

The militarization of Cuban society went further still. From the autumn of 1960, Castro had at his disposal a third force in the shape of the 800,000-strong Committees for the Defense of the Revolution (CDRs), whose task it was to track down saboteurs and oppositional groups. CDR members were nothing other than "block wardens" for spying on the local area. Thus, under the pressure of external tensions, Martí's heir was step by step converting his country into a totalitarian state and gradually making an absurdity of the revolutionary quest for freedom.

One year after the rebel army entered Havana, it was already a risky business to criticize political developments. Anyone who openly opposed the Communist influence was considered an opponent of the revolution and a friend of the United States. Opposition was tantamount to subversion. Even those who tried to remain neutral came under suspicion. "There are no neutrals," Castro said, "there are only partisans of the revolution or enemies of it." And: "To be a traitor to the revolution is to be a traitor to the country."[42] The extent to which the Communists had by then penetrated the power apparatus may be gauged from a confidential report by Werner Lamberz (then secretary of the East German youth organization, the FDJ, and later a member of the SED's Politburo) to state and Party leader Walter Ulbricht. Referring to a conversation on June 13, 1961, with Cuban PSP leader Blas Roca, on the margins of a session of the executive committee of the International Federation of Students, Lamberz wrote: "Already in the first stage of the revolution, a number of conditions were created which facilitated a rapid transition from the anti-imperialist to the anti-capitalist revolution." Especially in the period from May to November 1959, the Cuban Communists had waged "a resolute struggle against the anti-communism [that was being] disseminated by some leaders of the 26th of July

Movement and the 13th of March [Directorio Revolucionario]."
The period from early January to late February 1959 had been
one of "dual power of petty-bourgeois elements who represented
the interests of Cuba's national bourgeoisie." Both President
Urrutia and Prime Minister Miró Cardona had belonged to this
category.

"This period of dual power ended in February 1959," Lamberz
continues, "when Fidel Castro became prime minister and these
right-wing petty-bourgeois elements were excluded from the
government. A change in the relationship of forces then ensued
within the government."[43] What Lamberz does not say is that
during Castro's revolution the Communists at first had a timor-
ous or wait-and-see attitude. Blas Roca told him that "often the
Party's work is not visible from the outside, but it exists," and
that the PSP "developed the theoretical programme for the Cuban
revolution and helped to shape the decisive actions of the revolution" – which was quite simply untrue.

It is true that, once Castro's victory was at hand, the Communists hurried to ensure that they had an early share in it. Already
on December 17, 1958, an appeal for Moscow's help from the
comrades in Cuba landed (in the form of a confidential memorandum) on Walter Ulbricht's desk: "The leadership of the Cuban
Socialist People's Party has turned to the CC of the CPSU with
a request that it support the fighting people of Cuba with a
solidarity campaign." The Batista dictatorship, it went on, "after
the fiasco of its attempts to crush the democratic and national
liberation struggle of the Cuban people, has recently initiated
widespread terror." Batista, "with the active support of American
imperialist circles," was said to be "preparing another open armed
intervention by the USA in Cuba."[44]

Castro's old friend and correspondent from his prison days on
the Isle of Pines, the former Orthodox Party general secretary,
Luis Conte Agüero, publicly criticized his growing tendency to
use power arbitrarily against those who did not think in the same
way as himself. In March 1960, when he tried to read an open
letter to Castro on television, he was forcibly prevented by people
from G-2. In the end, he took refuge in the Argentinean embassy
and applied for asylum.[45]

Critical media were gradually reduced to silence during the period up to May 1960. Newspapers, radio, and television stations were expropriated or closed down – for example, the former house organ of the pro-Batista oligarchy, the *Diario de la Marina,* and soon after (when it attacked the measures against the *Diario de la Marina* as an attack on press freedom) *Prensa Libre.* The remaining papers, such as the Communist *Hoy* and the 26th of July organ *Revolución,* were as loyal to Castro as most of the closed ones had been to Batista.

This provoked the Catholic Church, most of which had anyway come out against the revolution, to denounce the latest developments from the pulpit; and members of the clergy who had initially been sympathetic now also took their distance. Even Bishop Pérez Serantes, the old friend of Castro's family who once saved his life, wrote a pastoral letter in which he said that "the frontier between the church and its enemies was now clearly defined." "It can no longer be said that the enemy is at our door, for in reality he is already inside, loud and strident, as if he was at home here." With Communism there could be "absolutely no cooperation of any kind."[46] Already in spring 1959 the leaders of the Cuban Revolution were being warned against "utopian levelling."

The measures against opposition platforms were also, however, a reaction to the growing number of attacks and sabotage actions, mostly organized by Cuban exiles working with the CIA in Florida. Early in 1960 an anti-Castro guerrilla force, the so-called Second National Front, began operating in the Escambray Mountains in central Cuba; its leader was a former comrade of Castro and Guevara, a passionate anti-Communist called Eloy Gutiérrez Menoyo, who received funds and weapons from Miami. Although revolutionary troops managed to isolate this guerrilla campaign, Castro himself estimated that it then numbered as many as 5,000 men, and it took until 1965 for it to be finally broken up.[47]

There were also several incidents where small civilian aircraft carried out terror attacks on people on foot and on industrial plant, or dropped fire bombs on sugar factories and plantations, killing people and causing great damage to the national economy. Papers found on a dead American pilot after one such attack proved that the organizers were based in Florida.

One of the most spectacular operations of this kind was the work of Castro's own former pilot and air force chief, Pedro Luis Díaz Lanz, who changed sides in late June 1959 and emigrated to the United States. On October 21 of the same year, in a kamikaze-style bombing and strafing raid, he flew low over Havana itself and managed to kill two pedestrians and wound another 45. Next to him in the aircraft was said to have been a CIA special agent by the name of Frank Sturgis, who had once fought with the rebels in the Sierra Maestra (a photo exists of him with Castro), become head of Castro's secret service in the air force, and then, like Díaz Lanz, gone into exile in Florida. It remains unclear whether he had been working throughout for the CIA. But in any event, he continued his close association with Díaz Lanz in subsequent years, and the two men became key figures in the clandestine operations and assassination attempts mounted against Castro by the CIA and the American Mafia.

5

Old Enemies, New Friends

The great powers at the gates

Following the victory of the revolution, Castro always expressed in public a wish to reach agreement with Washington. Rationally, there was a lot to be said for such a pragmatic attitude, since Cuba's economic dependence on the United States was too great to permit a sudden turning away. Emotionally, in his innermost being, he seemed more inclined towards a break. This is easy to understand if we bear in mind the documentary evidence left behind by Batista's men, as well as Cuba's long history of relations with the United States, and Castro's own experience of a dictatorship which, in waging war on its own people, had received military and other forms of support from the mighty neighbor to the north. "When I saw the rockets that they fired on Mario's house," he angrily wrote on June 5, 1958, in a letter to Celia Sánchez, "I swore that the Americans are going to pay dearly for what they are doing. When this war is over, I'll start a much longer and bigger war of my own: the war I'm going to fight against them."[1]

In the US capital, meanwhile, it was thought that the same grip as before could be kept on the sugar island 50 miles south of Florida; numerous observers attribute the later complete loss of Cuba to precisely this self-assurance. As one government analyst put it in an internal report: "We were probably so . . . fully persuaded of Cuba's total dependence upon the US that we could not recognize the face of Cuban nationalist pride and apparently found it difficult to take Cuba or Castro seriously."[2]

Nor did US politicians have any inhibitions about looking to the realm of psychopathology for explanations of the Castro phenomenon. Bonsal, the new ambassador in Havana, considered that the Comandante suffered at times from "mental instability;" President Eisenhower thought in the winter of 1959–60 that he was beginning "to look like a madman," who, like Nehru in India, worked himself up into a frenzy;[3] a CIA report claimed that his policies had nothing to do with the policies and actions of the United States, but only with his own "psychotic personality;"[4] and Vice-President Richard Nixon came away from a three-hour meeting with Castro, during his trip to the United States in April 1959, with the impression that he was "either incredibly naive" or "under communist discipline."[5] Nixon did, however, recognize "those indefinable qualities which make him a leader of men," and thought he would be "a great factor in the development of Cuba and very possibly in Latin American affairs generally."[6]

What especially angered official America were Castro's "David against Goliath" gestures – for example, his statement in the presence of journalists, a week after entering Havana: "Yes, I tell you, two hundred thousand gringos will die if the United States sends marines to Cuba."[7] As to the man who was to be his toughest adversary in Washington, future president John F. Kennedy, Castro still sneered at him in September 1960 at the UN General Assembly as "an illiterate and ignorant millionaire" who "has read some novels or even some Hollywood film about guerrilla warfare."[8] This would prove to be a big mistake.

For Kennedy was clearly one of the few people in Washington with a relatively sophisticated view of Cuba, and he was not afraid to take the Eisenhower administration to task for its record on the matter. At a later-forgotten election rally in Cincinnati, he explained his view of the causes of the Cuban Revolution: "Fidel Castro is part of the legacy of Bolívar, who led his men over the Andes Mountains, vowing 'war to the death' against Spanish rule."[9] Kennedy could see that someone as ambitious and full of himself as Castro would not be content with the little stage of Cuba.

This became apparent during Castro's early trips abroad: to Venezuela in January 1959, the United States and Canada in April, and from there directly to Argentina, Uruguay, and Brazil. His first stay in New York in the uniform of a victorious revolutionary, three and a half years after his fundraising tour in a double-breasted suit, had the air of a triumphal march through an enemy country. Traveling with a 70-strong delegation, he was greeted with a mixture of sympathy, curiosity, and enthusiasm by enlightened middle-class opinion; more than 30,000 flocked to hear his opening speech in New York's Central Park. Only official Washington gave him the cold shoulder, Eisenhower preferring to dally in the country playing golf and to leave his vice-president, Richard Nixon, to meet the Cuban leader. For more than a month already, serious thought had been given at the highest levels to the possibility of eliminating him.[10] A little later, at the end of the year, Castro made his first contact with the Soviet Union, when Tass news agency correspondent Aleksandr Alekseiev appeared for an audition bearing a bottle of vodka, several tins of caviar, and cordial greetings from the Soviet government. In February 1960, a Soviet trade fair that had previously been in Mexico and New York moved to Havana, and Soviet deputy premier Anastas Mikoyan visited the island for the opening ceremony. On February 13 he and Fidel Castro signed the first trade agreement between the two countries, whereby the Soviet Union undertook to buy 1 million tons of Cuban sugar per annum over the next five years. In return, Cuba would purchase crude oil and derivatives, steel, paper, grain, fertilizer, and machinery, on the basis of a 12-year loan of $100 million at a rate of interest of 2.5 percent. Diplomatic relations, which were broken off during the Batista dictatorship, were finally restored in May 1960.

Meanwhile, the United States blocked a $100 million dollar loan by a consortium of European banks, and intervened on the international market to prevent the sale of Western arms to Cuba. When Belgium tried to press ahead regardless, the French freighter *Coubre* and its consignment of Belgian weapons blew up in Havana Harbor, on March 4, 1960, killing 81 and injuring more than 300. A Belgian expert said that sabotage was the most likely cause,[11] and at the funeral for the victims Castro held the United States responsible. For the first time he ended his speech with the battle-cry that he would subsequently use to close all his public appearances: *"Patria o muerte, venceremos!"* – "Fatherland or death, we shall prevail!"

In July 1960, Raúl Castro traveled to the Soviet Union and agreed with Khrushchev an extensive program of military aid. An increase in Florida-based acts of sabotage, together with rumors of an imminent American ground operation, led Khrushchev to warn the United States on July 9: "The Soviet Union . . . is extending a helpful hand to the people of Cuba. . . . If it became necessary, the Soviet military can support the Cuban people with rocket weapons."[12]

At the same time, the land reform dispute was escalating into a major crisis, as the powerful United Fruit Company – for which CIA boss Allen Dulles and his brother John Foster Dulles (the foreign minister who died in 1959) had both once worked – refused to give up 15 percent of its land and found itself expropriated on April 4, 1960. At Washington's request, Texaco, Esso, Shell, and Standard Oil refineries then refused to comply with the Cuban government's order to process oil imports from the Soviet Union – whereupon their branches in Cuba as well as other US companies on the island (a total of 36) were likewise placed under Cuban government control.

On July 5, President Eisenhower moved to inflict a sharp blow on Cuba's sugar-dependent economy, cutting 700,000 tons from the US purchase commitment for the year 1960. This reduced the share of US imports in Cuba's total sugar output to 35 percent, down from 59 percent (2.4 million tons) in 1959. US ambassador Bonsal later remarked: "The suspension of the sugar quota was a major element in the program for the overthrow of Castro."[13] Two weeks previously, in a televized speech, Castro had spoken of an impending American "Dagger Law" that would stab the revolution in the back, and warned that "if we lose our entire sugar quota, they could lose all their investments in Cuba."[14] A month later, the Cuban government went a further step down that road by countering the Dagger Law with a "Machete Law" of its own, which did not actually expropriate all American companies in Cuba but placed them under Cuban guardianship and set a limit on their repatriation of profits. At the same time, the

Soviet Union demonstratively helped Castro out by declaring its readiness to add the US sugar quota to its own for 1960.

It took a fortnight for the other major Communist power, the People's Republic of China, to enter the arena with an undertaking to buy 500,000 tons of Cuban sugar per annum over a five-year period at world-market prices. Under US pressure, the Organization of American States (OAS) now issued the "San José Declaration" condemning "the attempt of the Chinese-Soviet powers" to take advantage of the political, economic, or social situation in the Americas. Washington did not, however, manage to push through a condemnation of Cuba.

Castro's response came in August 1960, with the nationalization of US-owned industrial and agricultural firms on the island, followed by the banks in September, immediately before his departure to attend the UN General Assembly in New York. Upon his return, the axe fell on the 550 or so large industrial and commercial businesses still in private foreign or Cuban hands, as well as the remainder of the banks (except for the Canadian). On October 15, he announced on television that the revolutionary program set out in his "History Will Absolve Me" speech from the dock after Moncada had been accomplished. Apart from small private businesses – and even their turn would come a few years later – capitalism had been virtually eradicated in Cuba by the second anniversary of the revolution. Household names such as Esso, Standard Oil, Texaco, Swift, Goodyear, Procter & Gamble, Colgate-Palmolive, Sears, Ford, Chase Manhattan, and First National Bank, as well as other firms and consortia, lost a billion dollars in investments. The American Mafia alone had to write off 100 million dollars in the tourist industry, according to Santos Trafficante, one of its chieftains in Cuba.[15]

Although Castro knew that he had most of the population behind him, his egalitarian program had devastating consequences for the middle classes. Self-employed professionals, doctors, engineers, technicians, scientists, economists, and other experts left the island in ever increasing numbers – a total of 200,000 highly qualified citizens between 1960 and 1962.[16] They mostly settled in Florida, where many of them – scorned by Castro as *gusanos*, or worms – joined one of the groups opposed to the regime in Havana.

When Castro went to New York in September 1960, official America greeted him with icy hostility through to sheer hatred. Apart from Nikita Khrushchev, whose arrival on the *Baltika* in New York Harbor had been made "humiliatingly unpleasant" by the US authorities, Castro seemed to attract "concentrated official wrath" on himself alone – to quote a report written at the time by the chief correspondent of the Munich-based *Süddeutsche Zeitung*, Hans Ulrich Kempski.

> Attributes such as murderer, hangman or butcher, applied to Khrushchev on placards and press articles, sounded well-nigh respectable in comparison with the outpourings of hate that any public mention of Castro's name provoked. Whereas, the previous year, he had been wildly cheered for five whole days in New York, he was now reviled as a hairy rat, a hobo and a ravisher of young girls, whose greatest pleasure was to hold a knife to any American's bare throat.[17]

While the 8,000 or so Cuban exiles living in New York waved little welcoming flags on the streets, the tabloids printed "reports and pictures of anti-Castro demonstrations – not explaining, of course, that it was always a question of the same little handful who had turned out days earlier in front of the UN building to march with placards and bowed heads around a flower-bed. At no time had more than twenty-five people been involved, sometimes there had been only three."[18]

Although Cuba was (and is) a member of the United Nations, its 85-person delegation were not at first able to track down any suitable hotel in New York that was prepared to take them. With great difficulty they eventually checked in to the Hotel Shelburn, but its astronomical prices soon forced them to look elsewhere. In a show that gained a lot of media attention, Castro and his horn-tooting column then drove through Manhattan to the head-quarters of the UN and demanded emergency accommodation from its general secretary, Dag Hammarskjøld, warning that they would otherwise camp out in Central Park. In the end, the delegation found the ideal place to stay, in terms of provoking "straight" America, and raised the Cuban flag over the Hotel Theresa on 125th Street, right in the middle of Harlem. "The Theresa has for thirty years been the nerve center of negro politics in the North," wrote Kempski in another article. "No white man can normally get a room here. The fact that Castro, the propagandist of racial integration, can take the risk and manage it must operate as a signal to black people and a dangerous affront to White America."[19]

The American media tried to fool the public into believing that the Cubans had wound up in a brothel, and were holding orgies or killing chickens in their rooms. Meanwhile, however, Castro effectively set up court there. Besieged by reporters like no other president or government leader, cheered by thousands of black and latino supporters in the local streets, he received the radical black leader Malcolm X, Indian premier Jawaharlal Nehru, Egyptian president Gamal Abdul Nasser, and the leader of the other world power, Nikita Khrushchev.

Kempski's reports from New York in September 1960 are worth quoting at greater length, because they draw an early picture of Castro's personality as it would impress itself on the public mind in subsequent years. The revolutionary already knew how to present himself as a talented political leader, determined to use a novel style in drawing attention to the demands of the Third World, and it soon became clear to friends and enemies alike that the new arrival on the world stage was a shrewd and intelligent man at once tactically astute and uncompromising. By now 34 years old, aware of the impact of his external image and resolute charm, Castro knew how to use the media and his own public appearances in taboo-breaking ways that would win support for his revolution, especially from up-and-coming generations.

He was also aware of the deeper symbolism and public effect of his decision, alone among those at the General Assembly, to continue wearing his uniform for the occasion. Kempski noted:

What he wears is not some smart parade-ground gear, but crumpled olive-green battledress. His shirt is open at the collar. . . . His

97

whole get-up looks as if the titan from the islands has just completed a stand-up fight. His face is a little bloated, but has a healthy colour. His shaggy, matted beard makes the long dark-brown cigars almost disappear between his bulging lips. He has a way of lazily eyeing his surroundings which expresses complete self-confidence, and whose hypnotic power you are unable to escape, at least in the first moment. Castro's deep voice is husky, but also cracked – which may be precisely why it captivates many of those who hear it. Given the youthful vigor that conjures up a picture-book ideal of a victorious warrior, his voice suggests that this colossus of a man smokes and drinks and roars in prodigious measure.[20]

Castro and Khrushchev, who had not met before, both knew how to ridicule the role of villains in which the American media had cast them, by putting on a highly public display of mutual affection at a plenary session of the UN General Assembly. "When Khrushchev went up to Castro . . . , the American journalists swore out loud. For them and the American public, it felt like the worst of nightmares that New York, of all places, should be where the unequal pair were first able to embrace and cover each other with kisses." And it was also on the occasion of the UN summit that the world was first able to enjoy one of Castro's marathon speeches, which would become another of his famous (or infamous) trademarks. During this appearance, the Cuban leader already gave us a glimpse of his ambition not only to revolutionize Cuba, but to carry his model to the rest of the Third World.

Kempski has left an impressive description of that historic debut:

His pocket is the size of a suitcase, and looks quite heavy as well. Fidel Castro carries it in front of him as he comes to the rostrum. Those assembled in the UN's domed hall are suddenly prey to the terrible thought that the pocket holds Castro's manuscript; they give expression to their feelings with a noise like the steam escaping from a weary locomotive. . . . A rumor is going around that Fidel Castro will speak for six hours – a suspicion strengthened when he opens his pocket. But he has no manuscript, only a huge thermos flask. . . . Castro has already been eight days in the city. . . . He engages the people's nervous curiosity all the more, as many Americans unhappy about their country's previous Cuba policy cherish the hope that in the end he will prove to be a politician who is not on the side of the Communists. . . . Finally he is there, before the General Assembly of the United Nations. He is wearing his usual battle fatigues, freshly washed and even ironed. . . . He is the only speaker not to make use of any aids. His sentences are carefully chosen, and are delivered as slowly as if he wanted to impress each individual word for ever on his listeners. He never slips up, never repeats himself. His expression is controlled, his gestures sparing. He speaks Spanish in a melodiously rising intonation, with a touch of sadness.

Fascinated is the only word for the attention with which the Assembly listened to him. Mostly looking straight up, Castro sounded "like the hero of a tragedy," or like a man alone at the Wailing Wall voicing the torment of his people.

It took him four and a half hours. He by no means slammed shut the door leading to the United States, nor did he behave at all like a Communist. Rather, he gave the impression of being a reluctant ally of world communism, who saw a Cuban-style popular front as the only way out. He wanted people to believe that this was because Washington had tried, through constant acts of aggression, to keep the island in a semi-colonial status. His evidence may be demagogically distorted, but it is not pure lies. . . . Castro gave much food for thought in the audience he left behind. . . . This positive impact, exceeding all expectations, was nevertheless weakened by the noisy support from Khrushchev and his entourage . . . , like that of a fan at a football match who has lost all restraint.[21]

Khrushchev's message could no longer be disregarded: Cuba, like it or not, had a new and powerful friend. Very soon it would come in useful, when private American creditors hit by the expropriations persuaded the US authorities to confiscate Castro's turboprop aircraft. In the end, Khrushchev had to lend him the means to fly back to Havana.

The CIA, the Mafia, and the Bay of Pigs

On January 7, 1959, one day before his triumphant entry into Havana, Castro received news that the United States had officially recognized his Urrutia government. On January 10 US Ambassador Smith, a friend of Batista's within the State Department, had to hand in his resignation, and on February 19 Philip W. Bonsal arrived in the Cuban capital to take his place. For the first time in many years the post was now occupied by a career diplomat, who, unlike his predecessors, had a command of the Spanish language as well as ample diplomatic experience in Latin America (most recently, as US ambassador in Bolivia). On March 6 he had his first interview with Fidel Castro, at the latter's villa in Cojímar. "Friendly, cordial and knowledgeable about Cuba – a good Ambassador" was Castro's verdict, as reported in *Time* magazine.[22]

Yet, by March 10, high-ranking members of the US administration were beginning to think of Castro as a dead man walking; that was the day when his assassination featured on the secret agenda of a National Security Council meeting in Washington.[23] "It remains a mystery," writes Szulc, "why the National Security Council discussed Castro's liquidation within five days of his first encounter with the American ambassador." Possibly it had something to do with fears that the United States might lose more than just Cuba. Castro's first trip in January, to Venezuela, had already set the alarm bells ringing. As Jacob Esterline, then CIA station chief in Caracas, later put it: "It seemed to me that something like a chain reaction was occurring all over Latin America after Castro came to power. I saw . . . that a new and powerful force was at work in the hemisphere."[24]

As the year wore on, the State Department and CIA increasingly concluded that the Castro regime should, like the Arbenz government in Guatemala, be removed through an invasion supported by local opposition forces. On December 11 Colonel J. C. King, head of the CIA's Western hemisphere division, wrote a memorandum to CIA boss Allen Dulles and his colleague Richard Bissell (who, as deputy director for covert operations, had already had responsibility for the removal of Arbenz in 1954), in which he recommended getting tough with Castro: that is, proceeding to eliminate him. "Many informed people," he wrote, "believe that the disappearance of Fidel would greatly accelerate the fall of the present government."[25]

Already in late October President Eisenhower, evidently reeling from the Matos affair, had ordered the CIA to fund the anti-Castro groups linking Florida with the clandestine opposition inside the country. At one point, Castro later revealed, there were approximately 300 "counter-revolutionary organizations;" but since many *gusanos* were actually secret servicemen "we knew more about what they did than they knew themselves."[26]

In March 1960, at a meeting of the CIA landing task force, Colonel King intimated to his superiors that "unless Fidel and Raúl Castro and Che Guevara could be eliminated in one package, . . . this operation [would] be a long drawn out affair."[27] And on March 17, under pressure from Vice-President Nixon, Eisenhower finally gave the green light for an invasion and instructed CIA boss Allen Dulles to train up a force of Cuban exiles. In a parallel process, the opposition inside Cuba was supposed to fan the flames of unrest and to undermine the system through selective attacks. According to a secret CIA memorandum written on May 5, 1961, after the Bay of Pigs adventure,[28] 800 sabotage operations destroyed 300,000 tons of sugarcane in the period prior to the invasion; another 150 arson attacks devastated 42 tobacco warehouses, two paper factories, a number of shops and "twenty-one apartments belonging to Communists;" and bombs were set off at a power station and the railway station. Eisenhower gave strict orders that the United States should officially appear to have had nothing to do with all this.

It did not escape Castro's notice that from autumn 1960 the CIA was engaged in extensive operations to bring down the revolutionary government. On October 20, 1960, Ambassador Bonsal was summoned to Washington for "consultations," and in the closing months of his presidency Eisenhower imposed the first embargo on Cuban exports, with exceptions only on humanitarian grounds. In December the contract for the purchase of Cuba's 1961 sugar crop was suspended. On January 3, 1961, two years after the revolution and two and a half weeks before John F. Kennedy's inauguration as president, Eisenhower finally broke off diplomatic relations with Cuba.

Decades later Kennedy's special adviser, Arthur Schlesinger Jr, noted that "the assassination project was initially an integral part of the invasion scheme."[29] He quoted Dulles's deputy director at the CIA, Richard Bissell, the man directly responsible for the invasion, as having said: "The assassination was intended to reinforce the plan. . . . Later, the Mafia became associated with the plan when [the CIA's link to the Mafia, Robert] Maheu brought in Mafia bosses [Salvatore 'Momo'] Giancana and [Johnny] Roselli."[30] Roselli was head of the Mafia in Las Vegas, the city built up as a gambler's paradise after the loss of Cuba. Giancana ran the show in Chicago, and it was later claimed that he had shared a mistress with President Kennedy: Judith Exner. Santos Trafficante, who had meanwhile become Mafia boss in Miami, was also included in the plans.

In August 1960, with Dulles's approval, Bissell approached Colonel Sheffield Edwards with a view to establishing contact with the Mafia.[31] Four days before Castro's September trip to the UN General Assembly one of Edwards's men, Jim O'Connell, met Maheu at the Hilton Plaza Hotel in New York and let him in on the assassination plan. Maheu arranged a number of further meetings with O'Connell, Roselli, Giancana, and Trafficante, both in New York and in Miami.[32] Bissell informed Dulles that "contact had been made with the Mafia."[33] A sum of $200,000 was set aside within the invasion budget for the murder operation.[34]

On October 18, 1960, J. Edgar Hoover at the FBI surprised Bissell with a memorandum showing that he knew of Giancana's involvement in the CIA plot to assassinate Castro:

> During recent conversation with several friends, Giancana stated that Fidel Castro was to be done away with very shortly. . . . He allegedly indicated that he had already met with the assassin-to-be on three occasions. . . . Giancana claimed that everything had been

perfected for the killing of Castro, and that the "assassin" had arranged with a girl . . . to drop a "pill" in some drink or food of Castro's.[35]

The girl in question was Marita Lorenz, Castro's former German girlfriend. She claimed that one day a CIA agent had shown her a photo of her aborted fetus in the Habana Libre suite and told her in reference to Castro: "He did that to you!" Suffering from shock, and disappointed at the course of their affair, she then allowed herself to be drawn into the CIA-Mafia plans to assassinate the Cuban leader.[36] Agent Frank Sturgis talked her into visiting Castro in Havana, to kill him with an almost untraceable pill specially prepared from shellfish toxin by the CIA's Technical Services Division. "I got the order to recruit her," Sturgis later recalled. "From a secret service point of view she was pure gold. And I cultivated her until she was ready to poison Castro."[37] She is supposed to have been promised 2 million, then 6 million dollars, for her part in the operation.

Robert Maheu claims that on March 11, 1961, at a meeting in the Hilton-Fontainebleau Hotel at Miami Beach with Mafia bosses Trafficante and Giancana, he handed over the poison and $10,000 dollars in cash to the Cuban exiles' link-man to the Mafia, Manuel Antonio Varona. Marita Lorenz says that she eventually received the pills from Frank Sturgis, concealed them in her make-up box, and set off for Havana. Shortly afterwards, when she met Castro again at his Habana Libre penthouse for which she still had a key, she was overcome with emotion and lost the heart to go ahead. "Love proved stronger," as she later put it.[38] She threw the deadly poison into the bidet and flushed it away. Immediately afterwards, Castro is supposed to have said: "Did they send you to kill me?", and in a challenging gesture he threw his personal revolver onto the bed beside her.[39] "I was kind of stunned that he should ask me that," she recalled. "You can't lie to him. He said: 'Nobody can kill me.'" Then they made love again and said goodbye.[40]

To a CIA agent in the hotel lobby, she nodded an agreed signal to make him believe that the order had been carried out. Completely disheartened, but without any obstruction from Castro or his people, she then returned to Miami. Castro himself never said anything in public about the affair, while shortly afterwards Marita Lorenz became the mistress of former Venezuelan dictator Marcos Pérez Jiménez and had a daughter by him. With his short rotund figure, quite unlike that of the large bearded revolutionary, he served as the model for the dictator in Gabriel García Márquez's *Autumn of the Patriarch*. She got to know him when she was collecting several hundred thousand dollars for the anti-Castro operations of her exiled Cuban friends in Florida.

Two years later, a barman with the evocative name of Santos de la Caridad (Saints of Charity) very nearly executed another assassination attempt at the Habana Libre when Castro ordered a milkshake late one night. But the botulism pills had become stuck to the inside of the hotel's freezer, and he was unable to remove them in one piece. Castro's security service learned of this only in late 1964, after the hotel employee was arrested as a member of an underground anti-revolutionary cell and made a confession. They also realized that he must have had the poison pills for nearly a year before the opportunity suddenly arose to take advantage of Castro's nocturnal thirst. After many years in jail, he was eventually shipped off to Miami.[41]

Further assassination attempts ended in failure or were rejected as impracticable. One plan was to give Castro a box of poisoned cigars, another to contaminate his diving-suit with highly infectious tuberculosis bacteria, yet another to lace his goggles with a substance that would cause all his hair and beard to fall out and make him look ridiculous. More seriously, a Havana-based agent with the code name NOTLOX planned to kill Castro with a bazooka round at a boxing match that he was due to attend at the Sports Palace in the capital on April 9, 1961, just a few days before the Bay of Pigs landing, but the scheme was eventually called off because of rivalry between different anti-Castro groups. In a speech on the day before the scheduled assassination, Castro characteristically poked fun at the CIA: "We believe that the Central Intelligence Agency has absolutely no intelligence at all. . . . Really, none of them, the Central Intelligence Agents, are intelligent. They should be called the Central Agency of Yankee Cretins." Castro knew: "For months the Central Agency of Yankee

Cretins has been preparing on the soil of Guatemala and the soil of other countries ruled by puppets of imperialism, military bases and armies of mercenaries to attack our country." And he threatened: "When they place a foot here, . . . they will learn the fury of the people who will fall upon them."[42]

Castro was therefore informed of what was brewing. Besides, the *New York Times* had reported it on the same day. Already in November 1960 the Cuban secret service had discovered the training camp in Guatemala, and early in April 1961, a few days before Castro's speech, the CIA picked up a report from the Soviet embassy in Mexico that April 17 had been set as the date for the landing of an invasion force. The new president, John F. Kennedy, who had inherited the plan from his predecessor and allowed it to go ahead only with considerable unease, angrily remarked that Castro "doesn't need agents over here. All he has to do is read our papers."[43] On April 12 Kennedy declared at a press conference "that there will not be, under any conditions, an intervention in Cuba by United States armed forces, and this government will do everything it possibly can . . . to make sure that there are no Americans involved in any actions inside Cuba." Referring to the recent indictment of a US citizen for "plotting an invasion of Cuba . . . to establish a Batista-like regime," he maintained that this "should indicate the feelings of this country towards those who wish to reestablish that kind of administration inside Cuba." A final point, which became especially significant over the coming days, allowed him to wash his hands of the invasion in the event of failure: "The basic issue in Cuba," he asserted, "is not one between the United States and Cuba; it is between the Cubans themselves."[44]

The CIA and State Department had considered several possible landing sites before deciding on the Bahía de Cochinos (Bay of Pigs), on a stretch of coast some 30 miles long between Playa Larga and Playa Girón, just in front of the Zapata swamps. For this reason it was to be known as Operation Zapata. In Washington no one suspected that Castro knew this lonely and deserted region better than almost any other on the 2,500 miles of Cuba's coastline, for it was planned to become a major rice-growing area and he had often been there on official visits.

Two days before the target date there was a crucial "softening-up operation." Castro recalled in conversation with Frei Betto:

A surprise attack was made on all our air bases at dawn on April 15, 1961, to destroy the few airplanes we had. I stayed up the whole night at the command post [in a house in the Vedado area of Havana], because there were reports that an enemy force that had been detected just off the coast of Oriente Province was going to land. Raúl was in Oriente. . . . Almeida was sent to the central part of the island; Che was sent to the western part; and I stayed in Havana. Every time it seemed the United States was going to invade Cuba, we divided up the country.[45]

The raids on the airfields at Havana (Campo Libertad), Cienfuegos (San Antonio de los Baños) and Santiago de Cuba were flown from Nicaragua. And it was also in Nicaragua, in the jungle-cleared town of Puerto Cabezas on the Caribbean coast, that the invasion force of Cuban exiles assembled after its year of CIA training in Guatemala.

The bombers that carried out the attacks were American B-26s, painted with Cuban national emblems to create the appearance of a military revolt. So that the rest of the world should believe this, an aircraft specially filled with bullet-holes in Nicaragua made an "emergency landing" in Miami, where the pilot astounded reporters with a story that he and others had flown through a hail of bullets to wipe out the entire Cuban air force. This immediately fell flat, however, when a journalist with expert knowledge identified it as a US aircraft by its metal nose (Cuban B-26s had perspex noses) and made the deception public. Even more embarrassing was the fact that the truth came out just as the US ambassador to the United Nations, Adlai Stevenson, was lying that the United States had had nothing to do with the attacks. The claim that Castro's entire air force had been destroyed was also false. "We still had more airplanes than pilots: eight planes and seven pilots," Castro recalled.[46]

Castro may have already suspected where the landing would occur. Early in April, during what seemed to be a random trip to the Zapata swamps, he suddenly turned to one of the journalists accompanying him and said: "You know, we should place a .50-calibre heavy machine gun there, just in case."[47] And on April 16, the day after the bombing attacks, the district commander Juan Almeida duly played safe by stationing a militia company along the Playa Girón.

Invasion Brigade 2506, so named after the identity number of Carlos Rodríguez Santana (a volunteer killed on September 8, 1960, during a training exercise in Guatemala), was then putting to sea off Puerto Cabezas over a period of three days. The fleet consisted of eight cargo ships chartered from an exiled Cuban shipowner and the United Fruit Company, plus six escort vessels. Their "host," Nicaraguan dictator Anastasio Somoza, turned up in person to see them off and asked them to bring him back a lock of Castro's beard. The force numbered 1,511 men. A unit of 117 airborne troops was kept in readiness, together with 11 B-26s awaiting orders to provide air support.[48]

A new moon was up as the ships rendezvoused before the Bay of Pigs. A CIA radio station on Swan Island off Honduras (actually inhabited mainly by lizards) finally gave the signal in the form of a cryptic news report, which Bissell's political coordinator, CIA agent and amateur author of spy thrillers Howard Hunt, had composed to throw Castro's secret service off the scent, as well as to place on standby the counter-revolutionary groups supposedly ready for action in Cuba. "Alert! Alert! Look well at the rainbow. The first will rise very soon. Chico is in the house. Visit him. Place notice in the tree. The tree is green and brown. The letters arrived well. The letters are white. The fish will not take much time to rise. The fish is red."[49] Shortly before one a.m. on April 17, 1961, Operation Zapata finally got under way – commanded by the two CIA agents Grayston Lynch and William Robertson. By daybreak the invaders had managed to establish themselves on the beach.

Just before the landing began, one of Almeida's motorized patrols had noticed lights flashing out at sea and initially assumed that a boat was in distress. But when they came under heavy fire from divers and a landing boat, sustaining a number of casualties before they were forced to retreat, there could no longer be any doubt that an invasion was under way. An hour later the survivors reached the nearest town, Jagüey Grande, in their jeep – and around 2.30 they made contact with Fidel Castro at his "Punto Uno" headquarters in Havana.

The commander-in-chief, who at that time had more than 25,000 well-equipped troops and 200,000 lightly armed militia at his disposal, immediately sent to the area artillery and armored units as well as an elite militia battalion of 870 men. At 4.00 he rang one of his last remaining pilots, air force veteran Enrique Carreras, who since the raid on San Antonio de los Baños near Cienfuegos had been sitting in his one-seater Sea Fury complete with missiles. Castro tersely described the situation and ordered: "I want you to sink those ships! Don't let those ships go!"[50] At first light two Sea Furys and one B-26 bomber soared up and attacked the fleet lying off the Bay of Pigs. At 6.30 Carreras scuttled the largest ship, the *Houston*, with its load of ammunition, fuel, and 150 men from the 8th Battalion. A second ship, the landing-craft *Barbara* containing the CIA command staff, was badly damaged and fled full of holes back out to sea. Then, at 9.30, Carreras sank the freighter *Río Escondido*, which had been carrying a 10-day reserve of food and ammunition, as well as medical supplies and telecommunications equipment. "God Almighty!" radioed William Robertson from the *Blue Beach*, "What was that? Fidel got the A-bomb?" – "Naw," replied his CIA colleague Grayston Lynch, "that was the damned *Río Escondido* that blew."[51] All the other ships in the invasion force now kept their distance, leaving some 1,350 men from the "2506 Brigade" to fend for themselves ashore.

In subsequent dog-fights, four of the exiles' 11 B-26 bombers were shot down. Castro also lost four planes from the tiny "air force" that had survived the initial raids, although the one belonging to "Grandad" Carreras (as his comrades called him) escaped intact. Castro was thus left with just two Sea Furys and three T-33 fighters, whereas the invasion force requested, and soon received, new aircraft from the United States for use by Cuban crews. On April 18, when things were looking grim for the invaders, they were again able to deploy some 20 bombers; four of these were now flown by American crews, but two were soon shot down and four members of the Alabama Air National Guard lost their lives. Castro later displayed their bodies as proof of US involvement in the invasion.

Meanwhile, Castro's ground troops sustained heavy losses in an assault on the well-armed beachhead. Carlos Franqui, who at the time had been chief editor of *Revolución*, recalled:

> We lost a lot of men. . . . But the real factor in our favor . . . was the militias: Amejeiras's column embarked on a suicide mission. They were massacred, but they reached the beach. . . . This frontal attack of men against machines (the enemy tanks) had nothing to do with guerrilla war; in fact, it was a Russian tactic, probably the idea of two Soviet generals, both of Spanish origin. . . . One of them, . . . a fox named Ciutat, . . . was sent by the Red Army and the Party as an adviser and was the father of the new Cuban army.[52]

Two weeks after the failure of the invasion, the CIA's paramilitary operations chief, Colonel Hawkins, wrote in a 48-page report of a highly successful sortie with six bombers, "two flown by Americans," against a column of Cuban troops stretching nearly 20 miles. He claimed that many tanks and more than 20 lorries full of soldiers were destroyed by napalm, bombs, missiles, and machine-gun fire, and – on the basis of intercepted radio messages – that the Cuban side had at that point suffered 1,800 casualties, mostly from air attacks.[53] Afterwards, the Cubans officially reported losses of just 176 dead and 300 wounded.[54]

In any event, the fighting was over after just 65 hours, when the invasion force ran out of ammunition. In the early morning hours of April 19, cut off from any supplies and encircled by some 20,000 Cuban troops, Brigade 2506 surrendered. A total of 114 had fallen or drowned, and a further 1,189 were marched off to prison.[55] The rest managed to escape on board the fleeing ships, in rubber dinghies, or on foot through the swamps.

The captives included a number of wanted killers from the days of the Batista regime, whose job, if the invasion had been successful, had been to ensure that Somoza got his lock of Castro's beard – or, in other words, to wipe out the leadership around Castro. Fourteen of them were tried for their activity under Batista: five were executed, and nine sentenced to 30 years' imprisonment.

None of the nearly 1,200 prisoners was initially charged with participation in the invasion, as Castro was again eager to convert his military victory into a major propaganda coup on the world arena. In a spectacular event that became known as the "Havana interrogation," Castro personally discussed with the prisoners in front of TV cameras both the invasion and his revolution. Castro asked in a speech on May 1:

> What kind of people were these, who came here to fight the workers and peasants? We have . . . established that among them were roughly 800 sons of wealthy families. Altogether, these 800 individuals owned 372,000 hectares of land that the Revolution has now expropriated, 9,666 rental properties, 70 industrial companies, ten sugar plants, two banks, five mines and two newspapers. . . . The rest of the thousand prisoners included 135 professional soldiers from the Batista army; the remainder came from the declassed petty bourgeoisie and the lumpenproletariat.[56]

Right from the start Castro made it clear that he had no interest in keeping the prisoners, and he made an offer (doubtless with intent to humiliate) that the United States should supply 500 tractors in return for them. Only a year later, after they had been tried by a military court and sentenced to terms in a labor camp, did the US give up its opposition to any deal of that kind. On December 23, 1962, 20 months after the invasion, they were finally released in exchange for US medical supplies to the value of 53 million dollars.

Two days after the Bay of Pigs fiasco, President Kennedy had accepted full responsibility for its outcome, as "the responsible officer of the government."[57] This was also the view of the CIA: if the US aircraft carrier *Essex* and its escort had been lying some 50 miles off the coast and been told to take no action, the blame for this rested with the White House and the State Department. Indeed, many CIA people and Cuban exiles never forgave Kennedy's refusal in advance to allow the intervention of US forces, especially in the form of massive air attacks. What they failed to appreciate was the wider political context of the Cold War, which meant, for example, that the Soviet Union was waiting for an opportunity to absorb the Western part of Berlin into the

GDR, and that the US president – out of consideration for his NATO allies – must not engage in any military action that might provoke this.

The gulf between the CIA and the White House is shown in the previously quoted report by the CIA's head of paramilitary operations, Colonel Hawkins. Complaining of the extent to which military requirements were subordinate to political affairs, he argued that certain "restrictions" would have to be overcome if the cold war against Communism was ever to be won, and bluntly demanded a greater willingness to take political risks as well as a greater presence and influence of military experts in the President's circle of advisers. Schlesinger, one of these advisers, later considered:

> When Kennedy said that whatever happens, there will be no American military involvement . . . he meant it. They did not understand that he meant it. . . . Kennedy would go to great lengths to avoid escalation of a crisis, especially a military crisis. He refused to escalate at the Bay of Pigs; he refused to escalate in the Berlin crisis; he refused to escalate in the Cuban missile crisis. . . . He was essentially a very cautious foreign-policy president. . . . Bissell and Dulles apparently didn't understand this and the country paid a terrible price for their willful misunderstanding of the President.[58]

Whereas Hawkins claimed that, at the time of the Bay of Pigs, Cuba had been "ripe for an uprising," that Castro's navy had been planning a putsch, and that Castro had deployed only militia forces but no army or navy units to repel the invasion, we can read in a "Top Secret" report by Kennedy's security adviser, McGeorge Bundy: "Particularly important was the failure to estimate accurately the proficiency of the Castro forces. . . . Hope was the parent of belief."[59] Special adviser Schlesinger, for his part, noted:

> For the reality was that Fidel Castro turned out to be a far more formidable foe and in command of a far better organized regime than anyone had supposed. His patrols spotted the invasion at almost the first possible moment. His planes reacted with speed and vigor. His police eliminated any chance of sabotage or rebellion

behind the lines. His soldiers stayed loyal and fought hard. He himself never panicked. . . . His performance was impressive."[60]

In November 1961 Allen Dulles was removed from office, along with his deputy, General Charles P. Cabell, and Bissell, following the production in October of a 150-page internal CIA report by the agency's inspector-general, Lyman Kirkpatrick. This top-secret document, which only became public in 1998 and of which there appears to have been only a single copy, exposed those responsible for the operation to devastating criticism.[61] It specially emphasized the fact that the CIA had greatly exceeded its powers by allowing support for anti-Castro Cuban rebels to mutate into a military project of its own; it then "became so wrapped up in the military operation that it failed to appraise the chances of success realistically," so that its agents ended up "playing the invasion by ear." Its operational budget had skyrocketed from $4.4 million to $46 million. A resistance force of 30,000 Cubans supposedly waiting on the island had never actually existed. It was not Kennedy's refusal to intervene but the CIA's own incompetence which had been the "main cause of the disaster." Bissell's command structure for the invasion had been "anarchic and disorganized" – indeed, all the planning had been "frenzied."[62] Bissell had obviously misled the President and, in the face of highly sensitive operations, made it impossible for him to retreat into a position of "plausible deniability." Attorney-General Robert Kennedy even accused Bissell of deceiving his brother in the White House with an old map from the year 1895.[63]

The air raids of April 15 were scarcely over when Castro ordered mass arrests of all the usual suspects – a list that included nearly everyone on whom the invasion force could count for support. Thus, by the time the white flag was raised at Playa Girón, somewhere between 100,000 and 250,000 people were detained in prisons, sports halls, or other holding centers. Others, such as the Catholic bishops – who had long taken their distance from the revolution – were placed under house arrest. Castro had no scruples about including the old family friend Bishop Pérez Serantes in Santiago.

112

Early in the year the revolutionary government had already begun to take more severe measures against the opposition. Using his militias and a neighborhood watch system, Castro had succeeded in almost completely crippling the resistance – as Hawkins acknowledged in his secret memorandum of May 5.[64] But it was only in late 1961/early 1962 that the outside world came to hear of a dozen trials before revolutionary courts of 37 "counter-revolutionaries," nine of whom were sentenced to death and executed.[65] The most active period had been the first half of March, when round-ups led to the capture of numerous contacts of resistance organizations in Florida. One of these was the first agriculture minister after the revolution, Humberto Sorí-Marín, a man who so hated Castro that he gave the CIA advice on how best to remove him with plastic explosive at a mass rally;[66] he was sentenced to death on April 18 and executed on April 19, the day on which the Bay of Pigs adventure collapsed.[67] Sorí-Marín, shuttling back and forth between Cuba and Florida, had been involved in acts of sabotage and the construction of a "transitional government" (handpicked by the CIA to exclude any of Batista's obvious henchmen), which was supposed to take power after a successful invasion. In fact, all its members belonged to the Revolutionary Democratic Front (FRD), a political umbrella organization for Cuban exile groups in the United States. The intended prime minister was none other than José Miró Cardona, the man who had already once before been appointed the man of the transition – under Castro in early 1959.

During the days of the invasion, however, the CIA choreographers treated this exile government in rather a peculiar manner. Before it could get up and running, Howard Hunt gave orders for Miró Cardona and his cabinet to be taken to a building at the Opa-Locka air base in Miami, where the CIA held them incommunicado for several days. "Government statements" distributed to the media after the beginning of the invasion, such as the one claiming that "Cuban patriots" had begun the "liberation" of Cuba, actually came from a public relations agency in New York with which the CIA occasionally had dealings. When the invasion ended in failure, the puppet government was still in a state of shock because of the way it had been treated, but the CIA consoled its members by flying them to Washington, where they were received by a disconsolate Kennedy.

Fidelismo

After April 19, 1961, "Playa Girón," the strip of beach on the Bahía de Cochinos on the south coast of Cuba, came to stand in Cuban history books for the fact that the awesome American superpower was far from almighty and invincible. A modern version of the biblical tale of David and Goliath came into being, in which Washington's defeat at the Bay of Pigs gave Castro legendary status as a victorious hero. Carlos Franqui, who, like so many of Fidel's friends, grew disenchanted and turned his back on the revolution, wrote: "His enemies were totally discredited and he became the incarnation of the revolution."[68]

Castro now had a free hand to go his own way. On the day when the victims of the air raids of April 15 were buried, he later told Frei Betto, "I gave not only a military but also a political response: I proclaimed the Socialist nature of the Revolution before the fighting at the Bay of Pigs. . . . At the Bay of Pigs [the people] were fighting for socialism."[69] The next step came within a fortnight, at a mass rally on May 1, 1961, when he officially declared Cuba a "Socialist state." At the same time, he finally retreated from his earlier decision to hold elections under the 1940 Constitution: "The Revolution has no time to waste on such foolishness." The 1940 Constitution was "too old and outdated;" the revolution had "exchanged the conception of pseudo-democracy for direct government by the people."[70]

Castro immediately follows up words with deeds. "For a political task that required a cadre who was completely trustworthy, . . . we sometimes chose an experienced member of the Communist Party. Sometimes it was safer to do this than to choose a younger comrade who had less experience."[71] The problem with the "younger comrades" from the 26th of July Movement was that they mostly came from the countryside, and unlike the strictly led and trained Communist cadre they were uneducated and less disciplined, often unable even to read or write. "The People's Socialist Party was a more homogeneous organization than ours; it was a working-class organization with better political education."[72]

On July 26, 1961, the eighth anniversary of the attack on the Moncada Barracks, Castro announced the fusion of his old 26th of July Movement with the remnants of the Directorio Revolucionario and the PSP into an alliance called the Integrated Revolutionary Organizations (ORI), the forerunner of the Communist Party of Cuba (PCC). In 1961, Castro turned mainly to the 50,000-strong PSP to implement his mass literacy campaign right down to the remotest corners of the island. He wanted Cuba to become in a few years the model for underdeveloped societies elsewhere in the world.

The kind of services asked of the PSP naturally came at a political price. Used by Castro, patronized by Raúl and Che, remote-controlled by Moscow, driven by their own ambition, the old Communists of the PSP got straight down to dominating the key structures of the ORI and building up their power in the military and security apparatus, so that the revolution would soon be under their control. Castro's old comrades in the 26th of July Movement were progressively sidelined. Uneasy and suspicious, they watched with growing bitterness as their Comandante allowed the control centers of the revolution to fall into the hands of people who had dismissed the struggle against Batista as a sectarian adventure and opportunistically stood aside until the hour of victory. The chief architect and beneficiary of this evolution was the power-hungry PSP leader Aníbal Escalante, who, partly because of his good connections with Moscow, was appointed by Castro as general secretary of the ORI National Directorate.

Carlos Franqui, the 26th of July man and founder of *Radio Rebelde*, acrimoniously described the consequences:

Any opposition was automatically considered counterrevolutionary, automatically seen as fomented by the CIA. . . . The victory at Girón [Bay of Pigs] could have been the beginning of a setting to rights of internal errors, of a cessation of Party politics, of a recovery of the disaffected, of understanding that within Cuba there was no counterrevolution. Just the opposite took place. . . . The most heavily attacked groups were the old underground fighters, the independent unionists, the Directorio, the independent students, Catholics, members of the Ortodoxos, professional people, technicians, and peasants. . . . The Communists hated my crowd even more than they hated the capitalists we had overcome, because they could not stand the idea of a radical revolution that was not inspired, directed, and organized by the Soviet Union. Now, with the new powers Fidel had graciously granted them, they were destroying the revolution with all their hate and fury. Fidel gave the green light. Raúl organized the persecution with Ramiro Valdés and Security.

Franqui experienced the atmosphere as ever more oppressive: "Fear, the mortal enemy of our revolution, grew like a weed."[73]

When the Cuban apparatchiks set about purging the ranks, they did it precisely where the revolution had found its most fertile soil: among the artists and intellectuals. The dream of combining social justice and artistic freedom soon proved to be an illusion, as the breakthrough to a new age seemed to be ending before it had even really begun. Any criticism was seen as a counter-revolutionary act that served imperialism. Among those who were denounced at this time and subjected to humiliating internment in a labor camp were many who believed in something other than socialism: Catholics, Protestants, and members of the *santería* cult popular among Afro-Cubans. Male and female prostitutes, homosexuals and pederasts had to wear prison uniforms with a large letter "P" on the back for *pimpillos* (pretty boy or girl – in other words, rent boy or prostitute). Franqui tells us that Interior Minister Valdés, who was already familiar with the ways of the Soviet, Chinese, East German, and Vietnamese comrades, once bragged to the laughing Castro brothers about an especially sinister device he had obtained from Czechoslovakia: a machine that could detect homosexuals.[74]

Fortunately, the policy of deliberate humiliation soon came to an end, after cultivated Communists such as Carlos Rafael Rodríguez (who was aware of the negative impact abroad) made indignant representations to Castro. Beneath the surface, however, the persecution continued. What happened in the months after the Bay of Pigs victory was only the beginning of a creeping censorship and restriction of cultural freedom.

The excesses and overreactions during those months reflected the nervousness of the Cuban leadership at the acts of sabotage, infiltration, and incitement orchestrated from Florida, which by no means fell away after the Bay of Pigs. "What the imperialists cannot forgive us," Castro said on April 16, 1961, "is that we have made a socialist revolution under the noses of the United States . . . and that we shall defend with our rifles this socialist revolution!"[75] The Cuban and Soviet secret services, which began working closely together after Raúl's visit to Moscow in autumn 1960, discovered at the last minute two CIA plots (also involving governments in Central America and Venezuela) to assassinate the Máximo Líder, one in June and one in July 1961.[76] The attempt with a telescopic-sight rifle planned for July 26, at a mass rally to commemorate the attack on the Moncada Barracks, was intended to eliminate not only Fidel but also his guest of honor on the platform: Yuri Gagarin, who on April 12 of that year had beaten off the American competition and become the first man to circle the earth in a space capsule.[77] On another occasion, Cuban exiles smuggled into the country planned with opponents inside to fake an attack by Castro's "revolutionary armed forces" on the US naval base at Guantánamo, providing the pretext for the US general staff attached to the President to occupy the island with 60,000 troops, in line with a decision already taken in April.

On December 1, 1961, Castro further angered Washington by taking a decisive step in the direction of Moscow. In a four-hour radio and television address to mark the fifth anniversary of the *Granma* landing, he surprised the world by declaring: "I am a Marxist-Leninist and I shall be a Marxist-Leninist until the day I die."[78] Then, a few months later, the ORI was converted into the Marxist-Leninist United Party of the Socialist Revolution (Partido Unido de la Revolución Socialista – PURS). When the American journalist Lee Lockwood asked Castro in 1965 whether he would have come to power if he had already embraced Marxism in the

Sierra Maestra and espoused a socialist program, the revolutionary leader admitted:

> Possibly not. It would not have been intelligent to bring about such an open confrontation. I think that all radical revolutionaries, in certain moments or circumstances, do not announce programmes that might unite all of their enemies on a single front. Throughout history, realistic revolutionaries have always proposed only those things that are attainable. . . . Furthermore, the degree of development of the people's revolutionary consciousness was much lower than it was to be when we came to power. In those days, there existed many prejudices against Communism. Most people did not know what Communism really was. I myself, when I was a secondary school student, had more or less the same prejudices as did any young man who had been educated in a parochial school. . . . I remember that I had the ideas which I had heard in my own house, from parents, from my family, and which I heard from my teachers and professors. Many people had no other idea of Communism except what the enemies of Communism told them about it.[79]

In the Sierra Maestra, then, Castro did not go so far ideologically as to propagate his revolution as Marxist – contrary to his claim in 1985 that he had already been "Marxist-Leninist" at the time of the Moncada attack. In 1965 he told Lee Lockwood that his development in that direction had been a much longer process, constantly driven by external influences and internal reflection.

> Nobody is born a revolutionary. A revolutionary is formed through a process. It is possible that there was some moment when I appeared less radical than I really was. It is possible too that I was more radical than I myself knew. Ultimately, a revolutionary struggle is like a military war. You have to set for yourself only those goals that are attainable at a given moment. . . . If you ask me whether I considered myself a revolutionary at the time I was in the mountains, I would answer yes, I considered myself a revolutionary. If you asked me, did I consider myself a Marxist-Leninist, I would say no, I did not consider myself a Marxist-Leninist. If you asked me whether I considered myself a Communist, a classic

Communist, I would say no, I did not consider myself a classic Communist. Today, yes, I believe I have that right. I have come full circle. Today I clearly see that, in the modern world, nobody can call himself a true revolutionary who is not a Marxist-Leninist.[80]

Lamberz, the East German SED functionary, wrote in his report of June 1961 on Fidel Castro:

> To the question how one should understand Fidel's declarations in the first half of 1959 – when he expressed such views as: "The revolution must give bread and freedom, but without terror," or "We don't want a red or a green revolution, a revolution of the left or the right" – Comrade Roca explained that Fidel Castro has always been a friend of the Party.

Although such declarations "should also be ascribed to Castro's ideological views at that time," they were "essentially" made with "tactical considerations" in mind.[81]

Blas Roca claimed to Lamberz that the PSP had been in contact with Fidel Castro since 1947, "when he was still a student" and the Party organized "joint actions with him at the university." Raúl, who also studied at Havana University, became a member of the Socialist/Communist Youth in 1952. "Both also began at that time to study Marxism-Leninism, but had mainly liberal-democratic views." Another interesting claim, however, is that before Fidel went into Mexican exile in 1955 there were "common agreements between him and the [Cuban] Party leadership," and that "throughout the period of the armed struggle he kept in close contact with the Party."[82] It is well known that the Party had close contact of this kind with Raúl, but not with Fidel (if we leave aside the visit by Carlos Rafael Rodríguez to the Sierra Maestra).

Nevertheless, in 1961 when Fidel publicly announced his conversion to Marxism-Leninism, the Cuban people was by no means so far advanced. How could it have been? The ideology had no place of note in Cuba's history; it was more in the way of a marginal phenomenon – even if, in Castro's view, "Martí's thinking contains such great and beautiful things that you can become a Marxist by having his ideology as a starting-point."[83] Besides, Castro concedes that "Martí did not explain why society was divided into classes." And since people were used to living in a class society, many of them had difficulty completing the radical turn and giving up individual freedoms.

Even the friends in Moscow whom Castro assumed to be overjoyed with his rapprochement were surprised and not exactly delighted by his latest step. But this mainly had to do with foreign-policy factors. "We had trouble understanding the timing of his statement," Khrushchev wrote in his memoirs. "Castro's declaration had the immediate effect of widening the gap between himself and the people who were against Socialism."[84] Vladimir Semichastny, then head of the KGB, expressed in a report to the Central Committee of the CPSU open criticism of the Cuban revolutionary leader:

> Castro's speech on the socialist character of the Cuban revolution, and the subsequent creation of a Marxist-Leninist party, proceeded without sufficient preparation of the laboring classes, thus intensifying the class struggle in Cuba and alienating from the revolution a significant portion of the petty bourgeoisie, the intelligentsia, the backward portions of the working class, and the peasantry, and also a series of Castro's revolutionary fighters, who were not ideologically ready for these changes.[85]

It is true that Castro was himself not prepared for these changes and was by no means the experienced Marxist-Leninist that he liked to present himself as. "Fidel Castro and his supporters," we read in a GDR diplomatic report of April 1962, "are, as it were, joining Marxism-Leninism relatively unburdened." Of course, such things were not openly said in official reports, nor, above all, in public statements. But Eastern-bloc diplomats trained in political dialectics, who usually exchanged impressions among themselves and especially discussed and agreed them with the Soviet embassy, had for a long time considered that Castro was not yet what he promised to be. In 1962 there was no more than a favorable mention: "Fidel Castro made considerable advances in appropriating and creatively applying Marxism-Leninism. But this knowledge was not yet sufficiently grounded, and often enough there were plainly visible deviations."[86]

The ideologization of public life during those months of mounting external threat went together with dramatic developments in the supply situation inside the country. On March 12, 1962, Castro had to introduce rationing of staple foods. Cubans learned to live with a little book of coupons, the *libreta*, which was supposed to guarantee everyone a fair share of food and other provisions. This accompanied the Cuban Revolution like a ghost. From now on lard, vegetable fats, rice, and beans in the whole country, soap, detergent, and toothpaste in Havana and a few other towns, and beef, chicken, fish, eggs, milk, and certain vegetables only in Havana, were subject to strict rationing.

While Castro blamed this on the United States and its "brutal blockade," Che Guevara made no bones about identifying causes nearer to home. On television he complained: "We made an absurd plan, disconnected from reality, with absurd goals, and with supplies that were totally a dream."[87] Since the revolution the country had been living beyond its means. The hectic attempt to industrialize agricultural land in accordance with the Soviet model was failing at the first fence, owing both to incompetence and to lack of infrastructure. Waste and sloppiness, encouraged by the increased money supply in circulation, were making things worse; the national economic check was not covered. According to an internal report by the East German ADN news agency: "All the measures announced and propagated were, it is now clear, based not upon consideration of objective possibilities but upon the subjective views of individuals. It was thus often wishful thinking which was served up in public as the reality."[88] Theodore Draper wrote in his work on the theory and practice of "Castroism" that, after 1960, the Cubans behaved as if "the Soviets had given them not a $100-million five-year credit but an unlimited account."[89]

Soon Castro had a convenient person to blame for the malaise – namely, ORI general secretary Aníbal Escalante – and he was probably not even wide of the mark. When Castro removed Antonio Núñez Jiménez (who was obviously not up to the job) as director of the National Agrarian Reform Institute (INRA) in charge of economic policy, and replaced him with the reliable PSP leader and economics expert Carlos Rafael Rodríguez, the latter's Party comrade Escalante criticized the decision on the grounds that he had not been consulted beforehand. At this point, Castro thought the time had come to make a clean break with what he saw as the Stalinist machinations of Escalante and his associates. A suspicion had long been forming that Escalante wanted to outmaneuver Castro through a creeping coup d'état – a suspicion that was fueled in February 1962 when Castro, his brother, and Che Guevara suddenly seemed to disappear from the scene for a considerable while. Some rumors went so far as to suggest that they had been deposed by the Communists, or were even being held prisoner by them.

On March 12, however, Castro returned to the public eye and announced his rationing program. In a series of appearances beginning the next day, he then set about undermining Escalante's position – initially through vague allusions that did not mention him by name. From March 20 the political execution followed in installments: first at a public session of the ORI leadership body, then in a television interview on March 26 that accused Escalante of serious errors. "He allowed himself to be swept away by personal ambition, and the result was that he created a series of problems – in fact, he made a chaos of the country." Escalante allegedly exploited the situation and built up a system of privileges and rewards totally dependent upon his own person.

> He appointed [PSP] members to the National Directory with a Nazi "Gauleiter" mentality instead of a Marxist mentality.... Didn't he know anyone else? No, because while the people here were fighting, he was hiding under his bed.... Some people began to wonder: but is this communism, Marxism, or socialism? This high-handedness, these abuses, these privileges, is it really communism?[90]

The next blow immediately fell upon Escalante's followers in the ORI, where a Party secretariat was formed with Fidel Castro as leader and Raúl as deputy. Escalante himself was allowed to pack his bags and go off into "exile" in Moscow. The second prominent victim of the "purge" was the Soviet ambassador in Havana, Sergei Kudryatsev, considered one of the men behind Escalante who had been pulling the strings. Castro categorically demanded that Moscow replace the diplomat, whom he violently abused as a "shithead" and "son of a bitch."

In a secret report in November 1963, the recently appointed GDR ambassador informed East Berlin, on the basis of a conversation with Escalante's longstanding comrade, PSP general secretary Blas Roca, that Escalante had provoked Castro's reaction with his "sectarian methods" as ORI general secretary.

> In his fever for power he began to issue orders to military leaders, asked ministers to report to him, and issued them with instructions. . . . Aníbal tried to make political commissars in the FAR [the Revolutionary Armed Forces] subject to himself. He gave them instructions and demanded reports from them. Such behavior aroused mistrust of the Party in Fidel.[91]

For the PSP, this meant a considerable reversal within the Integrated Revolutionary Organizations, the ORI. The East German comrades still angrily maintained in 1964:

> Among the effects of Aníbal Escalante's sectarian politics, was the reemergence of all Fidel Castro's previously known weaknesses resulting from deep petty-bourgeois roots. His petty-bourgeois origin, his still-defective knowledge in the field of Marxism-Leninism, his insufficient experience of taking into account the interests and problems of the international workers' movement in building a new social order on a national scale, as well as strongly marked emotional tendencies and a certain pragmatism were especially in evidence during his appearances before the people.

These features, combined with "the generally lagging construction of a [Communist] Party and the lack of political/ideological unity in the leadership of the Party [the PURS]," meant that [it] was still quite impossible to speak "of a collective leadership and responsibility for action, . . . of collectively made decisions."[92] Nevertheless, the reaction of the Soviet government to the fall of its protégé, Escalante, was astonishingly calm and pragmatic.

On April 11, when Castro had only just emerged victorious from the power struggle, the Soviet Party daily, *Pravda*, paid tribute to him as his country's leader and sharply condemned Escalante's "sectarian" conduct. At the First of May celebrations in Moscow, Cuba even rose above Yugoslavia to take twelfth place in the list of countries bringing fraternal greetings. According to "Kremlinological" criteria, this meant that the Caribbean island had been accepted into the community of socialist states.

Although the liaison was not for either side a "love match," and indeed remained for the USSR until the end a political "forced marriage," Khrushchev now began to shower Castro with favors. One calculation was to avoid slighting Castro, so that he did not seek the embrace of China. After his arrival in Moscow, Escalante had already warned the Kremlin that under Che Guevara's influence Castro might go off and flirt with China. Indeed, the Cubans had been quietly forging closer links with Beijing, since Havana did not feel that it had enough support from Moscow for its attempts to export the Cuban Revolution to other Latin American countries. But Moscow, in stepping up its relations with Havana, now seized the chance of shifting the East–West balance to its advantage through the positioning of a new satellite in the middle of the other superpower's sphere of influence.

"Mongoose" and "Anadyr"

On November 30, 1961, the day before Castro publicly signed up to Marxism-Leninism, President Kennedy gave the go-ahead for a new covert operation against Cuba, the most extensive ever undertaken by the CIA against another state. "Operation Mongoose" – so called after the greyish-brown Asian viverrine famous for its ability to attack and kill even the largest and most venomous snakes – would be allocated 400 CIA officers, several hundred motor-boats, and an annual budget reputedly in excess of 50 million dollars.

Cuba, as the president's brother, Attorney-General Robert Kennedy, put it to CIA director John McCone, had "top priority;" "all else is secondary – no time, no money, effort or manpower is to be spared."[93] In government circles in Washington the story was that the president had decided "to utilize all resources to unseat Castro."[94] On his brother's advice, the president appointed to head Operation Mongoose a South-East Asia expert in "special operations" under the Eisenhower administration, Brigadier-General Edward Lansdale, who was to be the inspiration for Haudegen, the main character in Graham Greene's novel *The Quiet American*. Lansdale was set up in the Pentagon and placed under Robert Kennedy's direct supervision. To his colleagues in the CIA he was known as a braggart. Or, more bluntly, "Lansdale was a nut" – the words of Samuel Halpern from Task Force W, the Cuba department in the CIA control room.[95]

When the new planning began to overthrow Cuba's revolutionary government, the CIA still had only 28 agents on the island. "After the Bay of Pigs, they [the Cubans] cleaned house. And they did a fine job," Halpern asked his superiors to bear in mind.[96] As before, he saw Castro's elimination as the prerequisite for success, and toward the end of 1961 he wheeled in Mafia drugs-trafficker Rolando Cubela, the killer of Batista's secret police chief. For CIA agent Desmond FitzGerald, the architect of several attempts on Castro's life, Cubela was something like "Robert Kennedy's special representative" in this matter.[97] Ronald Steel, in his biography of Robert Kennedy, makes it sound highly plausible that the Kennedy brothers were fully in the picture and backed the assassination plans, although no one has ever been able to prove that they actually gave the orders.[98]

Castro's embrace of Marxism-Leninism had the effect that, within just a few weeks, 13 Latin American governments – mostly under pressure from Washington – broke off diplomatic relations with Havana. At the summit of the Organization of American States (OAS) held in January 1962 at Punta del Este in Uruguay, Che Guevara's forceful interventions were unable to prevent his country's exclusion from the organization by a two-thirds majority of 14 out of 21 votes. The official justification spelled it out that "ties to Marxism-Leninism" were "incompatible with the

Inter-American system." Still, to win the fourteenth vote necessary to carry the decision, the US ambassador to the OAS had to dig deep at a dinner with little Haiti's foreign minister; the Uruguayan daily *El Día* reported that he promised to come up with 5 million dollars, ostensibly for a new airport in Port-au-Prince.[99] On February 7, 1962, the United States government imposed a total economic blockade of Cuba, causing the loss of $600 million in foreign currency earnings.

At the same time, there was a growing number of reports that Washington had decided to press ahead with another landing on the island. At a three-hour White House dinner with Alexei Adzhubei, Khrushchev's son-in-law and editor of the Soviet government daily *Izvestiya*, President Kennedy drew a striking parallel between Cuba and Hungary. He further aroused suspicions by alluding to the American presidential elections in 1964: "If I run for reelection . . . ," he told Adzhubei, "Cuba will be the main problem of the campaign, [and] we will have to do something."[100] Against this background, a day after the imposition of the US economic blockade, the Presidium of the Supreme Soviet gave the go-ahead on February 8, 1962, for a program of military aid to Cuba. On February 21, three weeks after Adzhubei's get-together with Kennedy, KGB Chief Semichastny informed Soviet Foreign Minister Andrei Gromyko and Defense Minister Rodion Malinovsky of what he had learned about a new invasion plan.[101]

On February 20 General Lansdale had presented to the "Special Group (Augmented)," or SGA, a top secret 26-page schedule setting out six stages for a coup in Cuba. The document submitted to the committee supervising Operation Mongoose, under US chief of staff Maxwell Taylor, also contained an option for "decisive intervention by US forces."[102] Already on February 7, the day when the blockade came into force, Admiral Robert Dennison, commander of US Atlantic forces (CINCLANT), had called a meeting of the joint chiefs of staff in Norfolk, Virginia, to make all necessary preparations for a landing on "Day X." President Kennedy and his advisers demanded that a military strike should be successfully carried out against the Castro regime within two to four weeks. On February 22, five days before the session of the UN Security Council, the invasion plan was ready in the safes of the supreme commander and the US general staff. Many years later, at a conference held in 1992 in Havana to review the missile crisis, the US defense secretary in 1962, Robert McNamara, admitted: "If I had been a Cuban leader at that time, I might well have concluded that there was a great risk of a US invasion. And I should say, as well, if I had been a Soviet leader at that time, I might have come to the same conclusion."[103]

In the spring of 1962, Soviet–Cuban relations were already so close that, as Khrushchev wrote in his memoirs, loss of the newly gained partner "would have been a terrible blow to Marxism-Leninism [. . .] and gravely diminish[ed] our stature throughout the world, but especially in Latin America."[104] In April, Khrushchev first floated to his defense minister, Malinovsky, the idea of stationing nuclear missiles in Cuba.[105] Khrushchev later wrote:

> In addition to protecting Cuba, our missiles would have equalized what the West likes to call "the balance of power." The Americans had surrounded our country with military bases and threatened us with nuclear weapons, . . . and it was high time America learned what it feels like to have her own land and her own people threatened.[106]

After all, according to present calculations, the US numerical superiority in nuclear warheads at the time of the Kennedy administration was somewhere between 9:1 and 17:1.[107] The United States had installed, along the border between NATO-member Turkey and the Soviet Union, five launching sites for nuclear-tipped Jupiter medium-range missiles, capable of reaching Soviet cities such as Kiev, Odessa, and even Moscow. The siting of missiles with ranges of 1,100 and 2,200 kilometers at America's very gates would at a stroke have doubled the number of nuclear missiles directly threatening cities and military targets in the United States, since all the Soviets had had pointed at America until that time had been the well-known intercontinental SS-7s or R-16s.

On May 20 Khrushchev discussed the topic with his deputy Anastas Mikoyan (himself an expert on Cuba), Defense Minister

Malinovsky, Foreign Minister Gromyko, Politburo member Frol Kozlov, and the KGB man in Havana closely in touch with Castro who was soon to become Soviet ambassador in the Cuban capital, Aleksandr Alekseev. "Comrade Alekseev," he said, "we have decided or are about to decide to put medium-range missiles with nuclear warheads in Cuba. What will Fidel say about this?" "He will be scared," came the answer, "and I don't think he will take them."[108]

After the Politburo "unanimously" decided on May 24 to offer Castro the stationing of the missiles, a high-ranking Soviet delegation secretly flew to Havana four days later by a round-about route through Conakry in West Africa. The group included the man in charge of Soviet strategic forces, Marshal Sergei Biryuzov, disguised as "engineer Petrov." "He asked me what would be required to prevent a US invasion," Castro recalled, and they began discussing the option of medium-range missiles. "We were informed," Castro continued, "that they would deploy 42 missiles." He discussed the matter among his closest circle.

> We did not like the missiles. If it was a matter of our defense alone, we would not have accepted the missiles here. But do not think it was because of the dangers that would come from having the missiles here, but rather because of the way in which this could damage the image of the Revolution in Latin America.[109]

In the end, it was also a "moral question:" "I thought: if we expected the Soviets to fight for our cause, to take risks for us, and if they were even prepared to go to war for our sake, it would have been immoral and cowardly not to allow the presence of the missiles here." The next day he informed the emissary from Moscow: "If it serves the purpose of strengthening the socialist camp and also defending the Cuban Revolution, we are prepared to instal the number of missiles . . . you consider necessary in our country."[110]

After Castro's agreement, the Presidium of the Supreme Soviet decreed on June 10, 1962, the hitherto most spectacular military aid program in Soviet history. Khrushchev wanted to make the Caribbean island the first nuclear power outside the Warsaw

Pact, albeit with the weapons under Soviet control. The original plan, evidently later revised, envisaged the installation of 40 mobile launching pads: 16 for IRBMs (intermediate-range ballistic missiles) of the R-14 (SS-5) type with a range of 2,200 nautical miles, and 24 for MRBMs (medium-range ballistic missiles) of the R-12 (SS-4) type with a range of 1,100 nautical miles. Each of these installations was to comprise two missiles – one as a reserve – and one nuclear warhead. Each of the warheads would have an explosive power equal to three megatons of TNT, roughly 225 times that of the atomic bombs dropped on Hiroshima (13.5 kilotons). The idea was to send the missiles to Cuba together with an army of 50,874 men (soldiers, officers, military advisers, and instructors from the Soviet armed forces), including four elite motorized units 2,500-strong and 250 armored vehicles, one intelligence regiment, one reconnaissance battalion, one battalion of technicians, two tank battalions equipped with the latest T-55 tanks, one helicopter regiment, one squadron of transport aircraft, one flight of 42 Mig-21 fighters, and 42 light bombers of the Ilyushin-28 type. In the end, a total of 41,902 men were stationed on the island. (According to Defense Secretary McNamara writing 30 years later, the CIA had long assumed that no more than 10,000 men would be based there.[111]) At that time, according to US estimates, Cuba itself had more than 275,000 soldiers, reservists and militia – which made it the largest military power in Latin America. In addition, the planned shipment from the Soviet Union included "rocket launchers" for 80 tactical cruise missiles to be used for coastal defense, with a range between 25 and 100 miles and explosive power up to that of one Hiroshima bomb, and the Ilyushin-28 bombers were to have carried six 12-kiloton atom bombs along with their conventional bomb load. Then there were 24 anti-aircraft batteries, with 144 conventional ground-to-air SA-2 missiles – the type that shot down U-2 pilot Gary Powers on May 1, 1960, at a height of 23,000 metres over the Soviet Union. Another decision provided for the construction of a naval base for the latest Soviet nuclear submarines. A fleet of 18 ships, including four destroyers, was to patrol the Cuban coast. And, to keep an eye on the US coast, Moscow wanted to deploy 11 submarines, seven of them capable of carrying three medium-range ballistic missiles, each with an explosive power equal to one megaton of TNT.[112]

In mid-July Moscow began shipments: over the next three months a fleet of 85 cargo and passenger vessels would run at least 150 trips across the Atlantic, carrying troops and matériel to the island nearly 4,500 miles away. It was one of the largest and most secret logistical operations ever undertaken by the Soviet Union; its name, "Operation Anadyr," so called after a river in North-East Siberia that flows into the Pacific, was supposed to confuse enemy intelligence. Despite all the speculation and rumors, Kennedy trusted the assurances of the Soviet leadership that only weapons of a defensive character would be sent to Cuba. In mid-September, however – as Khrushchev's deputy Mikoyan later maintained – the CIA received via the West German intelligence service (BND) the first concrete proof of a shipment of Soviet nuclear missiles to the island.[113] Khrushchev's plan of confronting the Americans with a fait accompli after the November Congressional elections had almost, but not quite, worked out.

Right from the start Castro was against Khrushchev's secretiveness.

> It did us a lot of harm. Kennedy trusted in what he was told. . . . So in the eyes of world public opinion, Kennedy gained moral force. . . . What other advantage did it give him? That when the missile sites were finally discovered on 14 October, the United States had an enormous advantage . . . the initiative in the military realm was put in [their] hands. They . . . could afford to choose one option or another, a political option, a quarantine, or a surprise air attack on those installations.[114]

Fearing a preemptive strike, Castro sent Che Guevara and his military adviser Major Emilio Aragónes to Moscow. "You don't have to worry," Malinovsky told them, "there will be no big reaction from the US side. And if there is a problem, we will send the Baltic fleet."[115] Khrushchev did not yield.

The only thing that was eventually made public, on September 2, was a mutually agreed communiqué on Soviet arms aid to Cuba.

This stated that, because of "imperialist threats," Cuba had asked the Soviet government for arms supplies and technical instructors, and that Moscow had acceded to the request. Two days later, to be on the safe side, President Kennedy told his press officer Pierre Salinger that the United States would regard the stationing of "offensive weapons of any kind" on Cuba as a threat to American security and would under no circumstances tolerate it. On September 13 he once more personally reaffirmed this stance, despite the fact that two days previously a Soviet government statement had declared that "the arms and military equipment sent to Cuba are intended solely for defensive purposes."[116]

The Soviet ambassador in Washington, Anatoly Dobrynin, who had not been kept filled in by Khrushchev, later wrote that the Soviet leader "grossly misunderstood the psychology of his opponents." "Had he asked the embassy beforehand, we could have predicted the violent American reaction. . . . It is worth noting that Castro understood this. . . . But Khrushchev wanted to spring a surprise on Washington; it was he who got the surprise in the end."[117] Looking back on the events, Kennedy's special adviser, Theodore Sorensen, and his security adviser, McGeorge Bundy, indirectly confirmed Castro's reading of the situation at the time. A publicly admitted stationing of Soviet missiles in Cuba, in response to the stationing of US missiles in Turkey, would, in Sorensen's words, have made it "much more difficult [for Kennedy] to mobilize world opinion on his side."[118]

Thirteen days on the brink of a third world war

On October 4, Robert Kennedy hauled over the coals "Operation Mongoose" chief Edward Lansdale. "Nothing is moving forward," he yelled.[119] The overthrow of Castro had been planned for that very month, but CIA analyses suggested that the popular uprising against Castro which it saw as a precondition for US military intervention was more unlikely than ever to happen. On the same day, the Soviet freighter *Indigirka* put in at Mariel near

Havana; it had on board 45 nuclear warheads for medium-range missiles, 36 warheads for cruise missiles, 12 nuclear warheads for tactical Luna missiles (subsequently added to the delivery schedule), and 6 atom bombs for the Ilyushin-28s. A total of 114 shipments had reached Cuba since July, and another 35 were due. Already delivered were 36 R-12 (SS-4) medium-range missiles.

Four days later, Cuban President Osvaldo Dorticós warned the UN General Assembly in New York against making Cuba the trigger for a new world war. "If we are attacked, we will defend ourselves; we have sufficient means with which to defend ourselves." And he added a remark that must have made everyone sit up and take notice: "We have indeed our inevitable weapons, the weapons which we would have preferred not to acquire and which we do not wish to employ."[120] After Dorticós's return to Havana, Castro confirmed – as if to subvert Khrushchev's secretive approach – that the Americans could no longer mount an invasion with impunity. "They could begin it," he said, "but they would not be able to end it."[121] On October 10 the Republican senator from New York, Kenneth Keating, finally made the claim that nuclear weapons were already in Cuba; it would appear that CIA chief and fellow-Republican John McCone, or someone in his circle, had supplied him with secret service reports not yet available even to President Kennedy. In contrast to the White House, McCone gave no credence to the Soviet smooth talk; he was convinced that the unusually high traffic in the shipping lanes did not have an innocuous, conventional explanation, but indicated that Soviet nuclear missiles were being installed in Cuba. Nevertheless, McCone does not seem to have had tangible proof at that time.

On October 13, 1962, shortly before midnight, Major Richard S. Heyser left on a U-2 spy flight from Edwards Air Force Base in California to check Keating's claim. More than six weeks had elapsed since the last such mission over Cuba, and that had suddenly revealed the existence of bases for conventional Soviet SA-2 ground-to-air missiles. But, in order to avoid giving Castro the opportunity to shoot down another U-2, further flights had been temporarily suspended. Finally, on October 14,

Major Heyser's glittering jet flew over a cloudless Western Cuba and photographed especially the area around San Cristóbal, where agents on the ground had reported activity by sizeable Soviet units within large sealed-off zones. Late the next afternoon, when the miles of film were developed and studied by experts at the CIA's National Photographic Interpretation Center (NPIC) in Washington, they confirmed the worst fears: the Soviet Union had indeed been building a nuclear weapons base in the backyard of the United States. Further U-2 flights would reveal the construction of nuclear launch pads at other places on the island.

On the morning of October 16, the president's security adviser, McGeorge Bundy, suddenly showed up in his bedroom at the White House and presented the U-2 photographs. Amid great secrecy the President's circle of advisers, which has gone down in history as the Executive Committee of the National Security Council (or Ex Comm, for short), met shortly afterwards in the Cabinet Room of the White House for its first crisis session. "Now, as the representative of the CIA explained the U-2 photographs that morning," Robert Kennedy later recalled, "we realized that it had all been lies, one gigantic fabric of lies. . . . We had been deceived by Khrushchev, but we had also fooled ourselves."[122] During the next 13 days, between Thursday, October 16 and Sunday, October 28, 1962, the world confronted – to quote Defense Secretary Robert McNamara – "the greatest danger of a catastrophic war since the beginning of the nuclear age."[123]

Five options came up for debate among the 15 to 20 members of Ex Comm: (1) an immediate air strike to destroy all the known missile sites; (2) more extensive air strikes against the missile sites as well as other military installations; (3) the second option plus the landing of American troops, the occupation of the island and the overthrow of the Castro regime; (4) instead of immediate military attacks, a complete blockade on all military sea transport to Cuba, until all strategic weapons were dismantled and withdrawn; (5) talks with the Soviet Union to reach a political "deal," trading the withdrawal of US medium-range missiles from Turkey and Italy for the removal of Soviet missiles from Cuba.

Given the unfavorable nature of the general political situation, the first three options carried a great risk of rapid escalation up to nuclear war. Option five, involving a negotiated solution, was rejected on the grounds that Soviet duplicity over the stationing of the missiles had severely damaged the basis for trust. Option four seemed to be a feasible middle way, which, if the Soviet Union tried to break the blockade, still left room for options one to three. While Defense Secretary McNamara argued for a blockade, his Joint Chiefs of Staff (JCS) voted for an immediate military attack. One group wanted this to be limited to the 52 missile installations and warhead depots already located, while another group favored surprise attacks on all 2,002 military targets, including some 1,500 defensive positions.

For five days the president and his advisers fought it out to find the right solution, favoring now one and now another option. Kennedy found himself sorely tested in the process. On Thursday, October 18, Soviet Foreign Minister Gromyko arrived on a long-planned visit to the White House. During talks lasting more than two hours, he announced that, after the US Congressional elections, the Soviet Union would feel "compelled" to take a harder line over Berlin. At the same time, Kennedy voiced his concern over the growing Soviet military presence in Cuba, while Gromyko emphasized its defensive character and expressed his own worries about a US invasion of Cuba. The president had difficulty keeping his composure. He noted indignantly to his advisers:

> Gromyko, in this very room not over 10 minutes ago, told more barefaced lies than I have ever heard in so short a time. All during his denial that the Russians had any missiles or weapons, or anything else, in Cuba, I had the low-level pictures in the center drawer of my desk, and it was an enormous temptation to show them to him.[124]

But since it had not yet been decided how the US would react, he kept what he knew about the missiles to himself.

After a vote in the Ex Comm group, John F. Kennedy followed the majority recommendation of a "quarantine." Two further considerations strengthened his resolve in that direction. First, the head of the tactical air force pointed out that, even with a surprise attack from the air, it could not be said with certainty that all the missile sites and nuclear weapons would be destroyed.[125] Second, Kennedy thought that an attack on the missile sites or even an invasion of Cuba would provoke a Soviet riposte in Berlin. "They can't, after all their statements, permit us to take out their missiles, kill a lot of Russians, and then do nothing."[126]

After Congressional leaders and the NATO and OAS allies had been informed, the president gave a radio and television address explaining the situation to the public. His speech on Monday evening, at 7 o'clock Washington time, sent the world into shock. First he reported that launch pads for nuclear missiles had been built in Cuba, and asserted that the Soviet Union had thereby deceived the world with false assurances, violated the Charter of the United Nations and threatened world peace. Then he announced a military blockade of the island, which would be lifted only after all nuclear weapons had been withdrawn. Finally, he warned Moscow that a missile attack from Cuba on any other country in the Western hemisphere would inevitably result in a nuclear attack by the United States on the Soviet Union. He called upon Khrushchev to end "this reckless and provocative threat to world peace."[127]

In parallel with the blockade, an order was made for the world-wide mobilization of US forces. All strategic missile units went onto the highest level of alert, and 250,000 men (including 90,000 ground troops) were placed on standby for a landing in Cuba – an eventuality which the US general staff estimated would result in 25,000 casualties, even if only conventional weapons were used. In fact, Washington knew nothing of the battlefield nuclear weapons with which the Soviets and Cubans intended to fight off an invasion. Nor did the US President and his advisers have any idea that, already in July, Khrushchev had told his commander in Cuba, General Pliyev, to use his own judgment in employing these "minor" nuclear devices.

"The crisis erupted on the night of 22 October, and defense preparations occupied almost all of our time after that," Castro recalled 30 years later.[128] Within 72 hours, 420,000 soldiers and militia were ready to repel an attack.[129] The naval blockade on all military transport to Cuba, meanwhile endorsed by the Organization of American States, came into force at 10 a.m. on

Wednesday, October 24, 1962. Now it was clear. If Soviet freighter captains tried to break the blockade, or if they used the armed support of their escort submarines to resist inspection of their cargo, hostilities would erupt between the world's two super-powers. Tension began to mount all around the world. People grew extremely worried and spent their time sitting in front of radios or televisions, or emptying supermarket shelves to lay up reserves. Governments made provisions for evacuation and other emergency measures. Millions of dead were predicted in the event of a nuclear war.

In a dramatic race against time, the *Aleksandrovsk* just managed to put in at the Cuban harbor of La Isabela. At 10.32, President Kennedy received news that six other Soviet freighters, four of them carrying R-14 booster rockets, had heaved to upon reaching the blockade line 500 miles off the Cuban coast – a line patrolled by 63 ships of the US navy. After many anxious moments, the White House finally heard with relief that a total of 14 Soviet ships had turned around; the blockade was beginning to take effect. There was still no sign, however, that the missiles already in Cuba were about to be removed – on the contrary, the Soviets were working flat out to get the launch pads finished. The US general staff began cautiously to prepare for a landing. Fidel Castro, on the basis of reports from his secret service, was convinced that air raids and an American landing were to be expected on October 29 or 30.

On Friday, October 26, at one in the morning, he dragged Soviet ambassador Alekseev out of bed and, in a state of nervous excitement, told him that the odds were 20:1 in favor of a US invasion within the next three days. Over beer and sausages he eventually dictated a letter to Khrushchev tersely setting out his "personal view" of the situation. It took quite a while, for he was not satisfied until the tenth draft of the letter. Yet the crucial passage, stylistically awkward and convoluted, is still not easy to interpret. "Dear Comrade Khrushchev," he writes at the point in question, "if . . . the imperialists invade Cuba to occupy it at last, an aggressive policy of this kind represents such a great danger for mankind that after such a deed the Soviet Union should never permit circumstances to arise in which the imperialists might carry out a nuclear first strike against it." A US invasion of Cuba, he continues, would be "the time to eliminate such a danger once and for all, through an act of legitimate defense. Hard and terrible this solution would be, but there would be no other."[130]

The Soviets were puzzled. "At the beginning I could not understand what he meant by his complicated phrases," Alekseev later reported to Moscow. Finally he asked Castro point blank: "Do you wish to say that we should be the first to launch a nuclear strike on the enemy?" Castro then replied: "No. I don't want to say that directly, but under certain circumstances, we must not wait to experience the perfidy of the imperialists, letting them initiate the first strike and deciding that Cuba should be wiped off the face of the earth."[131] Alekseev's interpretation was that, in Castro's view, the Soviet Union should answer a US invasion of Cuba with a devastating nuclear first strike against the United States.

It was as if Castro had been prepared to avenge the violent demise of his revolution with the end of the world. All of his attempts over the years to explain away those sentences, or simply to blame errors of communication between Havana and Moscow or of translation between Spanish and Russian, have taken nothing away from their explosive nature.

Khrushchev certainly understood the content of Castro's letter in the same way that Ambassador Alekseev had done, but it was only on October 30 that he dealt with the matter in a long reply. In the manner of a paternal friend, the veteran of the Second World War gave his temperamental "foster-child" in Havana a lesson in world war and annihilation, writing:

In your telex message, you suggested that we should be the first to carry out a nuclear strike against the enemy's country. Naturally you must realize what that would have led to. It would have been not just a strike but the prelude to a thermonuclear world war. Dear Comrade Fidel, I consider your suggestion wrong, although I understand your motivation. . . . In such an event, the United States would doubtless have suffered huge losses, but the Soviet Union and the whole socialist camp would also have suffered a

great deal. . . . Above all, Cuba would have been the first to burn
in the fire of war. . . . We struggle against imperialism not in order
to die but to make full use of our possibilities, so that in this
struggle we win more than we lose and achieve the victory of
communism.[132]

Castro did not want to let matters stand like that in the historical record. The next day, in another letter to Khrushchev, he
conceded:

> I may have tried to say too much in too few lines. We were aware
> that in the event of a thermonuclear war we would be wiped
> out. . . . I did not mean to suggest, Comrade Khrushchev, that the
> USSR should have been the aggressor, because that would have
> been more than wrong, it would in my view have been immoral
> and disgraceful; . . . I meant to say that, after imperialism had
> attacked Cuba, the USSR should act without hesitation and never
> commit the mistake of giving the enemy the opportunity to carry
> out a nuclear first strike against it.[133]

Castro's blood pressure seems to have been peaking. The next
day, after US reconnaissance aircraft had crossed Cuba at treetop
height, he instructed his 50 air defense units to fire without
warning on any American plane entering Cuban air space. He
also ordered landmines to be laid in the area around Guantánamo.

Meanwhile, Khrushchev had signaled to Kennedy his willingness to make concessions, leaving Castro more or less in the
dark. "We have to get these missiles out of there, before the real
fire starts," he is supposed to have told his former speech writer
Fyodor Burlatsky.[134] In a long letter to the US President, which
was handed to the American embassy in Moscow at 9 a.m. on
October 26, the Kremlin leader agreed that Soviet ships bound
for Cuba would no longer carry any weapons, if the United States
declared that it would neither itself mount an invasion of Cuba
nor support an invasion by a third party. "Then the necessity for
the presence of our military specialists in Cuba would disappear."[135] This formulation indicated that the Soviets were willing
to remove the missiles; for, if the specialists left and took the
"ignition keys" with them, the missiles themselves would become

useless. When Kennedy had the translation of this letter in his hands, however, in the late morning of October 26, all systems were in place for the 24 SS-4 medium-range missiles based in Cuba. The actual warheads were kept in bunkers under strict supervision, but three and a half hours were all it would take to mount them and make the missiles ready for launching.

The next day, evidently under pressure from others in the Soviet leadership, Khrushchev sent a second letter to President Kennedy in which he introduced the idea of a package deal: Soviet offensive weapons would be withdrawn from Cuba in return for the removal of American Jupiter medium-range missiles from Turkey.[136] Unable and unwilling to become drawn, at least publicly, into missile-bargaining of this kind, Kennedy discussed the matter out with his team of advisers and decided to accept only the first offer of October 26. The key passage of his reply to Khrushchev stated that the United States would lift the quarantine and renounce an invasion of Cuba, as soon as the nuclear weapons had been removed under UN supervision and the Soviet Union had given assurances that it would not install such weapons in Cuba in the future. Privately, however, Kennedy also placed the future of the Jupiter missiles in question – so as not to weaken Khrushchev still further in relation to his comrades. That same evening, he had his brother Robert give an oral undertaking to the Soviet ambassador, Dobrynin, that the Jupiters would be withdrawn within five months.

While Washington and Moscow were preparing to settle matters over Castro's head, the missile crisis suddenly entered another critical phase. At 10.22, in line with Castro's orders as supreme commander, an American U-2 spy plane was shot down over Banes in eastern Cuba by a Soviet ground-to-air missile. This incident, in which the pilot, Captain Rudolf Anderson Jr, lost his life, threatened to upset everything that had already been achieved. But Kennedy resisted pressure from the Pentagon to hit straight back.

At nine o'clock the next morning, Sunday, October 28, Khrushchev's reply came in over several pages. The Soviet premier made it officially known that the missiles would be removed from Cuba and agreed to UN monitoring of the process.[137] The

"Executive Committee" received the message with jubilation, while hotheads on the Pentagon general staff doubted its authenticity and advised that, unless there was "irrefutable proof" that the missiles were being dismantled, the president should still order air attacks on the missile bases the next day, as well as an invasion of Cuba.[138]

In a letter to Castro that same day, Khrushchev tried to explain his missile decision as a quid pro quo for the Americans' renunciation of an invasion of Cuba. As if in awe of the Cuban leader's temperament, he implored him not to let himself be "carried away with emotion," adding "friendly advice" to show "patience, steadfastness and once more steadfastness" and to stop shooting at American planes.[139]

In his immediate reply, Castro defended himself by pointing out that there had been fears of an American air attack, but he also remarked that he had not wanted to sit idly by, "with limited weapons," while enemy aircraft carried out a surprise attack. In any event, Castro suspended his order to shoot down reconnaissance aircraft, but also made it abundantly clear that "we reject in principle any inspection of our territory."[140] This placed Khrushchev in a very awkward position and jeopardized his agreement with the Americans.

The tone of Castro's letter of October 28 to the Soviet leader was cool and composed. But in reality the Máximo Líder was boiling with rage, because no one had even consulted him during the decisive phase of the missile crisis; he had had to pick up the spectacular news from radio and press agency reports. "Son of a bitch! Bastard! Arsehole!" this is how Franqui remembers him ranting against Khrushchev. "He went on cursing, beating even his own record for curses."[141] In his eyes, all that Khrushchev had won was a minimal concession on Kennedy's part; much more could have been got out of it for Cuba and the Soviet Union. And yet, Castro knew only that part of the superpower agreement which concerned Cuba; he was not told anything about the American promise to remove the Jupiter missiles from Turkey, which was important in shoring up Khrushchev's weakened position within the Soviet leadership. He would first hear of this only the following spring, after the Jupiters had actually been removed.

Scarcely had the Soviet–American agreement of October 28 been made public when Castro demanded that it be revised in line with five points that went far beyond mere renunciation of a military invasion. These were: (1) lifting of the economic blockade imposed in February; (2) cessation of the acts of subversion and sabotage by Americans and their counter-revolutionary "mercenaries" inside Cuba; (3) ending of the "acts of piracy" by Cuban exiles based in the United States and Puerto Rico; (4) an end to violations of Cuban air space and territorial waters by US aircraft and ships; and (5) return of the US naval base at Guantánamo in eastern Cuba.

But it was too late for improvements. When UN General Secretary Sithu U Thant arrived in Havana on October 30 to discuss UN monitoring of the Soviet missile withdrawal, he met a revolutionary leader in an "impossible and intractable mood," "extremely bitter" about the Soviets, the Americans, and U Thant himself, whom he insulted as a "lackey of the imperialists."[142] At their second meeting, Castro became so abusive that U Thant broke off talks and flew back to New York filled with consternation. Castro was flatly refusing to allow UN monitoring of the missile withdrawal, on the grounds that it would constitute a violation of Cuban sovereignty. "Whoever tries to inspect Cuba," he said, "must come in battle array."[143] On November 2, Khrushchev sent the Soviet deputy premier, Anastas Mikoyan, to calm Castro down – a task that led to his having to stay in Havana for almost three weeks. Meanwhile, the United States further demanded the withdrawal of the 42 Ilyushin-28 bombers on the island. Khrushchev reacted angrily, but in the end he was prepared to give way on this matter too. Castro, fearing that he would be left completely defenseless, refused to give his consent, but on November 16 the Presidium of the Supreme Soviet again passed him by and approved the order to remove the bombers in the following weeks. At the same time, the issue of the missile inspections was solved without further reference to Castro, through the mechanism of aerial observation on the high seas.

On November 20, 1962, President Kennedy reported at an evening press conference that, with "all the nuclear weapons" now gone from Cuba, he was ordering an end to the quarantine.[144]

In fact, Kennedy was mistaken: there were still some hundred nuclear warheads on the island, the six atom bombs for the Ilyushin-28s, and the tactical nuclear warheads for the Lunas and the cruise missiles. The Americans appear to have known nothing of their presence on the island; Defense Secretary McNamara, for example, was completely taken aback when he learned of this 30 years later, at the 1992 "Havana Conference" on the crisis. Yet, on November 20, 1962, Cuban Foreign Minister Raúl Roa had committed the blunder of informing Cuba's ambassador to the United Nations, Carlos Lechuga, that their country's security was not endangered by the Soviet–American agreement, because the tactical nuclear weapons were still in place and would have to be preserved at all costs. When a copy of this report arrived, via secret service channels, at the Soviet embassy in Havana and landed on the lingering Mikoyan's desk, he grew worried and, without consulting Moscow, changed into reverse gear. "We have a law that prohibits the turning over of any nuclear weapons, including tactical weapons, to another country," he explained to Castro. "The Americans do not know that there are tactical atomic weapons here, and we will take them back not because the US wants us to but of our own volition."[145] Khrushchev subsequently backed Mikoyan's action, and so the remaining nuclear warheads were taken back to the Soviet Union.

More generally, Mikoyan was outspoken in his criticism of the Cuban leader: "What should not be lost sight of," he reported to the Kremlin, "is the difficulty of Castro's personality – his sharp pride."[146] "These are good people," he further lamented in a letter to Khrushchev, "but of a difficult character, expansive, emotional, nervous, high-strung, quick to explode in anger, and unhealthily apt to concentrate on trivialities."[147] Khrushchev was beginning to have doubts about Castro – since his behavior during the missile crisis was "just shouting and unreasonable" – and even about the future of the Soviet–Cuban alliance: "Either they will cooperate," he warned, "or we will recall our personnel."[148] Khrushchev instructed Mikoyan to make it clear to the Cuban leader how disillusioned they were growing in Moscow. "Cuba, which now does not want to confer with us, wants instead to lasso us, hoping that their actions will embroil us in a war with America. We do not intend to move in that direction."[149]

Castro became so agitated that it evidently took a toll on his health. The Soviet Ambassador, Alekseev, learned from Castro's doctors that during Mikoyan's visit he had been on the verge of a physical and mental breakdown and had had to take several days off from his duties to recover.[150] Nor had Mikoyan failed to hear of the scorn being directed at Khrushchev on the streets of Cuba: *Nikita, mariquita, lo que se da no se quita!* ("Nikita, you pansy, a gift is never taken back!"). Carlos Franqui's paper, *Revolución*, ran a week-long series of articles about the treacherous Soviet Union – until Castro ordered a halt.

Despite the differences of opinion, Castro's Cuba emerged from the October crisis more strongly tied than before to the Soviet Union. But, apart from the enormous economic and military aid that the Soviet Union and other socialist countries gave Cuba over the next 30 years, the relationship remained cool right up to the time when the USSR disappeared from the political map. It was a "marriage of convenience" which, for all the effusive gestures and brotherly kisses, involved only a material and no longer an emotional bond. Neither side was really happy with the other. Soviet personnel in Cuba led a ghetto-like existence, respected but not liked by the local population, known as *bolos* ("cones" or "nitwits") because of their ungainly appearance.

There has been much speculation about how close the world really was to the nuclear brink in October 1962. We can tell from Khrushchev's memoirs what would have been the consequences of an American attack on Cuba: "The Americans knew that if Russian blood were shed in Cuba, American blood would surely be shed in Germany."[151]

The horrific episode of the missiles was over by the end of 1962. The last Soviet ship carrying tactical nuclear warheads and Il-28 bombers left for home at Christmas, together with just under 24,000 of the nearly 42,000 Soviet troops stationed in Cuba during the installation of the missiles; that still left roughly 18,000 men. In late-April 1963, it was the turn of the American Jupiter missiles in Turkey to be withdrawn.

Castro's refusal to allow on-the-spot verification by UN observers meant that the US undertaking not to invade Cuba was never set down in writing. Nevertheless, both Kennedy and all subsequent US administrations have regarded it as a binding commitment, albeit with sometimes major reservations. Nor has there been any attempt of that kind in the years since the October crisis. "The exchanges [between Washington and Moscow] were sufficiently lengthy and detailed to constitute mutual assurances," wrote Nixon's security adviser and secretary of state, Henry Kissinger, in his memoirs.[152] He it was who, on August 7, 1970, finally confirmed the agreement in a diplomatic note to the Soviet chargé d'affaires in Washington. The White House therein noted with satisfaction that the Soviet Union had confirmed the validity of the 1962 agreements, which were defined "as prohibiting the emplacement of any offensive weapon of any kind or any offensive delivery system on Cuban territory." "We reaffirmed that in return we would not use military force to bring about a change in the governmental structure of Cuba."[153]

Three gamblers

In 1962, with Castro, Khrushchev, and Kennedy, the vagaries of history placed three political poker-players on the world stage, who each went to their limits of calculable risk in order to outplay the other two. Holding their breath in the spectator stands, the anxious peoples of the world watched the weeks-long trial of strength on the edge of the abyss. If the situation did not get completely out of control, this was due perhaps to each man's ability to place himself in the other's shoes, perhaps also to a mutual respect that helped them master emotions, personal vanity, and narcissistic disorders.

Castro found it most difficult to cope, because the other two had assigned him only a secondary role. Yet in those critical days, his characteristic way of operating – which involved stressing others out through outbursts of rage, personal offence, charm, sarcasm, and hour-long speeches, until their nerves broke or they gave up exhausted – was a recipe for success that assured him at least the applause of his fellow-countrymen. The fact that he too did not shrink from playing with fire is clear from his letter of October 26, in which he hinted at a preemptive nuclear strike in the event of a US invasion of Cuba. Although he did not care to admit it, Washington's eventual undertaking to refrain from an invasion in the future was a real achievement. But Khrushchev did perhaps miss a chance in his solo poker game with Kennedy. For we know today that, in the game-planning at the White House, even Defense Secretary Robert McNamara proposed greater concessions to the Soviet Union and hence indirectly to Cuba, such as a speedy relinquishment of the US naval base at Guantánamo.[154]

It was clear at the time, however, that the Americans would not be persuaded to give up other ways and means, short of an invasion, of removing Castro through covert operations and of ruining his system through an economic blockade.

The missile crisis was not only a trial of strength between the superpowers; it also revealed the vanities and characters of the main actors, and how they fought out their personal rivalries. Although branded a hothead, after his shoe-banging performance at the UN General Assembly in 1960 to gain the attention of the media, the 68-year-old Nikita Khrushchev saw himself in 1962 as having to teach the two "wild youngsters" a lesson. One of them he had condescendingly treated as an adventurer, when Castro had been preparing to overthrow Batista's puppet regime and to deprive the "Yankees" of their sink of iniquity; the other he had disparaged as a political greenhorn, after they met in Vienna in early June 1961, a man expected to be easy game in the East–West contest. But Khrushchev had underestimated them both. In the end it was they who taught him a lesson, and this eventually contributed in 1964 to his own downfall at the hands of Leonid Brezhnev, Aleksei Kosygin, and Nikolai Podgorny.

Castro and Kennedy both came from a younger generation, being at that time 36 and 45 years old respectively. They wanted to leave behind the times of old gangsters like Batista or case-hard power politicians like Eisenhower, and to offer new social perspectives and values to the rising generation – the one as a new-style revolutionary and socialist, the other as a liberal reformer of the freedom-centered American Way of Life. Both were sons of fathers with a pioneering spirit, who had traveled a rocky road to riches and high standing and sometimes strayed from the straight and narrow. John F. Kennedy and Fidel Castro were full-blooded politicians of above-average intelligence, brilliant analysts with a sure instinct, and good speakers with a charismatic radiance. Each had to assert himself against a hostile establishment; one had been a soldier during World War II, the other had waged a war of his own.

Many years later, Castro said to Tad Szulc:

At the time Kennedy was, in my opinion, unquestionably a man full of idealism, of purpose, of youth, of enthusiasm. I do not think he was an unscrupulous man. He was, simply, . . . very inexperienced in politics although very intelligent, very wise, very well prepared, with magnificent personal qualities. I can speak of experience and inexperience in politics because when we Cubans compare ourselves now with what we knew then about politics . . . we are really ashamed of our ignorance at that time.[155]

Secretly more fascinated than repelled by each other, they competed in the early sixties for nothing less than a favorable judgment in world history. For Kennedy the Bay of Pigs defeat was a minus point, for Castro it was a plus; the missile crisis made Kennedy a big winner and Castro a little winner. One factor that should not be underestimated is that both men had an alter ego in their power games: their closest confidants were their younger brothers, who also played an important role behind the scenes as secret emissaries, conciliators, "sweepers," tacticians, and strategists. Raúl Castro served as an ideological intermediary and lightning-conductor between Moscow and Havana; Robert Kennedy was the President's buffer in dealings with the US secret service and military, as well as being responsible for secret contacts with Khrushchev via unofficial KGB channels in the Soviet embassy in Washington. Even "Daddy" Khrushchev had a "spiritual brother" in the shape of his deputy Anastas Mikoyan, who was a personal friend and a master in political survival since the days of Stalin.

For the two younger leaders, then, the significance of the one in world politics was closely bound up with the significance of the other: the Bay of Pigs and the missile crisis, the struggle for influence in Latin America and the Third World, as well as a more general ideological contest, shaped the competition of the two young heroes for the sympathies of the James Dean generation, for which they embodied the breakthrough into a new age. Kennedy, the refreshing new American president, and Castro, the victorious revolutionary, became the first political pop-idols of the sixties. It was a decade that would be marked by student protests and the Vietnam War, when, amid the Cold War rituals of the older generation, Hermann Hesse's *Steppenwolf* suddenly acquired the status of cult book, flower power generated a new cult music, and Castro's charismatic comrade-in-arms Che Guevara became Jesus Christ for the "love and peace" youth. The anti-establishment revolt was coupled with a longing for death. When Che Guevara fell in 1967 on the edge of the Bolivian jungle, the left-wing protest generation hailed him as an icon of revolutionary martyrdom. And when Kennedy was murdered in 1963, a year after the missile crisis, he became myth, legend, and model for a liberal, tolerant America.

The mutual attraction among these opposing figures of world politics is also evident in the conciliatory gestures that they made to one another in the course of 1963. First, Khrushchev stood Castro a triumphant 40-day trip around the Soviet Union and lavished on him generous economic aid. Then, in June, Kennedy offered Khrushchev the hand of reconciliation, when he gave a speech to graduates of the American University calling upon US citizens to take a fresh look at relations with the Soviet Union. "No government or social system is so evil," he said, "that its people must be considered as lacking in virtue."[156] Khrushchev reacted enthusiastically, describing the speech as the best by an American president since Roosevelt. Shortly afterwards, the two countries signed an agreement halting nuclear tests in the atmosphere. And, so that the world should never again teeter on

147

the brink of nuclear war, a direct telephone link was established between the Kremlin and the White House: the famous "hot line."

At the same time, Castro and Kennedy also drew closer to each other. As we can see from secret documents first made available only in the late 1990s, contact between Havana and Washington resumed behind the scenes in January 1963, despite the Cold War rhetoric and covert CIA operations. The United States sounded out the possibility of a *modus vivendi* similar to that which existed with Communist Eastern Europe.[157] What the Americans would have liked most, according to a position paper by security adviser McGeorge Bundy in April 1963, was that Castro should take his distance from Moscow in rather the same way that Tito had done in Yugoslavia.[158] In such an event, the White House could envisage the lifting of the economic embargo and the resumption of diplomatic relations. So as not to alienate Castro in advance by making unrealistic demands, Kennedy even decided that the breaking of Cuba's ties with the Soviet Union and China would no longer be a prerequisite for American–Cuban dialogue.

The discreet contacts were pursued on several tracks: through the New York lawyer James Donovan, who in late 1962 had negotiated the release of the Bay of Pigs mercenaries for the United States; through the popular reporter for ABC television, Lisa Howard, to whom Castro gave a long interview in April and expressed an interest in the improvement of US–Cuban relations; and through the former journalist and American ambassador to the UN, William Attwood. Castro's representatives were his personal physician and adviser René Vallejo and the Cuban ambassador to the UN, Carlos Lechuga. Whereas Castro repeatedly involved himself in the feelers, Kennedy was content to leave the action to his brother Robert, security adviser McGeorge Bundy and his deputy Gordon Chase, special adviser Schlesinger, and UN ambassador Stevenson. Also there in the background was the CIA, whose head, John McCone, started making difficulties in May 1963, on the grounds that such a policy would cut against the CIA's anti-Castro operations. In September, however, the contacts were resumed, and by early November Attwood could report that Castro was "unhappy about his present

148

dependence on the Soviet bloc," and that "he would like to establish some official contact with the US, even though this would not be welcomed by most of his hard-core Communist entourage, such as Che Guevara."[159]

When Jean Daniel, a journalist from the French news weekly *L'Express*, traveled to Washington for an interview in late October, with the intention of flying on to Havana, Kennedy gave him an oral message for Castro in which he raised the prospect of lifting the embargo if Castro stopped supporting guerrilla groups in Latin America. But Daniel was unable to hand on Castro's reply. After a first meeting on November 19, the two men went together with Vallejo to the Cuban leader's house on the beach at Varadero, where the telephone rang for Castro around midday. At the other end of the line was the country's president, Osvaldo Dorticós. "What? Assassination?" Daniel heard his host ask, visibly disconcerted. Everyone gathered around the radio, and shortly afterwards it was reported that Kennedy was dead. When the American national anthem was then broadcast, Castro and his guests stood up and silently remembered the Cubans' arch enemy. "Everything is going to change," he told Daniel. "This is a serious matter, an extremely serious matter." Castro rightly suspected that attempts would be made to blame him for the assassination. After all, as recently as September 7 of that year, in an interview at the Brazilian embassy in Havana against the background of CIA covert operations against his own person, he had warned: "United States leaders should think that if they are aiding terrorist plans to eliminate Cuban leaders, they themselves will not be safe."[160] And had not Lee Harvey Oswald, the suspected assassin, been a member of a committee called "Fair Play for Cuba"? When serving in the Marines, he had been trained as a radar specialist in California and at an air base in Japan, and he spoke Russian. He had defected to the Soviet Union in October 1959 and married a Russian woman. Yet in 1962 he had returned to the United States, without being arrested and prosecuted for desertion, and had even had no difficulty obtaining a new passport. The milieu in which he had moved before Kennedy's murder had probably been made up of CIA, Mafia, and militant Cuban exiles.

When the first attempts were made to link Cuba with Oswald and the Kennedy assassination, Castro got his administrative departments to make some investigations of their own. He told Nicaraguan writer and former interior minister Tomás Borge:

> We discovered that an individual of that name and answering to that description had presented himself at our embassy in Mexico and asked for a visa to come to Cuba – I think it was a temporary visa, en route to the Soviet Union. Our personnel turned down his application. . . . I wonder why Oswald wanted to come to Cuba. . . . What would have happened if he had come to Cuba, gone on to the Soviet Union, returned to the United States and killed Kennedy?[161]

Later it turned out that he had been an Oswald double groomed by the CIA, who, on returning to the United States, apparently met bar-owner Jack Ruby, the man who would shoot Oswald at a Dallas police station after the Kennedy assassination. In the same conversation with Borge, Castro expressed his own doubts about the official verdict that Oswald had been a lone assassin.

> I have a lot of experience using telescopic sights, because I trained those who came on board the *Granma* [in 1956]. . . . It seemed extremely difficult – almost impossible – for anyone to fire so many shots at a moving target in such a short time – and do so with such precision that Kennedy was seriously injured three times. . . . When you use a telescopic sight, you have to bring the next bullet up into the breech of the rifle again and get the target back in your sights after you've fired the first shot. It isn't easy, and it takes time.[162]

In the endless speculation about the possible motives and instigators behind the Kennedy assassination, one finds again and again the names of people from circles that wanted Castro dead: the Mafiosi Johnny Roselli and Santos Trafficante (who later killed Roselli), and interlinked figures from CIA and Cuban exile milieux with some connection to Jack Ruby (who, well before the revolution, had had business links with Trafficante and the Cuba-based Mafia). Even Castro's German ex-girlfriend, Marita Lorenz, comes into the picture, for she later claimed before the Warren Commission and in her memoirs that her CIA friend, Frank Sturgis, who once talked her into the botulism attempt on Castro's life, had been mixed up in the Kennedy assassination.[163] Apparently she even heard some of the planning at the house of Cuban exile Orlando Bosch, in Miami. (Bosch later featured as the man behind a bomb attack on a Cuban transport plane, in which 76 people were killed off Barbados in October 1976. Owing to his CIA connections, he went unpunished under the CIA boss of the time and later US President George Bush, and a few years later, according to Hinckle and Turner, found a friend in George Bush's son Jeb (brother of George W. Bush), who served as governor of Florida in the late 1990s and scraped home in the presidential elections of the year 2000.[164])

A few days before the deadly bullets hit Kennedy, Marita Lorenz, Sturgis, and others, posing as members of a hunting club, drove two cars packed with guns to Dallas and put up at a motel there. It seems that among the group were Castro's renegade pilot, Pedro Díaz Lanz, and an inconspicuous man they called "Ozzie." Marita Lorenz, who had meanwhile followed a combat course with 5,000 men at a Cuban exile camp, says that she met him on other exercises and took a dislike to him; she used to joke that the slightly built man could barely hold up a rifle. This "Ozzie" was in fact Lee Harvey Oswald. During the night, she claims, two men commanding the others' respect made a brief appearance, one of whom she later identified as CIA agent Howard Hunt, who had been in charge of planning for the Bay of Pigs landing. Hunt handed over a thick envelope filled with money. The other man was a gangster type, who told Sturgis to send her out. She later identified him as Jack Ruby.

The theory that Bay of Pigs veterans from the Cuban exile community and the CIA were behind the assassination is based on the fact that they felt Kennedy had betrayed them and left them in the lurch. For Lyndon B. Johnson, however, Kennedy's vice-president and successor, the man behind the shooting was to be found in Havana. It had been a shoot-out as in the days of the Wild West: "Well, Kennedy tried to get Fidel Castro," he said in a TV interview, "but Fidel Castro got Kennedy first."[165]

At the time, there were also other conspiracy theories that featured Johnson in a prominent role. Kennedy's opponent in the presidential contest, Richard Nixon, who happened to have been in Dallas shortly before, speculated that Kennedy had wanted to drop Johnson as vice-president before the next elections.

A macabre footnote is that on the fateful afternoon of November 22, a CIA agent in Paris was handing over a specially prepared pen to Rolando Cubela, alias AM/LASH, the man the CIA had hired to kill Castro. The ballpoint, which was never actually used, contained a poison needle that would immediately kill its victim after the tiniest scratch.[166] At one point during their meeting, the telephone rang and the CIA agent was told by a Paris-based colleague that the President had just been shot.[167]

CIA agent Frank Sturgis was left untouched despite his clear links with Oswald, and some years later he even had the chance to make a name for himself by playing a major role in the undercover war against Castro. In June 1972, in fact, he was caught during the break-in at the Democratic Party's election headquarters in Washington, the famous Watergate complex. His accomplices, and even some of the men behind the operation, were part of Sturgis's old Cuba connection: Bernard Barker, a Havana-born American who had worked for Batista's notorious SIM police; Rolando Eugenio Martínez, the FBI's contact man in Cuba; two other CIA veterans, Félix Rodríguez and Rafael Quintero; and even Howard Hunt, the Bay of Pigs coordinator, man in charge of Cuban exile agents and – according to Marita Lorenz – a night-time deliverer of funds at a Dallas motel just before Kennedy's assassination. At the time of Watergate, Hunt was actually a White House adviser. The burglars brazenly maintained that they had been looking for evidence of Castro's financial support for the Democratic presidential candidate, George McGovern.

Let us recall. Immediately after the shooting of Kennedy, the names of Sturgis and Hunt, as well as other figures from the milieu of the CIA, organized crime and the Cuban emigration, were already repeatedly linked with the circle of acquaintances of Lee Harvey Oswald, the supposed assassin, and even with the assassination itself. And yet, in the report it issued in 1964, the

Commission set up to investigate the assassination, named after its chairman Senator Earl Warren, stood by the version that Oswald had acted alone. Doubts about the Commission were fueled by the fact that one of its members was Kennedy's sworn enemy, Allen Dulles, who had been sacked not long before as head of the CIA. Only at the end of the 1970s did a Senate Commission under Senator Frank Church (the Church Commission) accept the possibility that there had been a conspiracy to murder the President.

The only man who ever got a court to concern itself officially with the Kennedy case was former New Orleans district attorney Jim Garrison. In 1966 he began secret investigations, because Oswald's milieu of CIA and FBI agents and militant Cuban exiles operated mainly in New Orleans and had strange links that the Warren Commission never considered. Soon Garrison found that higher authorities and affected institutions such as the CIA and FBI were crudely hindering his investigations; attempts were made to blacken his name, and there were mysterious murders or deaths of potential witnesses. In the end, however, his application for an official judicial inquiry into Kennedy's assassination was turned down. He thought at the time: "The group around Operation Mongoose seems to have been the center of the JFK conspiracy."[168] Since no official legal body would touch the rather remarkable findings of Garrison's research, Hollywood director Oliver Stone took them up in his feature film of the nineties, *JFK*.

Just a few weeks after Kennedy's death, Castro tried to resume the feelers with the United States. In February 1964 Lisa Howard reported a verbal message from Castro to Kennedy's successor, Lyndon Johnson, in which the Cuban leader gave assurances of absolute secrecy, even if domestic political considerations forced Johnson to make "bellicose statements about Cuba" or even "to take some hostile action."[169] All he asked was to be informed of this beforehand. But there was no reaction from Johnson, either to this or to subsequent initiatives on Castro's part.

6

The Long March with Che

★

Moscow, Beijing, and Havana

"On 31 January 1963 . . . Khrushchev wrote me a lengthy letter, really a wonderful letter. It is 31 pages long . . . a beautiful, elegant, friendly, very friendly letter. Some of its paragraphs are almost poetic. It invites me to visit the Soviet Union. . . . Tempers had been cooling down by then; they had been quite hot. I accepted the trip."[1]

Castro set off on April 26. Khrushchev had his guest picked up with what was then the most modern Soviet long-haul aircraft: a Tupolev 114. Fears that it might be shot down meant that the date and route of the trip were kept strictly secret. In any event, the Tupolev's range did not permit a non-stop flight to Moscow, and so Castro made a refueling stop in Murmansk, where Khrushchev's deputy Mikoyan was waiting to receive him. Castro later recalled:

I got there by a miracle, because I had to fly in a TU-114 plane. It was a 16-hour flight. I think that it is a kind of bombardment in a plane like that. . . . The plane had four propellers, and it shook and vibrated, and we had to land blind. It was lucky that Khrushchev . . . had sent the best pilot in the Soviet Union, because he was the only man who would have been able to land in the middle of the mountains in Murmansk with such a fog that you could not see for five meters. On the third day, we finally landed . . . my part in all this could have ended that day. . . . I said: If this crashes, we will never even know why. I was sitting with the pilots watching the operation. Suddenly I said: I will get out of here. . . . I do not want it to happen that, instead of helping, I make things more complicated. I stayed sitting down until that monster landed.[2]

Flying, it would seem, was the one thing Castro feared.

Unusually, the Cuban Premier's trip to the Soviet Union lasted 40 days, nearly six weeks, from April 26 to June 3, 1963. It turned into a triumphal procession accompanied by cheering crowds. He traveled all over the country, visiting 14 cities and looking round both civilian and military installations. Although he came with a large entourage, he made a point of not bringing any of the old Communist leaders from the PSP, not even the dependable Carlos Rafael Rodríguez. Nevertheless, no state guest had ever been given such a spectacular reception, or been so lionized by the media. He wore the highest medals on his chest – including those of Hero of the Soviet Union and the Order of Lenin. As a rare honor, he was asked to make a speech at a mass rally on Red Square, and it was at the Kremlin wall that he stood beside the Soviet leadership for the military parade on the First of May.

It is true that, with an eye on Washington, the Kremlin refused a formal military alliance. But, in a joint statement issued on May 24 at the end of the official part of Castro's visit, the Soviet Union endorsed the five demands Castro had made of U Thant – including a US withdrawal from the Guantánamo naval base. Moscow was mainly concerned to emphasize its guarantees of Cuba's security, although they sounded like so much lip-service.[3]

After their tour was over, Khrushchev invited Castro to his summer house at Pitzunda, on the Black Sea coast, where he one day read out his correspondence with Kennedy from the time of the missile crisis. He also quoted – inadvertently, it would seem – from the secret agreement on the removal of American medium-range missiles from Turkey, in return for the withdrawal of Soviet nuclear missiles from Cuba. "It was the last thing that Nikita wanted me to hear," Castro recalled many years later, "since he knew my way of thinking, and that we were completely against being used as an exchange token."[4] This surprise was more fuel for Castro's mistrust. But apart from that, the two men used their seclusion to map out areas for future cooperation and to discuss ideological questions and differences.

This being 1963, ideological differences within the socialist world centered on the bitter struggle between the Soviet Union and the People's Republic of China. In principle, it was a question of which had more correctly used the teachings of Marx, Engels, and Lenin to find the way to a classless society: on the one side, the "right-wing" orthodox Soviet Communists had decided, after various setbacks, to decentralize the socialist-oriented state economy, to permit greater self-management at enterprise level, and to increase material incentives for the workforce; on the other side, the "left-wing" Chinese comrades condemned Moscow's adoption of the capitalist market and law of value within the socialist system as a revisionist betrayal of true doctrine. There were also major differences over foreign policy. Since the Twentieth Congress of the Communist Party of the Soviet Union (CPSU) in 1956, without any break during the Cuban missile crisis, the USSR had followed a line of "peaceful coexistence" with the other major nuclear power, the United States. It was in accordance with this policy that Moscow had been cautious about any active exporting of the Cuban Revolution to other countries; Cuba was supposed to serve as a kind of shop-window demonstrating the superiority of the socialist system, but the Kremlin was not prepared to give significant financial or logistical backing to guerrilla movements elsewhere in the Third World. For this reason, the Chinese Communists and their supporters abroad accused the Kremlin of leaving Third World revolutionary currents in the lurch, and of living on the backs of poorer countries by reducing the "export of revolution" mainly to the exploitation of their raw materials and other resources. This, it was claimed, further promoted the underdevelopment of the Third World and was neither more nor less than a variant of imperialism painted red.

The ideological conflict between Moscow and Beijing was increasingly brought up for discussion within the Cuban leadership, especially by Che Guevara. Following the victory of the Cuban Revolution, Castro had given his friend and guerrilla comrade operational responsibility for the country's economic planning and foreign policy. But Guevara, after an early period of enthusiasm, had watched with concern as Cuba's growing dependence on the Soviet Union reduced its room for maneuver both internally and externally, and, like the comrades in Beijing, he considered that Moscow's distinctive form of state capitalism was leading it on a false ideological path. Against this background, Castro could see that for Khrushchev the worst that could happen would be for Cuba to reach an understanding with the Chinese.

It is not true, however, that when Castro sat down with Khrushchev in Pitzunda he was already making eyes at the Chinese. Much less ideologically aligned than either his brother Raúl or Che Guevara, he set greatest store by the political leeway that allowed him to remain in charge at home and guaranteed Cuba a large degree of national sovereignty. But he also wanted to play a role on the international stage – and knew that all this would be much less of a problem with the Chinese than with the Soviets. Still, Beijing had too little to offer economically, militarily and politically, and carried too little political weight in the international balance of power. If Castro played the Chinese card, it would only be to push up the price he could expect from Moscow. The real danger for Soviet–Cuban relations came from Che Guevara, while for Moscow the most reliable partner in Cuba's ruling troika was the defense minister, Raúl Castro.

Since he first met Fidel Castro in 1955 in Mexico, Che had grown in his quiet way into the role of ideological brains of the revolution, and exerted ever greater influence over the commander-in-chief. Sheldon B. Liss, a student of Castro's political thought, writes:

From José Martí, Fidel learned how to blend humanism and "*cubanidad*" into a revolutionary package. Argentine physician "Che" Guevara helped him to approach revolution theoretically. Castro does not mention Che by name as often as he does Martí, but the ideas of his comrade-in-arms constantly appear in his speeches and motivate his actions. Fidel had read Marx and Lenin before he met Che. . . . But Che, with his more developed theoretical background, assisted Fidel in organizing the theory . . . and in fashioning a more coherent Marxist philosophy.[5]

"Nobody is born a revolutionary," Castro told US journalist Lee Lockwood in 1965. "A revolutionary is formed through a process. . . . At the time I met Che Guevara he had a greater revolutionary development, ideologically speaking, than I had . . . he was a more advanced revolutionary than I was."[6] In the Sierra Maestra they developed an almost brotherly relationship with each other, one outstanding feature of which was Castro's personal care and consideration for Che because of his frequent asthma attacks. However different they were in temperament, they both tended to wear themselves out completely for the cause of the revolution. "There is no doubt," Castro remarked, "that he has had influence in both the revolutionary fight and the revolutionary process."[7]

During those years Guevara was the only one, apart from Raúl, whom Castro would tolerate at his side; his worldwide popularity does not seem to have made the Máximo Líder think of him as a rival. In international circles he was the best advertisement for the Cuban Revolution, a media weapon useful for any number of purposes. With his exotic olive-green outfit, his black beret with a red star on a wild mop of hair, his shaggy beard and cigar in the corner of his mouth, he was the incarnation of a professional revolutionary for the protest generation all around the world. "El Che," as he was called in Cuba, gave the impression of being the gentler of the two, well-mannered and almost feminine, but from time to time also arrogant and exceedingly vain. Fidel Castro, by contrast, was in external appearance clearly a macho figure, with a farmer's earthiness like that of his father, more likely to crash about and to inspire fear in people. But appearances were deceptive: the reality was rather the opposite. Beneath his tough shell Castro was more open, more flexible, more tolerant and less dogmatic, and therefore far and away the wilier in everyday political affairs. In comparison, Guevara appeared to be a dogmatic revolutionary, coldly rigorous and unwilling to compromise.

In an article that appeared in June 1960 in *US News and World Report*, we can read under the title "Communists Take Over 90 Miles from U.S." that a "red dictatorship" was "in full control," and that Che Guevara, as the brains behind the revolution, exercised "dictatorial power over national finances" and was thus responsible for the confiscation of US assets.[8] For Castro, however, Guevara had "developed into a model person, not only for our people but for all peoples of Latin America; Che gave revolutionary steadfastness its highest expression."[9]

It is possible that, without Guevara, Castro would not have survived politically for long after the victory of the revolution, but would have been crushed between the middle classes and the orthodox Communists who had meanwhile jumped on the bandwagon. Whereas Fidel still adopted a moderate political tone toward the bourgeoisie, Che was already working behind the scenes with Raúl Castro to establish a Marxist-Leninist state. Fidel Castro was lucky to have had in Guevara a partner who, in the process of integrating into the revolutionary movement the Communist PSP founded back in 1925, could prove more than a match for power-hungry and Moscow-dependent dialecticians like Aníbal Escalante and Blas Roca.

Castro soon placed Guevara in key positions. He put him in charge of the secret group that planned the agrarian reform law promulgated in May 1959. From the end of November of the same year, Guevara was president of the National Bank running a new monetary policy that turned the country away from a free-market economy, and on February 23, 1961, he became minister of industry responsible for the construction of a Moscow-oriented Marxist-Leninist planned economy. In June 1959 he began his first foreign-policy assignment; he traveled until September to more than a dozen Asian and African countries, enlisting support there for the Cuban Revolution and forging new economic links. In February 1960 he signed the first trade agreement with the Soviet Union, and over the following months with China, Hungary, Bulgaria, North Korea, and the GDR. But, when he flew to Moscow for two weeks in late October 1960, to discuss trade issues at a "round table" with representatives of the socialist countries and to try to gain permanent observer status at the Council for Mutual Economic Aid, his request on behalf of the Cuban government was turned down. Moscow was of the view that it was too early for such a step.

The new man

"Fidel," Sheldon Liss writes, "contends that his political ideas, for the most part, result from *reflection*. He does not regard himself as a philosopher. Whereas philosophers formalize or explain the relations between ideas, Fidel informally interprets ideas."[10] His thinking is influenced by Martí, Marx, Engels, Lenin, and Mao, as well as by Gramsci, Hegel, and others.

> He very rarely puts pen to paper, as a thinker such as Mao Zedong would have. . . . He is more concerned with mobilizing forces around ideas. . . . He also has the ability to blend his ideas with those of others. . . . Historicism pervades Castro's thinking. He proceeds on the premise that all sociological phenomena are historically determined, all truths are relative, no absolute values exist, and all events are influenced by the past. He believes in a moral imperative in politics. . . . Castro, like Marx and Engels, . . . expects the superior morality of communism to elevate humanity. He believes that if a person has superior intelligence, it should be put at the service of humanity, but that individual should receive the same benefits as one with lesser intelligence. All owe society their maximum effort.[11]

In Guevara's view, Castro conveyed his ideas by the "intuitive method;" he was a master at this, and only someone who had experienced it could appreciate his special way of becoming one with the people. In his essay, "Man and Socialism in Cuba," Guevara goes into raptures about Castro's powers of suggestion: "In the big public meetings, one can observe something like the dialogue of two tuning forks whose vibrations summon forth new vibrations each in the other. Fidel and the mass begin to vibrate in a dialogue of growing intensity which reaches its culminating point in an abrupt ending crowned by our victorious battle cry."[12] Unlike Castro, Guevara did put pen to paper to express his ideas about Cuba's new political system; he thus became over time the chief theoretician of *fidelismo*. After his death, several volumes of his speeches, essays and thoughts about "the new man in Cuba" formed the intellectual basis of Cuban society, even though practice rarely was able to match the theory. The new man continually failed because of the old.

With the victory of his revolution, Fidel Castro refuted the orthodox Marxist theory that the capitalist system could be overcome only in an industrial society endowed with Marxist consciousness; he also showed that this could be achieved with a small group of non-Communists. Subsequently, Castro and Guevara agreed that Cuba's economic foundations and power structures had to undergo swift and radical transformation if the pendulum was not to swing back – a logical consequence of this was the removal from power of the bourgeois politicians who had been brought into the first post-Batista government under President Urrutia. For Castro and his leadership group, the point was to prevent the rule of the old elites from being gradually restored under the direction of Washington and Florida. At first, this by no means necessarily meant for him the establishment of a Marxist system, although it is true that the Communists in his milieu became more influential as the pressure mounted from the United States. Very soon this removed any chance of seeking a third way of "peaceful coexistence" between capitalism and socialism, under the aegis of a bourgeois left-wing government. One thing was clear: in order to involve the whole people in the revolution, there had to be radical changes and a new social consciousness had to be created.

Once the only alternative was counter-revolution, the pace of things speeded up. The moral values and principles that had proved themselves in the Sierra Maestra were now transferred to the realm of everyday life: selflessness and modest living, discipline and comradeship instead of egoism, material incentives and moral degeneracy. Guevara put it as follows in 1963, in a speech on "Party Militancy" that saw the 26th of July Movement as the engine driving Cuba toward socialism: "We have discovered that the process of the historical development of societies can, in certain cases, be shortened. . . . We were able to speed things up through the vanguard movement by shortening the various stages and establishing the socialist character of our revolution two years

161

after the Revolution triumphed."[13] The Cuban leadership wanted to gain acceptance for the idea that, with the support of an economically and technologically more developed Soviet Union, it could venture a "great leap forward" of its own.

In the early 1960s, the main aim was the conversion of Cuba from an export-oriented sugar monoculture to a modern industrial economy less dependent upon imports from abroad. "Industrialization depends upon land reform. We have already covered the first part of this road," Guevara said in 1960 in a speech on "revolution and egoism." "Our road is difficult, and our strength is the unity of the workers, the peasants, and all the underprivileged classes."[14] The agrarian population was indeed the strongest pillar of the revolution, because it had gained most from it through the redistribution of land. No longer was anything said of another group whom Castro had to thank for the victory over Batista: the liberal bourgeoisie. "Industrialization is built of sacrifices," Guevara warned. "A process of accelerated industrialization is no lark, and we will see this in the future."[15]

That future has been lasting dozens of years. No end was in sight more than a quarter of a century later, when Castro recognized: "We shall work hard and must work hard – for we are a third world country, we wasted centuries under colonialism and nearly sixty years under neocolonialism, and we have also wasted a few years under the revolution. We must make up for lost time."[16] Early on, in 1960, Guevara was still excited about the prospects:

> In ten years, we intend to raise the per capita income somewhat more than nine hundred pesos . . . [to] twice today's per capita. . . . At this moment the duties of the working class are to produce, . . . to produce without unemployment, produce more, create more wealth, more wealth that will be transferred into more sources of wealth; to economize as much as possible, not only on the level of the state, but on whatever level a real national saving is possible; . . . to organize, organize in order to bring the greatest force to the collective task of industrialization.[17]

Initially Castro and Guevara were convinced that, with the ideological and material backing of the Soviet Union, Cuba could progress faster than if it had to rely on itself alone. Guevara's idealistic goal was one day to do away altogether with material incentives and exchange-value, even if, as he noted in his 1963 speech on the tasks of the party, that was not possible at once:

> There are two things that are constantly conflicting and dialectically becoming part of the process of creating a socialist society. . . . On the one hand, material incentives are made necessary by our having emerged from a society that thought only of material incentives. . . . On the other hand, we still do not have enough to give each individual what he needs. For these reasons, interest in material things will be with us for a time during the process of creating a socialist society. . . . Material incentives will not play a part in the new society. . . . We must establish the conditions under which this type of motivation that is operative today will increasingly lose its importance and be replaced by nonmaterial incentives such as the sense of duty and the new revolutionary way of thinking.[18]

This brought Guevara into conflict with Soviet economic thinking. In his view, the material incentives, "economic calculation," enterprise viability and profitability that were central features of the Soviet economy did not advance the cause of socialism: "Pursuing the chimera of achieving socialism with the aid of the blunted weapons left to us by capitalism . . . , it is possible to come to a blind alley."[19] An article published in 1964, "On the Budgetary System of Financing," again expressed this heretical approach: "It is necessary to make it clear now that what we seek is a more efficient way of achieving communism."[20]

At the end of this "more efficient way" would be the "new man," whose incentive to work and goal in life would no longer be the egoistic accumulation of material goods, but rather a selfless moral duty towards society – a society which, in return, would care for him and his family. Castro and Guevara geared their new economic and social policy to this goal, launching an ambitious literacy drive, an extensive healthcare program, and a guaranteed basic provision for every citizen. The overcoming of Cuba's underdevelopment as a Third World country was thus a prerequisite for the creation of the "new man."

But Cuba's great leap forward was a failure. In the first phase of industrialization, Cubans still had a fairly good life: low rents, higher wages, and free healthcare gave a considerable boost to income; consumption and living standards rose. It was not long, however, before output was unable to keep up with demand. Supplies ran out after two years, and at one point even breeding bulls were slaughtered and eaten. In 1962, when food rationing was first introduced, annual economic growth was a mere 0.4 percent. From mid-1963 the Cuban economy slid into its worst-ever crisis, as gross national product fell by 1.5 percent. The new agricultural policy of "diversification against sugar mono-culture," which the revolutionaries themselves later came to see as amateurish, had chaotic and sometimes catastrophic results in many areas. Between 1961 and 1963 agricultural output fell by 23 percent; the sugar harvest, at 3.9 million tons in 1963,[21] was the worst since the end of World War II, down more than 40 percent from the post-revolutionary high of 6.9 million tons in 1961. As Castro's industry minister, Che Guevara was responsible for this disaster. The result was a foreign trade deficit that became a permanent feature of the economy.

A hard look at the realities eventually forced the leadership to move away from its idealistic positions. After a half-year experiment at 247 pilot enterprises employing 40,000 workers, it was decided in December 1963 that from the following January pay linked to productivity would be introduced in 4,000 industrial enterprises for a total of 400,000 employees. Whereas pay had been based on a proliferation of 25,000 skills and more than 90,000 wage-rates, the new system established just eight rates based on skill grades. For each percentage point by which workers exceeded their norm, they would receive a bonus – although this could not be higher than half their basic wage, and anything above that would fall to the state. Those failing to meet their targets would incur deductions up to half their basic wage. Even sugarcane cutters would now be paid by results, not in accordance with fixed rates or a simple hope that moral motivation and revolutionary enthusiasm would raise output above its previous levels. The new measures were introduced at the urging of Communists loyal to Moscow, and against the resistance of the Guevara faction.

This was the situation when the influential Soviet Politburo member Nikolai Podgorny arrived in Havana in December 1963. On January 12, 1964, Fidel Castro accompanied him back to Moscow, and ten days later, after detailed discussions with Khrushchev and Leonid Brezhnev, he and his hosts signed an agreement whereby the Soviet Union undertook over the next five years to purchase the bulk of the Cuban sugar crop at a price above the world-market rate.

In 1964, in a self-critical article for the journal *International Affairs*, Che Guevara finally admitted some elementary mistakes:

> Our first error was the way in which we carried out diversification. . . . The sugar cane areas were reduced and the land thus made available was used for the cultivation of new crops. But this meant a general decline in agricultural production. The entire economic history of Cuba has demonstrated that no other agricultural activity would give such returns as those yielded by the cultivation of sugar cane. At the outset of the Revolution many of us were not aware of this basic economic fact, because a fetishistic idea connected sugar with our dependence on imperialism and with the misery in rural areas, without analysing the real causes: the relation to the uneven trade balance. . . . Only a very solid productive organization could have resisted such rapid change.

Furthermore, it was discovered that "in many [industrial] plants the technical efficiency was insufficient when measured by international standards."[22] The quality standards of Eastern-bloc technology did not match those of the machines and equipment goods previously imported from the United States; nor were their technical specifications compatible.

Castro later told Tad Szulc:

> At the outset of the revolution, when we had to assume all the functions of the state and all the functions of the economy . . . we began this task without experts, just ignorant people who did not know what had to be done. . . . We suffered the consequences of different errors. Let us say that one error we committed was to want to jump stages, wanting to arrive at communist forms of [wealth] distribution, jumping over socialist forms of distribution

165

– and it is impossible to jump stages. The communist formula is: each must give according to his capacity and receive according to his needs. The socialist one is: each must give according to his capacity and receive according to his work.[23]

In other words, the satisfaction of needs was running ahead of performance; Cubans were living beyond their means.

As the focus now shifted to sugar production, Che Guevara's policy underwent a change that would be crucial for future development. The agreements meant a big step backwards, and the industrialization drive – which had anyway been making only slow progress – ran into the sand. After the disastrous sugar harvest of 1963, Castro announced that it would reach 5.5 million tons the following year, 7 million tons in 1965, and the magic figure of 10 million tons in 1970; all economic efforts would be concentrated on this goal. Guevara therefore had to write off his ambitious plan, so that "by 1970 we will have laid the foundations for our economy's development, based primarily upon our own technology and our own raw materials, mostly processed with our own machinery."[24]

If he had come only a little closer to his goal, this was not just because the massive task of conversion had placed far too many demands on a workforce lacking both the necessary skills and (never previously required) logistical capacities. In addition, the agreed supplies of machinery and plant from the Eastern bloc had arrived either too late or not at all. Often they had been of such poor quality that it would have cost more time and money to get them working than to let them rot and simply import the required goods.

Delays in the supply of such vital products as oil, as well as in the signing of annual aid agreements, were actually quite deliberate. They served as a means of disciplining Havana, so that it could not afford to stir up conflicts elsewhere in the Third World without taking into account the political and strategic interests of the Warsaw Pact – a course that would have forced Moscow to keep explaining itself in the international arena. Guevara especially irritated the Kremlin when he used the Trotskyist term "permanent revolution" in his speeches. In order to end this playing with fire, Moscow tied future economic aid to the condition that Cuba would refrain from supporting or instigating revolutions in the Third World.

To the outside world, the fraternal socialist countries displayed a perfect family life together with their questionable Cuban match, but behind closed doors they were extremely worried that things would not work out. Kennedy was right in sensing that Castro's political ambitions would not be limited to his own island. In one of the East German embassy's many "assessments" of political trends in Cuba, which were based upon a lively exchange of views with other Eastern-bloc diplomats, we read that in the summer of 1964 "ideological/political and theoretical confusion on basic political issues in the Party leadership," as well as petty-bourgeois "radicalism and nationalism" represented by "Fidel Castro himself," were leading to an "underestimation of the international relationship of forces with regard to Cuba and of the effectiveness of the policy of peaceful coexistence," and "an inclination toward 'violent solutions' in policy toward the USA, its Latin American lackeys and the Latin American liberation movement." Worldwide support for revolutionary Cuba, "and the pressure to use Cuba's well-founded example as the basis for the Latin American liberation struggle, in the sense of a kind of command post for the Latin American liberation struggle," were throwing up certain "tendencies" toward "nationalist arrogance." In the eyes of East European friends, Castro and his comrades were losing touch with political realities and falling into delusions of grandeur. The resulting "dangers for future development should not be underestimated," the report concluded.[25]

The demise of Che

Economic realities, the collapse of his utopian hopes, and ideological differences with Moscow gradually worked behind the scenes to deprive Guevara of power. Disappointed, he again took refuge in the role of foreign policy spokesman for the revolution, making long trips abroad that further aroused Moscow's suspicion. Already in July 1963 he had visited Algeria, whose president, Ben Bella, was an ally of Castro's, and it was at an economics seminar there that he surprised everyone with the admission that his concept of industrialization and diversification was not working. But his stay also served other purposes, for a few months later, in October 1963, a battalion of 800 Cuban soldiers and officers together with 70 tanks arrived to support the government in its military conflict with Morocco over the Eastern Sahara. Earlier, in 1961, Cuba had supplied the Algerian National Liberation Front (FLN) with weapons for its war of independence against France. Now Castro was taking the first steps in exporting the Cuban Revolution, not only with words and guns but with Cuban troops. In return, Ben Bella allowed the Cubans to escape international attention by secretly shipping through Algeria three tons of weapons for the Venezuelan guerrilla campaign to overthrow the government in Caracas.

In March 1964 Guevara traveled on an official mission to Geneva, where he represented Cuba at an UNCTAD conference on world trade and again drew attention to his country as champion of the Third World. "It must be clearly understood," he said, "and we say it in all frankness, that the only way to solve the problems besetting humanity is to eliminate completely the exploitation of dependent countries by developed capitalist countries, with all the consequences that implies."[26] Eastern-bloc delegations loyal to Moscow made him feel that he really did not belong among them, that he was a kind of strange and exotic creature. And the representatives of Latin American countries also kept their distance. He stayed away from Cuba for a good month, making side-trips to Prague and Paris, then meeting in Algiers a number of Congolese politicians who had gone into exile after the murder of nationalist leader Patrice Lumumba.

On July 3, 1964, came Guevara's first open loss of powers as industry minister, when a special autonomous ministry was created for the sugar industry. This did not seem to be a sudden jolt for Guevara; he anyway gave the impression of being increasingly bored and unenthusiastic. It was denied that he had quarreled with Castro. Then in October, while President Dorticós was away in Moscow, Nikita Khrushchev was replaced at the head of the Soviet leadership. The new rulers in the Kremlin, who gave "Operation Anadyr" as one of the reasons for the change, were Leonid Brezhnev as general secretary of the CPSU, Aleksei Kosygin as prime minister, and Nikolai Podgorny as head of state. Castro declined to fly to Moscow for the November march-past in honor of the socialist nomenklatura, thus taking the opportunity to mark his independence in the eyes of world opinion. In his place he sent none other than . . . Che Guevara. Fidel himself took his time before his next trip to Moscow: eight months.

On December 11, 1964, Che Guevara made a further major appearance on the international stage, when he spoke on behalf of Cuba at the United Nations in New York. With a deeper meaning behind his words – and certainly without consulting Castro in advance – he quoted at length from the revolutionary appeal of the "Second Declaration of Havana," which the Cubans had issued on February 4, 1962, in response to their exclusion from the Organization of American States: "Two hundred million Latin Americans," he read, are "sounding a warning note . . . that the hour of vindication . . . is now striking from one end to the other of the continent. That anonymous mass . . . is beginning definitely to enter into its own history, it is beginning to write it with its blood, to suffer and die for it."[27] With this speech he was unconsciously foretelling his own destiny. Even friends sensed that his time in Cuba was running out.

Rather than return immediately to Havana from New York, Che spent the next three months traveling in the Third World – not in Latin America, but in Africa and (for a stopover) China. He met leaders of the liberation struggles in the Portuguese colonies of Angola, Mozambique, and Guinea-Bissau, flew on to Mali, the Congo, Guinea, and Senegal, then to Ghana, Tanzania, and Egypt. Driven restlessly onward, he roamed the dark continent and tried to put together a front against neocolonialism in Black Africa. The alliances he formed during this time would lead later – as in the case of Angola – to a long Cuban involvement in Africa. The first and last stop on his tour was Algiers.

On February 24, 1965, a week after a new long-term agreement between Cuba and the Soviet Union had raised the sugar quota and the general level of trade between the two countries, Guevara made a speech at the "Second Economic Seminar of Afro-American Solidarity" in Algiers which marked his definitive break with the Soviet Union:

> Each time a country liberates itself, as we have said, it is a defeat for the world imperialist system ... and it is our international duty ... to contribute our efforts. ... From all this a conclusion must be drawn: The development of the countries which now begin the road of liberation must be underwritten by the socialist countries. ... How can ... mutually beneficial trade ... mean selling at world market prices raw materials which cost unlimited sweat and suffering to the backward countries and buying [from the socialist countries] at world market prices the machines produced in today's large automated factories? If we establish that type of relationship ... , we must agree that the socialist countries are, to a certain extent, accomplices in imperialist exploitation. ... The socialist countries have the moral duty of liquidating their tacit complicity with the exploiting countries of the West.[28]

This appearance in distant Algeria was Guevara's last as Comandante of the Cuban Revolution. When he returned to Havana on March 15, 1965, Fidel Castro, Raúl and President Dorticós picked him up from the airport. Behind closed doors, a dramatic exchange that was supposed to have lasted 40 hours then took place between Che (the "brains"), Fidel (the "heart") and Raúl (the "fist") of the revolution, as *Time* magazine had described them in August 1960. None of the three men subsequently said a word in public about what transpired, and Fidel Castro has imposed a news blackout on the matter. No records or notes have since emerged; all we have are rumors and stories at second or third hand. Franqui, referring to statements by Castro's loyal colleague Celia Sánchez, claims: "What is certain is that Guevara was ... energetically reprimanded, accused of indiscipline and irresponsibility, of compromising Cuba's relations with the USSR; Fidel was furious over his irresponsibility in Algiers."[29]

It later leaked out that Castro had been angry for several reasons. On the very day of Guevara's speech in Algiers, Raúl Castro had been in Moscow meeting the new Brezhnev leadership, and they had immediately confronted him with accusations against Guevara.

But Fidel was especially upset that Guevara should have raised such serious points in a faraway place like Algiers. Raúl suspected Guevara of Trotskyism, because of his attachment to the concept of world revolution – a charge to which Che replied by calling the defense minister an "idiot." In a confidential report to East Berlin, the correspondent of the GDR news agency ADN wrote that, according to "quite well-informed sources," Fidel Castro accused Guevara of "causing considerable damage to Cuba." "Guevara, for his part, is said to have complained that he had traveled all over the world for Castro and not even been given any recognition for it. He also reproached Castro with having 'pro-Soviet tendencies.'"[30] Guevara accepted responsibility for what had happened, but he refused to make a public self-criticism or to offer an apology to the Soviets. Eventually, "at the height of the altercation" – that is, after nearly two whole days and nights – Guevara apparently "lost control and slammed the door." Foreign diplomats – again according to the ADN report – supported the view that "Fidel Castro and Ernesto 'Che' Guevara had behaved like little children rather than politicians, although the burden of responsibility for the whole country rested on their shoulders."[31]

Just under ten years after their first meeting in Mexico, the friendship between the two men seemed to be over. On March 22, 1965, Guevara convened a final meeting at the ministry for industry, and was not seen again in public. Hurt and angry, suffering from a bad attack of asthma, he withdrew to a sanatorium for a few days and made up his mind to decamp from Cuba; his new revolutionary destination was to be the Congo. At dawn on April 2, without saying farewell to Fidel Castro (although he apparently left a letter for him), Guevara set off with two companions incognito on a roundabout route to Black Africa, his head closely shaven and his mouth newly fitted with false teeth. Officially a rumor was spread that he had left for the sugarcane cutting in eastern Cuba – a plausible story, since he was known to do that from time to time. Castro tried to dispel other speculations circulating among foreign correspondents: "All I can tell you," he said, "is that Comandante Guevara will always be where he can most serve the Revolution."[32]

It may be that the clash among the three top revolutionaries was about more than just Che's speech in Algiers. The background was that he and his friends in the state and Party apparatus had long been preparing a trial of strength over the future political direction of the Cuban Revolution. In fact, the quarrel itself coincided with the publication of a long letter from Che to the editor of the Uruguayan weekly *Marcha*, under the title "Socialism and the New Man in Cuba," which had the character of a manifesto and, with hindsight, his political testament. Despite the lack of success of his idea of forming a new man motivated only by moral duty to the revolution, Guevara once again summarized the theoretical bases of his thinking, in a way that caused quite a stir within the Latin American left, as well as in Moscow and Havana. Claiming for Cuba the vanguard political role in Latin America of which he still dreamed, he critically took up the subordination of the fraternal socialist countries to the dogma of Soviet policy.

Guevara had long been outside the country, without this being public knowledge, when his essay appeared in *Verde Olivo*, the central organ of the Revolutionary Armed Forces (FAR), on April 11, and in Carlos Franqui's *Revolución* on April 13. The fact that this was not prevented shows that Guevara still commanded a degree of respect and support that made him "untouchable," but perhaps it also reveals "that Fidel was personally very attached to Guevara and shared his lack of clarity on some important issues," as the GDR ambassador of the day wrote back to Berlin.[33] The uproar Che had caused behind the scenes is even more evident from an analysis written by the GDR embassy in Havana in late October 1965, immediately after the official foundation of the Communist Party of Cuba (PCC). Judging by this text, it is quite possible that Guevara had wanted to use his essay to make a decisive impact on the programmatic debate: that is, to ensure that the PCC evolved in a direction other than the one prescribed in Moscow doctrine.

The GDR embassy paper asserts that "the whole conception behind this work of Guevara's has its origins in petty-bourgeois radicalism;" it is strongly reminiscent of "the ideas disseminated by the Chinese leadership." "It should not be forgotten that here in Cuba Guevara was for some time described as 'Chino' (Chinese)." The "dangerous character of Guevara's conception" lay not only in the moment he chose to express it, but in the fact that "demonstrably" his platform had already been "fully worked out before his speech in Algiers." It was thus "clear that Guevara's speech in Algiers was not some isolated error of judgment, . . . but the conscious result of an entire way of thinking." Furthermore:

> One especially dangerous aspect . . . derives from the fact that it took place before the Party's founding congress, or, to be precise, with an eye on preparations for the congress. The platform singles out for praise a number of ideas that are still today unclear in Fidel Castro himself; it actually pulls him backward on other issues (e.g., the issue of individual material incentives in production) and attempts to tie Fidel Castro and his inner circle down once and for all.[34]

The embassy suspected that Guevara had tried "to set himself up as one of the leading minds (if not the leading mind) on the ideological/political and theoretical questions facing the PURS (Cuba's CP) and the whole of Cuba's socialist development. The role of the strongly emotional, more or less correctly acting pragmatist and people's tribune was apparently still intended for Fidel Castro." Guevara was indirectly accused of having wanted to stage a kind of palace revolt. According to information reaching the GDR embassy, the affair was made considerably worse "by Guevara's attempt to use his 'legendary' reputation to win over some high commanders of the FAR to the platform, thereby forcing Raúl Castro to endorse this line or at least to tolerate it." Even *Hoy*, the house organ of the Communists in Cuba, had dealt with Guevara's essay in July, "without polemicizing against the shoddy effort by name." Still, defense minister Raúl Castro had "severely reprimanded" the FAR's political leader responsible for its publication in *Verde Olivo*, and "other commanders" were even said to have been "dismissed or transferred to other functions."

The speech in Algiers had certainly played a role, but it was his essay which had brought to a head the "friction between the top leadership and Guevara." Instead of a further clash, however, the leadership apparently tried to allow the affair "gradually to sink into oblivion," so that Guevara could be "retained simply as a monument of a noble-minded liberation fighter (rather like Camilo Cienfuegos)." Fidel Castro himself, in his speech to the founding congress of the PCC, had been prepared to make only "a few critical observations." It had already been noted in a different context that the prevailing method in Cuba was "to send 'troublesome' people on 'holiday' or abroad for a longer or shorter time."[35]

Only Che's parents learned, from a farewell letter, that he was setting off for Africa's "heart of darkness:" "Once again I feel under my heels the ribs of Rocinante," he wrote sarcastically, appearing to sense that what lay ahead was a purely quixotic venture.[36] On the shores of Lake Tanganyika he rendezvoused with a force of just under 130 Cubans who had been sent on ahead by Castro. Using the cover name "Tatu," he joined the people around guerrilla leader Laurent Kabila (a shady despot, who in the late nineties finally managed to win power).

Che's mission was a failure and ended in disaster; the Africans had no fighting morale, Che fell ill with asthma and dysentery. He corresponded with Castro, who gave him protective support and later sent out emissaries, eventually Guevara's wife Aleida, to persuade him to return. On November 4, Castro wrote him a positive letter urgently pressing him to call off the expedition, a move that seems to have been dictated by concern for his seemingly desperate friend.

> We must do everything, except for the absurd. If in Tatu's view our presence becomes unjustifiable and futile, we must think of retreating. . . . We are worried that you will make the mistake of fearing that your attitude will be considered defeatist and pessimistic. If you decide to leave Tatu can remain the same, either returning here or staying somewhere else. We will support any decision. Avoid annihilation![37]

It was all over by the end of the year. The enterprise, as it were, dissolved itself – first, because the general political situation in the region changed and the war ground to a halt; second, because Guevara's authority over the troops evaporated when it leaked out that he no longer counted for much back home.

On October 3, 1965, his friend Fidel had made public Che's letter of farewell, in the run-up to the long-delayed congress winding up the Unified Party of the Socialist Revolution (PURS) and turning it into the PCC. Castro must have felt forced into this decision, because otherwise it would have been inexplicable why Che Guevara of all people should not have been made a member of the new Party leadership. Fidel Castro himself became first secretary of the Party.[38] Where Che was, however, remained a state secret after the congress. In the farewell letter, he had renounced all positions in the Party leadership and government, his title as Comandante of the Revolution, and his Cuban citizenship. "I have lived through some wonderful days, and I feel – by your side – proud to belong to this people precisely in the great, if sad, days of the crisis. If my last hour finds me elsewhere, may my last thought be of this people and especially of you."[39]

Guevara's letter has no date: Castro said only that he had received it on April 1, and this immediately aroused all manner of speculation about its authenticity. Its homage to Castro has never ceased to puzzle: "My only mistake was that I did not trust you even more right from the first moments in the Sierra Maestra, and did not understand soon enough your qualities as a leader and a revolutionary. . . . I am grateful for what you taught me, for your example, and I shall try to remain faithful in the final consequences of my action."[40] Some skeptics in Guevara's milieu have cast doubt on the obsequious personal references to Castro. But the homage might also be seen as bitter irony; Guevara knew well how to express this, especially when he felt deeply offended, and it would have been quite appropriate in his situation at the time. His future path was already mapped out in another sentence: "Other peoples of the world are asking for my modest efforts. I am able to do what is denied you, because you bear responsibility as leader of the revolution in Cuba. And so, the time has come when we must part."

After the collapse of the Congo adventure, Guevara hid himself away for several months in the Cuban embassy in Dar es

Salaam, the capital of Tanzania. At first he refused to consider going back to Cuba. In late February/early March he traveled to Prague and received a visit from Cuban friends and people sent by Castro. Already the plan seems to have been ripening in his mind to go to Bolivia, and to work from there to inspire revolution in Latin America. In July 1966, however, he showed up once more in Cuba and was welcomed by the Castro brothers. Again he withdrew to a sanatorium and did not appear in public; rumors later circulated that he had a complete mental and physical break-down, which would have been quite easy to understand. But his resolve to go to South America was unshakeable. Over the following months, a guerrilla force of some 20 men was put together to accompany him to Bolivia. Castañeda, in his biography, reports that Castro gave every support for Guevara's project, but that right up to the end he tried to get him to call it off, not least because he did not trust the Bolivian Communists, who had close links with Moscow and were no friends of Guevara's. Castañeda describes what was evidently Castro's last attempt to change his friend's mind, a final embrace, an expression of despair on Castro's face and obstinacy on Guevara's.

In November 1966 Guevara finally arrived via Europe and Brazil in the Bolivian capital La Paz, disguised as a Uruguayan businessman. On November 7 he reached the country estate near Santa Cruz that he had selected as a base; his comrades were already waiting there, to launch the jungle adventure that would be his final act of quixotry. In February of the following year, their radio broke down and Guevara no longer had any contact with Havana. Yet he managed to send out a last "message to the peoples of the world," which on April 16, 1967, appeared in the Cuban magazine *Tricontinental* on the occasion of the tricontinental conference in Havana. It contained the famous image of creating "two, three, many Vietnams."[41]

By summer, the government in La Paz, the CIA, and Moscow knew that Che Guevara was roaming the country in Bolivia. On July 26, 1967, Soviet premier Kosygin stopped off in Havana on his way from Washington, where President Johnson issued him with a reproach for Guevara's campaign. Kosygin passed this on to Castro, because Moscow had not been informed of Guevara's expedition. Apparently Kosygin threatened to cut Soviet aid to Cuba if Havana was unable to give up exporting revolution.

A few months later, on October 15, 1967, Fidel reported the death of Che Guevara and ordered a period of official mourning. On October 7 soldiers had surprised Guevara and his small band of guerrillas; he was wounded in the ensuing gun battle, jailed along with the other survivors, and taken to the village of Higuera, where he was interrogated by Bolivian officers belonging to a US-trained Ranger unit and by CIA agent Félix Rodríguez (who was also involved in the Watergate break-in in 1972). Then, on October 8, 1967, Guevara was murdered on the orders of Bolivian President Barrientos, in the little school at Higuera. His corpse was exhibited, photographed, and finally buried just beneath the surface of the airfield runway at Villegrande. Those in charge of the operation cut off his hands and preserved them in formaldehyde; they later turned up in Havana and are now kept under lock and key in the Museum of the Revolution. In 1997 his remains were dug up in Bolivia and taken to Cuba, where on the thirtieth anniversary of his death he was given a state funeral at Santa Clara, the site of his greatest victory during the civil war.

Many have tried to work out why Guevara had to die a hero's death in Bolivia, for that is how it soon came to be represented. Why, for example, did Castro not send an elite unit to get him out? One suggestion is that he sacrificed his comrade under pressure from Moscow; there was all manner of speculation about treachery by the KGB and the Bolivian Communists. The French leftist Régis Debray, who was arrested on his way to meet Che Guevara in Bolivia, claimed to Agence France Presse that, according to "various sources" (mainly three deserters), the military had already received information in March 1967 about Guevara's area of operations. Also at that time, in Camiri, a cross-country vehicle belonging to Guevara's German friend, Tamara "Tania" Bunke, fell into the hands of the police, containing notebooks with names, addresses, and telephone numbers of people involved in the conspiracy. When Che learned of this, he was horrified that the fruit of two years' work had been lost. He had first met the attractive Tania in East Berlin in late 1960, where she was working as an interpreter, and soon afterwards she traveled to Cuba. Guevara's biographer Daniel James has written that she was in fact an agent of the Stasi, the East German state security police. According to her controlling officer, Stasi lieutenant Günther Männel, who defected to the West in 1961: "I myself assigned Tamara Bunke to Guevara as an agent."[42]

But was Che not just simply responsible for his fate? Was he not the victim of inexplicable dilettantism, personal vanity and an overestimation of his abilities, or of a kind of death wish that many thought they could detect in him? Castañeda writes in his biography: "Fidel did not send Che to his death in Bolivia; nor did he betray or sacrifice him. He simply allowed history to run its course, fully aware of its inevitable outcome. Fidel did not shape the event; he let it happen."[43] Besides, what could Castro and Cuba have done with a revolutionary in early retirement, especially as he had consciously turned his back on the country? In death he eventually found his true destiny. His mystique as a latter-day martyr began then, the photographer Korda having intuitively supplied the picture which transfigured "El Che" as the most famous icon of the twentieth century.

Castro had every reason in the mid-sixties to condemn Che Guevara out of hand, seeing that his combination of ideological rigidity and superficial economic knowledge almost robbed the revolution of the victory it had achieved with so much difficulty. Yet Castro stood by him, because the two had become joined together and had a brotherly affection for each other. Perhaps the most accurate description of the relationship between them is the one given by Castañeda:

> During that long year of 1964, when he lost both friends and battles, undertaking endless struggles over topics crucial to the fate of the Revolution, Che discovered two indisputable facts about his role in Cuba. One was that Castro held him very dear indeed; he would back him in all his projects for Argentina, Algeria, Venezuela, and now Africa. Fidel never disputed the place Guevara had carved out for himself, or reproached him for his errors or outbursts. Che could nurture no grudges on that account. But Guevara also understood that Fidel, consummate politician that he was, did not really commit himself to Che's stances. He had to wage his own battles, and suffer his own defeats. Without ever

disputing his sporadic victories, Castro never extended Che Guevara his full consent. At times, he even sided with his opponents, either because *révolution oblige*, or because he simply did not agree with Che's ideas. Moment by moment, battle by battle, Che gradually realized he was alone: neither with nor against Fidel. But Castro was everywhere; lacking his support, Che had nothing, no ground to stand on. His situation was untenable: the slogan of neither marriage nor divorce with Fidel became unsustainable for Che. Nothing could have affected Che more than this tangle of ambiguities and contradictions – the half tones of his twilight in Cuba.[44]

7

Bad Times, Good Times

★

War and peace with Moscow

With Che Guevara's death, Castro lost not only a friend but an ideological mentor. As if to scotch the rumors, he demonstrated how strong the substantive agreement between the two men had been until the end, and how much their old friendship had survived differences in practical politics, when in November 1967 he again declined to take up an invitation to Moscow. This time, moreover, it was the celebrations marking the fiftieth anniversary of the October Revolution for which he sent a third-rank delegation in his stead.

Shortly afterwards, Castro provoked the Kremlin with a frontal attack on the arrested development of its orthodox brand of Marxism. Pay related to productivity, as well as the obligation for enterprises to prove their economic viability within a planned economy, reminded him of the old capitalist days. He therefore called for advances to the next stage, where the "new man" would be a central feature. The spirit of Che Guevara seemed to be finding a voice.

In Castro's eyes, the cautious reforms under Brezhnev in the Eastern bloc, especially in Hungary and Czechoslovakia, were further decentralizing the state-directed economy and introducing market elements into the system, thereby discreetly opening it up to the West and even to a more extensive regression. Castro's more centralist view favored *national* accumulation of the economic results that enterprises were able to achieve – whether these showed a gain or a loss. Investment in further development, and the funding of social policy, should also remain centrally controlled; only this could ensure that surpluses were fairly distributed, and that the whole population, both urban and rural, had access to healthcare, education and training, as well as housing fit for human habitation.

In mid-January 1968, at the end of a week-long international cultural congress in Havana that won him and his colleagues considerable attention, Castro took the opportunity to put Moscow-style attitudes in the ideological dock before several hundred artists and intellectuals from 70 countries, including Jean-Paul Sartre and Bertrand Russell:

> There can be nothing so anti-Marxist as dogma. There can be nothing so anti-Marxist as the petrifaction of ideas. And there are ideas that are even put forward in the name of Marxism that seem real fossils. . . . Marxism needs to develop, overcome a certain sclerosis, interpret the realities of the present in an objective and scientific way, behave like a revolutionary force and not like a pseudo-revolutionary church.[1]

Filled with disquiet, Castro made a statement to the effect that the working people were growing ever more distant and alienated from the real goal of an ideal classless society no longer ruled by money. Finally, he delivered a sweeping blow against the orthodox Communist parties, charging that they "remained completely removed from the struggle against imperialism," and that they preferred slavishly to follow the Soviet Union rather than take part in the "just struggle." "These groups," he went on, had not once raised "the banner of Che" since his death, and would "never be able to die like him, or to be true revolutionaries like him."[2]

The real reason why Castro had stayed away from the October celebrations in Moscow, and why he now decided to launch a blistering attack, was that Moscow had some responsibility for the fact that Cuba stood on the brink of economic collapse. Not only had Soviet deliveries been unreliable; in October, Moscow had denied a request that it should raise its oil exports to Cuba by 8 percent and replace the existing annual trade agreements with one lasting three years. Evidently intending to punish Castro for his lack of discipline, the Soviets then let the time pass when a trade agreement was due to be signed for 1968. Since Cuba was totally dependent upon Soviet oil supplies, Castro found himself compelled in January 1968 to announce precautionary rationing.

Nevertheless, the Soviets were only part of the problem. The Cubans themselves were the other part. Serious planning mistakes combined with erratic corrections and repeated improvisation, incompetence and mismanagement, constant interference by the Máximo Líder at every level, rash compliance with his spontaneous ideas and suggestions (which, though often correct, were not adequately coordinated) had been leading to chaos, especially in agriculture. In the end there was too little capital, and too little efficiency, to fulfill all the ambitious hopes. The last straw was that small businesses and small farmers had established a parallel economy in the shape of a flourishing black market, which was putting too much into the pockets of traders rather than those of the revolution.

The Soviets and their East European allies, who could rely on strong diplomatic missions to keep a tight and closely coordinated watch on events, and who for nearly a decade had been discussing and agreeing among themselves the level of political, economic, and military support to extend to Castro, continued to blame him personally for the problems in the economy. Nothing in his autocratic style of leadership seemed to have changed in the intervening years. Ever since 1960 GDR diplomats, for example, had been critically informing East Berlin of his "partisan manner" and lack of a socialist team spirit, and it may be worth quoting a few of their reports to help us understand the developing tensions between Cuba and the Eastern bloc. The way in which they characterized Castro over the years shifted between mounting irritability and resignation, giving a vivid impression of the cultural peculiarities and mentalities that clashed with each other at an international level.

It is interesting that the phenomenon of *fidelismo* is never mentioned in the reports, although, for the broad mass of the population, it is not "Marxism-Leninism" but this concept signifying the opposite of collective leadership which still today defines the political system in Cuba. The Cubans' identification with *fidelismo* means identification with a *caudillo*, with a figure who embodies and defends the national consciousness, whether as a Christian, a Marxist-Leninist, or a democrat. The *caudillo* is the product of their thinking; he is the nation's father figure, a patriarch, who may have his shortcomings but is still trusted and obeyed. Cubans, like most Latin Americans, have traditionally known how to cope with such a figure better than with a seemingly anonymous collective leadership, whether in a Communist or a democratic system. Lack of due consideration for this factor created a permanent misunderstanding of the Cuban Revolution and its leader – and not only in East European capitals.

For years, then, the GDR reports complained about the lack of "collective work in the leadership of the Party and state apparatus," without making the effort to find anything deeper than the trivial notion that that was what Castro was like. We read, for instance, in one confidential report from the GDR embassy in May 1964:

> He has not yet overcome . . . his original strong inclination to a partisan style of work, to nationalism and left radicalism, to personal decision-making on all important matters, to subjective evaluation of trends and their causes, to decisions purely his own on how to guide the popular masses from a basically emotional point of view (through speeches, discussions, etc.), to a dramatic "letting off steam" against the "main enemy" in difficult situations, and his violent reaction to suggested corrections of certain of his ideas and practices.[3]

In any event, it was recognized that "his person . . . is still surrounded with the legendary glory of a people's hero, of the leader of all Cuba's revolutionary forces," and that there was no way of getting around him. The "genuine and complete support of the broad masses" for Castro remained "very strong." "They have confidence in him, and equate the leading role of the Party with his behavior." This made it "even more difficult" for older leading comrades "to make effective corrections." He had a following especially among those strong "circles of middle functionaries, who have taken few or no steps to become real Marxist-Leninists." Against this background, "the holding of the Party's founding congress [and conversion of the PURS into the PCC] was still seriously in doubt in 1964."

The founding congress eventually took place in 1965, but even then it seemed more like a token event to keep Moscow and its satellites happy. The PCC leadership was, of course, not properly elected but chosen by Castro. And he kept his East European friends waiting another ten years before the first regular Party congress, originally scheduled for 1967 at the latest, met to adopt a program and statutes. So far, the East German comrades remarked, "Fidel Castro's speeches" constitute the "fundamental programmatic basis of ideological and political work;"[4] and for the time being there were no signs of a learning process, self-discipline, or readiness for a collective style of work, as required by the Party doctrine to which he now subscribed. As the Soviet embassy noted at the end of 1964, Fidel Castro himself remained "the root of all the considerable difficulties and imperfections." He still wanted "to have the only say in deciding all important issues," and had "evidently taken great pains to ensure that no one (not even his brother Raúl or a Party leadership committee) encroached upon his towering position on the inside or the out-side." In a confidential report on a conversation with the Soviet deputy ambassador, his GDR colleague wrote back to head-quarters that the Soviets did not think Castro was truly prepared "to develop collective leadership activity," because he did not want to "subject himself to the resulting discipline" or to encourage this in "the leading cadres around him, who are even more petty-bourgeois than he is."[5]

Castro's leadership style, marked by "constant suspicion" of other officials and "deficient knowledge about members of his own council of ministers," resulted in some "extremely curious phenomena." Thus, at one session of the Cuban Council of Ministers, at which Finance Minister Rom gave a report on the financial situation, "Fidel Castro listened to the report . . . and eventually asked the man seated next to him who this Rom was and whether he might have connections with the counter-revolution; after all, he (Rom) knew very many internal details about the country's economic situation, and that was a danger for the Revolution." In Cuba at that time, noted the comrades from the Eastern bloc, the type of functionary who prospered and found favor with the head of state was one who eagerly obeyed his every wink or nod. All of them reported for duty with the slogan: "*Comandante en Jefe, ordene!*" [Commander-in-chief, give us your orders!]. The Soviets regarded Ramiro Valdés, the interior minister in charge of state security, as an example of this kind of official.

In the end, however, for higher reasons of strategy, Moscow learned to live with the Caribbean party leader and his peculiarities, to accept him as he was. Whether or not the Cuban Party develops "in the way we know from our own parties, and the corresponding path of socialist construction is taken in Cuba, . . . we will still help them in either case," Soviet Ambassador Alekseev reassured his GDR counterpart Friedrich Johne, a former officer, in early June 1964. "So, we start from that assumption and support them as positively and as well as possible."[6] Three-quarters of a year later, when all of a sudden Alekseev's deputy aggressively demanded greater understanding for the Cubans and asked for them not to be judged "too harshly," the obvious ideological hardliners at the GDR embassy considered it "a kind of new tendency" on the Soviets' part and were rather disgruntled to hear of it.

Moscow's order for tolerance would be severely and repeatedly tested over the following years. In September 1964, the comrades in East Berlin were horrified by a report from Havana that Castro and "the left-radical extremists ever more closely surrounding him" had gone on a "real rampage," which "must be effectively stopped." It seemed that they had "wagered everything . . . on making it brutally clear in practice to those around them that they were deeply serious in their aims."[7] The "left-radical extremists" were Guevara supporters critical of Moscow: although Che was then no longer living in Cuba, he continued to have a large following to which the ideologically unpredictable Castro was thought to belong. And this group was trying to save not only Guevara's idealistic economic concept of the "new man," but also that of "world revolution." It became clear that, despite their disagreements, Castro's thinking was in many respects still similar to Guevara's, when, after the latter's departure from Cuba in 1965, he criticized the Soviet failure to give adequate support to North Vietnam against the American bombing that had begun in February of that year. He complained that "even the attacks on North Vietnam have not had the effect of overcoming the divisions within the socialist family."[8] And in May 1966 he even spoke of "ending the Vietnam War through the massive deployment of units of the socialist armies." The "escalation to world war" that would have been a likely consequence was "not accepted by him as an argument," the East German correspondent in Havana soberly remarked.[9]

Eastern-bloc diplomats noted that the Tricontinental Conference planned for Havana in spring 1967 was intended to ignite larger centers of conflict in Asia, Africa, and Latin America, and that there was even some idea of starting a revolution in a Latin American country. Che Guevara sent a message from Bolivia for the occasion, the famous "Message to the Peoples of the World," in which he called for the creation of "a second, third Vietnam in the world."[10] It was a carefully considered idea, more than just a slogan for students in revolt to carry on their banners in the streets of Europe. But the East Europeans, who were more interested in a policy of peaceful coexistence with capitalism, reported that Guevara's "left-extremist" supporters were urging "the creation of a Latin American Vietnam by concentrating all forces and sources of aid" on a single country. Their goal, it was claimed, was "to ignite simultaneous continent-wide actions from the victory or the flames of this revolutionary center, and, if possible, to commit the socialist countries more extensively than before." This "revolutionary center," the GDR embassy suspected in an alarm-raising letter of September 1966, "might be Venezuela." That was the country which Castro had first visited after the victory of the Cuban Revolution, and whose government had exposed itself by brusquely rejecting his request for a loan.

The comrades from Latin American Communist parties showed little enthusiasm for such ideas. Most of them had long been seeking to achieve power by peaceful means, through participation in elections. East European observers noted growing "outrage among Latin American Party representatives over the way in which the Cuban leadership was behaving," and warned that it was "plunging headlong into unintentional self-isolation, as a result of which it could only further lose responsible control over its own actions."[11] The Communist parties of Chile and Argentina, in particular, were reported to be putting up strong resistance to the Cuban thinking. Castro attacked them for this and accused them of not showing sufficient solidarity. The aim of his "frontal attack on the fraternal parties in Latin America," according to a GDR embassy analysis, was, "if not to win over the socialist countries, then at least to tie them down to their positions of patient waiting, hesitation and non-interference, so that unlimited freedom of action would be assured for undermining a number of CPs in LA [Latin America]."

The Venezuelan Communists strongly protested at Castro's attempts to interfere in their country's politics, arguing that his "intemperate speeches were tolerated [only] because Cuba stood in the front line of the struggle against imperialism." A Venezuelan Politburo statement of March 13, 1967, unusual for Communists in its unsurpassable frankness, claimed the right to pursue its own policy "without any interference." It went on:

> Cuba has creditably followed a hard revolutionary path . . . ; but we want to make it clear that we were never and will never be Cuba's agents in Venezuela . . . We . . . never accept being told what to do. Fidel Castro enjoys . . . again playing the role of judge over revolutionary activities in Latin America, the role of the super-revolutionary who has already carried out the revolution in the place of the Latin American Communists. . . . We categorically reject his claim to be the only one who decides what is and is not revolutionary in Latin America.[12]

Visibly affected by the aggressive tone of this statement, which was also widely distributed in the United States, Castro replied in a half-angry, half-scornful speech lasting several hours, large parts of which served a didactic purpose. He summed up in one sentence his verdict on the Venezuelan comrades and their role: "These so-called Communists . . . are getting together with the

187

political castes of the bourgeoisie to wage war on the heroic guerrilla fighters."[13]

The GDR mission noted, however, that a "considerable loss of prestige" among fraternal parties induced the Cubans "to give up their basic tactical line of simultaneously making the revolution throughout Latin America."[14] In this context, it is worth noting the false suspicion prevalent among Latin American Communists in the summer and autumn of 1966 that Che Guevara was already inside Venezuela, a country then shaken by political crises. They were not unaware "that for some time Cuban officers and men have been trained for use in LA [Latin America]." Possibly the original idea had indeed been for Guevara to trigger and lead a revolution in Venezuela, and he switched to Bolivia when he failed to receive any support from the Venezuelan comrades. He had also thought of returning from Africa to fight in his own homeland, Argentina, but the police detection and murder of an advance party of two close comrades had forced him to abandon that project.

Late in January 1968 Castro again provoked his Soviet friends, by arresting 37 members of a "sectarian micro-faction" inside the new Communist Party of Cuba who had been "conspiring" with Moscow. Most of those in question were well-known people from the old PSP, again led by Aníbal Escalante, who had been allowed to return from a brief exile in Moscow to take part in the founding of the PCC in 1965. In a speech to the Central Committee of the PCC, Raúl Castro raised the monstrous accusation that comrades from the CPSU, the East German Socialist Unity Party (SED), and the Czechoslovak Communist Party had been openly conspiring against the Cuban Party leadership; and that, in particular, they had leveled criticism at Castro's ideological and political conceptions. At a trial before a revolutionary court, Escalante and the others were charged with having worked with the KGB since 1962 to topple Castro. Apparently Escalante had tried to talk the Soviets into ending their aid to Cuba, in order to bring down Castro and replace him with a regime loyal to Moscow. But this time Escalante, who had been caught red-handed at a secret meeting with a Soviet officer, did not get off so lightly: he was sentenced to 15 years' imprisonment. After an early release, he became manager of an agricultural enterprise and died a few years later.[15]

Moscow and East Berlin were beside themselves over the accusations made by Cuba's Number Two, Raúl Castro:

> The open and sharpest-yet attack on the CPSU, our Party and other fraternal parties, which has come about through these internal measures within the [Cuban] CP, are a provocation against the unity of the international Communist movement. It is intended to discredit our parties before world public opinion, to undermine trust in the sincerity, honesty and correctness of their relations with fraternal parties. . . . It has raised anti-Soviet and anti-Marxist behavior to an official state attitude in Cuba.

The language of this internal statement issued by the International Department of the SED Central Committee could hardly have been sharper.

At the end of March Castro gave a further turn of the screw in the doctrinal struggle when, in an allusion to China's "Great Leap Forward," he launched a "Great Revolutionary Offensive" to nationalize all 58,012 remaining small businesses (from car repair shops to ice-cream stalls), denouncing them as relics of the bourgeoisie and offering them up on the altar of ideology.

The drive was announced in a speech lasting many hours before an audience of several hundred thousands. Taking aim at "those who do not work, the loafers, the parasites, the privileged, and a certain kind of exploiter that still remains in our country," he found it "an incredible thing" that "there still are nine hundred and fifty-five privately owned bars," and surprised his audience with a number of revelations: for example, that, according to "the results of investigations of these bars . . . , a great number of people who intend to leave the country are engaged in this type of business, which not only yields high profits but permits them to be in constant contact with *lumpen* and other anti-social and counter-revolutionary elements." Among the owners of hot-dog stands, he claimed, "there was the greatest percentage of those not integrated into the revolution . . . ; of forty-one individuals who answered this item, thirty-nine, or 91.5 percent, were counter-revolutionary." To general applause and laughter, he exclaimed:

Are we going to construct socialism, or are we going to construct vending stands? . . . We did not make a revolution here to establish the right to trade. Such a revolution took place in 1789 – that was the era of the bourgeois revolution, it was the revolution of the merchants, of the bourgeois. When will they finally understand that this is a revolution of socialists, that it is a revolution of Communists . . . that nobody shed his blood here fighting against this tyranny, against mercenaries, against bandits, in order to establish the right for somebody to make two hundred pesos selling rum, or fifty pesos selling fried eggs or omelettes? . . . Clearly and definitely we must say that we propose to eliminate all opportunities for private trade.[16]

From then on, there was still less to buy; everyday life was still more joyless. Cuba became the Caribbean island with the dreariest choice of leisure activities; Havana, a city legendary for its Parisian *joie de vivre*, sank to the cultural level of the rural province of Oriente. Under the watchful eyes of the Committees for the Defense of the Revolution, collective labor, thrift and abstinence became the defining elements of the Cuban zest for life.

After Castro further distanced himself from Moscow, refusing in February 1968 to send a Cuban delegation to the world conference of Communist parties in Bucharest where the consequences of the ideological rift with Beijing were to be discussed, the Kremlin answered in March with an intensification of economic pressure. Trade would not be increased, as in previous years, by just under a quarter, but only by 10 percent; and Cuba would have to deliver 5 million tons of sugar in 1969, even though the 1968 harvest would barely suffice to meet its obligations and to cover its own needs. In the end, the harvest was a mere 5.3 million tons, a million less than in the previous year and 3 million below the plan target, and all the forecasts were that the results for 1969 would be even lower. Thus, at the end of the first decade of the revolution, Cuba's sugar arrears to the Soviet Union were fast approaching a total of 10 million tons, and it was increasingly doubtful whether Castro's undertaking to achieve a harvest of 10 million tons in 1970 could be achieved.

In the middle of 1968, Moscow seemed to be gradually nearing the point when it would say enough was enough. In July, in an explosive letter sent in "strict confidence" to Party leader Walter Ulbricht, the East German foreign minister, Otto Winzer, said that the Soviet ambassador in Havana had raised with his GDR counterpart the question of "whether, given that the Cuban side was evidently unwilling to develop friendly relations, Soviet aid and support could continue as before."[17] Under the rules of the game in Eastern-bloc diplomacy at the time, such a grave option would not have been casually tossed out; it served as a disguised warning, with the possible consequences certainly present in the minds of both men involved in the conversation.

Castro seemed to feel – as if the message had finally reached the person for whom it was intended – that the Soviet leaders' patience with deviationists was running out. Things must have suddenly become crystal-clear a few weeks later, when Moscow set a brutal example by occupying Czechoslovakia in the early hours of August 21, 1968, with a force of Soviet, East German, Polish, Hungarian, and Bulgarian troops, to provide "fraternal support" (for someone or other) against the reform Communism of the Alexander Dubcek government. It was true that the Kremlin could not simply move against Castro by means of a similar attack by land. If the recent Escalante affair had really been a Moscow-directed conspiracy, then the next option, after its collapse, would be one day to proceed in the way that the ambassador had outlined.

Yet the crushing of the "Prague Spring" – a move that aroused great controversy in the socialist camp – offered the practical politician in Castro an unexpected and spectacular opportunity to return to the Moscow fold. On August 23, after two days of silence, he surprised everyone with a dialectical balancing-act on television which left nothing wanting in clarity: "What cannot be denied here," he began, "is that the sovereignty of the Czechoslovak State was violated. . . . And the violation was, in fact, of a flagrant nature."[18] But he also said: "We acknowledge the bitter necessity that called for the sending of those forces into Czechoslovakia; we do not condemn the socialist countries that made that decision."[19] Condemning the liberal reforms in Czechoslovakia and other socialist countries, he stressed that it had been absolutely necessary to prevent Czechoslovakia from "falling into the arms of imperialism."[20]

Nevertheless, relations with Moscow did not improve overnight. On the centenary of Cuba's first liberation struggle, he gave a patriotic speech in the east of the island praising José Martí and other heroes of Cuban history, and failed to say a single word about Marxism-Leninism, socialism, the Communist Party, or the Soviet Union. And again in 1968 he sent only third-level figures from the Cuban leadership to the annual commemoration of the October Revolution in Moscow. A rapprochement must have been taking place behind the scenes, however, because all of a sudden everything seemed to change and the friendship was booming again. On the tenth anniversary of the victory over Batista, Castro made a speech filled with praise for the Soviet Union. In February 1969, a new trade agreement was signed that took account of the difficulties facing the Cubans: the Cuban trade deficit with the USSR was already 4 billion dollars; military aid over the previous decade was estimated by Castro to have totalled 1.5 billion dollars.[21] Throughout 1969 there was again a busy exchange of official visits, and in June the Cuban delegation to a conference of Communist parties in Moscow finally condemned the "sectarianism" in Beijing. The Kremlin was content. Shortly afterwards, in July, a squadron of eight Soviet ships put into Havana, and when Soviet defense minister Marshal Andrei Grechko visited the Cuban capital in November he was seen cutting cane beside the Castro brothers.

★

Ten million tons

Castro officially called 1970 "the year of the ten million tons." But it became a year of only 8.5 million tons. At least this was the largest sugar harvest in Cuba's history, but it was still 15 percent below the ambitious target. For Castro it was a personal defeat, the worst in his career as a revolutionary: "The ten million ton harvest represents far more than tons of sugar, far more than an economic victory," *Granma* quoted him as saying in October 1969. "It is a test, a moral duty for this country. [Therefore] we cannot fall a single gram short of the ten million. . . . Even one pound below the ten million tons – we say this before the whole world – would be a defeat, not a victory."[22]

The propaganda machine had wound the whole country up for the target, invoking the Bay of Pigs spirit of victory. Additional land had been sown, so that 1.4 million hectares were available. New methods permitted several cycles of sowing and harvesting during 334 days from July 1969 to July 1960, instead of the usual three months at the turn of the year. Even the weather played its part. All other economic activity had to slow down, because virtually the whole population – mothers and children, school and university students, industrial workers, pensioners, white-collar workers, army personnel – assembled with machetes for "voluntary" work in the sugarcane fields, to lend a hand to the 250,000 professional cutters. Nearly every day Fidel Castro himself put in four hours.

Even Christmas was abolished for 1969. Already on January 3, 1969, Castro had deleted it from the calendar, on the grounds that every day had to be used for the record harvest: "Now begins a year with eighteen months. The next New Year's celebrations will be on 1 July, the next Christmas between 1 and 26 July [1970]."[23] (When Cuba later reverted to the old calendar, the promised reintroduction of Christmas was not part of it. Only in 1997 did the festivities appear again, when the Pope requested it shortly before his visit to the island.)

Yet all the effort was of no avail; the target of 10 million tons had been set too high. Worse, the rest of the Cuban economy fell between 20 and 40 percent, as men and machinery were mobilized for the sugar harvest.

When Castro appeared before the waiting crowd on July 26, 1970, for the commemoration of the Moncada attack, he did not try to put a gloss on things. In a self-critical speech, he offered the resignation of himself and the Cuban Party leadership, although naturally none of those listening wanted that. Even in defeat, Cubans were prepared to follow their charismatic leader. Besides, what alternative did they have? "We proved incapable of waging what we called the simultaneous battle. . . . The heroic effort to raise production, to raise our purchasing power, resulted in dislocations in the economy, in a fall in production in other sectors, and in general in an increase in our difficulties." Recognizing "the responsibility of all of us and mine in particular," he stressed:

> The battle of the ten million was not lost by the people, it is us, the administrative apparatus, the leaders of the revolution who lost it. . . . Most of the time we fell into the error of minimizing the complexity of the problems facing us. . . . there are comrades who are worn out, burned out; they have lost their energy, they can no longer carry the burden on their shoulders.

Finally, he spoke of the need for greater democracy at leadership levels, more effective delegation of responsibilities, and critical analysis of the course of the revolution:

> It is easier to win twenty wars than to win the battle of development. The fight today is not against people, . . . we are fighting against objective factors; we are fighting against the past, we are fighting with the continued presence of this past in the present, we are fighting against limitations of all kinds. But sincerely this is the greatest challenge that we have had in our lives and the greatest challenge the Revolution has ever faced.[24]

Despite all the efforts, falling output in the transition from the first to the second decade of the Cuban Revolution also revealed a waning of revolutionary energy among the population. Guevara's and Castro's concept of "moral incentives" was no longer working. Absenteeism was spreading dramatically at the workplace: in August and September 1968 alone, some 20 percent of employees took time off, and in Castro's home province of Oriente the figure in August was as high as 52 percent. "Perhaps our greatest illusion," Castro said, "was to have believed that a society . . . could become, at a stroke, a society in which everyone behaved in an ethical and moral fashion."[25] Somewhat resignedly, he was at last indicating a willingness not to insist on "moral incentives" as the only motivation for work. At the same time, he called upon the workers "to democratize themselves, to constitute a strong and powerful labor movement."[26]

The last thing Castro had in mind, however, was political pluralism. What he wanted was a way of channeling criticism of the system: employees should be more closely involved both in decision-making processes and in responsibility for production; the problem of idling could then also be better controlled. Together with a comprehensive reorganization of the Confederation of Cuban Workers (CTC) over the next three years, a new "anti-slackers" law was introduced in 1971 which prescribed severe penalties for the "work-shy." Material incentives (already used for a time between 1963 and 1966) were again envisaged as a means of increasing work motivation and therefore productivity. Castro argued:

> Together with moral incentive, we must also use material incentive, without abusing either one, because the former would lead us to idealism, while the latter would lead to individual selfishness. We must act in such a way that economic incentives will not become the exclusive motivation of man, nor moral incentives serve to have some live off the work of the rest.[27]

By 1972 the whole governmental apparatus was reformed and restructured. Collective leadership responsibility was supposed to have at last replaced Castro's personal decision-making, so that, in day-to-day politics, there would now be limits to his ability to extend his rule into literally every area. This new degree of predictability in Cuban politics was also a concession to the Soviet fund-providers. Yet Castro's position in power was untouched, as his own person stood above the law and his authority to set guidelines was as absolute as before.

The next step towards a formal institutionalization of the Cuban Revolution was the drafting and adoption of a constitution. Soon after the victory of the revolution, Castro had moved away from his original intention to reintroduce the 1940 Constitution that Batista suspended in 1952, and had ruled instead on the formal ground of the Basic Law promulgated early in 1959 and of thousands of subsequent laws and ordinances. In 1974 a commission was set up under the 76-year-old Blas Roca, a long-time Communist, to prepare a new Constitution; a first draft was published half a year later and presented for public discussion in all the structures of society.

This Constitution of "the state of all workers and farmers and all other toilers by hand and by brain" mainly followed the Soviet model. The Communist Party (PCC), as the "highest leading force of society and the state . . . in the construction of socialism and . . . the formation of a communist society," was the supreme political authority. One novelty was the introduction of "People's Power" (*Poder Popular*) as the organ of local self-administration. Unexpectedly, the issue of whether candidates for the National Assembly should be directly elected by the people to avoid manipulation, or whether they should be sent there by local bodies, the *poderes populares*, gave rise to such heated debates that a decision was postponed when the main body of the text was submitted to a constitutional referendum on February 15, 1976. After this pruned draft was adopted by 97.7 of the vote, the central drafting commission under Castro's chairmanship blocked all impulses toward direct democracy from below. In the 1990s, a change to the system finally allowed the population itself to elect candidates for the National Assembly. But for the time being, "the National Assembly [would be] composed of members selected by the local assemblies." Preparations were made for 3,000 delegates to vote on the issue at the five-day congress of the PCC in December 1975; it would be the first regular congress of the Communist Party of Cuba, permitted only after Castro's annoyance with the old Communists and the comrades in Moscow had subsided, and they in turn had given him unqualified recognition.

The Constitution finally came into force on February 24, 1976. Castro took over as head of state from Osvaldo Dorticós, who became a government minister as well as a member of the PCC Central Committee and Politbureau. (Dorticós committed suicide in 1983, at the age of 64.[28]) Castro was thus unrestricted leader of the Cuban Revolution, in effect the Máximo Líder for life: head of state and Party, but also commander-in-chief of the armed forces and (as chairman of the 31-member Council of Ministers elected by the National Assembly) prime minister. His brother

Raúl was his deputy in all posts, as well as having his own position as defense minister.

If Castro had not changed tack in the early seventies and made his peace with Moscow, his position after the "year of the ten million tons" would scarcely have remained so uncontested. But as it was, the Soviet Union could soften the blow to his reputation, and the economic consequences of a defeat for which he readily blamed himself, by agreeing to supply additional goods and loans. In June 1972, following Castro's first trip in eight years to the Soviet Union, Cuba was accepted as the ninth member of the Eastern bloc's Council for Mutual Economic Aid. The Soviet Union hoped thereby to share out among Comecon's member-states the economic costs of Cuban integration. But for Cuba, ten years after the missile crisis, it meant economic and military guarantees as well as recognition as a full member of the socialist community.

In December 1972 Castro was again in Moscow, to take part in the celebrations marking the fiftieth anniversary of the founding of the USSR. The agreement on further economic cooperation that he signed with Brezhnev involved, in his own words, "extraordinary concessions" to the Cubans: the purchase price for Cuban sugar nearly doubled; Moscow granted not only a moratorium until 1986 on nearly 4 billion dollars of debt but a suspension of interest payments for 25 years; it also accorded Cuba a further loan of 300 million dollars, payable in three tranches at a favorable rate of interest. The "golden seventies" of relative prosperity were beginning for the Cubans; very soon, by the middle of the decade, nearly half of all Soviet development aid was going to the island state. Its hard-currency income from exports of sugar, as well as from other goods such as nickel, tobacco, citrus fruit, and fish, gave the Cuban government some leeway and enabled it to make some purchases in the West: for example, cars, machinery, locomotives, hotel equipment, furniture. In 1975 Cuba received even more loans from West European banking consortia, as well as 200 million dollars from Argentina, where 60,000 US automobiles were produced under license for Cuba. At first, the United States certainly tried to intervene behind the scenes at every level, but it was an era of detente and the cold warriors were on the defensive.

Towards the end of 1974, on the initiative of US Secretary of State Henry Kissinger, secret contacts were established with the Cubans. On July 29, 1975, the United States even voted in the OAS to end the diplomatic and economic sanctions imposed against Cuba 11 years before. Many Latin American countries restored relations with Havana. And the new US administration under Gerald Ford declared certain trade restrictions "temporarily" suspended, especially the ban on US corporations maintaining business contacts with Cuba through their overseas subsidiaries.[29]

On January 28, 1974, 15 years after the victory of the revolution, not quite 14 years after Deputy Prime Minister Mikoyan had made the first official Soviet trip to the country, Leonid Brezhnev, general secretary of the CPSU, touched down in Havana for a week-long visit. It was the first time that a Soviet Party chief had ever been to Latin America, and the signal was not lost, either on Washington or on the socialist bloc and the Third World. Brezhnev's journey to meet Castro was tantamount to a benediction: not only were all the sins of the past forgiven, but Cuba became the model for revolutionary struggle. The exalted guest went with Castro in the tracks of the revolution, beginning with a visit to the Moncada Barracks in Santiago de Cuba. It was estimated that a million people gathered for the central rally to greet the two men, at the foot of the José Martí memorial in Havana.

The joint Soviet-Cuban statement reported their "complete agreement of views about the present world situation and the foreign-policy tasks of the socialist states." Cuba paid tribute to the "peace program" of the Soviet Union, and unity also prevailed with regard to "general and complete disarmament, the prohibition of the use of force in international relations, and the ban for all times on the use of nuclear weapons."[30] In reality, Castro had been skeptical or even dismissive regarding the first signs of East–West detente in the early 1970s. He feared that a rapprochement between the superpowers would bring the opposite of security for small countries such as Cuba, since they would feel able to use the umbrella of detente to strike at them with greater impunity.

Less than three weeks later, the GDR state and Party leader, Erich Honecker, followed Brezhnev to Havana, where he received an equally magnificent welcome. He too stayed a week, and went out to meet the people all over the island; his entourage was so enthusiastic that plans were announced to produce a film and a picture book about the visit. Behind closed doors, however, there was a lot of hard talking: Castro had already prepared the East German leader – as he had Brezhnev – for the possibility "that we will have to review our whole sugar policy, since all we have is sugar."[31] In other words, the comrades would have to pay more for their sugar. Castro gave his visitors from East Berlin a dramatic lesson in Caribbean economics, which climaxed in the observation that Cuba's income from sugar and its few other products would in the current year be equivalent to only "40 percent of world market prices," while its spending on necessary imports would be "10, 15 or 20 percent above world market prices."

Castro angrily reproached the Eastern-bloc states with reselling reasonably priced Cuban sugar at higher prices on the world market: "To take one example, 100 percent of the sugar that we export to Poland is re-exported." This reselling of Cuban sugar by fraternal socialist countries had the effect of pushing down the price which Cuba (as one of the two or three largest sugar-exporting countries) was able to obtain for what it had to sell directly on the world market for foreign currency. In this way, Castro argued, "we lost millions and millions in convertible currency" over the past years.

Only the Soviet Union, Castro said in praise of it, had improved the situation in the last year by increasing the price it paid for Cuban sugar; "the other countries have done nothing." Cuba therefore demanded a solid agreement on "rational trade, fair trade and balanced trade," on the basis of equal rights. "We can no longer play the role of beggar and keep modestly knocking every day on the doors of foreign trade departments," Castro declared. He also seems to have referred in passing to other typical problems in trade relations. "Twenty-three percent of the goods that we were supposed to receive from the GDR in 1973 have not arrived in our country. We do not know when we shall get them. In some of these cases there were shipping difficulties, in others there were supply difficulties."

Honecker too had many grounds for complaint – after all, the other Comecon countries generally saw Cuba's slow economic growth in a critical light, not least because it was constantly exposed to the moods and sudden ideas of the Máximo Líder. Honecker let himself indulge in criticism wrapped up in gentle irony: "There is a lot of spontaneity, but naturally the hand of the Party is felt." But on one thing he made himself unmistakably clear:

> I would like to state categorically that until now we have not acted out of stinginess in our economic relations with Cuba, but have always based ourselves on Cuba's significance as the first socialist country in the Americas. . . . And if there is a greater advantage on one side, it must lie not on our side but on Cuba's. That is our position.

Just a few weeks later, Castro was able to take Honecker and his Eastern-bloc counterparts at their word. To the joy of the Cubans, the CPSU Politburo decided in the spring following Brezhnev's visit that the 200 rubles a ton agreed in December for Cuban sugar would be raised to 325 rubles a ton for the years 1974 and 1975. Castro immediately passed news of this to the other Comecon states, and let it be understood that he expected them to match the Soviet Union. Such a decision on their part, he wrote in May 1974 to Honecker, would correspond "not only to the spirit" of their mutual relations but also "to conditions on world markets," where the price of sugar was more than 400 rubles a ton.

Into the Third World

The Kremlin had also wanted Brezhnev's visit to underline the importance it attached to the Third World. Cuba's outstanding role as spokesman for the Third World, and its growing agreement with Moscow on questions of development policy, were demonstrated by the fact that Brezhnev did not include any other country in his trip. Above all, the Soviets hoped that Castro's influence and reputation in the Third World would win credibility and influence for themselves in neutral developing countries that were shy of drawing too close to either of the superpowers.

In the early seventies, Castro not only corrected and redefined Cuba's relationship with the Soviet Union, but also developed a new line in foreign policy. Che Guevara's failure and death, as well as the weak resonance of his call to create "two, three, many Vietnams," had caused Castro to draw away from any simple exporting of revolution. The strengthening of social-revolutionary forces, which were winning influence and power in several Latin American countries not through armed struggle but by peaceful means, also forced Castro to do some rethinking. For he now had to recognize that there were other paths than violence to national emancipation and social transformation.

The very special Cuban experiences of guerrilla warfare could not easily be transferred to other countries, even if here and there attempts were made to precipitate a revolutionary situation (for example, by the Tupamaros urban guerrillas in Uruguay). At most, Guevara's book on guerrilla warfare[32] met with passionate approval only among European drawing-room revolutionaries or political loose cannons such as Germany's Baader-Meinhof terrorist group. In Peru in October 1968, a progressive military government had come to power not through a popular revolution but through a putsch from above, and yet the generals there had nationalized a large part of industry, decreed an extensive land reform and expropriated North American oil corporations. In 1970, the bourgeois socialist Salvador Allende had won the presidency not through arms but through a tight electoral victory, even though the CIA had tried to prevent this with years of covert operations. And in other parts of Latin America, especially in Brazil, the "liberation theology" emanating from within the Catholic Church and favoring social justice throughout the continent had won ever greater support and influence in oppositional circles.

Castro, albeit somewhat reluctantly, instrumentalized these currents for his own ends. He formulated his new line in

November 1971, during a state visit to Chile that was his first trip abroad for seven years, and his first in Latin America for 12 years. Like someone on a visit to relatives, who suddenly does not want to leave, he remained not the planned ten days but a full twice as much, traveling the 3,000-mile length of the country from the Atacama Desert to Patagonia. The wearing journey became a triumphal procession for him but caused considerable discomfort to his hosts, under siege as they were from a strong political right. It soon became clear that a Havana–Santiago political axis would be ideal for Castro's internationalist concept of revolution; and he was already friends with Allende, from the time before the election when the Chilean had paid several visits to the Cuban. When Castro was asked along the way whether he supported the Chilean road to socialism, even though it did not correspond to the course taken in Cuba, he gave a statesman-like answer: "Not only did we find no contradiction, . . . we will always look with satisfaction on every new variation that may appear. And let every variation in the world make its appearance! If all roads lead to Rome, we can only wish for thousands of roads to lead to revolutionary Rome!"[33] By "revolutionary Rome" he meant his dream of (left-wing) Pan-American unity.

Castro's goal – to build the broadest possible anti-imperialist front, not only in America but throughout the Third World – forced him into rhetorical restraint and dialectical flexibility. The professional revolutionary was more and more assuming the role of a statesman, which increased both his international reputation and his popularity at home; it flattered national pride and freed the country from the oppressive diplomatic isolation of the sixties, giving Cuba a certain weight again in the world. At a time when, in those latitudes, the upper classes and oligarchies were jealously watching over their national interests, so jealously that (until the early nineties at least) they undermined any attempt to create a Mercosur along the lines of the European Economic Community, Castro developed for the nitrate miners of northern Chile the vision of a common Latin American market, "a union of sister nations that may become a large and powerful community in the world of tomorrow."[34] Such reasonable and constructive ideas on the part of their arch-enemy disturbed the strategists in Washington more than his usual polemics had done. For if they fell on fertile ground, they would certainly endanger for a long time to come the powerful economic interests of the United States in Latin America.

Castro was able to report, years later, that the CIA had been planning to have him killed – first in Chile, then on his journey back through Peru or Ecuador; and that assassins disguised as Venezuelan journalists had been equipped via the US embassy in La Paz with the most up-to-date precision weapons and submachine guns. One device was a television camera specially adapted to function as a firearm: "It was straight in front of me," he said, "but they didn't shoot."[35]

The shooting took place a couple of years later, when a military putsch prepared with the help of the CIA put a bloody end to Chilean president Salvador Allende and his government and plunged the country into nearly 17 years of dictatorship under General Augusto Pinochet. According to our present knowledge, Allende avoided falling into the hands of the military by shooting himself in the Moneda Palace in central Santiago – apparently with a submachine gun given to him as a present by Castro in 1971.

During his visit, Castro seems to have had a suspicion of what was in store for Chile: his moderate account of a trip to "revolutionary Rome" strays from time to time into the militant rhetoric of the revolutionary from the Sierra Maestra. "For America to become united and become Our America, the America Martí spoke of, it will be necessary to eliminate the very last vestige of those reactionaries who want the peoples to be weak so they can hold them in oppression and in subjection to foreign monopolies."[36]

A few months after his Chile visit, inspired by his growing reputation and his new image as an (outwardly) moderate revolutionary, Castro boarded his Ilyushin-62 on May 3, 1972, and set off for a two-month trip that would include his first stay in the Soviet Union for eight years and reach a climax with Cuba's admission to Comecon. Altogether, he visited ten countries. First, as if in the tracks of Che Guevara, he traveled to Africa, where Cuba had for years been overtly or covertly supporting liberation movements and left-leaning regimes. He visited Guinea,

Sierra Leone, and Algeria (in the company of a conspicuously large military delegation), refined old relationships or cultivated new ones such as with Hoari Boumedienne in Algeria, who in the mid-sixties had overthrown Castro's and Guevara's friend Ben Bella. Then he flew on to Bulgaria, Romania, Hungary, Poland, the GDR, Czechoslovakia, and finally the Soviet Union.

In December 1972 Allende made a return visit to Cuba, the last time he would ever meet Castro. On September 11, 1973, the Cuban leader, coming straight from the fourth Non-Aligned Conference in Algiers, learned in Hanoi of Allende's overthrow and death.

On February 21, 1974, five months after the putsch in Chile, Castro told GDR leader Honecker (who was then in Havana) of his impressions and conclusions from his visit to Chile. "Since my visit to Chile, I had seen the strength of reaction, the fascism, the government's weaknesses and its powerlessness. I had . . . the impression that the government's only chance of saving itself was to go on the offensive, a mass popular offensive." Given "the sabotage in international loans, a large foreign debt, a government without any foreign currency, and the high food prices," Allende could only "with great audacity . . . have had any chance of survival." Castro continued: "I think that in that situation the only option was to try to arm the popular forces. Naturally it would have been dangerous, but it was more dangerous to do nothing. . . . For the enemy was mobilized, the fascists were mobilized, and the masses were nowhere to be seen because the government had not mobilized them."[37]

Castro did not want to lose Chile as a base for revolutionary missionary work on the Latin American mainland. And, having seen early on the latent danger facing Allende, he was prepared to help him out with limited military support: he sent an elite contingent of Cuban soldiers to act as his bodyguard and military advisers, headed by his then-trusted friend Antonio de la Guardia (whom Castro had executed 18 years later for alleged drug-trafficking).[38] "When the coup took place," he confided to Honecker, "there were in our embassy enough weapons for a battalion, automatic weapons, armour-piercing weapons, and there was also a force of special troops." But Allende did not want them to get involved in fighting, any more than he had allowed his Communist allies in Popular Unity to undergo paramilitary training.

The putschists around Pinochet always sought to justify their brutal coup, and their subsequent persecution of opponents of the dictatorship, by arguing that a real "war" was on against the Cuban-backed leftists of the MIR (Movimiento de Izquierda Revolucionario), who subscribed to Che Guevara's path of armed guerrilla struggle. In his conversation with Honecker, Castro admitted that there actually were links with the MIR, which was then operating underground. But, although there was some readiness to give them support, the scale of it was in the end only quite small.

Castro also told Honecker that Cuba had insisted that the situation in Chile "required arming and that Unidad Popular must prepare for it." According to the (uncorrected) stenographic record of the conversation, Castro claimed that a few months before the coup Allende had given his consent "for weapons to be given to Unidad Popular forces." The components of Unidad Popular – Socialists and Communists, as well as the United People's Action Movement (MAPU) of the Christian left – had preferred Allende's peaceful road to the MIR's armed struggle. But Castro now dressed this up to sound as if those parties had not been "prepared" for arming: "They had got some weapons, but much fewer than we wanted to give and could have sent."[39]

"The largest part" of the weapons stored in the Cuban embassy had been intended "for the Communist Party." "A few weeks before the coup we asked them to collect the weapons. They did not collect them." So, if it is true – as Castro claimed – that a few months before the putsch Allende agreed (contradicting his own stated policy) to the distribution of weapons to Unidad Popular members, he appears to have withdrawn his approval shortly before the actual coup. This can be the only explanation – assuming the stenographic record is correct – for Castro's statement: "We had handed out some weapons and said, we won't disregard Allende's instruction, but if the coup takes place we will give you the weapons." When the military finally struck, "we couldn't give them any, because the fascist groups quickly surrounded the embassy." The Cubans thus had "to take two-thirds of the weapons out of the country." "But," Castro let it be known, "a third of the weapons have remained there, and with the support of our Soviet friends we gave them to the MIR. We wouldn't hand them out on the day of the coup, but only later. Now there are no longer any weapons in the embassy. They have a fair number of automatic weapons."

"But now we are not interfering," Castro finally indicated in February 1974. Partly this was because he felt uneasy about the MIR people: "They had conflicts with Allende, and Allende was right. . . . They had really extremist positions." The Havana–Santiago axis was therefore in ruins. "The situation is difficult, the persecution is great, the struggle is hard. . . . If there is no energetic resistance, Unidad Popular will not win another electoral victory in twenty years' time," he concluded, with near-prophetic foresight.[40]

In 1975 Cuba was gradually drawn into the civil war in Angola. After left-reformist army officers overthrew the dictatorship in Portugal in 1974 and announced that the Portuguese colonies of Angola, Mozambique, Guinea-Bissau, and the Cape Verde Islands would be give independence, the three parties to the Angolan civil war signed an agreement in January 1975 at the Portuguese town of Alvor (the so-called Alvor Accords), which envisaged free elections and full independence for Angola by November. "One would have expected the US to back it to the full," wrote the former diplomat and State Department Cuba expert Wayne S. Smith. "Instead – incredibly – the Ford administration moved to do the exact opposite, to shred the Alvor agreement."[41] The reason soon became clear: namely, that Agostinho Neto's Marxist MPLA (Popular Movement for the Liberation of Angola) would emerge as victor from the elections. Thus, at a moment when Washington was finally giving up Vietnam as lost, the CIA pumped in money, weapons, and mercenaries and got Holden Roberto's rival FNLA (National Front for the Liberation of Angola) to break the agreement. It was not long before the conflict had turned into a surrogate war between the United States, China, and South Africa on one side, and the Soviet Union and Cuba on the other.

In the spring of 1975, the MPLA sent a request to Havana for military assistance, and in May Cuba responded with 250 advisers. Then in late September, after the hostilities had spread, Castro launched "Operation Carlota" (so called after the black female leader of a Cuban slave revolt in the nineteenth century) to send equipment and troops to Angola. By early October 1,500 Cuban troops were already stationed there; by February 1976 the figure was ten times higher, 15,000; and after 1977 as many as 36,000 were there at any one time. Castro announced that his troops would stay for as long as they were needed. Ten years later they were still there. More than 200,000 Cuban soldiers had been sent out in rotation for a period of duty.

Castro himself created a kind of command post in Havana, interfering in strategy and tactics in ways that were not always to the liking of Cuban officers. It is true that the Cubans were largely responsible for the rapid victories that followed, but the war dragged on until the late eighties because of the military and political inability of the Angolans. For Cuba, which in the seventies gained a high degree of self-confidence from the military engagement, the Angola campaign in the eighties took a growing toll economically, politically, and socially. No charge was made for the support given to the Angolans. And it was not only heroes who came back alive and well from the faraway African country: there were also coffins and young cripples making the 7,500-mile crossing.

In 1984, when Cuba had 40,000 soldiers there, Castro feared that the Angolans would want to "prolong their presence indefinitely." In late July, in Cienfuegos, he told GDR Politbureau member Hermann Axen of disunity, lack of principle, money-making and corruption among the Marxist leadership of the African country, and even of acts of violence against the civilian population. Moreover, "experienced Cuban advisers and experts who had been active there for years were being dismissed, and advisers brought in from Western countries [with whom] private money-making deals" could be struck. Without the Cubans, the opposition UNITA would for long have been ruling the country. In his secret report, Axen further quoted Castro as saying: "Incapable of stabilizing the internal political situation, . . . [the MPLA leadership] was seeking compromises with the enemy and even making a bargaining chip of the Cuban troops in order to create ostensible advantages for themselves." There was no unity in the Politbureau and government; it was impossible to rely on them. Yet, despite these accompanying phenomena, the Cuban troop presence was to last until 1991.[42]

Castro always stressed that the military aid to Angola corresponded to his own estimate of the situation, and that his troops had in no sense been sent as Cuban "gurkhas of the Soviet empire," as Washington claimed. "The Soviets absolutely did not ask us. They never said a single word on the subject. It was exclusively a Cuban decision," he said in a television interview to US journalist Barbara Walters.[43] To Tad Szulc he declared: "The Angolans asked us for help. . . . Angola was invaded by South Africa. . . . Therefore we could never have done anything more than just to help Angola against an external invasion."[44] Soviet sources confirm this account: "The idea for the large-scale military operation had originated in Havana, not Moscow."[45] Even black African states not well disposed to Angola or Castro show him respect for the operation. "The West had underestimated the extent to which Blacks in general, and Africans in particular, abhorred the Nazi-like apartheid regime in South Africa," writes Carlos Moore in his study of "Castro, the Blacks and Africa."[46]

In his engagement against underdevelopment and imperialism, in Africa's struggle of South against North, black against white, the "white" Castro knew how to use the fact that the cultural roots of colonial Cuba lay in Africa, and that a majority of the Cuban population was descended from African slaves. It was mainly black troops and black generals who once fought Cuba's war of liberation against Spain. "We are a Latin-African nation," Castro once said. "African blood flows through our veins."[47] This makes it clear why he did not necessarily need an impetus from Moscow to go ahead. "In keeping with the duties rooted in our principles, our ideology, our convictions and our very own blood, we shall defend Angola and Africa."[48]

The Swiss sociologist Jean Ziegler made a key point when he wrote: "In November 1975, Cuban regiments, three-fourths of which were made up of black troops, disembarked at the port of

Luanda and pushed the invaders back. . . . Black Cubans had blocked the way of white South African tanks and paratroopers."[49] Castro was convinced, then, that the Cuban Revolution had a chance of survival only if it exported its political and moral principles and worked to achieve prestige, respect and therefore restraint in the international community, most of which was composed of Third World states. Against this background, "Operation Carlota" established Castro's reputation as a leading Third World figure more securely than ever before.

Subsequently, Castro and his diplomats spun a dense global web of relations with Third World states. With the Soviet Union and a modest economic prosperity at its back, Cuba was even able to afford to elaborate its own concept of development aid. For Cuban diplomats brought with them not only military advisers and secret service experts, but also teachers and doctors. Thousands of volunteers fanned out to help Cuba's new friends overcome underdevelopment through literacy campaigns, the building of a health system, and other social institutions. By the end of the millennium, according to Castro, Cuba had sent more than 25,000 doctors alone to the Third World. He has always stressed the idealistic character of these expensive missions: "Our homeland is not just Cuba; our homeland is also humanity."[50] But they were not quite as selfless and idealistic as all that: Castro's medium-to-long-term aim, after all, is the construction of a worldwide anti-imperialist front against the United States. Only if the Third World and the newly developing nations are united among themselves and speak with a single voice, will they be able to change in their favor the terms of trade with the First World. That was their only value for the Soviet Union. Seen in this light, its financial and economic aid to Cuba was rather like an investment of political capital expected to yield a high rate of return.

In 1976 Cuba's engagement in Africa led to fresh tensions with the United States. At first, the new Carter administration continued the talks begun under his predecessor Gerald Ford to bring the two states closer together. These talks even survived acts of terrorism by anti-Castro exiles, evidently directed by the CIA: for example, the bomb explosion on board a Cuban airplane soon after it took off from Barbados, on October 6, 1976, which caused the death of 73 people. Those who took part in the attack – including the well-known Cuban exile and CIA collaborator Orlando Bosch – were soon discovered and, in some cases, arrested in Venezuela. Four years later, however, the charges against them were dropped because of "lack of evidence;" they walked free in the interests of US "national security."

Despite these and other operations originating in Florida, semi-diplomatic relations in the form of "representations of interests" were restored between Cuba and the United States in September 1977, 16 years after the closure of their respective embassies. But as Cuba was meanwhile increasing instead of reducing the number of its military personnel in Angola, the Carter administration suddenly issued an ultimatum making the continuation of secret talks between the two governments dependent upon a Cuban withdrawal from Angola – a condition which for Castro was unworthy of discussion. His response combined derision with delusions of grandeur:

> What moral basis can the United States have to speak about Cuban troops in Africa? What moral basis can a country have whose troops are on every continent? . . . when their own troops are stationed right here on our own national territory, at the Guantánamo naval base? It would be ridiculous for us to tell the United States government that, in order for relations between Cuba and the United States to be resumed or improved, it would have to withdraw its troops from the Philippines, or Turkey, or Greece, or Okinawa, or South Korea.[51]

In fact, the Cubans soon found themselves present in another African theater of war. Early in 1978 Cuba intervened in the war between Ethiopia and Somalia, this time – unlike in Angola – expressly at the request of the Soviet Union. By February 15,000 Cuban troops were waging a counter-offensive and driving Somali forces out of Ogaden.

It was a precarious business. Originally Somalia and the Soviet Union had been allies: the USSR had a military base at Berbera in the strategically important Horn of Africa, while the USA supported the military regime that took over after the fall of

Emperor Haile Selassie in 1974 – that is, until Mengistu Haile Mariam emerged from the ruling junta in February 1977 to seize power for himself. In the wake of the brutal repression that ensued, the Carter administration withdrew support from Mengistu, the self-declared Marxist, who thereupon sought a rapprochement with the Soviet Union. Moscow found itself in a doubly awkward position. On the one hand, both it and Havana had always supported the striving for independence of the Ethiopian province of Eritrea, and now they were expected to make a U-turn and stand up for the territorial integrity of the Ethiopian state. On the other hand, they were allied with Somalia, precisely because Ethiopia had for long had designs on Ogaden in the Horn of Africa. This alliance soon broke down, of course, and Somalia's President Mohammed Siad Barre also felt compelled to change camps. He made enquiries in Washington, received military support, invaded Ethiopia to support the independence movement there, and drove the ruler in Addis Ababa into such a tight corner that he had to turn to the Soviet Union for military help. Moscow, as we have seen, then delegated to Castro the task of dealing with the Somalis.

The following year, Castro was able to count on new friends and allies in his own hemisphere. In March 1979 Maurice Bishop took power through a putsch on the Caribbean island of Grenada, and in July the Cuban-supported Sandinista Liberation Front succeeded in overthrowing and driving into exile the Nicaraguan dictator Anastasio Somoza. In both cases, Castro sent technicians, doctors, teachers, and military advisers. Remarkably, he warned his Nicaraguan comrade Daniel Ortega not to install a Cuban-style Marxist system but to preserve a mixed economy. He also advised him – in vain – to develop good relations with the United States.

In the autumn of 1979, the now 53-year-old Castro was at the height of his international reputation, an "elder statesman" of the Third World, so to speak. His country was a respected member of the international community, and 35 countries were receiving civil and military support from Havana. In September Castro acted as host to the Sixth Non-Aligned Conference in Havana, with the participation of 94 member-states and liberation movements.

This automatically made him official spokesman of the organization for the next four years – a goal which he and Cuban diplomacy had long been working to achieve. His close ties of dependence on the Soviet Union meant that this was not an uncontroversial decision, and Yugoslavia's head of state, Josef Broz Tito, as well as representatives of the People's Republic of China, were especially hostile. His answer to the Chinese was that they were betraying the cause of the Third World by supporting United States policy against the Soviet Union.

"We have many close friends at this conference, but we don't always agree with the best of them," he said at the opening session. And he tried to allay doubts about his role by assuring delegates: "We will work with all member countries – without exception – to achieve our aims and to implement the agreements that are adopted. We will be patient, prudent, flexible, calm. Cuba will observe these norms throughout the years in which it presides over the movement."[52] Castro bridged the ideological differences by setting out the main problem for all those present: the combination of the underdevelopment of poor countries with their dependence on the financial policy of the world's major economies. The next month, as spokesman of the Non-Aligned Movement, he presented the decisions of the Havana conference to the General Assembly of the United Nations in New York, demanding an end to the arms race and a redistribution of the resources thereby freed for development of the poorer countries of the world. He laid special emphasis on what would become his main political plank in the following years: that is, the search for a way out of the "debt trap."

In his view, the international financial organizations bore the main blame for the fact that the developing countries had accumulated a debt mountain of $300 billion. In 1978 alone, the debt was estimated by the World Bank to have been in excess of $51 billion. "The international monetary system prevailing today is bankrupt," he said. "It must be replaced! The debts of the least developed countries . . . must be cancelled!"[53] Less than a quarter of a year later, however, his moral authority and credibility as Third World spokesman would be severely damaged when Soviet troops marched into Afghanistan. The country was not

212

only a member but a co-founder of the Non-Aligned Movement. Castro suddenly found himself between two stools, for when the Non-Aligned Movement voted on a UN Resolution on Afghanistan, Cuba lined up with eight other members against a majority of 56 countries (with 26 abstentions) which condemned the Soviet invasion. He thereby lost the chance to take a seat on the UN Security Council on behalf of the non-aligned countries. His role as spokesman then unfolded in an unspectacular manner over the next few years.

The revolution devours its children

In the late 1960s, after attempts to bring forth the "new man" in Cuba came to an end with the death of Che Guevara, the fearless poet Heberto Padilla, well known for his biting irony, caricatured such efforts in a piece called "Instructions for Joining a New Society:"

> One: Be optimistic.
> Two: Be well turned out, courteous, obedient.
> (Must have made the grade in sports.)
> And finally, walk
> as every member does;
> one step forward
> and two or three back:
> but always applauding, applauding.[54]

Padilla's book *Outside the Game*, with its criticism of the development of a revolution he had once celebrated, provoked the supreme guardians. But he went on regardless. They left him alone a while longer, partly because he had influential friends at home and abroad, and partly because Fidel evidently held a protective hand over him. In March 1971, however, he suffered the fate he had already predicted in another poem:

213

Cuban poets no longer dream
(Not even at night). . . .
Hands seize them by the shoulders
Turn them about.[55]

Men from the G-2 secret police arrested him and threw him in jail.

Thirty-two days later he was set free, after a sharply worded open letter to Castro from noted European and Latin American intellectuals had been published in the French daily *Le Monde*.

With the same vigor with which we defended the Cuban Revolution from the first day, seeing it as exemplary because of its respect for human beings and its struggle for freedom, we now ask you to spare Cuba the dogmatic obscurantism, the cultural xenophobia and the repressive system that Stalinism has imposed on the socialist countries, and which bear an alarming similarity to the things that are currently reported to be happening in Cuba.[56]

Among the signatories were Jean-Paul Sartre and Simone de Beauvoir, Hans Magnus Enzensberger, Mario Vargas Llosa, Carlos Fuentes, Susan Sontag, Pier Paolo Pasolini, Alberto Moravia, Alain Resnais, and Gabriel García Márquez.

Padilla's release on Castro's orders had a price: the insubordinate poet had to make a public "self-criticism" and call upon other writers to follow his example. His obsequious confession, however, turned into a parody of actually existing socialism: "I have committed many, many errors, that are really inexcusable. . . . And I feel . . . truly happy . . . with the possibility of beginning my life over again with a new spirit." His humiliating period behind bars, he now characterized as an opportunity for "reflection." And what he said about his interrogators has the ring of scorn and derision: "If I have learned anything from the state security comrades, it is because of their humility, their simplicity, the sensitivity and warmth with which they carry out their humane tasks." He also regretted his description of the Writers' Association as a "hollow shell of pretentious nobodies," and castigated the malicious demon that was still within him. He had even been unfair and ungrateful toward Castro, and he would "never tire of repeating this." Then the poet mentioned "similar errors" he had committed, which, thanks to the "generosity of our revolution," had not landed him in the same trouble. "Let us then be soldiers!" he concluded. "For, comrades, we live . . . in the glorious trench of the present-day world, in the trench facing imperialist penetration of our country and of Latin America." And finally, repeating Castro's own favorite formula so that it had a subtly servile effect: "Fatherland or death! Venceremos!"[57]

Many critics, taking Padilla's "confession" at face value, called him a coward who had betrayed his wife and friends; others recognized the text as purest satire. Left-wing intellectuals divided into one large group (including Mario Vargas Llosa from Peru and Jorge Edwards from Chile) who broke with Castro over the affair, and a smaller group (including Gabriel García Márquez) who forgave his behavior as a regrettable slip. Padilla himself – who, during a similar period of disgrace ten years earlier, had been sent to Moscow to stand next to Aníbal Escalante and translate for him at press conferences – now had to earn his keep in Havana translating literature from English. He was not able to publish his own work, but ten years later, in 1981, he was allowed to go to the United States after Gabriel García Márquez intervened on his behalf. He died in December 2000 in Alabama, at the age of 68, having found a means of livelihood at the university there.

At the First National Congress of Education and Culture in April 1971, held in Havana under the shadow of the Padilla affair, Castro angrily attacked his West European critics for their open letter in *Le Monde* and described them as "despicable agents of cultural imperialism." "So they are at war with us," he mocked. "Magnificent! Our doors remain closed to them – indefinitely."[58] The declaration at the end of the congress was accordingly an "ideological monstrosity" (Tad Szulc). Cuba's cultural development had to be geared to the masses, it said, "contrary to the tendencies of the elite. . . . Socialism creates objective and subjective conditions that render feasible a true creative freedom while rejecting as inadmissible those tendencies that are based on a criterion of libertinage and aimed at concealing the counter-revolutionary poison of works that conspire against revolutionary ideology." In future, "political and ideological reliability should be taken into account" in appointments at universities, the media and cultural institutions. No more invitations should be made to foreign authors or intellectuals "whose work and ideology are at odds with the interests of the revolution;" and "cultural channels may not serve for the proliferation of false intellectuals who plan to convert snobbism, extravagance, homosexuality and other social aberrations into expressions of revolutionary art."[59]

"It seems incomprehensible," Szulc comments, "that Fidel Castro could intellectually tolerate such insults against his beloved revolution on the part of his own ideologues."[60] What comes through here is the Soviet hand in reorienting the Cuban leadership in the sixties and early seventies. "For the Soviet advisers, the freedoms and privileges of intellectuals (so far the favorite children of Castroism) had long been a thorn in the side of the Caribbean revolution," wrote Walter Haubrich, one of the best analysts of Latin American politics and culture, in the *Frankfurter Allgemeine Zeitung*.

> In the army and police, as well as among Cuba's old Communists who were now gaining influence, criticism grew louder of the privileged living conditions of artists, film people, scientists and writers. The years after the Padilla affair thus became one of the darkest periods for Cuban culture. A Stalinist bureaucrat by the name of Pablón was appointed culture minister. Ruthless operators in the Party and army found a new scapegoat for the mistakes of the revolution and the declining popular support: they were the fault of homosexuals among the artists and intellectuals.[61]

Only in the mid-seventies was the grip on cultural life slightly relaxed.

In the late sixties and early seventies, however, a veritable laager mentality prevailed against critics in Havana's political scene. Actually Castro did not need it. Scarcely any politician in the twentieth century, anywhere in the world, had won such a degree of support among intellectuals and artists as that which the revolutionary Fidel Castro enjoyed. Even his critics accorded him open or secret respect. He embodied the dreams of postwar intellectuals and made them a reality, and in death Che Guevara still lent them an air of mystique.

The judgment of intellectuals has always been important for Castro, whose sure feel for the media has led him to make use of them time and time again. At first there was hardly a writer who remained impervious to his fascination and charisma: Cubans such as Guillermo Cabrera Infante, Norberto Fuentes, Armando Valladeres, José Lezama Lima, Jesús Díaz, Pablo Armando Fernández, Alejo Carpentier, Antón Arrufat, Heberto Padilla; other Latin Americans such as Gabriel García Márquez, Mario Vargas Llosa, Carlos Fuentes, Octavio Paz, Julio Cortázar, Pablo Neruda, and Jorge Edwards, as well as countless writers from Western Europe such as Hans Magnus Enzensberger in Germany, expressed their sympathy with him. The affection soon cooled, however, with the growing "Sovietization" of cultural policy (which tolerated only what served the ruling doctrine), the censorship and complete desolation of the media, and the persecution of dissidents, even those who saw themselves as critical supporters. Fidel Castro, still less his brother Raúl or Che Guevara (who counted as the most dogmatic and ideologically rigorous of all), had no idea how to handle the kind of independent mind who was quite capable of making fun of himself as well as others. Many artists who lived in the United States or Europe during the Batista years – for example, the writer Alejo Carpentier or the painter (and friend of Picasso's) Wilfredo Lam, whose Afro-Cuban surrealism hangs in the world's great galleries – lived for a short time as guests on the island before returning disappointed into "exile." The transfer of prominent artists and intellectuals to the diplomatic service, and their assignment to attractive posts as cultural attachés (like Carpentier in Paris) or even ambassadors, was a method for governments to save face that was certainly not invented by Castro.

After the victory of the revolution, Castro and his inner circle believed at first that intellectuals would let themselves be socialized and remodeled as easily as the production conditions in agriculture and industry. This unbalanced attitude to freedom of speech and artistic expression soon made itself felt. On the one hand, Castro promoted intellectual freedoms and scope for creation;

the founding of the Casa de las Americas in 1960, under Haydée Santamaría, a comrade since the Moncada days, made possible a broad publication program. But then in 1961, in the wake of the Bay of Pigs operation, he allowed the Communist hardliners of the PSP to act on their fear of uncontrollable ideas, intellectual conflict and subversive humor by officially encouraging a sentence of death on the cultural magazine *Lunes*.

Lunes was the Monday supplement of Franqui's newspaper *Revolución*, the voice of the 26th of July Movement, which for a short while blossomed into one of the most interesting cultural magazines in Latin America, with a print run of around 250,000 copies. The chief editor was the respected writer Guillermo Cabrera Infante (author of *Three Trapped Tigers*, among others), and he had working with him a number of young poets such as Antón Arrufat, Pablo Armando Fernández, Heberto Padilla, and José Álvarez Barragano. Franqui recalled:

> Our thesis was that we had to break down the barriers that separated elite culture from mass culture. We wanted to bring the highest quality of culture to hundreds of thousands of readers. . . . We published huge editions with pictures and texts by Marx, Borges, Sartre, Neruda, Faulkner, Lezama Lima, Martí, Breton, Picasso, Miró, Virginia Woolf, Trotsky, Bernanos and Brecht. . . . Even *Lunes*'s typography was a scandal for left- and right-wing prudes.[62]

In June 1961, immediately after the victory at Playa Girón, when "the greatest number of writers and artists felt united with the revolution,"[63] heated debates took place on three successive Fridays concerning the future role of artists and intellectuals in the revolutionary process. The debates served as a preparation for the first "Congress of Writers and Artists" in August 1961, at which the country's intellectuals were to be brought politically under a single line and grouped for the future into a National Union of Writers and Artists (UNEAC), under the chairmanship of Castro's favorite Cuban author, Nicolás Guillán.

The Friday meetings eventually degenerated into a grand inquisitorial judgment on the freedom of opinion and intellectual expression practised in *Lunes*, and of the criticisms it had published of the crude seizure of power by pro-Moscow Communists. Virtually every Cuban artist of note took part in the proceedings. Seated opposite them were Castro, in the presiding chair, President Osvaldo Dorticós, Carlos Rafael Rodríguez, Education Minister Armando Hart, and Castro's friend from university days, Alfredo Guevara, director of the Cuban Film Institute (ICAIC). Castro opened the first session with the words: "Whoever is most afraid should speak first." The one who came forward was Virgilio Piñera, author of tales of fantasy. "Doctor Castro," he said, "have you ever asked yourself why any writer should be afraid of the Revolution? And since it seems as if I'm the one who is most afraid, let me ask why the Revolution is so afraid of writers."[64]

Castro's answer to the question of what would be culturally permissible in Cuba was tantamount to a death sentence on *Lunes*. In his closing "words to intellectuals," he distinguished three groups: those who completely identify with the revolution; sympathizers who associate themselves with the revolution but do not actively contribute to it; and those with whom nothing can be done: the counter-revolutionaries. His call to integrate the sympathizers seemed at first like an outstretched hand:

> The Revolution must find a way to these intellectuals and writers. The Revolution must . . . act in such a way that those sections of artists and intellectuals whose attitude was not from the beginning revolutionary can find a place in the Revolution where they can work and develop, and where their creative spirit – even if they are not revolutionary writers and artists – should have the chance and the freedom to express itself within the Revolution.

But then he drew the boundaries of artistic freedom: "This means: in the Revolution everything, against the Revolution nothing. And there should not be a special law for artists and writers. It is the main principle for all citizens. It is a fundamental principle of our Revolution."[65] The limits of tolerance were clearly defined:

> Does this mean, for example, that we will tell people what they must write? No. Everyone should write what they want, and if

what they write is no good then that's their hard luck. We don't tell anyone what to write about. . . . But we will always judge their literary work through the prism of the Revolution. That is . . . a right of the revolutionary government that must be respected, just like the right of every individual to write what they want.[66]

In practice, this meant that anything which did not look nice "through the prism of the Revolution" would not be published. Since paper was in short supply, moreover, it was not difficult to hand back awkward work to its author. Norberto Fuentes found that out, as did Antón Arrufat, Pablo Armando Fernández, and others.

It was not long before the paper shortage put an end to *Lunes*, a cultural magazine that was deemed to stand outside the revolution. (Its parent paper, *Revolución*, kept going for four more years, but its turn would come too.) Defamed as a house journal for intellectuals "mainly opposed to the national cultural heritage,"[67] *Lunes* was alleged to feature "decadent outlooks" and to be under the influence of the 26th of July Movement as well as the United States and France. Finally, in a surprise coup in October 1965, shortly after the founding congress of the Communist Party of Cuba, Castro engineered its merger with the old PSP mouthpiece *Hoy* (Today) into a new central organ of the PCC Central Committee, *Granma* ("Grandmother"), named after the motorlaunch in which Castro landed in December 1956 before heading into the Sierra Maestra. The incident was real-life political satire. Castro gave advance notice of its journalistic standards when he said in all seriousness during a trip to the Soviet Union that the Communist Party daily, *Pravda* (meaning "Truth"), was the best newspaper in the world. So it was that *Granma* became a kind of official gazette of the Cuban Revolution, as journalistically attractive throughout its decades of existence as the telephone list of an army barracks.

All this throws considerable light on the relationship of forces in Cuba during the period shortly after the victory of the revolution, if one considers the ruthlessness with which the PSP's pro-Moscow ideologues and their spiritual comrades among

Eastern-bloc diplomats systematically denounced the 26th of July Movement, describing it, for example, as a gathering-place for all manner of "partisans, terrorists, anarchists and adventurers"[68] – the kind of people with whom an upright Marxist-Leninist would have nothing to do. In so dismissing the true victors of the self-sacrificing struggle against Batista as a "petty-bourgeois radical movement" that had emerged in 1955 from the Ortodoxos party (a "fake opposition" run by "capitulators"), they grossly falsified the historical truth and covered up their own pitiful role during the revolution.

The East European diplomatic version of history, influenced by the PSP, suppressed the fact that the 26th of July Movement was only formally founded after Castro's release from prison in 1955, and that its real origins went back to his attack on the Moncada Barracks on July 26, 1953. Now, the very people who – as Castro once mockingly pointed out – "hid under their beds" during the revolution were trying to deny any historical credit to Cuba's only really successful revolutionary movement since the days of José Martí. The chief editor of *Revolución*, Carlos Franqui, a loyal and fearless if also critical comrade of Castro's since the fifties, was shamelessly portrayed as a man grouping around him "elements who do not stand on the ground of Marxism-Leninism and wish to distort the emerging revolutionary development." In 1968 Franqui, feeling thoroughly disillusioned, left for exile in Italy; he was now a *persona non grata* in Cuba, to such a point that, in line with an old Moscow practice, he was brushed out of an official photograph showing him alongside Castro. And yet, the PSP did not manage entirely to delete the name of the 26th of July Movement from the historical record. Castro himself ensured that that would not happen, by making that day the main national holiday to commemorate the beginning of his revolution – and not the equally important January 1, 1959, the day of his eventual victory.

The Writers' Union and the Cultural Congresses also eventually put in some practice in cultural allegiance to Moscow. Writers repeatedly landed in prison for acts of insubordination, went unpublished, or were driven out of the country when the State Book Institute declined their work. Especially cynical was the ending of copyright in April 1967 – a socialization of intellectual property which meant that all works now belonged to the nation. Writers and artists received a salary and accommodation from the state; they were no longer supposed to be dependent upon the laws of the market, but only on the Party bureaucrats who awarded a livelihood to "cultural producers."

Alexander Dubcek's "Prague Spring" initially aroused some hopes among Cuban artists. But, after Castro's approval of the Warsaw Pact invasion of Czechoslovakia, his brother Raúl – the "Green Olive" – opened fire with a series of articles denouncing "bourgeois" intellectuals and "counter-revolutionary" literature. The occasion for these was the annual prize awarded by the Writers' and Artists' Association (UNEAC) and the Casa de las Americas for the best literary works of the year. Despite the opposition of Castro's favorite Nicolás Guillán and UNEAC officials loyal to the Party line, the jury (which included foreign writers such as Jorge Edwards) chose three authors who were then out of favor: Padilla, Antón Arrufat, and Norberto Fuentes. The Casa de las Americas was permitted to publish their texts, but only on condition that it added a UNEAC editorial note certifying that they were "ideologically in conflict with our Revolution."

Sheldon B. Liss writes, in his study of Castro's political and social thought:

> Once the revolutionaries took power in Cuba, Fidel . . . sought to produce and nurture a new generation of intellectuals to analyse Cuba's past and help guide its future. By the time he took over, Fidel had developed a bit of the moral and intellectual arrogance that causes disdain for others who do not have the benefit of the answers that Marxist analysis provides. He wanted to surround himself with advisers who shared his privileged insights. . . . Castro endeavored to create an intellectual cadre to become the conscience and the critic of society. He understood that although intellectuals did not play a major role in the early phases of the Revolution, he needed them as a support group to sustain it. He wanted the new intellectuals either to be, or to appreciate, activists. He wanted them to devise solutions to societal problems and to actively engage in solving them.

In this respect, of course, Castro was hardly different from other politicians who like to have intellectuals as temporary conversation partners, advisers or clowns for intervals in politics, given a freedom to say what they please that would not be granted to others.

Yet there are limits to such freedom, and anyone who goes beyond them can easily see the favors withdrawn – under socialism as under capitalism. It is hardly surprising, then, that since 1959 intellectuals in Cuba have generally been in agreement with government policy. What "critics often fail to realize," writes Liss, "is that in a socialist society intellectual work is deemed a part of the socialization process. . . . Castro does not see Cuba as a pluralistic society, whose diverse ethnic groups develop their own cultures. He attempts to unify society by having all people relate to the same cultural composite."[69]

This helps us to understand why, with some exceptions, the quality of Cuban literature was quite poor in the ensuing decades. Many authors remained silent, became "unpolitical" or, as in the case of Miguel Barnet, suffered a crisis of creativity. Barnet eventually came to an accommodation with the regime, and was soon sitting as a deputy in the National Assembly and representing Cuba at UNESCO. Anyway, in the nineties Castro appointed as culture minister the writer Abel Prieto, a Politbureau member considered to belong to the Party's liberal spectrum who, in his new role, fought to achieve some leeway in cultural matters. Thus, Cuban cinema again commands considerable international attention – for example, Fernando Pérez's *Life Is To Whistle*, an everyday fable which has earned several distinctions abroad because of its fascinating, lightly worn images, its music and its satirical overtones.

The longer the Comandante has ruled, the more has it been the case that what good writers and artists produce in exile is impregnated with bitterness (as in Jesús Díaz), vapid anti-Communism (Guillermo Cabrera Infante), or banal sex (Zoé Valdés). Cabrera Infante's hatred for Castro soon went so far that he no longer smoked Cuban cigars and no longer spoke to people who visited Cuba.[70] "The works of Cuban exile literature," judges Walter Haubrich, "are in danger of becoming interchangeable.

For their authors have been living in a shared routine of every-day nothingness, and their experiences in the alien outside world have again been similar to one another."[71]

The decades of restrictions are all the less understandable if one considers that Castro's educational policy succeeded in making Cubans a reading nation, ahead of most other Latin American countries. Books – when they are available despite the paper shortage – cost only a fraction of what people have to pay in Chile or Mexico. Selected classics of world literature, including contemporary foreign authors such as Günter Grass, have always been very reasonably priced, though in small editions. For decades, Castro made sure that state-commissioned pirate editions were available to the population.

His conduct is also incomprehensible because we know that he has been a manic reader all his life. He is not known to be particularly interested in other spheres of culture. When he went to New York in the spring of 1959, for example, and his companions advised him to visit the Museum of Modern Art, he decided to go instead to the Brooklyn Zoo. Nor is music his thing. "I have a very bad ear for music," he told his friend Tomás Borge. "I like classical music and . . . have a real soft spot for marches." But "I have to blame nature because it didn't give me musical genes, a good ear for music or a good singing voice."[72] His real passion has always been the written word: "I've always read as many books as I could, and it makes me sad that I don't have more time for reading. I suffer when I see libraries and lists of book titles of any kind, regretting that I can't spend my life reading and studying."[73] He has read historical biographies, "all the books ever written about the French Revolution, many about the Bolshevik Revolution, countless numbers about the Mexican Revolution, and also many about the Chinese Revolution." In prison he made his reading more systematic and organized real classes "with courses in philosophy. We read a lot of world literature. For two years, I spent between 14 and 15 hours a day reading, except for the time I spent writing manifestos, messages and letters in invisible ink: lime juice." He read Dostoevsky, Romain Rolland, Victor Hugo, and Balzac. In his Mexican exile and the Sierra Maestra, he read nearly "all the books ever written . . . about World War II." Various specialist books followed after the victory of the revolution, "70, 80 or 100 books on agriculture." One of his aims in reading this kind of book was to turn the material to practical use – often to the regret of those around him, and not always with the intended effect.

As Castro's revolution grew in years, the turn came for books on ancient Rome, Greece and Egypt, early Chinese culture, and the old Indian cultures. But contemporary writers are also on his list, especially Latin American writers such as his friend Gabriel García Márquez. But not only they. "Last night, I was reading a little novel called *Perfume*, by Patrick Suskind. It's an unusual subject, very interesting and pleasant. . . . Suskind's book teaches you a lot. It's incredible what I've learned about perfumes, even about the technology of perfume making." His favorite, though, is Cervantes's *Don Quixote*, which he has read "five or six times, at least." And what of Cuban writers? Surely someone like himself, having "such a great love of literature," must also have close links with Cuban writers – asked Borge guilelessly. And the answer he received tells us a lot: "With some, but not many. . . . Because of my work . . . ; I'm a slave to it. . . . contact with writers hasn't been in the immediate sphere of my work. . . . I haven't been able to cultivate that, Tomás; my workload hasn't made that possible."[74]

Santiago de Cuba.
Nov 6 1940.
Mr. Franklin Roosevelt,
President of the United
States.

My good friend Roosevelt
I don't know very En-
glish, but I know as much
as write to you.
I like to hear the radio, and
I am very happy, because
I heard in it, that you will
be President for a new
(período)
I am twelve years old.
I am a boy but I think very
much, but I do not think
that I am writing to the

1 Letter from the (according to official sources) 14-year-old Fidel Castro to President Franklin D. Roosevelt: "I am twelve years old."

2 "Finca Mañacas:" Castro's birthplace near Birán in eastern Cuba. Photography is not welcomed.

3 The father: Ángel Castro.

4 The mother: Lina Ruz.

5 Fidel Castro's great model: José Martí. A statue in Cienfuegos.

6 The Havana palace of dictator Batista, later the Museum of the Revolution.

7 Fidel Castro in the 1950s.

8 Naty Revuelta with their newly born daughter Alina, 1956.

9 Fund-raising for the revolution at New York's Palm Garden, 1955.

10 Adversary Fulgencio Batista and his country. A view of the Sierra Maestra, 1958.

11 He started with just a few people: the guerrilla leader in 1957. Second from the left: Che Guevara. Kneeling in front of Fidel: his brother, Raúl.

12 A holy image around his neck, a gun in his hand: Fidel Castro in the Sierra, 1958.

13 January 8, 1959: the victor enters Havana. Left, wearing a hat: Camilo Cienfuegos.

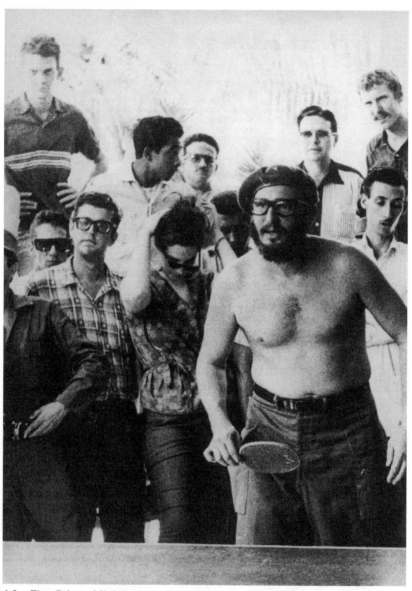

14 The Prime Minister playing table tennis, 1967.

15 The orator . . .

16 . . . and his audience.

17 Fidel Castro and Che Guevara, 1960.

18 A lifelong hero for women.

19 Visiting US Vice-President Richard Nixon, 1959.

20 After the missile crisis: with Nikita Khrushchev in Moscow, 1963.

21 With his brother, Raúl, 1975.

22 With Gabriel García Márquez in Havana, 1986.

23 At the summit of non-aligned nations in Havana, 1979.

24 An unusual outfit: in suit and tie at UNESCO, Paris, 1995.

25 A historic event at the Vatican, 1996: the Jesuit boarder Fidel Castro invites Pope John Paul II to Cuba.

26 Quo vadis, Cuba?

8

Alone against All

★

Exodus to Florida

On April 1, 1980, a bus crashed through the barrier outside the Peruvian embassy in the Havana district of Miramar. There was an exchange of gunfire between the Peruvian security guards and Cuban militiamen posted at the gate, one of whom was killed. The six people inside the vehicle asked for political asylum.

Castro was so incensed that he removed all further "protection" from the embassy. The news spread like wildfire that no one would be prevented from entering the grounds, and within five days 10,000 people were occupying nearly every square inch, some even perched on roofs and trees. A week after the original incident, US President Jimmy Carter intervened to declare: "We see the hunger of many people on that island to escape political deprivation of freedom and also [of] economic diversity. Our hearts go out to the almost 10,000 freedom-loving Cubans who entered . . . the Peruvian Embassy just within the week."[1] As the tension mounted, the Peruvian government showed no willingness to accept a single one of those wanting to leave Cuba, and in mid-April – evidently on the initiative of the United States – Costa Rican President Rodrigo Carazo offered to set up an air link to ferry the refugees to his country. *Granma* reacted to this scornfully on April 18: "To travel to the US, there is no need to make a stop in Costa Rica. It costs less and is quicker to travel directly to Key West, some 90 miles away."[2] Shortly afterwards, Castro got his interior minister to announce that anyone in the embassy grounds could go home, pack their bags and leave for wherever they liked. The port of Mariel, west of Havana, was opened specially for this purpose, and the authorities let it be known that boats could cross over from Florida to pick people up. Castro saw an opportunity to rid himself at a stroke of discontented *gusanos* (worms).

Two boats hurried across from Florida to pick up relatives. The next day there were dozens of boats, soon hundreds, and in the end thousands – an exodus of unexpected proportions. People flocked down with their families from all over the country, occasionally clashing in the streets of Havana with the Committees for the Defense of the Revolution (CDRs). Castro organized the propaganda offensive. On May 1, 1980, in a speech to a crowd of a million on "Revolution Square," he exclaimed: "In our country, we don't need those who don't have revolutionary genes, revolutionary blood, minds adapted to the idea of a revolution, and hearts adapted to the effort and heroism of a revolution. After all, those who lack these qualities are an insignificant part of the people."[3] He spoke of them as riff-raff, using not the Spanish word *canalla* but the German *lumpen*, which has become part of an international revolutionary language. Does it allude to Marx's concept of a "lumpenproletariat?" "The idea of sending boats to pick up the lumpen arose spontaneously in Florida. Then all we had to do was tell them that we wouldn't shoot at them because they weren't coming to make war, and that we would show them every courtesy."[4]

The United States, whose president, Jimmy Carter, had horrified his own officials by announcing on May 5 that the refugees would be "welcomed with open hearts and open arms," was now overwhelmed by the sudden rush. It is estimated that by the end of September, when Castro responded to US pressure and blocked the outflow, some 125,000 people had poured across from one port to the other. Among them, as Castro cynically remarked, were a number of "chicken thieves" for whom the prison gates had been thrown open; in fact, there were several thousand common criminals in their ranks. Numerous inmates of psychiatric institutions also found a new home in the United States. It was later discovered that as many as 26,000 *marielitos* (as they were called,

227

after the port of departure) had served prison sentences, many apparently for political reasons. But the figure included 4–5,000 serious criminals, who, soon after landing in the United States, found themselves back behind bars in the penitentiaries of Georgia, Louisiana, and Arkansas.

In the end, the "Mariel boatlift" was a dubious victory for each of the two heads of state. The public sense that Carter had ceded to Castro's pressure and been made to look small was a factor in his defeat at the hands of Ronald Reagan at the next presidential elections. Castro also managed to cause a blip in the career of another Democratic politician, for it was in the wake of a revolt by newly exported Cuban criminals at Fort Chaffee that future President Bill Clinton was voted out as governor of Arkansas in 1980.

It remains true, however, that even without the crooks and psychiatric inmates the influx of refugees was by no means as welcome as Washington outwardly showed. There were simply too many of them. Whereas, in March 1980, the US government had set a quota of 19,500 for the acceptance of Cuban refugees on grounds of political, racial, or religious persecution, those who had been crossing from Mariel had economic rather than political motives, and presented fewer occupational skills than the previous average. Furthermore, the United States had to deal at the same time with boatloads of refugees from Haiti, a Caribbean island hit by political instability. Worldwide attention to the issue meant that it was morally impossible to treat the two groups in different ways, and so both won the right to stay in the United States.

In the white-dominated community of Florida, this sudden influx led to growing social problems and a bitter struggle over jobs and housing, as well as to a rise in crime. This time, moreover, there were many black Afro-Cubans among the refugees, and they were viewed as competitors by blacks already living there. The Cuban exile community, in particular, was far from happy at the prospect of having to share the cake with so many unexpected relatives. True, none of Carter's political rivals in the Democratic Party or among the Republicans directly opposed acceptance of the Cubans, but there were unmistakable hints that the resources were not enough to integrate such a large number.

All these fears and worries were camouflaged, however, by the Cuban hardliners' media-effective reproach that Carter had cooperated with Castro by accepting everyone the enemy had thrown at him. In their view, Castro had emerged victorious over Carter and the United States.

That is not how things looked at first. Pictures of the exodus on the world's television screens caused Castro an undeniable loss of face, as it became clear that he had underestimated the degree of discontent among his citizens and the preparedness of many to pack up and go. One factor fueling rejection of the system had probably been the officially permitted visits to the island by Cuban exiles in the two years before the Mariel episode; the guests had left behind not only a good hundred million dollars in badly needed foreign currency, but also presents packed at home for their needy relatives. And they told a thousand and one fabulous tales about the glittering world not so far from the shores of Cuba, where milk and honey flowed and it seemed to be Christmas the whole year round.

This had its corrosive effect, and in the end Castro's familiar device of allowing people to leave the country, as a safety valve for domestic political tensions, led to an uncontrolled rush that no one had anticipated. Economically, the cost–benefit calculation did not work out, since the loss of skilled labor was so huge that it outweighed the additional foreign-currency revenue from relatives' visits. On the other hand, Castro had accepted a similar brain drain before, and he would put up with it again in the future.

The exodus of 1980 had a long pre-history in which the United States had served as a haven for political refugees from Cuba. It was there that one of the most prominent exiles, José Martí, had spent 1895 preparing the liberation war against the Spanish. And, on the eve of Castro's revolution on January 1, 1959, 125,000 Cubans were living in the United States, most of them awaiting the end of the Batista regime. Castro had numerous supporters and sympathizers among them who, despite official obstacles, gave him political, financial, and material assistance (including supplies of weapons). Some 85,000 of them returned to Cuba in the first year after the fall of the dictatorship, while just under 74,000 (mostly upper-class people or members of Bastista's repressive apparatus) left the island. In almost three years between 1960 and the missile crisis of October 1962, a further 196,000 – mainly from the middle classes – turned their backs on the revolution. Castro did not try to stop them. Subsequently the figure averaged 12,000 a year, before climbing again from 1965 as a result of political repression and mounting economic problems. At that time, 20,000 people are thought to have been in prison in Cuba for political reasons.[5]

In 1965, as ever more "illegal emigrants" made for Florida in small boats and inflated rubber tyres, Castro decided for the first time to handle things in the "Mariel" way, through what became known to Cubans as Operation Camarioca. On September 28 he announced that participation in the revolution was a voluntary matter; anyone who preferred to leave and had relatives in Florida could arrange for a boat to pick them up at Camarioca Harbor on the Varadero Peninsula. Within a month, some 5,000 people had taken up the offer and left for Florida. A few days later, faced with the sudden rush, President Johnson signed a new order lifting all restrictions on Cuban immigration: "I declare here this afternoon to the people of Cuba that those who seek refuge here in America will find it. The dedication of America to our traditions as an asylum for the oppressed is going to be upheld."[6] On November 6, the first US–Cuban agreement on emigration was signed, and by 1971 more than 260,000 people had flown across in a US-funded airlift. Permission was given only to those who had relatives in the United States, or men who were no longer of an age for military service, and anyone leaving automatically lost Cuban citizenship as well as all their personal possessions. Having registered on the waiting list, they were usually dismissed from their job, ordered to vacate their flat, and sent to work in agriculture.

Cuba's East European allies – especially representatives of the GDR – were horrified by Castro's opening of the route to Florida, which completely contradicted their own way of dealing with such matters. They were especially alarmed when he announced that 200,000 people had applied to emigrate, but the word in unofficial circles was that the figure was as high as half a million. There were even fears "that, by the end of the year [1966], the number of people wishing to emigrate might be so high that every fifth Cuban would be planning to leave the country."[7] In one of his confidential reports to the government in East Berlin, the ADN correspondent in Havana, outwardly a journalist, described Operation Camarioca and the emigration agreement with the United States as the "greatest error in Cuban internal politics," and criticized Castro for his unwillingness to "revise" it.[8] As if a more humane socialism prevailed in the GDR, the East German ambassador noted in a report to his superiors in mid-October 1965:

> In this context, the serious question arises as to why the Cuban Party does not instead fulfill its essential duty to offer all citizens . . . a clear perspective within socialism, and struggle to win over each individual through the method of persuasion. Here we again see the effect of the poorly differentiated class analysis and immaturity of the Cuban Party leadership. . . . There is also the question of the material damage that such a procedure might cause, the medical profession and the technical intelligentsia being just one case in point.[9]

Referring to a leading Communist from a South American country, the diplomat asked for it to be borne in mind that "this procedure on the part of the CP of Cuba is by no means calculated to make the Cuban example appear more effective in Latin America."

In a further letter some two weeks later, the ambassador wrote that the "Soviet, Czechoslovak, Polish, Hungarian, Mongolian and other comrades from socialist diplomatic missions have reached similar views to our own;" namely, that the "mass emigration" represents "a retreat in the face of imperialist propaganda, and a consequence or aspect of the inadequacy of the Cuban Party's work with people." He stressed that his interlocutors had "supported our Party's policy vis-à-vis West Germany and West Berlin" – a policy that required GDR soldiers to shoot at people trying to escape the country at its heavily guarded borders. He assured his superiors that he had had no trouble explaining this on the spot: "On questions directly concerning our own problems, we naturally always defend our Party's policy – there can be no doubt about that."[10] Around that time, Western diplomats and journalists heard of "a protest by the GDR ambassador to the Cuban foreign ministry" concerning its emigration policy. Yet, according to the ADN correspondent, "attempts to use the emigration operation as an argument against the GDR's anti-fascist defensive wall, and thus artificially to construct conflicts between Cuba and the GDR, . . . were of no avail."[11]

At first, Castro did not allow himself to be deflected by criticism from his socialist brothers. But the persistently high number of people seeking to leave Cuba, and the resulting loss of skilled labor, finally induced him to put an end to the "freedom flights" in April 1973. Castro reproached the Nixon government with trying to use its emigration propaganda to undermine the political system in Cuba. There were also critics inside the United States of the large-scale emigration from Cuba: exile circles took the position that it only shored up and stabilized the Castro regime. In any event, the number of emigration permits now sharply declined, and for most people the only way of leaving was to cross the open sea illegally. Between 1959 and 1980 (the year of the Peruvian embassy incident followed by Operation Mariel), a total of 800,000 people are estimated to have left the island.

As after Camarioca, the Mariel period also led to negotiations between the United States and Cuba to put the refugee problem on a stable footing. But it was not until four years later, in December 1984, that an agreement was finally reached whereby Cuba undertook to allow 3,000 political prisoners to leave for the USA and to take back 2,746 "chicken thieves" and "lumpens;" new visa regulations would in future enable up to 20,000 Cubans a year to travel to the USA. The agreement, which Cuban exiles saw as raising the Castro government to the status of a negotiating partner with the same rights as Washington, was nevertheless suspended by Castro just a few months later. This came in response to a new tightening of economic sanctions by the Reagan administration, which suddenly clamped down on tourist trips to Cuba after the number of US tourists traveling to the island had risen to 40,000 a year; the only exceptions would be for diplomats, journalists and scientists, and private individuals on urgent family business. At the same time, the amount of money that Cuban exiles were permitted to transfer to family members in Cuba was limited to $1,200 a year. The measures culminated in the approval of a broadcasting license for Radio Martí, a government-funded propaganda station set up by the US authorities at the instigation of the militant Cuban American National Foundation (CANF). Castro felt he had been cheated.

In November 1987 the "migration agreement" was reactivated, even though Castro had been unable to secure an end to the Radio Martí broadcasts. But since the United States, in the following years, handled the issuing of visas in a very dilatory manner, fewer than a third of the maximum of 20,000 Cubans a year actually received permission to leave. The evident aim of this was to raise indirectly the pressure inside Cuba. There were further occupations of diplomatic premises in 1990, including those of the Federal Republic of Germany, and more and more people chose the sea route to get away from the drabness of life at home. The next great exodus began in the summer of 1994, when the collapse of the Soviet bloc and a further tightening (since 1992) of the US embargo brought the economy to the brink of ruin. Between July and the end of September, nearly 35,000 panic-stricken Cubans made off on small boats, rafts, or rubber tyres. There are no reliable figures about the number who lost their lives at sea.

It has been estimated that, between Castro's victory and the end of the millennium, a total of more than a million Cubans left the island – that is, 10 to 15 percent of its present-day population. The majority of these settled down in the United States, especially Florida. In fact, the state is today politically controlled by Cuban exiles and their mostly Republican friends, who have family roots in Cuba. Miami has come to be known as "Havana North," while the name "Little Havana" remains more widely used for the area around Eighth Street, Calle Ocho. For generations a large number of Cuban exiles have lived there. Originally they came in the belief that Castro would fall within a few months and they would be able to return; but then that generation started dying off – often extremely embittered – while others assimilated and gradually turned into a second and third generation. Many young people no longer travel to the land of their parents and grandparents, especially if they have built a life for themselves in the United States and entered into family ties. Apparently only a half of their elders would now like to return to Cuba, and such a move becomes harder, the longer Castro holds out. The exiles have long since become an immigrant community.

What unites people in "Havana North" is the adversary in "Havana South." But there is no agreement among them about how he should be removed and what should come next. Still today, in the area around Calle Ocho, the only people who are welcome are those who express undying hatred of Castro, support the economic embargo and oppose any talks with the regime in Havana. Less militant opponents, who are prepared to consider some dialogue, do not have an easy time of it in these circles.

There have been repeated attempts to create some kind of a united front. Three days after the occupation of the Peruvian embassy in Havana, a National Convention took place between April 4 and 6, 1980, at Bayfront Park in Miami, attended by 400 delegates and 100 guests from various Cuban exile organizations. It set up a "Cuban Patriotic Council" that was supposed to unify the whole of the anti-Castro opposition, with Manuel Antonio Varona as its president. He had been involved in preparing the Bay of Pigs invasion, and belonged to the José Miró Cardona government set up by the CIA to replace Castro in the event of its success. In March 1961, acting as the CIA link to the American Mafia, he had taken delivery of the pills intended to kill off the Cuban revolutionary leader. But in the early eighties, when the multi-millionaire building contractor Jorge Mas Canosa founded his Cuban American National Foundation (CANF), he soon replaced the less presentable Tony Varona as Cuban "president in waiting." Later, the CANF too came under suspicion of involvement in terrorist operations against Cuba.

Since 1959 Miami had also been the center of subversion against the Castro regime. Here Cuban exiles worked intensively with the CIA, sometimes also with Mafiosi who had a score to settle with Castro for the loss of their cushy positions in Cuba. It has been estimated that the CIA hired as many as 12,000 agents among the Cuban exiles for covert operations against Castro's Cuba.[12] They composed the best-known terrorist outfits, with

234

imaginative, martial-sounding names such as Alpha 66, Omega 7, Abdala, Command Zero, El Condor, Cuban Power 76, Scorpion, and (an association of Bay of Pigs veterans) Brigade 2506, responsible for nearly all the assassination attempts and sabotage actions inside Cuba or against Cuban interests abroad. In July 1980, for instance, a background paper of the GDR ministry for state security drew up a long list of bomb attacks carried out by these organizations against Cuban offices in New York as well as in Europe.[13]

Whether in the circles around Lee Harvey Oswald (Kennedy's ostensible assassin) and his own killer, Jack Ruby, or in connection with the break-in at the Democratic Party's Watergate headquarters during the 1972 election campaign, or after the bomb attack that killed 73 people on a Cuban commercial aircraft soon after take-off from Barbados in October 1976, or in a series of other bombings, murders and attempted murders, we again and again come across the same Cuban exiles and CIA agents acting in one way or another as wire-pullers or actual operators. The list includes the former Cuban paediatrician Orlando Bosch; CIA agent Frank Sturgis (who fought under cover in the Sierra Maestra and was later Marita Lorenz's "control"); the Cuban exiles' former link to the Mafia, Tony Varona; the CIA's coordinator of the Bay of Pigs invasion, Howard Hunt; the head of the CIA's "Task Force W," William Harvey, responsible for attempts to assassinate Castro; and a number of others.

A situation report drawn up by the GDR ministry for state security "on the counter-revolutionary anti-Cuban terror scene, with special reference to the 'Alpha 66' terror organization" reached the following conclusion in May 1982: "Analysis of the individuals comprising 'Alpha 66' reveals close collaboration with the CIA. According to information from fraternal Cuban bodies, as well as to reports in the Western press, individual members have been recruited as CIA agents." In connection with the murder in Washington in September 1976 of Salvador Allende's former foreign minister, Orlando Letelier, the situation report further claimed that Alpha 66 "and other counter-revolutionary anti-Cuban organizations had planned and executed the operation in close collaboration with the DINA (the Chilean secret police)."

The president of Alpha 66 had "close links with the Chilean junta" and received "funding from there." The organization also had at its disposal "a wide network of safe houses in the United States, Latin and South America, and to some extent also in Europe. . . . It was known to have collaborated closely with the neofascist 'Fuerza Nueva' group in Spain."[14]

A founder member of Alpha 66, Eloy Gutiérrez Menoyo, had once been a guerrilla companion of Castro's and Guevara's. When Communist influence over political developments increased after the victory of the revolution, however, he broke with his old comrades and recruited the "Second National Front" in the Escambray region in central Cuba. Until the middle of the sixties, this counter-revolutionary guerrilla band managed to keep Castro's revolutionary armed forces busy. But Gutiérrez Menoyo himself was captured in 1964 and spent the next 22 years in jail. In the mid-eighties, when Castro eventually allowed the physically broken man to go into exile, Gutiérrez Menoyo did not join any of the radical anti-Castro groups – as he had every reason to do – but founded as a counterweight to the CANF a moderate group called "Cambio Cubano" (Cuban Change), which called for an end to confrontation and a dialogue with Havana.

Rectificación and perestroika

On January 11, 1980, Celia Sánchez, the woman at Castro's side since the days in the Sierra Maestra, died of lung cancer at the age of 59. The doctor's daughter from the little town of Manzanillo, in Castro's home province of Oriente, was five years older than Castro and from 1959 until her death was thought of as "mother of the nation." But she was more than that. After Castro, in 1957, took her from the plains to be with him in the mountains, she became (and would remain) the most important person in his life, forming together with his Alsatian dog "Guardién" a kind of family. In 1959 her small flat on Calle 11 in Miramar became his place of study and refuge, at times when he needed to flee his headquarters on the top floor of the Habana Libre (the rebaptized Hilton hotel) or the monstrous Palace of the Revolution that had been built as a ministry in Batista's time.

Throughout, she organized Castro's everyday life behind the scenes. She had more influence than anyone else in his milieu on political life and the decisions he made; and she screened him so effectively that, after his mother's death in August 1963, he virtually ceased to be a private individual for the outside world. Whether the source was a secret service or someone wanting to appear important, all the stories about his occasional affairs, a legitimate son, seven illegitimate children and innumerable grand-children, good or bad relations with his siblings, as well as various personal habits, preferences, hobbies and disorders, usually were and remained nothing more than rumor. What has been authen-ticated is that relations broke down with his younger sister Juana (who left the country in 1964), as they did with his daughter Alina. Juana Castro has pulled her brother to pieces in all her various public statements, describing him as nothing other than a "despot." Nor has Alina had many good words to say about him; it emerges from the bitter memoirs of this former model, several times married and several times divorced, that she never came to terms personally or socially with her role as daughter of the Máximo Líder, who for his part did not exactly prove a caring father. In 1998 she went to live in Spain.

No outsider knows whether Celia Sánchez was more than a rigorous companion and a loyal comrade. She knew of Castro's love affairs, and many a woman learned to fear her power. But Naty Revuelta, Alina's mother whom Celia Sánchez kept on the sidelines and Castro sent off to Paris for a time in 1964, survived her into the new millennium, living in her house in Havana and sticking by Castro and his embattled revolution. Celia Sánchez may have been Cuba's and Castro's "First Lady," but after divorcing Mirta Díaz-Balart he appeared to be married only to the revolution. On the other hand, he had free and steady relationships with women, such as the eight-month romance with German captain's daughter Marita Lorenz or, immediately after-wards, with the "dark rose of Bogota," Gloria Gaitán, daughter of Colombian opposition leader, Jorge Eliécer Gaitán, whom

Castro much admired and who was murdered soon after they met in 1948. It was, as she later said, a "romantic friendship."

At roughly the same time, the Argentinean child psychiatrist Lidia Vexel-Robertson claims to have had "an intense but proper romance in the Hispanic tradition" with Castro, which lasted for a number of months.[15] An attractive woman, who worked at the Mount Sinai Hospital in New York, she first met Castro in 1959 at an embassy reception during his trip to the USA, where he was accompanied by Marita Lorenz (though he presented her as the girlfriend of his bodyguard Jesús Yáñez Pelletier). When rumors of a marriage began to circulate, Celia Sánchez is supposed to have put an end to the relationship by threatening "drastic measures" – at least that is the version that Bourne attributes to Vexel-Robertson. There is also a suspicion, however, that Castro set Celia up to do this, because he felt under too much pressure. Vexel-Robertson later married another *barbudo* and returned to live with him in the United States.[16]

Apart from Naty Revuelta, with whom he took up again for a while and never completely broke contact, the years following the revolution also saw Castro begin a steady relationship with Dalia Soto del Valle from Trinidad, an old colonial city on the south coast of Cuba. She too was a beauty from the former upper classes, and it is said that Castro had five sons with her. Alina claims that long before the revolution, in 1948 or thereabouts when he was still together with Mirta Díaz-Balart, he fathered another son with a passing acquaintance called Amparo, during a trip to the East. This child, Jorge Ángel, would thus have come into the world at more or less the same time as Fidelito.

In later years, people in Havana also heard of a relationship with a dancer from Tropicana or a beautiful dark-haired interpreter. And, even in the fortieth year of the revolution, when stories were circulating in the foreign press that he was infirm, a conversation partner in Havana was able to report that Castro was seeing a mulatto girl who was as pretty as a picture. People like such stories, but no one knows what is true and what is invention. "Really, the only thing I keep to myself is my private life," he said at the age of 65 in a conversation with Tomás Borge. "I don't have anything more, and it's something. I think that a person's private life shouldn't be used for publicity or politics – as is so commonly done in that capitalist world . . . – I've maintained these views throughout my life."[17]

Earlier in life, he was a passionate skin-diver and deep-sea fisherman: once, at the beginning of the revolution, he won a cup for the largest catch together with Ernest Hemingway, who owned a house near Havana (now a museum) similar to the one in Key West. It is known that Castro likes to cook, which does not exactly fit the picture one has of him. "The best thing is not to boil either shrimp or lobster," he told Frei Betto, "because boiling water reduces the substance and the taste and toughens the flesh. . . . Five minutes of broiling is enough for shrimp. Lobster takes eleven minutes to bake or six minutes on a skewer over hot coals. Baste only with butter, garlic and lemon. Good food is simple food."[18]

A meal for him always included good wine and then a cigar, his favorite being the Corona Especial with the brand name "Cohiba" that he himself introduced after the revolution. For a long time this was available only to a privileged circle of smokers, and many politicians would receive a box from him for Christmas. Nowadays "Cohiba" is freely obtainable: it counts alongside "Trinidad" and "Robaina," both also Cuban, as one of the best and most expensive brands in the world. He told the New York magazine *Cigar Aficionado*, in an interview in summer 1994:

> I should explain that. I got used to smoking in my early years. My father was a cigar smoker, and he really appreciated a fine cigar. . . . I remember when I was a teenager in high school. I was about 15 years old. I had lunch with my father when he presented me with a cigar. So he introduced me to cigars and he also taught me to drink wine. . . . He liked wines from Rioja. I always smoked cigars and, on very few occasions, cigarettes. But I . . . was always a cigar smoker . . . until I was about 59 years old.[19]

He enjoyed smoking cigars for 44 years – except up in the Sierra Maestra, although even there he could not do without tobacco altogether. In May 1958, when the rebels were surrounded during Batista's great offensive, he wrote desperately from his headquarters to Celia Sánchez: "I have no tobacco, I have no wine, I have nothing. A bottle of rosé wine, sweet and Spanish, was left in Bismarck's house, in the refrigerator. Where is it?"[20] He finally gave up on August 26, 1985, during an anti-smoking campaign for which he wanted to serve as a model. Since then, he is said not to have smoked even in secret. His love of cigars no longer goes beyond occasional sniffing or finger-rolling.

Castro likes to spend weekends in a simple beach house, together with friends such as Colombian novelist Gabriel García Márquez. It is not known whether he also sometimes unwinds at the farm in Birán where he was born. The remote property, set in an idyllic landscape, is well maintained and watched over by men in uniform, who politely but firmly send foreign visitors on their way. Castro is said to have kept his old habit of spending the night in different places, either in Havana or elsewhere on the island. Before the Pope's visit to Cuba, a bon mot was doing the rounds in answer to the question of where he slept at night: "Everywhere – like Jesus Christ!" But usually at night, when a column of three old bullet-proof Mercedes limousines with heavily armed guards drive him home through empty streets, the destination is a complex of government houses screened off from the outside world in the diplomatic area of Siboney, in West Havana. García Márquez has a similar "guesthouse" at his disposal nearby, for when he is in the country, and Castro likes to drop in and discuss matters with him until the early hours of the morning. The writer is one of the few personal friends who have remained, as well as being one of those whose opinion Castro values. His influence is so great that he often plays a mediating role in relation to political prisoners, as he did at the time of the Padilla affair.

Celia Sánchez's death in 1980 tore a great hole not only in the life of the then 63-year-old Castro, but also in the Cuban leadership nomenklatura. For a long time, the Máximo Líder appeared completely devastated to those around him. Then, on the Moncada anniversary on July 26, one of the two female participants in the attack on the Batista Barracks – Haydée Santamaría – took her own life. The director of the Casa de Las Americas – the publishing house often in the firing line of cultural bureaucrats and intellectuals – was said to have had personal problems, in that her husband Armando Hart, also a pro-Castro revolutionary from the earliest days, wanted to separate from her. But the death of these two women, who, together with Raúl Castro's wife Vilma Espín, embodied female emancipation under the revolution, was rather like a bad omen.

Soon the struggle for survival was again breaking out on all fronts. When Ronald Reagan took over as US president in January 1981, the promising (if inconsistent) detente initiated by his Democratic predecessor Jimmy Carter came to an end. The trade embargo was further tightened, and Washington declined to renew a fishing agreement signed by the two countries in 1977. Because of Cuba's support for the Sandinist revolution in Nicaragua and the guerrilla struggle in El Salvador, the Reagan administration even considered for a while a total sea blockade of the island.

In October, Moscow succeeded in scoring an own goal on the little Caribbean island of Grenada, when the ambitious Soviet-backed finance minister, Bernard Coard, ousted the popular prime minister (and friend of Castro's), Maurice Bishop. In the ensuing power struggle, Bishop was killed by soldiers who had sided with Coard. Then the United States used the putsch as the pretext for an invasion, and on October 26 just under 9,000 US soldiers landed on the island. At the airport, the first-ever direct military confrontation took place between US and Cuban forces.

At the time of the landing, there were nearly 800 Cubans on the island: 636 construction workers employed at the airport, 43 military advisers, and the rest diplomats. Of these, 24 were killed during the invasion, and 642 were taken prisoner and displayed to the world in a camp surrounded by barbed wire. All the White House claims about at least 1,100 professional Cuban soldiers, who were supposed to have built arms depots and planned to take over the island, soon turned out to be untrue and had to be officially withdrawn.

Despite the loss of Grenada as an ally, things had been changing in Cuba's favor in Latin America. Since 1977, when the OAS (with a US supporting vote) loosened restrictions on contacts, the island state had managed to break out of isolation. Diplomatic relations were restored with nearly all Latin American countries, and the arc of cooperation in the first half of the eighties stretched from offers of military assistance for the right-wing Argentinean regime during the "anti-colonialist" Falklands War,[21] to both civilian and military aid for the Sandinistas in Nicaragua and the left-wing FMLN liberation movement in El Salvador. "When we were asked for teachers after the victory of the revolution in Nicaragua, 29,000 volunteers came forward," Castro proudly reported. "At the beginning [of 1959], we didn't even have enough doctors to send to the interior of our own country. Today we have doctors in 25 Third World countries – more than 1,500 doctors are working in the Third World."

Cuba also established links with the major continental economies, such as Argentina, Brazil, Mexico, and Venezuela, which in turn offered it loans. During those years the Third World generally was sinking ever deeper into a debt crisis vis-à-vis the First World. In Latin America, this was so dramatic that the eighties are thought of in retrospect as the "wasted decade." Only Cuba seemed to be doing better – for the time being. "In these years of crisis, 1982, 1983 and 1984, . . . the economies of Latin American nations as a whole declined by 9 percent while Cuba's grew by 24; this is for the 1982–84 period. Last year our economy grew by 7 to 8 percent, during 1984."[22] In the seventies and early eighties, even the sugar harvests were so good that between 1981 and 1985 Cuban economic experts were looking forward optimistically to the future. Given the stable prospects, Castro allowed only a cautious opening to the market in the mid- to late seventies. From 1976, private individuals were again allowed to offer their services as electricians, plumbers, hairdressers, motor mechanics, and so on – a course followed up in 1980 with the authorization of private farmers' markets and housebuilders.

The positive economic data for the first half of the eighties were not immune from crisis. After all, although the US blockade had been in place since 1962 and Cuba had been a member of Comecon since 1972, figures produced by Julio Carranza Valdés at Cuba's American Studies Center (CEA) have shown that "right into the seventies approximately 40 percent of Cuba's foreign trade was with capitalist countries."[23]

The Cuban economy was therefore hard hit when the Reagan administration stepped up its embargo, and when a collapse of world sugar prices, from 27 cents a pound in 1980 to 4 cents a pound in 1985 (the lowest in real terms since the thirties depression), dramatically reduced foreign currency earnings.[24] Neither the good harvests, which in the first half of the eighties averaged 7.5 million tons, nor the sizeable Soviet sugar price subsidies could come near to compensating for this drop.

The slump in oil prices after 1985, combined with a rise in the dollar exchange-rate, had similar effects. For, until then, Cuba had been able to obtain some $500 million, or a good 40 percent of its foreign currency, by reselling up to a quarter of the 12 million tons of crude oil that it imported each year from the Soviet Union.

As the terms of trade changed, Cuba's debt to the West climbed from $2.8 billion in 1983 to $3.6 billion in 1985 and more than $6 billion in 1987, while with the Eastern bloc it reached $19 billion, or its peso equivalent, by 1987. When Cuba tried to renegotiate its debt in summer 1986 at the Paris Club, the Americans pressed for the application to be turned down, and the island suddenly found itself with its back to the wall – especially as the repayment of billions of dollars in loans from the Soviet Union was due to begin that same year. Communist Cuba, which had long had a good reputation in Latin America for debt servicing, now saw no option but to declare a moratorium on repayments, which in turn led indirectly to a freeze on Western loans and a further exacerbation of the country's plight.[25]

Castro, whose credibility and authority had suffered from his justification of the Soviet invasion of Afghanistan, responded to the worsening situation by making the Third World debt crisis the central theme of his foreign policy in the mid-1980s. All the levers of his propaganda machine were used to mobilize world opinion, and his reputation in the Third World shot up when he made it clear: "I think this is the key problem of our time."[26] Since Washington had anyway shut him out of the world economic system dominated by the industrial countries, he was able to address the North–South problem in a direct and open manner, and to press the kind of demands that state leaders dripfed by the North could not afford to raise. The shaky social stability of most developing countries was indeed dependent on their major lenders, especially the World Bank and the International Monetary Fund, for which Cuba was just a white speck on the map. According to official statistics, in just the first half of the 1980s the Third World transferred to the industrial nations a total of $325 billion in interest and $321 billion in debt repayment.[27] Latin America's accumulated debt alone – overwhelmingly to North American banks – was put at roughly $350 billion.

Castro took a fighting stance in his conversations with Betto: "This is totally untenable. . . . Mathematics shows that [the debt] can't be paid." Emphatically demanding "total cancellation of the debt – both capital and interest," he justified this by the history of relations between the First and Third Worlds: "Our countries have been and continue to be plundered." He then proposed a reform of international monetary policy:

> An essential aspect of our thesis is that the . . . rich and powerful creditor states assume responsibility for the debt to their own banks, allocating 12 percent of their military spending – which now amounts to $1 trillion a year – for this purpose. . . . The Third World [would have] an additional $300 billion purchasing power each year as a result of the cancellation of the foreign debt and the establishment of a system of fair international economic relations.[28]

He warned that the USA and IMF, with their "selfish, absurd policy," might provoke a social explosion in the Third World. And, speaking as a statesman – rather different from his former image as a professional revolutionary – he considered that social upheavals would carry the Third World back rather than genuinely forward. "I'd rather have an orderly way out of the crisis . . . than an uncontrollable explosion. Even more important than one, two, three, four or five revolutions, at this point, is to come out of this crisis, to establish the New International Economic Order and to create the conditions for development."[29]

Castro's involvement in the debt debate was, however, increasingly driven by economic difficulties inside Cuba, which had to face not only the US embargo but ideologically motivated discrimination on the part of the World Bank, IMF, and other financial organizations and private banks. But it also had itself to blame. Since the seventies – as in the early sixties – Cubans had been living and consuming beyond their means; they had spent scarce reserves of foreign currency or loan money to pay for too many imports. Meanwhile the productivity of Cuban firms had continually declined: outlays had risen but output fallen. A swollen bureaucracy worked inefficiently, corruption was spreading, private farmers' markets and small firms allowed the profit motive, envy and class contradictions to reemerge. The common good took second place, as material incentives prevailed over what was left of moral ones.

Castro was disappointed and furious with the way things were going. In 1985 he ditched the new Five-Year Plan and kicked those responsible for it out of their jobs, because the figure work was based on credit and on income that belonged to the realm of fantasy. At the National Assembly in early January, the Cuban leader angrily complained as he had in the sixties that "a sectorial spirit has reigned in all the organizations, in all the ministries."[30] Instead of a plan for everyone, everyone was planning for himself. JUCEPLAN, the central planning authority that had operated since 1960 in accordance with the Moscow model, was frozen out of the picture, and the quinquennial congress of the Communist Party, the body that normally approved the Five-Year Plan and future targets, was postponed until February 1986. Castro set up a special coordinating group of his own to formulate a new plan, a cost-cutting budget very different from those of the past. When the congress finally took place in 1986, it decided on major new measures to steer the economy onto more viable paths; it launched a campaign in this spirit under the title *Rectificación de los errores*.

The Spanish word *rectificación*, like the rather more formal English "rectification," carries a sense of "correction," "improvement", or "reformation." In Moscow, Mikhail Gorbachev had been general secretary of the CPSU since March 1985, and what *perestroika* (or "restructuring") was to him *rectificación* was to Castro. However, the common features did not go much beyond this rough terminological equivalence in respect of a new policy. Castro understood by *rectificación* a consolidation of the old, a "re-Cubanization" of the revolution, whereas Gorbachev meant *perestroika* to denote a radically new departure.

Thus in May 1986, for example, Castro put an end to the limited reforms of 1976 that had allowed individuals to provide services and to set up street stalls on a market basis, as well as the measures of 1980 that had cleared the way for private farmers' markets. At that time Gorbachev was moving in the opposite direction, toward the introduction by stages of a "regulated market economy." Castro wanted to go back to orthodox Marxist-Leninist principles, to central planning and control; Gorbachev aimed at further decentralization and enterprise autonomy, gradually involving partial integration into the Western capitalist system. While Gorbachev appeared in large parts of the world as the bright new hero of the Soviet Union, and even won growing sympathy inside Cuba, Castro forcefully counterposed the myth and egalitarian austerity associated with the dead hero Che Guevara and his time.[31] "Perestroika," the *New York Times* quoted him as saying in 1989, "is another man's wife. I don't want to get involved."[32]

Since 1959 Castro had repeatedly given the order for "corrections" – always under direct or indirect pressure from Moscow. After the collapse of Che Guevara's great leap forward into industrialization, he had to beat a retreat into sugar monoculture; the failure of the 10 million tons harvest in 1970 eventually forced him into a Moscow-style decentralization of the Cuban economy and a delegation of authority, responsibility, and influence, hence a partial loss of his own scope for control. The rectification campaign, however, did not involve such a bending to the Kremlin's model for the Communist world. Rather, Castro used it as an opportunity to free himself from Moscow, and to breathe new life into the original fighting spirit of the revolution. "What has made us powerful and invincible in the face of economic and political aggression and military threat?" he asked in July 1986 at a conference on enterprise management. And he gave the answer himself: "Morale, an unselfish spirit of social altruism: that was the raw material that made our people. It is more important to safeguard the consciousness of workers and act honestly than to meet the plan."[33]

Castro believed that a recentralization of economic processes could strengthen control over production and performance, check sloppiness and mismanagement, raise productivity in the state economy, rebuild social equality, and overcome the crisis. In line with Che Guevara's teaching on the "new man," moral incentives would once more have pride of place over material incentives – or, in translation, since resources were no longer sufficient to meet the expectations of consumption and social benefits that had grown in recent years, it was necessary to produce more than ever for lower levels of income and welfare.

For Cubans, the reforms begun in the mid-eighties were the most drastic they had experienced, because it was becoming clear that – although the problems facing Moscow and Havana were qualitatively the same and differed at most only in scale – they had reached the parting of the ways. With his conservative turn, Castro suddenly ended the limited opening to the market and took from his fellow-countrymen an element of freedom and *joie de vivre* that had been won through great effort. This led the *New York Times* to label him a "fossil Marxist," while in the eyes of its columnist William Safire he was the "Ceauşescu of the Caribbean."[34] Where others saw elements of a market as an opportunity to guarantee a basic food supply that was never secure in the planning model, Castro laid greater emphasis than ever on the danger of ideological divisions and creeping disintegration of the system (and therefore of his own power). With an eye on events in Eastern Europe and reactions to them in the West, he began to toy with the concept of "inflexible" socialism. Shortly after the fall of the Berlin Wall, *Granma* quoted him as saying: "Now there are two types of socialists, two types of communists: good and bad ones, as defined by imperialism. . . . Those who do not submit to imperialism . . . they call inflexible. Long live inflexibility."[35]

To follow Gorbachev and expand the private sector would, in Castro's view, lead Cuba into chaos, so unprepared organizationally and mentally were both the population and the state apparatus. It would be necessary to dismantle the Cuban Revolution and build a completely new political system virtually overnight, creating a highly explosive vacuum at the center of the tense relationship between Cuba and Florida. To expect that of Castro and his leadership would indeed have been politically naive, or even irresponsible.

Castro soon gave a glimpse of the direction he wanted to take. The authorization of private services and private farmers' markets had, he said, "created a class of newly rich who are doing as they please."[36] He accused certain independent farmers of making 50,000 to 60,000 pesos (1 peso = 1 dollar) from a one-hectare field of garlic. At that time, it was known that there were "1,800 millionaires in Cuba and nearly five times as many with more than half a million pesos, most of whom wanted to leave Cuba."[37] These people had sown among the population traditionally "capitalist attitudes," such as idleness, self-interest, and materialism. Castro hit out at enterprise managers who, "dressed up as capitalists but without capitalist efficiency," conspired with their employees to deceive the state – for example, by lowering output targets so that the plan could be easily fulfilled and earnings increased through extra bonuses.

Castro described in exaggerated terms how many regularly earned money in their sleep. A manager might say to a worker: "Sleep on the floor and I'll pay you extra for abnormal conditions."[38] Until the mid-eighties, when the "rectification" process was introduced, output targets were indeed so often reduced that nearly every Cuban worker was easily capable of fulfilling them four or five times over. "Although we recognize that there is room for bonuses under socialism," Castro explained, "they must be the result of good work . . . not because of trumped-up profits."[39] In all sectors people were busy lining their own pockets. Products and spare parts were stolen from state enterprises, sold on the sly or taken for use at home; good-quality agricultural produce landed on the counters of private farmers' markets, while poor-quality stuff was traded in the state sector; construction material and machinery disappeared and ended up in private housebuilding; workers tried to arrange early retirement so that they could use their pension to set up a private business. Castro was not afraid to denounce shortcomings all over the country, and exposed to ridicule officials such as those at the MINCONS (Construction Ministry): "[If you] appeal to the MINCONS and say to them . . . please build a day-care centre in Guanabacoa because there's a new factory . . . MINCONS couldn't build a single day-care centre, not one!" Just to make the request "was enough to make them faint." And he mockingly suggested how the comrades there might answer: "How can you ask such a terrible thing, to build a day-care centre in Guanabacoa with all the commitments we already have and all the projects that we never finish?"[40]

It was against this background that Castro eventually announced: "We're rectifying all those things – and there are many that strayed from the revolutionary spirit, from revolutionary work, revolutionary virtue, revolutionary effort, revolutionary responsibility." "Rectification" for him meant "revolution within the Revolution," a move against those who were negating "Che's ideas, revolutionary thought, style, spirit and example."[41] On the twentieth anniversary of Guevara's death, the Cuban propaganda machine presented the ideological course correction associated with *rectificación* as a revival of the revolutionary idealism of the sixties.

Previously, any return to dogmatic positions had occurred when decisive economic measures or political changes were about to happen, and when it seemed essential to close ranks to keep the revolution on course. The state and Party leadership handed down from above the ideological framework within which the *rectificación* was to be interpreted over the following years. It was thought necessary to keep a tight rein on society, since the population was being asked to swallow things which, in Western societies too, would hardly be accepted without grumbling or revolt. Abolition of the popular farmers' markets was just one measure in an austerity program which stretched into every sphere of the economy, and which, on closer inspection, by no means always corresponded to a strictly Marxist definition of purity.

Boston sociologist Susan Eckstein writes:

In sum, "rectification" in practice diverged from and at times contradicted the rhetoric of the campaign. While assigning new life to Marxist-Leninist and Guevarist moral principles, the government and Party implemented certain reforms and tolerated practices of the preceding period that involved market features, that undermined revolutionary and prerevolutionary won gains, and that led living standards to drop.[42]

The urgent need to balance the state budget left Castro with little choice. Thus, the problems of socialist Cuba – and many of the ways of tackling them – resembled those to be found in capitalist Third World countries. As Eckstein points out, "many other Third World governments implemented neoliberal economic reforms in response to similar fiscal crises at the time."[43]

One outcome of the restructuring of Cuba's state economy was a change in social standards as rapid and extensive as the kind familiar from neoliberal performance-oriented societies. In order to boost the efficiency of the system, decisions were taken to increase work targets, to link bonuses more closely to output, and to punish abuses. Castro himself called into question a number of social gains, eventually enlisting the support of the trade unions, with the result that there were no longer unconditional guarantees of job security or wage levels. Promotion no longer came automatically with length of service, but also depended on workers' skills and qualifications. Pay was related to output, and average incomes even declined slightly during this period. To cut down on the extravagant and overpowerful bureaucracy, nearly 23,000 posts in state and enterprise administration were eliminated in the course of 1988. Although officially there was no unemployment, it was actually running at 6 percent. In future, when manpower was short, it would be permissible and indeed necessary for workers to perform tasks outside the narrow sphere for which they were qualified. *Multioficio* – more or less, "multiservice" – became the magic formula through which bottlenecks were supposed to be overcome.

The housing shortage was still a major problem in the eighties. Although in 1982 the government again allowed the construction of private housing, the unsatisfied demand rose sharply throughout the country between 1971 and 1985 – from 755,000 to 888,000 units. In the capital the situation was described as "explosive." "The collapse of more houses in the old town is to be expected in the event of heavy rainfall; 56,000 people are currently living in hostel accommodation," the GDR embassy reported to East Berlin in 1987.[44] Because of the continuing drought, the "supply of drinking water is also a growing problem. In some localities, all of it has to be delivered by tankers. There are plans for expensive drilling – down at least 100 meters – to open new wells." At the same time in the eighties, the number of nursery school places was 20,000 short of requirements.

To bring some immediate relief, Castro revived the so-called "microbrigades" and "construction brigades" from the 1970s, which worked on a piece-rate plus bonus system from 12 to 15 hours a day. The "microbrigades" were made up of students, school-leavers, pensioners, and housewives, while the "construction brigades" recruited fairly well-paid and ideologically unobjectionable "model workers" from other enterprises as a kind of "rapid deployment force" on the socialist building-site front. In 1990 up to as many as 40,000 people belonged to this prestigious vanguard of the working class, roughly 1 percent of the country's 4-million labor force; some brigades had more than 1,000 members. The conditions they enjoyed were special in every sense: they lived in superior housing, received better food, could buy luxury goods on favorable terms – and, above all, earned higher pay, up to 60 percent more than the average monthly wage of 185 pesos.

Workers who did not belong to one of the brigades were called upon to do voluntary overtime. In 1987, for example, some 400,000 men and women responded to the Party's appeal for "forty hours of voluntary work on community projects," eventually putting in a total of 20 million extra hours. Two years later, more than 2 million workers obeyed the call to work a "Red Sunday" without extra pay, on the occasion of the seventieth anniversary of the Russian October Revolution and the Sixteenth Congress of the Cuban Trade Union Federation, the CTC.

While Castro hit out at capitalist attitudes inside the country, the need for foreign currency led him to seek alliances with the ideological devil in the form of joint ventures between Cuban state enterprises and foreign corporations. Companies were set up at home and abroad with Western participation: Cubatabaco,

Caribsugar, Cubanacán, Gaviota, Cubapak, Cimex, Banco Financiero and others, concentrating on biotechnology (where Cuba played a major world role), tobacco, and, above all, tourism (especially the magnificent beaches of the Varadero Peninsula). The Panama-registered Cimex, involved in the tourist industry in 17 different countries, was the largest of the joint companies: it was associated with 12 corporate partners, and had more than 48 subsidiaries. Gaviota, founded in 1988, specialized in high-level tourism and came under Raúl Castro's defense ministry. The development of tourism as a source of foreign currency increased the number of people visiting the island by 150 percent in the course of the eighties, until it reached more than 320,000 in the year 1990. (The figure was scheduled to reach 2 million by the end of the millennium, bringing in more revenue from abroad than any other sector of the economy.) But all the new efforts to earn foreign currency were unable to offset the losses resulting from lower prices on world commodity markets. Cuba therefore had to keep cutting back its imports from Western countries, and against his will Castro found that he was more dependent than ever on the Soviet Union and the Eastern bloc. In 1986, the launch year for both *rectificación* and *perestroika*, more than 86 percent of Cuba's foreign trade was with other Comecon countries.

The encrusted bureaucracy also got a taste of the new dynamic born of necessity. In order to create the right conditions for the rectification campaign, Castro broke up old structures, fired incompetent officials, made personnel changes everywhere from the Central Committee to the heads of ministries, and embarked on a major rejuvenation of the apparatus. In elections to the Party's leading bodies, at the congress held in February 1986, sweeping changes were introduced under the slogan "Renewal or Death." A total of 40 percent of those elected to the Central Committee, and 50 percent of the new Politbureau, had never served on those bodies before.[45] Castro wanted to take account of the fact that a half of Cuba's population of 10 million had been born since the revolution, and another way he showed this was by taking 20 well-trained members of the Communist Youth (UJC) to work as advisers by his side. This constantly replenished reservoir would also provide him with his future ministers – one being the young paediatrician Carlos Lage Dávila, who was later made responsible for planning economic policy and helped lead the country into the new millennium as Castro's deputy in the Council of State. The up-and-coming revolutionaries chosen by Castro traveled the country in his company or on his behalf, to track down and rectify serious irregularities.

Although Cuba rolled back the private sector just as Gorbachev's Soviet Union was giving it a boost, market instruments were deployed in both countries to overcome the crisis. The difference was that in the one case the state itself kept charge of those instruments, while in the other it handed them over to the free market. Cubans were not spared neoliberal shock therapy – but it was ordered not by their own government but by erstwhile friends and allies. The Cuban media spelled out more and more clearly for its viewers the negative consequences that Gorbachev's reforms and the worsening economic and political crisis in the Soviet Union were having for the social security of the population there, as well as the knock-on effects for Cuba itself. Cubans learned that they could expect from Soviet-style liberalization not a higher standard of living but chaos and unemployment. They could picture to themselves that the kind of economic and political transformation which would follow the mass return of exiles from Miami would in all probability be far less peaceful than the changes in the Eastern bloc. This helps to explain why the magic words "perestroika" and "democracy" lost a lot of their force among the Cuban population.

In fact, perestroika was only part of a dual political concept; the other part was *glasnost,* or "openness." Once again Castro's understanding of the term was different from that of the Soviet general secretary. In Cuba too "we have glasnost," he said in 1988 in an interview for the US television channel NBC. "We have always had it. No party in the world has been more self-critical than the Communist Party of Cuba. None. Examine our history and you will see glasnost on a large scale."[46] But in Cuba the word "glasnost" was equated with an "opening" not in the sense of the Spanish word *apertura,* but at most with *sinceridad,* or frankness. It was openness behind closed doors, and in the limited space of ideological principles that had already been laid down.

This was also true for intellectuals, although they were encouraged to take part in the rectification and to advance criticisms of the political stagnation and bureaucratic inefficiency. "Whereas Soviet *glasnost* had opened up a Pandora's box of demands that threatened to undermine the fragile stability of the USSR, the Cuban version, if it could be called by the same name, was a decidedly controlled and limited affair," wrote Sebastian Balfour.[47] The controlled character of the *rectificación*, and the fact that it never led, as in Eastern Europe, to street power and the fall of the Communist regime, was not only due to the ubiquitous presence of Cuba's state security. It was also the result of a basic ideological unanimity in Cuba about the hard times ahead.

In a speech in Havana on the thirtieth anniversary of the Cuban Revolution, at the beginning of January 1989, Castro still officially dismissed speculation about growing political differences between Cuba and the Soviet Union. At the same time, however, he made it quite clear that he intended to stick to his course.

> What I can assure you . . . is that the revolution is not going to change. I think the secret of this revolution is having been loyal to principles from start to finish, having been loyal for thirty years and being willing to continue that way for another thirty or hundred years. . . . There is only one honorable way to survive under conditions as different as those Cuba has had to face over the last thirty years; loyalty to principles and never letting yourself be intimidated by anything, not letting anyone or anything change the pure and straight line of the revolution.

The message was crystal-clear, as were those to whom it was addressed. Castro did not forget to thank the Soviet Union and its deceased leaders for the help Cuba had received in previous decades. "We will never forget the support received at key moments, when we did not lack the weapons needed for our defense. We will never forget the economic cooperation, the just trade relations."[48] All the more did he complain behind the scenes about the revisionist policy of the new Soviet leader, who was trying to cure the ills of socialism "with capitalist medicine."

In his book *Castro's Final Hour*, the US journalist Andres Oppenheimer quotes from a revealing dialogue in January 1989 between Fidel Castro and Gabriel García Márquez, a supporter of Gorbachev's reform policy. "Don't get me wrong, I'm not against the principles of Perestroika," Castro said. "But it's an extremely risky policy. It's leading the Socialist world back to capitalism." García Márquez suggested that, on the contrary, "perhaps it's the beginning of true socialism, of socialism with a human face." To which he replied: "No. Believe me, Gabo, it's going to be a disaster."[49] Yuri Pavlov, former Soviet ambassador and director of the Latin American department of the foreign ministry under Gorbachev, later recalled: "Castro was one of the few foreign leaders who saw that Mikhail Gorbachev's *perestroika* could get out of control and wreck the very system it was intended to improve."[50]

The Soviet imperium collapses

On April 2, 1989, 15 years after Brezhnev's trip to Cuba, Soviet leader Mikhail Gorbachev and his foreign minister Eduard Shevardnadze arrived for a three-day visit. In the five previous years Castro had already met Gorbachev at least three times, more often than any of the latter's predecessors in a similar period of time. The first occasion was in February 1984, at the funeral of Brezhnev's successor, Yuri Andropov, who had died at the age of 70 after just 15 months in office. At the time Gorbachev was responsible within the Politburo for the struggle against corruption in the country's ruling apparatus. And a year later, in March 1985, when Konstantin Chernenko died in his turn, a generation change was completed with the surprising appointment of Gorbachev as general secretary of the Communist Party of the Soviet Union. Castro simply conveyed his congratulations by telephone. But the Twenty-seventh Congress of the CPSU in 1986 offered Castro the chance to pay a courtesy call on the new Soviet leader. The 59-year-old veteran revolutionary had a three-hour conversation with Gorbachev in the Kremlin on the afternoon of March 2, the Russian's birthday. Already *perestroika* was beginning to make itself felt.

In November 1986 Castro was again in Moscow, for the annual celebration of the October Revolution. More important, however, was the meeting of general secretaries and Central Committee first secretaries of Communist parties from Comecon countries, at which Gorbachev tried to drive home the urgency of economic reforms. "It is no secret," he had written on September 2 in his letter of invitation, "that the structure and forms of economic relations among our countries, both bilateral and multilateral, have come into conflict with the need for rapid and comprehensive strengthening of the economy as well as an acceleration of scientific and technological progress."[51] In his opening words to the closed meeting in November, Gorbachev then reminded everyone present that "in the present period of historical development" the Comecon countries faced "an inexorable choice:" either socialism greatly quickened its pace, adopted the most modern positions in science and technology, and convincingly demonstrated the superiority of its way of life, or else it remained mired in problems and difficulties, lost its dynamism and was driven "into a corner."[52] Castro, attending his first meeting of Comecon leaders in 14 years, seemed in his contribution eager to mark a distance from the new course, by emphasizing that Cuba belonged "partly to a different world, the Third World." He dressed up as self-criticism his old critique, taken over from Che Guevara, of the way in which Soviet economic policy watered down the Communist ideal. We wanted to complete a historical leap in short order, he said; we copied a number of good experiences from the socialist countries, but also copied well many bad experiences. Nor did he forget to mention that Cuba was still "dependent upon help from the fraternal countries, especially the Soviet Union." If the Comecon countries ceased paying more than the world-market price for sugar, "the people of Cuba would be condemned to go hungry."[53]

Despite their divergences expressed in the terms *rectificación* and *perestroika*, the two leaders seemed to have found a direct rapport with each other, in a relationship of mutual respect. There was thus great excitement as the time approached for Gorbachev's trip to Cuba. Western politicians and commentators, brimming with impatience and political naivety, expected that the Soviet Party leader would force Castro's *rectificación* onto the tracks of *perestroika*. But Gorbachev seemed determined to dash the hopes of all those who could scarcely wait for Castro's rule to end. For a start, it looked as if he did not want to damage the decades-long relationship with Cuba by openly compromising his host.

Factors associated with both internal and external policy played a role in this. Perestroika did not mean for Gorbachev naively and needlessly giving up the strategically not insignificant position on the Caribbean island, or vexing friendly Third World countries in which Castro still enjoyed a high reputation. And so, he evidently preferred for the time being to maintain an obliging attitude toward the Soviet Union's difficult ally. Besides, at that time he could scarcely apply any coercive measures against Cuba, both because Castro's friends among orthodox Communists in the Soviet apparatus were still too powerful, and because a shortage of foreign currency meant that the two countries were still all too dependent upon each other economically. Havana needed Moscow's oil, and Moscow needed Havana's sugar and nickel. Nevertheless, Castro seemed unsure and concerned about what was in store.

One of the most important people accompanying Gorbachev was Yuri Pavlov, who had been involved in preparing the trip. Part of the reform wing of the ruling apparatus in Moscow, he saw Castro as a Stalinist and felt a deep antipathy toward him. Later he wrote:

> When the talks began, Castro was visibly nervous. He apparently feared that Gorbachev would try to win him to his new creed, drawing him into discussing the polemics he wanted to avoid. He need not have worried. After the preliminaries were over, the Secretary General of the CPSU Central Committee asserted, "I am not going to impose on you my model. You can do whatever you think fit." From then on, Castro relaxed.[54]

The tension had never been greater since the missile crisis of 1962. For Cuba's political and economic existence ultimately hung on one word from Gorbachev, the man whose policy Castro had long considered a betrayal of the principles of Marxism-Leninism. It was a paradoxical situation: this stubborn man of all people, who for decades had been difficult for Moscow to discipline and bring into line, was now, with his Caribbean ideological mish-mash of *fidelismo,* presenting himself as the last defender of an outmoded doctrine.

Castro had long feared another betrayal as in the 1962 missile crisis, when the Soviet Union would once again sacrifice Cuba's interests on the altar of world politics.

> There are two kinds of survival and two kinds of peace, the survival of the rich and the survival of the poor; the peace of the rich and the peace of the poor. That is why the news that there may be peace, that there may be detente between the United States and the Soviet Union, does not necessarily mean that there is going to be peace for us.[55]

The centerpiece of Gorbachev's visit was a speech before the Cuban National Assembly. Though at first appearing jovial and conciliatory, the Soviet leader used the opportunity to signal in diplomatic language that he expected some rethinking from Castro. Aware of his own popularity among Cubans, he warned Castro not to be left behind by history and developed his oft-quoted theme that "life punishes those who arrive late:"

> Human civilization is at the crossroads. It is moving, as it were, from one phase to another. One cannot yet predict what its new image will be like. But one thing is already clear, namely, that today success will come to those who keep pace with the times and draw appropriate conclusions from the changes produced by the advent of high technologies and the decisive role of science and intellectual effort. . . . Either we continue moving down the old much-traveled track toward even greater stagnation and the economic, social, and even political dead-end, with the ensuing risk of being pushed to the sidelines of progress, or we embark on an arduous but vitally important path of our society's revolutionary renewal, of imparting to socialism a new qualitative dimension that would meet the highest standards of humanism and progress.[56]

There was some hard talking as Castro and his guest visited the sights of Havana. When his chief negotiator, Vice-President Carlos Rafael Rodríguez, and his six-man team tried to discuss the shape of the next trade agreement with their Soviet counterparts under Vice-President Vladimir Kamenzev, they discovered that it would run for not five years but only one year, and that only the basic framework would be decided at government level. The finer points, including the range and conditions of the commercial exchange, would have to be directly negotiated between individual enterprises – and, what is more, settled in convertible currency, on a dollar basis.

Castro did not show any obvious reaction to the Soviet general secretary's speech. Instinctively, however, he appeared to sense that the Moscow reforms had released centrifugal forces that could no longer be reined in, and that they would soon carry Gorbachev and the whole Soviet system into a blind alley. This made him all the more determined that his revolution would politically outlast Gorbachev. In Camagüey for the Moncada anniversary celebrations on July 26, 1989, just a few months before the collapse of the German Democratic Republic and two years before the Soviet Union itself became history, he made a speech full of foreboding:

> We warn imperialism that it shouldn't have so many illusions about our Revolution, thinking that our revolution won't be able to stand firm if there's a catastrophe in the socialist community. If, tomorrow or another day, we should wake up to the news that a huge civil war has broken out in the Soviet Union or even that the Soviet Union has disintegrated . . . Cuba and the Cuban Revolution would keep on struggling and keep on standing firm.[57]

The others who kept on struggling and standing firm were the comrades in the GDR, with whom (next to Moscow) Cuba had had the closest political and economic relations in the Eastern bloc since the 1960s. Apart from numerous trips at Politbureau or ministerial level and by a wide range of Party and trade union organizations, as well as an intensive program of student exchanges, there were four state visits by one side or the other in the space of eight years. Twice, in 1972 and 1977, Castro went to the

GDR, and twice, in 1974 and 1980, Honecker traveled to Cuba and received the kind of reception only previously given to Soviet state and Party leader Leonid Brezhnev. In addition, the two men met a number of times at Eastern bloc summits, as in 1984 and 1986 in Moscow.

Castro knew of the ideological reliability of the SED apparatus and shared its critical and anxious view of developments in the Kremlin. Straight after Gorbachev's visit to Cuba, therefore, he sent Politbureau member and Central Committee secretary, Jorge Risquet, to discuss with Honecker and Hermann Axen from the Politbureau in East Berlin and, more generally, to fill in the GDR leadership about his talks with the CPSU general secretary. From the notes on Honecker's meeting with Risquet on April 17, 1989, it emerges that Gorbachev "personally showed extraordinarily great understanding for Cuba's path, its problems and its specificities," and that he "in no way adopted a paternalist attitude or tried to impose his will." The East German leadership's unease about Gorbachev's course in Moscow, and its sympathy with Castro's uncompromising stance, led Honecker to follow on and state that "Cuba's steadfastness . . . as underlined in Fidel Castro's speeches during M. Gorbachev's visit," was "very highly appreciated" in the GDR. "We are in agreement with the Cuban fraternal party that the complex nature of present international trends calls for a very firm position to be taken. . . . Vigilance is therefore always required. On this question we fully agree with Fidel Castro."[58]

If we compare the minutes, it turns out that on April 13 Risquet expressed more frankly with Axen than with Honecker "a certain concern" in the Cuban leadership about "the increasingly serious difficulties in the Soviet Union."[59] Despite Gorbachev's instructive explanations, "the leadership of the [Cuban] CP continued to view with concern certain elements in the development of socialism." In some countries, a gradual abandonment of the leading role of the Party was already discernible, and in Cuba's eyes one position after another was being given up. A gradual development of socialist countries toward capitalist relations would apparently have to be taken into consideration. "Risquet spoke of a discrepancy between the way in which M. Gorbachev explained things and theories and viewpoints propagated by the Soviet media."

The Cuban certainly made no secret of Havana's worries about a US intervention. Axen reported him as saying:

> In view of the fact that Cuba is not a member of the Warsaw Pact, Cuba must have a central idea about how it can use its own forces to resist attacks by the USA. Apart from the regular armed forces, there are two million Cubans under arms, well trained and motivated, who have enough deterrent potential to dissuade the USA from an attack.[60]

"Of course, there are two kinds of Communists: those who let themselves be killed easily, and we Communists who won't let ourselves be killed easily. What can still scare us, who 27 years ago had the experience of the October [missile] crisis? . . . Nothing in the world can make our revolutionary people quake in our boots," Castro scornfully thundered at his Moncada rally in late July 1989, to continual applause interrupted with shouts of "Fidel! Fidel! Give it to the yankees!" In bitter defiance he added: "[Never before] has a US administration acted with such crazed triumphalism or given speeches so confident of victory as this one is doing now." The Bush government speaks as if "the community of socialist states is on its way out, [as if] socialism is finished and will end up in the dustbin of history that the great strategists and creative geniuses of the socialist movement reserved for capitalism itself."[61]

Yet it was the supposedly stable GDR which found itself there a few months later. Shortly before, in early September 1989, Fidel Castro's brother Raúl had paid another top-level visit to East Berlin, on his way to the conference of non-aligned states. In retrospect, his conversation with Politbureau member Axen eerily registers how unprepared the GDR leadership was, even in its inner circles, to contemplate the reality that would soon lead to the fall of the Wall. Cuba's number two, referring to the threat of US military intervention against Panama and to fears that this might "have immediate knock-on effects for Cuba and Nicaragua," expressed his "great satisfaction" at having such "reliable allies." "The stability of the GDR," the minutes record him as saying, "is of exceptional importance for us. It can be safely said that trends in the GDR are stable and dynamic. . . . The GDR is a solid barrier, a firm bulwark on that sensitive frontier in the heart of Europe."[62]

Soon the GDR and other Eastern bloc states were falling like dominoes. Only Cuba held out. But, in comparison with what the country soon had to face, the *rectificación* period would appear as a mere prelude to the unknown. Castro had to steer the country into an economic and political storm at the end of the century, without knowing how long it would last, whether he would be able to ride it out, or whether at the end he would find himself captain of a wreck.

The fall in world sugar and oil prices in the eighties, leading to Castro's debt moratorium as an emergency response to Cuba's inability to repay creditors in both East and West, had a number of fateful consequences. The block on further Western loans suddenly left Cuba looking at a 30 percent shortfall in foreign currency, so that the island could no longer afford the imports via countries other than the United States (mainly of technology) that had been running at US$1.6 billion a year. This situation arose at the very moment when the shock therapy administered to the bankrupt socialist economies of the Soviet Union and Cuba was leading them in diametrically opposite directions, under the names of *perestroika* and *rectificación* respectively. Yet, instead of loosening as quickly as possible Cuba's dependent economic ties to the socialist bloc, Castro was compelled by sheer necessity, and against all reason, to bind the country to it still more firmly.

At one point, when the dependence on the Eastern bloc was already around 90 percent (two-thirds of it on the Soviet Union alone), Cuba and the USSR agreed in the protocol signed during Gorbachev's visit an 8 percent increase in mutual trade from 1989 to 1990 that carried it to a record level of 9.2 billion rubles.[63] Everything was now being gambled on one card. But on the Soviet side, too, there was still a strong interest in the extension of trade relations. Thus, the paper *Sovietskaya Rossiya* quoted Leonid Abalkin, vice-president of the Soviet Council of Ministers, as saying:

The supply of [4 million tons of] Cuban sugar satisfies up to 30 percent of the Soviet domestic demand; 20 percent of the cobalt produced in the USSR is derived from [Cuban] nickel-cobalt concentrate. Without the supply of [30,000 tons of] Cuban nickel, the factories in the Urals would not be able to produce high quality steel. [Cuban] shipments of citrus fruits represent the base 40 percent of our national market. If we did not have these levels of [Cuban] supplies, it must be understood that we would feel quite differently, for we would have to pay capitalist countries between 1.5 to 2 billion dollars for the same production. Similarly, the Cuban economy would not be able to survive without the supply of Soviet petroleum.[64]

This was the same Abalkin who, in April 1990, a year after Gorbachev's visit, spent a week in Havana working out a new annual (rather than quinquennial) basis for trade agreements between Cuba and the Soviet Union. The outcome was a joint protocol that envisaged a further increase in trade up to a volume of $14 billion.

Back in Moscow, Abalkin came under heavy fire, as the Soviet Union was no longer in any position to meet the delivery obligations he had agreed in Havana. Of the 700 or so products on Cuba's list, the Soviet planning authorities had access to only a tenth – including oil, rice, and spare parts for vital production plant. All the rest were subject to direct negotiations with individual enterprises.

Soon after Gorbachev's visit to Cuba, the disintegration of the Soviet Union accelerated to such an extent that economic and political–military ties began to unravel altogether. All agreements and previous arrangements to which the Cubans still clung as their final hope became virtually worthless from one day to the next.

On September 28 Castro gave a gloomy report on relations between the two countries:

At this moment we do not know what the level of our trade with the USSR will be next year. Right now no one knows how much they are going to pay us for our sugar, for our exports, or how much they are going to charge us for the products they supply us, or how much fuel we are going to receive. No one knows anything about this right now despite the fact that there are only three months left before the end of the year.[65]

At that time, the Soviet Union was already nearly 2 million tons behind with its oil deliveries – more than 15 percent of the usual annual quantity. Moreover, as a result of the crisis in the Gulf, the price of crude oil soared from $14 a barrel to $40 between the middle of 1990 and late September, further limiting Cuba's ability to purchase oil on the free market.

"But," according to Castro, "the really brutal cuts took place at the moment when the USSR collapsed and we had to face what was in effect a double blockade [from the USA and now, indirectly, from Russia]."[66] As 1991 turned into 1992, the facts and figures of Cuba's economic decline pointed to a looming catastrophe – a direct result of the dissolution of Comecon in June 1991 and the Soviet Union in December 1991.

Within three years, the oil deliveries fell by nearly a half from the 1989 figure of 13.3 million tons, and they had to be paid for at the world-market price instead of the earlier preferential rate. Nothing was left any more for reselling – besides, it would no longer have been economically advantageous. At the same time, the Soviet side halved the price it was prepared to pay for Cuban sugar. According to Castro:

> One of our most serious problems is our grave shortage of convertible currency. . . . There used to be convertible currencies and settlement currencies: the ruble, the GDR mark, the currencies of the socialist countries. Today we must pay for everything in convertible currencies, especially for the fuel that keeps the country moving. And we have a special problem with fuel, which makes the situation extremely acute.[67]

In the early years of the revolution, Cuba received 8 tons of fuel for 1 ton of sugar. "Today, since oil fetches a monopoly price and sugar on the world market gets, as we have often said, a junk price, a minimal price, we can buy only 1.4 or 1.5 tons of oil for 1 ton of sugar."[68] By 1993 Cuba had to worry whether it would receive even a quarter – 3.3 million tons – of the 1989 oil delivery, and whether at least 1.5 million tons – a third of the former total – would be taken in return. Since the old Eastern bloc economies were increasingly using market criteria and demanding transactions in hard currency, Cuba's import capability shrank at least 70 percent by 1992, from $8.1 billion to $2.2 billion. As supply problems became dramatically worse, Castro's complaints had something desperate about them. "Where are we to get the foreign currency for food . . . ? Where are we to get foreign currency for the medicine we need every day? We know that some three hundred different medicines are lacking. Where are we to get raw materials like cotton or fertilizer base?"[69] No answers were forthcoming.

On July 26, 1993, the fortieth anniversary of the Moncada attack that marked the heroic beginning of Castro's revolution, the country and the leadership celebrated in a mood of deep depression. "The year 1992 was hard," said Castro in his speech for the occasion, "but, as if our trials were not enough, very bad signs appeared in another respect to make our situation more acute. The second half of 1992 was very dry, and the first half of 1993, in terms of climate, was really hellish." To make matters still worse, the storm of the century swept across the island, "at a time when there is usually not any bad weather or cyclones." He spoke of damage "estimated at approximately one billion dollars." "Our sugar production, which in 1992 was 7 million tons, . . . fell back sharply. [. . .] Output in 1992–93 fell to 4.28 million tons, that is, down 2.75 million tons. . . . In the year we lost income of approximately 450 million dollars. . . . And for this year we expect imports of approximately 1,719 million dollars."[70]

After 1992 there were no more loans from the former Eastern bloc – which, according to Castro, had until recently amounted to some $1.5 billion a year from the Soviet Union and approximately $160 million from the rest of Eastern Europe. Cuba's accumulated debt to the old Soviet republics was difficult to calculate in those turbulent times. Estimates fluctuated, depending on the partner and the interests at stake, between 15 and 25 billion rubles: that is, at the most favorable exchange-rate, roughly $2 billion, and at the least favorable rate (the 0.62 rubles to the dollar used for trade with the West) more than $15 billion. The hard-currency debt was on top of that: another $6.5 billion.[71]

The oil situation was repeated in relation to other vital supplies. At the time of Gorbachev's visit, Cuba still received 100 percent of its wheat from Eastern bloc countries, 100 percent of its vegetable oil, 63 percent of its powdered milk, and 40 percent of its rice. Thus, in the year of the end of the Soviet Union, Havana could feel happy if Moscow still met 40 percent of its supply commitments to Cuba. An expected delivery of 100,000 refrigerators suddenly failed to materialize, as did 128,500 washing machines. The production of clothing ground to a halt because zips were not being delivered, and beer could no longer be brewed because Czechoslovakia and Germany failed to come up with the agreed 45,000 tons of malt. So it was across all branches of the economy.

More and more often, Cuban trade delegations had to return home empty-handed. With a touch of gallows humor, Castro mocked the quality of the things that did arrive: for example, the Hungarian Ikarus buses, which had such a huge fuel consumption that they needed a gallon every 4 miles and poisoned the city with their exhaust; or the Bulgarian forklift trucks, which would never have been offloaded anywhere but in Cuba. As if it was all the same in the end, he angrily announced that Cuba would no longer take Eastern Europe's "junk." Former "fraternal countries" did not even keep to firm contracts, and simply cut off agreed credit lines. Poland, Hungary, the Czech Republic, and Slovakia were now struggling to gain entry into the European Union. And German reunification killed off the republic from which Cuba had received the most development aid, and which had been not only a major supplier of military hardware but also a competent partner and adviser on internal and external security.

It borders on a miracle that, despite all the prophecies, the crisis did not produce social unrest in Cuba or quite simply lead to its collapse. If there were no mass revolts, no violent clashes, no bloody repression, this was partly due to the iron grip of the security apparatus. Another reason was probably the widespread feeling of resignation. It is also true, however, that Castro still managed with his speeches to get the people to pull together in the face of each new challenge. He seems to be one of the few political talents in history capable of wearing down resistance through speeches that often last several long hours.

Signs of the end of the Cuban–Soviet partnership began to appear soon after Gorbachev's visit. The mood noticeably cooled, even if the official rhetoric still tried to patch up the ever larger tears in the relationship. In the summer of 1989, the Cuban censorship suddenly banned the Spanish-language editions of *Moscow News* and *Sputnik* from sale in street kiosks. The magazines were much sought after among young people, because they described with unusual candor the political changes in the Eastern bloc, and presented political alternatives to Marxism-Leninism that were poison for Castro's autocratic system. As there were few copies in circulation, they were snapped up and passed from hand to hand at black-market prices. A leading article in the Party paper *Granma* justified the ban by attacking those in the Soviet Union who:

> deny the leading role of the [Communist] Party and demand a multiparty system, advocate the free market, exalt foreign invest-ments, have rediscovered popular [political] participation and question internationalism and solidarity aid to other countries. . . . With pain and bitterness we have had to confront the consequences of this confusion, of all these ideas, in young people who have been poorly instructed in terms of ideology and history, a state of affairs for which we are responsible.[72]

Soon afterwards, Soviet people also disappeared from the island. In 1989, at the time of Gorbachev's visit, some 5,000 Soviet technicians (mainly engineers) and 7,000 "military advisers" and their families were stationed there. Still in February 1990, against the background of the renewal in 1989 of the friendship treaty with Cuba that reaffirmed the need for a Soviet military presence, Gorbachev declared: "The military threat has not disappeared; the United States and NATO maintain offensive doctrines and concepts. At the same time, they are maintaining their armies and military budgets; that is why we need an army which is well prepared and well equipped."[73]

Until the end of his days as general secretary of the CPSU and head of the Soviet state, Gorbachev tried to keep a balance between reformists and conservatives on the Cuban issue too, and refused to abandon in a rush allies of such long standing. When the United States wanted Cuba to be brought for judgment before the UN Human Rights Commission, Moscow parted company with its former East European allies and stuck by Cuba's side. Whereas Russian President Boris Yeltsin, in his role as spokesman for the reformers, wanted to end all further support for Castro's Cuba – on the grounds that it was a police state from the Brezhnev era – the old Communists argued for aid to be maintained at least as long as the United States refused to normalize its relations with the Caribbean island.

But Washington, thinking that Castro's fall was imminent, was not about to opt for normalization. The screws were indeed turning on Cuba, and there no longer seemed to be any escape as the ending of the East European commitment intensified the effects of the US embargo. The Bush administration tried to help things along a little. "Freedom and democracy, Mr Castro! Not sometime, . . . but now!" the man in the White House could be heard saying. Only if Castro permitted free elections and a UN investigation of human rights abuses, only if he gave political prisoners their freedom and ended "subversive activities in Latin America," would there be a prospect of improved relations. Of course, even in the form of their presentation, these conditions were meant to bring about a rejection by the other side, so that this could be immediately used against Cuba.[74] Susan Eckstein noted:

> Washington maintained a hard line toward Cuba while improving relations not only with Gorbachev's Communist government, . . . but also with China after Beijing's repression of a prodemocratic movement. . . . To justify his China policy, President Bush used the opposite rationale that he articulated in his Cuban stance. He argued that isolating China was not the best way to pressure for democratic reform.[75]

Whereas Gorbachev still resisted political pressure to give up the Soviet link with Cuba before Washington was visibly prepared to restore normal relations with Havana, the Bush administration exploited the growing economic difficulties of the Soviet Union and tied any further economic assistance and development loans to Moscow's ending of its military and economic relations with Cuba. One bilateral agreement, for example, specified that the USA would purchase nickel from the Soviet Union, but only on condition that not an ounce of it was of Cuban origin. In 1992 Russian President Yeltsin was helped out with a loan so that he could buy 2 million tons of sugar on the world market, instead of from the Cubans at a more favorable price – with the result that Cuba was stuck with its sugar harvest. And, although in 1992 the General Assembly of the United Nations again recorded a clear vote for an end to the US embargo against Cuba, the West European states – particularly Germany, Spain, and Sweden – supported Washington's persistent efforts to bring Castro to his knees through the withholding of development aid.

According to official estimates, the collapse of the Soviet Union cost Cuba roughly \$5.7 billion in 1992 alone.[76] The Caribbean island had lost 70 percent of its purchasing power in the space of three years, and the great American power was still tightening the garrote to choke the life out of Castro's system. In 1993, at the summit meeting in Vancouver with bankrupt Russia's President Yeltsin, Bill Clinton made further financial assistance to Russia dependent upon its suspension of all oil deliveries to Cuba.

By then, the military alliance between Moscow and Havana was already a thing of the past. The last Soviet technicians had left the island almost unnoticed not long after Gorbachev's promises to the contrary: the first 1,700 having departed in 1990, and the rest in the following year. Autumn 1991 also saw the withdrawal of the last Soviet military units. After Russian President Boris Yeltsin had defeated in August 1991 the abortive putsch by Moscow's old-style Communists against Soviet President Gorbachev, the Moscow reformers were able to assert their will and to clear the way for the return of troops based in Cuba. Until then Castro had been able to count on his strong lobby in Moscow, especially in the Kremlin's military apparatus, but now that was being rapidly stripped of its power.

269

For Castro there was a strong sense of *déjà vu*: another "betrayal" by the friends in Moscow. As before, when Khrushchev ordered the removal of Soviet missiles in October 1962, Castro first heard from a news broadcast that all Soviet units had been instructed to pull out.[77] Gorbachev himself announced the measure on September 16, 1991, ironically enough when he was standing beside US Secretary of State James Baker. On the same occasion, he also let it be known that the Soviet Union – whose days were clearly numbered – was prepared to place all its future economic relations with Cuba on a world market footing. Moscow anyway no longer had the means to subsidize the Cuban economy.

Along with the Soviets, diplomats of other East European states also gradually left the island. The large embassies of former Warsaw Pact countries shrivelled into caretaker missions; reunified Germany installed its representatives in the former embassy of the GDR.

Moscow's only interest was the huge listening system at Lourdes near Havana, where every year more than 2,600 specialists eavesdropped on the United States and Latin America. In autumn 1992, the new Russian-dominated CIS signed a 20-year contract for the right to use the facilities, but it was only in 1994 that the two sides agreed on the terms of payment. Havana wanted a million dollars a year for the service, and they eventually settled on a sum of $200 million.[78] (The contract was finally cancelled in 2002, under President Putin.)

The electronic spy station – similar to the ones operated by the United States on the Teufelsberg in Berlin, at Bad Aibling in Bavaria, and elsewhere along the Iron Curtain – became a kind of bargaining-counter against the 44-square-mile US naval base at Guantánamo in the east of the island. Gorbachev's foreign minister Pankin did in fact demand that, after the Soviet troop withdrawal, the United States should pull out its own 2,000 men from Guantánamo and hand back the land they had appropriated in violation of international law. But Washington was deaf to such appeals. In later years – especially at the beginning of the new millennium, when American plans to build a national missile defense again aroused the hostility of the Russian military – the listening post near Havana acquired new political and military significance.

In the difficult juncture following the departure of the friends from Eastern Europe, Cuba made its peace with an old "enemy:" the People's Republic of China. Already in 1990 Beijing was Cuba's second-largest trade partner, with a rather modest total approaching US$600 million. A five-year agreement governed the exchange of Cuban sugar, citrus fruit, nickel, iron, medicines, and medical equipment for Chinese food, bicycles, and financing of industrial plant. The relations remained limited: China too wanted to see hard dollars on the table. But the old ideological differences seemed to be safely buried in December 1995, when Castro visited the Great Wall as a guest of the Chinese state.

The brother's power

On July 13, 1989, Fidel Castro demonstrated to friends and enemies alike, in a way that stirred public opinion, his determination to do everything in his power to maintain the same ground rules for the revolution. At dawn, following a spectacular trial before a military court, a firing squad executed the 49-year-old "hero of the revolution," General Arnaldo Ochoa Sánchez, a prominent commander of the Angola campaign and for many years a close comrade and personal friend of Castro's. Three other senior officers and employees of the defense and interior ministries died together with him, ostensibly for high treason against the revolution in connection with drug-trafficking, illegal business deals, and corruption. One of them was the 50-year-old Captain Antonio de la Guardia, a top secret service agent, with the reputation of a kind of Cuban James Bond, who had formerly headed an elite combat unit under the interior ministry.

The affair gave rise to numerous conjectures at home and abroad, because it was set against the background of the debate over *perestroika* and *rectificación*. Already in earlier years, in Africa, Ochoa was said to have been outspoken in his criticisms of the political course of the Castro brothers. Cuban exiles in nearby Miami immediately suspected that he had become a danger to

Raúl Castro in particular. The hero of Angola was a charismatic leader of frontline troops and – unlike Fidel's younger brother – as popular among the masses and the Party hierarchy as among the Fuerzas Armadas Revolucionarias (FAR). Not only did he have credit, as it were, for safeguarding the independence of Angola and Namibia; he had won for Castro, despite heavy losses, a surrogate war against the United States, in which the CIA had backed the right-wing Angolan UNITA forces against the left-wing MPLA of future President Agostinho Neto. Ochoa and those executed with him represented a progressive, reform-oriented wing of the FAR that had recently been gaining in strength. At the time of his arrest, the General was on the verge of being appointed supreme commander of the armed forces in the west of Cuba, the most important of the three defense sectors, which included the capital and Havana province.

At his trial, which was shown in censored excerpts on nation-wide television, Ochoa admitted that he was guilty of illegal business deals on a grand scale. He justified himself by saying that the foreign currency earned in this way had not been for his personal use but exclusively to remedy shortages of food and medicine for his troops, and to build much-needed infrastructure such as a military airfield in Angola. The charge that Ochoa had been directly involved in drug-trafficking did not seem proved beyond doubt, unlike in the case of the three others executed with him. Apart from the four death sentences, another ten men received long terms of up to 30 years' imprisonment, as did Brigadier-General Patricio de la Guardia, twin brother of the executed Antonio de la Guardia. The pre-trial investigations uncovered an extensive underground world of business dealings centered on Panama, in which senior Cuban officers, including several generals and employees of the defense and interior ministries, had lined their own pockets.

A few weeks later José Abrantes, a personal friend of Castro's who lost his job as interior minister at the beginning of the Ochoa trial, was sentenced to 20 years' imprisonment, along with Diocles Torralba, former transport minister and father-in-law of Antonio de la Guardia. They too had been found guilty of involvement in the corruption cartel. Less than two years later, Abrantes succumbed in prison to a heart attack, but before his death he apparently told Patricio de la Guardia that Castro himself had known of occasional cocaine transactions that the Colombian Medellín cartel had routed through Cuba. *Miami Herald* reporter Andres Oppenheimer, who won the Pulitzer Prize for uncovering the Iran–Contra affair under President Reagan, claimed that, according to statements by la Guardia's relatives and former Cuban secret service agents, Abrantes had accused Castro of instructing him to sell via Eastern Europe, for $50 million, 10 tons of cocaine confiscated by the Cuban coastguard.[79] No convincing proof of this grave charge was ever produced, and in any event the deals were said to have spun out of control and developed behind Castro's back.

It is still shrouded in mystery whether the drugs and currency network served only to enrich its organizers, or whether it also involved a conspiracy to discredit the Castro brothers by associating them with drug-trafficking. What was proved, however, was that the trial defendants had entered the shadowy drugs world through close official and unofficial contacts in Panama. In the late eighties Panama, with its Canal Zone inhabited by 13,000 troops of the US "Southern Command," was a banking paradise that gave the Cubans a gateway to the world and constituted a kind of Hong Kong of the Caribbean and Central America. With its intertwined and unsupervised access to currency markets and money-laundering facilities, this little country was as attractive to serious businessmen and politically correct governments as it was to Colombian drug-traffickers and their middlemen. Panama's ruling clique around General Antonio Manuel Noriega was at the disposal of anyone prepared to give it a share. And when it was a question of helping a country to get round an embargo, the pickings could be especially rich. Using Panama, Cuba was able to sell export goods for dollars and purchase Western technology and consumer goods to an annual value of at least $60 million. But Castro did not trust Noriega an inch and had a personal antipathy for the corrupt general.

As early as 1986, the US media revealed that for at least ten years Noriega had been on the CIA's payroll. While he enabled it to channel through Panama weapons for the anti-Sandinista

Contras in Nicaragua, the CIA in return shut its eyes to his dealings with the Medellín cartel that was flooding the United States with cocaine. As to the Cubans, Noriega gave them permission to use Panama as a foreign currency hub in exchange for supplies of military equipment. He seemed to need these rather urgently, since the peace process in Central America meant that his services in sowing conflict there were no longer required in Washington. In the middle of 1987, in fact, his links to the Colombian drug-dealers suddenly put him on the hit list of the Reagan administration.

At Christmas 1989, US troops occupied the whole of Panama. Noriega, who hid for days with friends and in the Vatican Embassy, eventually gave himself up and was taken in chains to the United States, where he received a long prison sentence for drug-trafficking. His disappearance from the political scene also cut Cuba's Panamanian link to non-socialist markets.

It was already known in Batista's time that Cuba's 3,000 miles of coastline and more than 3,000 offshore islands made it a paradise for drug smugglers. After the victory of the revolution, it was not only the CIA's saboteurs who came and went illegally: many a member of the Cuban exile community also made a fast buck there in the depths of night. Such activity lined private pockets, but it also filled the war chest for use against Castro – apparently with the approval of the CIA. At the same time, quite a few smugglers fell into the hands of the Cuban coastguard.

In 1985, four years before the Ochoa trial, Castro told the *Washington Post* of his concern at the island's use as a staging post for the drugs trade. "Of all the Caribbean countries, Cuba is the one that has the largest number of drug traffickers in jail. . . . We've really become the police of the Caribbean and we often wonder why, since the United States doesn't pay us for this service." Others would have been quite happy to pay him – not for keeping an eye on things, but for looking the other way. But, he insisted, that had always been out of the question. "I assure you that we've had plenty of offers. You know how brazen these underworld characters are. We would practically have solved our foreign exchange problems, but we're not interested in that kind of money." Why not? Ideologically speaking, would it not be a legitimate contribution to the ruin of the capitalist system? "I don't know whether it has to do with morals or the fact that I studied the catechism or studied all about Christian morality in Christian schools, but to me it is a question of Christian morality and Marxist-Leninist morality, and that's what we go by."[80]

In the months after the Ochoa trial, when the days of Noriega's rule already seemed to be numbered, there were several major purges in the Cuban security apparatus, the ministries of culture, agriculture, and construction, and the tourism and film industries. The fact that the interior ministry was placed under the defense ministry, and its top echelons replaced with loyal army officers, points to the dramatic nature of the events. It may be that the Ochoa affair was no more than the tip of an iceberg.

The new boss at the interior ministry, which was also responsible for the personal security of the state leadership, was the second-highest officer in the FAR, General Abelardo Colomé Ibarra. He had been a close companion of Ochoa's in Angola, but he was also one of the panel of military judges who had passed sentence of death on Ochoa and the others. In the ensuing purges and reshuffles, more than two-thirds of FAR officers in the west of the island (where Ochoa had been due to assume command) were replaced.[81]

Nearly a decade later, in June 1998, a journalist and former employee of Cuba's Prensa Latina news agency, Raúl Martín, told *El Nuevo Herald* (the Spanish-language edition of the *Miami Herald*) that between 1987 and 1989 he had been involved in a covert KGB operation against Castro, the aim of which had been to work with discontented elements in the army to overthrow Castro and open the way to a Cuban version of *perestroika*.[82] It was completely unsuccessful, however, because at that time Cuban intelligence was keeping a close watch on Soviet military experts and KGB people in the country. Was Ochoa perhaps a new Aníbal Escalante within the officer corps? The answer, if there is one, lies in the Cuban secret archives. As far as official propaganda was concerned, the Ochoa case served as a warning that corruption and counter-revolution had still to be ruthlessly hunted down.

It was not only the Ochoa affair that convinced the Castro brothers of the need to restructure their security apparatus. Events in Eastern Europe and signs of decomposition in the Warsaw Pact confronted Cuba's military and secret services with a quite new challenge: the island was now completely on its own in the Western hemisphere. The first task was to prevent *perestroika* from seeping into the most politically sensitive of all domains. For some time Cuba's Revolutionary Armed Forces, with help from the Soviet Union and Eastern Europe, had had the reputation of being one of the best-trained and best-equipped armies in the Third World. It was able to field 300,000 men when a US invasion threatened in the early sixties, and it still numbered 250,000 at the end of the decade. By the mid-seventies it was down to just under half that strength, but then it expanded again in response to Cuba's growing international commitments. In 1990–1, when the Warsaw Pact (of which Cuba was not a member) began to unravel, the London-based Institute for Strategic Studies put an estimate of 180,500 on the FAR. By the mid-nineties that figure had gone right back down to 105,000.

For a time, Cuba counted as the numerically strongest military power in Latin America. It was also the only Third World country which, over a long period of time, deployed large contingents of troops in an overseas region of conflict – in this case, Africa. No other developing country played such an active and influential role in providing "international solidarity," both civilian and military, in regional conflicts. Despite thousands of dead and wounded in Angola (precise figures are not available), Washington's calculation that it would become Cuba's Vietnam-style national disaster proved to be wide of the mark.

After a first intervention on Algeria's side in its border conflict with Morocco in 1963, Castro sent troops three years later to Congo (Brazzaville), where they helped to shore up the military regime for almost a quarter of a century. In the early seventies, Cuban soldiers also appeared in South Yemen and Syria. But these were all small expeditions, in comparison with the contingents of up to 70,000 men later based in Angola and Ethiopia. Altogether, it is estimated that 300,000 Cubans served at various times outside their country. In Latin America, Washington's declared sphere of interest, Havana's military role was limited to advice and instruction for its political friends in Surinam, Grenada, and Nicaragua, as well as for the guerrilla movements in El Salvador, Guatemala, and Colombia; the bulk of its effort went into civilian assistance in humanitarian fields.

The end of the Soviet Union, however, brought an end to Cuba's foreign military commitments. After Angola, South Africa, and Cuba worked out and signed a comprehensive peace plan for southern Africa, the last Cuban troops were on their way home by May 1991. Castro then declared that Cuba's high-prestige but costly military support for liberation movements and friendly governments in the Third World was at an end.

Cuba's growing political and economic isolation, especially as a result of developments in Eastern Europe, forced the country's leadership not only to ensure that its armed forces were still loyal to the regime, but also to include them in the necessary restructuring of society. The size of the standing army had to be drastically reduced, the period of military service shortened, and the modernization of combat units put on ice. But, above all else, military doctrine had to be adjusted to the new conditions: the tasks required of soldiers, whose loyalty was more indispensable than ever, had to be redefined in a convincing manner. In other Latin American countries, similar cutbacks would long have raised the danger of a coup. If Cuban troops remained exceptionally loyal in these difficult times, military experts put it down to the success over the years in creating a high degree of identification between the armed forces and the nation and its political leadership.

This may have been due to the fact that in Cuba, unlike elsewhere in Latin America, the traditions of the armed forces were rooted not in the nineteenth-century struggle for independence from Spain, but directly in the person of Castro and his revolution.[83] The victory on January 1, 1959, shattered the old Batista army, and any useable remnants were integrated into the newly formed Fuerzas Armadas Revolucionarias. The doctrine of this new "people's army" then consistently involved a mixture of conventional and guerrilla warfare, based on a combination of Soviet training and the experience of the Castro brothers and Che Guevara (the latter written up in the form of a guerrilla manual).

277

Along with permanent readiness to defend the country against the arch-enemy to the north, the army saw its role as one of providing military support for Castro's internationalist commitments in the Third World. Overseas expeditions, such as the one in Angola, made a major contribution to the development of national consciousness among the soldiers and the population at large – despite growing concern over the high number of casualties and a sense of disillusionment at not being able to win the Third World over to the Cuban model.

The internationally recognized efficiency and fighting morale of the Cuban army had a deterrent value that should not be underestimated, even if Washington was never prepared to admit this in public. Castro's concept of defense involved turning Cuba into a second Vietnam in the event of a US invasion. The fact that for decades the United States dismissed any thought of a landing on Cuba was thus not due only to Kennedy's promise at the time of the missile crisis; it was also bound up with the possibility that it might turn into another lengthy, costly, and ultimately disastrous enterprise.

Significantly enough, rumors began to circulate that a military option was again under consideration in Washington just at the moment when the collapse of the Soviet Union and growing economic difficulties were affecting the Cuban military and its capacity for defense. For not only the reductions in troop strength, but also the withdrawal of the Soviet brigade, the shortage of spare parts, and the lack of technical modernization soon rubbed the shine from the once-proud FAR. According to US State Department figures, in 1990 Cuba still received military support from the Soviet Union in the order of roughly $1.5 billion, but after 1990 it got nothing more. The delivery of "several dozen" MIG fighters, agreed many years before, had still not happened.[84] As to morale, it is true that a few men in the upper ranks of the air force went over to the United States, and in April 1999 Castro's chief bodyguard, a ranking captain, defected to the US embassy in Santo Domingo, on the margins of a summit meeting of the Association of Caribbean States. But there was no sign of the rapidly collapsing morale hoped for in the West, still less of an actual disintegration of the armed forces. Not the least reason for this was an awareness in the officer corps of what awaited it if the system went under; the Cuban exile community had always made it plain how impatient it was to regain control of the island and to clear up the political and military hierarchy.

Of course, it would not be as easy to pull off as people in Miami imagined. It was not just a question of the Revolutionary Armed Forces; there was also the MTT (Milícia de Tropas Territoriales), a kind of armed civil guard set up in 1980 to cover the whole island, which had as many as 2 million members by the mid-nineties. The founding of the MIT, in response to the aggressively anti-Cuban rhetoric with which the Reagan administration accompanied its official duties, was supposed to provide support units for the regular army, in accordance with the Cuban military conception of an "all people's war" (*guerra de todo el Pueblo*). In addition, there was the 100,000-strong Ejército Juvenil de Trabajo (Young Labor Army), a paramilitary force set up in 1973 to help with the harvest, to which the least well-qualified soldiers and officers belonged. These auxiliaries helped to offset, at least quantitatively, the successive thinning out of the professional army.

One political question of major concern (not only abroad) in connection with the ideological reversals of the early nineties was whether the Cuban military would be deployed if the worsening supply crisis led to disturbances inside the country. But this became a topical issue only once, when public demonstrations of discontent took place in the summer of 1994 in Havana and a mass exodus similar to the one of 1980 began to take shape. Thousands of Cubans risked their lives trying to escape the prevailing gloom on anything that floated. Castro held back the army and avoided an escalation, and eventually it was the United States which refused to accept all the refugees and asked Castro to find an end to the situation. The regular police had only to intervene and it was all over. There were no bloody clashes in the streets. Order was restored virtually overnight.

Nevertheless, the army general staff let it be known in this connection: "[W]e would rather use our weapons against the foreign aggressors, but we warn its internal fifth column that our revolutionary people have never had a vocation to be puppets.

If anyone tries to strike our cheek, we will not turn the other. Instead, we will act with firmness."[85] The final option of the Cuban leadership probably would be to use the army against the civilian population, but it is by no means certain that this would produce results. For, unlike in other Latin American countries, where the military has always been a kind of state within the state and has more often pointed its guns at its own citizens than at external enemies, such action in Cuba would contradict the FAR's strong awareness of itself as a "people's army."

It must be appreciated that Cuban civil society – in its organization, activity, and language – has always also been a militarized society, rooted in the Sierra Maestra guerrilla tradition that was able to survive and win through only with the help of the population. The unbroken capacity for rapid mobilization of the masses, whether for rallies or for harvest labor, is typical in this respect. Whereas rulers elsewhere feel an identification of the people with the military as a threat to their power, it has fallen to Cuba to bring about a fusion of civilian and military society in the political-cum-military concept of the revolution.

In the nineties it was especially clear that not only the interior ministry, but also such key bodies as the transport ministry, the ministry for heavy industry, the communications ministry and the sugar ministry were being run by generals. Of the 1,700 delegates to the Fourth Party Congress in 1991, 240 belonged to the armed forces; military men constituted powerful factions in the Central Committee and the Politbureau, as well as in lower Party structures right down to local level. This helps to explain the unavoidable "self-discipline" of the Cuban population in hard times. On the other hand, Castro has in the Milícia de Tropas Territoriales a large civilian force which, should the need arise, could be used to hold the soldiers and their commanders in check. A military putsch would thus carry a high risk of failure, as well as threatening to develop into a civil war.

It is testimony not only to Castro's great self-assurance but also – for all the prophecies of doom – to the enormous stability of his system, that he could allow a fifth of the population to bear arms in the dramatic economic circumstances of the eighties and nineties, without having to fear that the guns would be suddenly turned on him. For Castro, of course, this kind of civil defense is not a militarization of society but an expression of its democratization:

> We don't just have the vote, we have the weapons in the hands of the people. Can a people who have weapons in their hands be enslaved? Can a people who have weapons in their hands be oppressed? Can a policy be imposed on a people who have weapons in their hands? And how is such a miracle possible unless there is total identification between the people and the nation, between the people and the Revolution?[86]

This Cuban variant of the "citizen in uniform" idea makes the penetration of society by oppositional forces appear a hopeless enterprise. It also permits the use of soldiers as a reserve army in agriculture and industry in times of necessity – a kind of crisis management that would be unthinkable, or probably lead to an uprising, in other Latin American countries. From Argentina to Venezuela, such a request would offend the pride of the military. But not in Cuba. In 1991, when the Soviet imperium was falling apart and the Soviet presence in Cuba was being wound up, Castro set out a new line of advance: "[O]ne of the Armed Forces' missions at this time is to help the economy."[87] As in the sixties and seventies, soldiers and officers now had to change for work in the factories, the fields, and the bureaucracy. The ending of Soviet military assistance meant that the armed forces had to make a sharp turn toward self-sufficiency, whether it was a question of spare parts for equipment, or farming and stock breeding, or the production of ammunition and their own multipurpose aircraft, the AC-001 Comas. Military maneuvers off the Cuban coast, and the heightened fears of a US invasion following the Gulf War, made the army leadership pull out all the stops to build huge underground tunnel systems for the storage and protection of weapons and equipment. The armed forces also involved themselves more and more in civilian activities, especially joint ventures with foreign, mostly European and Canadian, investors in the tourism industry. This was supposed to lift some of the burden of military expenditure from the state budget. And, indeed, in

1995 the high command reported that it had managed to fund a third of the military budget from its own efforts and its own enterprise – a kind of self-help that would again be unimaginable anywhere else in the world.

War economy in peacetime

Cuba was now all alone. Surrounded by enemies and opponents, the government saw only one possible path if it was to avoid falling into line with the "new world order:" the path of autarky. For Castro, this was personally and politically the greatest challenge of his life, but also a macabre opportunity for genuine independence under the least favorable circumstances.

"Socialism or death! *Venceremos!*" From September 1990, Castro's rhetorical formula with which he always ended his speeches was put to such a test that he could not have imagined it in his worst nightmares. The country seemed to be plunging into its death agony. Without pausing for breath, it had to move from *rectificación* to the *período especial*. Julio Carranza Valdés, from Cuba's Center for American Studies (CEA), argues that changes introduced in the period of "rectification" had not provided for "any structural adjustments such as the economy would later have to make, when the crisis of the socialist camp broke with full force."[88] And Castro thought that:

> in no historical epoch did any country find itself in the situation in which ours found itself, when the socialist camp collapsed and we remained under the pitiless blockade of the USA. No one imagined that something as sure and steady as the sun would one day disappear, as it happened with the disintegration of the Soviet Union.[89]

The "special period" was Castro's answer to neoliberalism, even if everyone doubted his judgment. Although his decision to hold out seemed like political adventurism, he scarcely had any other choice if he was not simply to throw in the towel. And so, he put his trust in his own instinct and his unbroken will to political survival. His security services would have given him a reliable picture of the limits of endurance of the Cuban population, and he seemed convinced that he could ask of it the extra sacrifices of a "war economy in peacetime," without provoking a mass revolt. In October 1991, just a few months after old-style Communists had launched their abortive coup in Moscow, when the dissolution of the Soviet Union was already hard fact and Cubans had been through a summer of growing deprivation, Castro announced at the opening of the Fourth Congress of the Communist Party of Cuba: "We will defend ourselves on our own, surrounded by an ocean of capitalism. . . . The Cuban people went its own way during the long years of the American blockade, relying on the solid pillars of the socialist camp and the Soviet Union. Those pillars have collapsed."[90] Cubans now had to accomplish a "real miracle:" that is, "to produce more milk, meat, rice and vegetables with minimal amounts of fodder, fertilizer and herbicide."

People hoped that, under these oppressive conditions, Castro would at least allow the reopening of the farmers' markets that had helped to keep the population supplied with food in the eighties. But he was convinced that such a step would immediately spur corruption and produce a dangerous inequality. The main task was to ensure "that whatever we have we distribute evenly among everyone." And he promised: "Not even in the special period will we have beggars, there won't be anyone without food . . . no one will be left out in the street."[91]

The *período especial* meant – in 1991, for instance – that everyone with a ration book received just under 200 grams of fish every ten days, half a kilo of meat a week (or alternatively, only chicken for up to 50 days at a time), three to four eggs a week, half a kilo of rice, 500 to 750 grams of sugar, 125 grams of beans, and 25 grams of coffee. Cooking oil and flour were rarely available, and there were few vegetables or fruit, no jam, virtually no butter, milk only for small children, old people and those in special need; the bread allowance was 250 grams a day. Soap, detergent, toilet paper, and matches were not often seen. The lack of chlorine made it advisable to boil water, but there was also a shortage of methylated spirits to use as fuel. Every two years, citizens were entitled to buy four underpants or bras, two pairs of socks, one shirt or blouse, and 4 meters of material for trousers or dresses. Castro appealed to women to wear or recycle old clothes for the next five years – the estimated length of the special period.

> Everything that can help to counteract the terrible blow is being discussed not only in the National Assembly, but also in the hundreds of thousands of meetings that take place in factories, production and service centers, trade unions, universities, secondary schools, and all the organizations of farmers, women or flat-dwellers and other organizations of a social character.

And again: "The little we have will be distributed with the greatest degree of equality."[92]

The restrictions most likely to be strengthened were those on journalistic products. The papers *Juventud Rebelde* ("Rebel Youth") and *Trabajadores* ("Workers") began to appear only weekly, with a reduced size and printrun. The army paper *Verde Olivo* ceased publication, and the Party paper *Granma* appeared with a smaller number of pages and in a reduced format. Because of the paper shortage, virtually the only books to be published were for use in schools. Television broadcasts were limited for the time being to 48 hours a week.

The economy measures, together with falling output in every sector, led to a rise in unemployment and also in underemployment, which at times affected up to a third of all employees. On the other hand, more and more people failed to show up at work, partly because they had to spend as many as 15 hours a week standing in queues and fighting for food that was often not there. To cut down on absenteeism, the government eventually allowed others to keep someone's place in the queue – for a price.

One of the most important economies was the slashing of energy consumption by 50 percent. The Juragua nuclear power station being built with Soviet help near Cienfuegos might have brought some relief: Castro hoped that it would halve oil requirements from the early nineties. But when the Soviet Union pulled out its technicians and the "special period" hit the country, the uncompleted edifice remained as a ruin in the landscape. Castro had to write off $1.2 billion in Cuban investment for the project and make the head of the nuclear program redundant – none other than his son Fidelito, who had a doctorate in nuclear physics. Nor was Cuba's own offshore oil production sufficiently developed to offer more than slight relief. In the end, nearly half of all industrial enterprises – mainly those dependent upon old Eastern bloc technology – had to order a full or partial shutdown. Textile production came to an almost complete standstill, as did the cement, nickel, and chemical industries. As time passed, moreover, the electricity supply was sometimes working for only six or seven hours a day. Another of the "precapitalist" survival strategies was to lay up the country's 90,000 petrol-guzzling tractors and replace them with 9,000 ox-carts – with dramatic consequences for agricultural production. Machine labor was replaced with manual labor, especially in sowing and reaping, and even 70 percent of the 1993 sugar harvest was brought in by hand. Bus, taxi, and car transport was cut by up to 50 percent, and the few personal vehicles on the road mostly belonged to state enterprises, organizations, and ministries. People queued for two or three hours at bus stops, to get a place in or on one of the packed *camellos* ("camels"), municipal buses so called because of the hump-like structure in their middle.

Cuban society almost literally stopped moving – until the Comandante had the saving idea that the mass of the population should ride back to the future on horse-drawn carts and bicycles. Still filled with optimism, he knew how to sell this to people: "The special period also has its positive sides – like the fact that we are now entering the age of the bicycle. In a sense, this too is a revolution." For, in the end, cycling was good for one's health. Although Cubans were by no means a nation of cyclists and many had first to learn how to ride the new means of locomotion, he went into real raptures: "I have no doubt that in the summer we'll see whole clouds of cyclists heading for the beaches of our capital."[93] Nearly a million machines were bought from China, and sold to students for 60 pesos each and to employees for 120 pesos. The Chinese also helped build five factories around the country, with the capacity to produce half a million bicycles over the next five years. At the same time, 60,000 tricycles were supposed to cover half the transport of goods. The armed forces too were required to use the new vehicles, so that at the annual May Day parade soldiers rode past the state and Party leadership on olive-green bicycles. Soon a half of all households had purchased at least one, removing a third of the burden from car and bus transport and covering a quarter of all journeys to work. When supply failed for a short time to keep up with demand, the number of bicycle thefts increased and people had to cart their 55-pound machines into their offices and homes. And, however healthy it was, it also cost energy and sharpened the hunger that was becoming less and less easy to still. "Daily calorie consumption," Castro reported, "fell from 3000 to 1900, and daily protein consumption from 80 to 50."[94]

Thus, Castro set out an ambitious food program which, instead of suggesting a return to an earlier phase in the development of *Homo sapiens*, reflected the struggle for survival of a relatively advanced agrarian and industrial society located somewhere between the First and Third Worlds. The aim, as we have seen, was pure self-sufficiency. Twenty thousand hectares of sugar land was set aside for the production of rice, fruit, and vegetables. Fish farms and 1,800 chicken farms (producing 10 percent more eggs and poultry), as well as 1,000 dairies, were supposed to come into being over the next ten years. In the cities, back yards, railway sidings, waste ground, ornamental gardens and balconies were converted into "victory gardens" for the growing of fruit and vegetables. By the middle of 1992, there were more than a million such places looked after by tenants, neighborhood welfare groups, and students. Vegetable production was supposed to rise 50 percent within five years. But such huge advances in survival techniques failed to happen, simply because the system was so inaccessible and earlier omissions and neglect began to take their toll. Thus, a high percentage of products – some estimates put the figure at almost a third – went bad as a result of transport problems, improper storage, or defective refrigeration. A lot was stolen, however, and ended up on the black market – where at least it reached the final consumer.

As Fidel Castro still opposed the reintroduction of farmers' markets and insisted that all produce must be distributed by the state, people continued to rely on the thriving black market when they wanted or needed something on top of their ration. For, under the counter, it was miraculously possible to find almost everything, at astronomical prices. Unofficial figures (which need to be treated with caution) estimate that between 1989 and the middle of 1993 turnover on the black market shot up from the equivalent of $2 billion to $14.5 billion, outstripping the volume of state retail trade with its fixed prices.[95] With average monthly earnings running at 200 to 300 pesos, the price of a black-market chicken rose from 70 to 200 pesos in the space of a year. Half a kilo of lard cost 10 pesos, a packet of cigarettes 5 to 10 pesos. Traders wanted 500 pesos for a pair of jeans, or 300 for a pair of shoes.

All the inventiveness and organizational talent lacking in the official approach to scarcity appeared to be concentrated in the black market. Over the years, the Soviet military and technical personnel based in the country supplied (and joined) the 60,000 *negocieros* of this shadowy world, and before their final departure they sold off anything that would make a fast buck, even weapons and uniforms. Cubans also stole what there was to steal, mostly at work, in agriculture or from stocks intended for the tourist industry. The crime rate was a source of concern, despite drastic measures such as the rounding up of whole rings of criminals specializing in theft, speculation, bribery, illegal currency trading, or the receiving of stolen goods in and around the port of Havana. Not infrequently, high state officials were also implicated: for example, at the tourist center of Varadero, the chief airport customs officer was found to be the head of a gang. The criminals seemed to have contacts everywhere, even in the police and at the various ministries. In 1991 the railway parcel service had to be closed down, because too many consignments (often containing food) were being stolen en route. In the same year, weapons were handed out to farmworkers so that they could protect themselves against armed robbers who wanted to steal the fruits of their labor.

The survival program was only formally based on doctrinal purity; it harked back to capitalist and pre-capitalist elements as well as socialist ones. "This is no time for theorizing but instead for advancing, resisting and overcoming," Castro told the Federation of University Students in December 1990.[96] And shortly afterwards, he raised the question: "How could a capitalist country accomplish this?"[97] To put people in the mood for the "zero option" of complete economic isolation, he had less and less recourse to the exhortations of Marxism-Leninism. Official discourse had long preferred the word "fatherland" to "socialism," and in this hour of need Castro returned to the original roots of his revolution, dramatically presenting the "special period" as one more episode in Cuba's long struggle for national independence. Thus in April 1991, on the thirtieth anniversary of the Bay of Pigs, he strengthened the leadership's resolve by appealing to the spiritual fathers of the independence struggle:

> We will tell the imperialists, no, you can't do what you want with us! . . . And if we have to put up with material deprivation, we will put up with it, because we can never forget that those who began our independence struggle spent ten years in the woods . . . and when some of them got tired and thought that it was impossible to fight under such difficult conditions . . . and wanted peace without independence, [Antonio] Maceo said "No!" And, along with Maceo, the best representatives of that heroic people said "No!" . . . That is who we are: the heirs of Maceo . . . the heirs of Martí.[98]

The country presented a curious picture in the early nineties, a cross between impending collapse and burgeoning confidence. The grand Hotel Nacional, a Mafia stronghold in Batista's time, had no life in it. The huge propaganda board on the Malecón, Havana's wide seafront promenade, defiantly announced: "*Patria o Muerte – Venceremos!*" ("Fatherland or death – we shall conquer!").

Expectations were great in October 1991 when the Fourth Party Congress eventually met in an atmosphere of privation, after months of preparation and several postponements. The gathering had been preceded by nearly 90,000 local meetings around the country, where more than 3 million citizens had taken part. A wide-ranging questionnaire had solicited the views of more than a million people about a series of issues concerning everyday life and the state of the Revolution. Never before – and not again, unfortunately – did the Cuban people have such an opportunity for democratic rank-and-file participation. Perhaps they took it too seriously. For Castro was confronted with an endless list of complaints about the wild inefficiency and horrendous incompetence of the bureaucracy, and he was reminded of the massive criticisms of the Party and state apparatus following the failure of the campaign in 1970 for the 10 million tons harvest.

The congress recommended a set of constitutional amendments to the National Assembly, including a form of direct election of deputies to the national assembly of the one-party state. Previously the ordinary population had voted for only 150 regional assemblies. These then chose the members of 14 provincial parliaments, from the ranks of which the 600 or so members of the National Assembly were finally appointed. Now, in the run-up to parliamentary elections, those entitled to vote would be able to choose directly at local and regional level, in 14,686 constituencies, among several candidates for the National Assembly, even if all came from the ranks of the only permitted party, the PCC.

The procedure was a sham, however, for in the end there would still be only one candidate for each seat in parliament, and that one candidate would be a Party loyalist who had been gone over with a fine toothcomb. It was true that, as Castro pointed out, the candidate needed more than half of the votes. But, because of the nature of the election process, it was unlikely that any candidate would receive too few votes. Instead of choosing the full list of candidates in their constituency, voters would have the option of going into the booth, selecting individual candidates, and "voting" others off the list. But it was exceptional for anyone to do this, observed by everyone else around; nor was there much point. With the vote for candidates always well above 90 percent, few ever adopted a procedure that took time and made them look conspicuous. Besides, at that point in the election process there were no alternative candidates and no oppositional contenders.

Of course, anyone dispatched to the really influential and powerful structures – the Central Committee and Politbureau of the PCC, the Council of State – ultimately remained subject to the will of the Máximo Líder.

Another recommended change to the Constitution was, however, seen as the signal for a cautious opening of the political system: namely, the deletion of the duty to raise all Cubans only in the spirit of Marxism-Leninism. This came at a time when belief in the doctrine had anyway begun to evaporate; the more patriotic *fidelismo*, though still with a socialist orientation, was again on the upswing at Party schools. But, from now on, men and women professing allegiance to any of the Christian denominations would be allowed to join the Communist Party. The discrimination against Church members in the allocation of jobs and college places, which had been the norm since the sixties, was supposed to become a thing of the past. "There's no country in the world," Castro claimed, "where the people participate in shaping their future as much as in ours. . . . No other regime is as democratic as a socialist regime."[99]

Nevertheless, the restructuring of the leadership apparatus that took place on Castro's instructions was quite spectacular. The number of Party members was reduced by two-thirds, the number of Central Committee secretariats halved from 19 to 9, with a corresponding reduction in the number of jobs. Further down, local Party functionaries found themselves relieved of their posts; whole networks were dissolved. Delegates to the congress replaced more than half the 225 members of the Central Committee and more than half of the 25-person Politbureau. The new members of these bodies came almost exclusively from the generation of 30- and 40-year-olds, representing a broader spectrum of occupational groups than before – even including the field of culture.

But the congress disappointed hopes of a material improvement. The tense situation in the country was reflected in the fact that this important congress took place far from the capital, in Santiago de Cuba, not coincidentally the heart of Castro's traditionally rebellious native province. Accredited foreign journalists were not permitted to attend, and even had to leave the island for the duration. Those who failed to do so were expelled.

After the Party Congress, political observers, journalists, and diplomats concluded from Castro's obvious immobility and the initial lack of economic liberalization that the days of "Castroism" were numbered, that its collapse was looming on the horizon. They were strengthened in this view when, at the concluding rally, the nation and the world saw on their television screens a Máximo Líder with a bunker mentality who could control himself only with difficulty, as he fiercely reaffirmed that he would rather go down with the revolution than abandon the socialist road. A multiparty system was "fake pluralism," he grumbled. Never would Cuba "stumble into the trap of making large or small concessions."[100] He accused the USA of "hegemonism" and compared it to Hitler's Germany. To be sure, in recent months Washington had further tightened the blockade and exerted ever more ruthless pressure on firms and governments in other countries because of their trade links with Cuba.

The population directly felt the effects. It was hardly possible any more to import food containing important vitamins, or powdered milk for young children. As a result, deficiency diseases began to assume epidemic proportions, although the more or less functioning health system fairly soon managed to bring these under control with the help of European governments. After the Party Congress, however, the economic decline turned into a free fall toward catastrophe. Not even the *libreta* ration-book could guarantee a basic supply of food, as there was no longer the minimum to go round. The transport system virtually collapsed, as the lack of spare parts and fuel made itself ever more sharply felt. And more and more of the ever scarcer goods rotted away.

In July 1992, three-quarters of a year after the Party Congress, the Cuban National Assembly adopted its recommendations in the form of a number of laws and constitutional amendments. The state form of the "dictatorship of the proletariat," which had been enshrined in 1976 at the height of the Cuban–Soviet friendship, was simply deleted. The father and hero of the revolution was no longer Karl Marx but again José Martí – and, with him, Fidel Castro. In order to underline this claim to leadership, Castro could be seen almost daily on television or in public campaigns, including in his new position as president of the "National Security Council" that had been reconstituted because of recent events. The Constitution also incorporated the new religious freedom and guaranteed the freedom of opinion, so long as this was exercised in accordance with the socialist principles of society. Anyone who, in the Party's opinion, contravened those principles would have to face the newly formed "rapid deployment force" of the interior ministry and its so-called *actos de repudio* (acts of repudiation or rejection). These repressive groups, unpopular and highly controversial among the public and even inside the Party, were the other side of the charisma of *fidelismo*, whose "repudiation" of oppositional activity involved the crudest threat or application of force.

They descended upon the dissidents who reappeared on the scene in greater numbers during the *período especial*. In one such incident, the well-known poet, Maria Elena Cruz, and the former philosophy professor and chairman of the small "Cuban Commission for Human Rights and National Reconciliation," Elizardo Sánchez, were set upon with cudgels. Released after nine years' imprisonment, Sánchez was again beaten up for disturbing public order and slandering the head of the state and Party, and then sent back to prison.

In order to keep some control over the growing discontent, boredom and lack of prospects, especially among young people, the leadership made some scanty attempts to increase the range of leisure options. At the same time, many were sent off to work in agriculture. As some compensation for the loss of more than 30,000 one-year scholarships to study in the former Eastern bloc, the age at which people were allowed to travel abroad was reduced from 45 (for men) and 40 (for women) to 20 for both sexes. Their favorite new destination was the United States, which at that time was issuing only a fraction of the agreed annual quota of 20,000 visas. This was not the only reason why the liberalization of travel was rather a cosmetic measure; young people also needed money which they did not have – with the exception of black-market dealers.

The Party's youth organization, the UJC, organized large open-air rock festivals with popular groups, to take young people's minds off the drabness of the "special period." Hardly anyone was more popular among Cuban youth than the talented UJC chairman Roberto Robaina, who customarily behaved in a rebellious manner toward the fossilized veterans of the revolution. But not toward Castro. At the organization's congress in 1992, Robaina and the UJC offered their loyalty and affection and paid him bombastic tribute "with all our hearts, as we would honor a beloved father."

Robaina was one of the stars among those younger Party leaders who would soon be called to high office, in a move designed to integrate the new generation and to assure it of a place in the post-revolutionary society. Already the next year, when he was still not yet 40, Robaina was appointed Cuba's foreign minister. Another member of the youthful elite upon whom the Party pinned its hopes was Carlos Lage, the man responsible for the country's economic program since the beginning of the *período especial*.

Robaina was able to hold out for six years as foreign minister, before Castro decided that he was not sufficiently strong in character to withstand the ideological – and, to be sure, also material – temptations of capitalism. In the late spring of 1999, he suddenly fell into the void and ended up in a political "reformatory." There were even rumors that, shortly before, he had been preparing to decamp with his family to Spain.

9

The Eternal Revolutionary

★

Class struggle on a dollar basis

Alone among the great hopes of the rectification and the special period, Carlos Lage managed to survive politically alongside Castro into the new millennium. There was no shortage of attempts by the old guard to lever out the slightly built family man, who looked rather inconspicuous in the shadow of the Great Chairman. Many of them saw as a betrayal the dollarization of the economy that he promoted after 1993, the intensification of foreign capitalist participation in Cuban enterprises, and the gradual, still very cautious opening to the market. But it obviously proved difficult to get rid of him. Unlike other fast-rising men in the Party, Lage did not expose himself to animosity because of any materialist inclinations. It was often heard that, despite his prominent position, he lived in modest accommodation in central Havana and still dropped his children off at school before riding into work by bicycle. So long as Castro gave him protection and he did not make any serious mistakes, his position seemed assured.

Of course, Lage did not pursue "creeping privatization" or "denationalization" of the Cuban economy on his own initiative; he had Castro's backing for it. The state and Party leader countered orthodox doubts with dialectical flexibility, as so often when his back has been against the wall: "We're not dogmatic, no, we're realistic," he once said. "We do all this with a practical attitude, we're not violating any principles of socialism."[1] Julio García Olivares, a member of the Central Committee and at that time chairman of the Cuban Chamber of Commerce, expressed this ideological acrobatics as follows: "We have to think like capitalists but continue being socialists."[2] One of the amendments to the Constitution adopted by the National Assembly in July 1992 specifically guaranteed the participation and ownership rights of foreign investors.

Under the umbrella of socialism, a number of additional measures with a neoliberal ring succeeded in overcoming bureaucratic obstruction. In particular, labor law governing such matters as working hours and protection from dismissal was no longer regarded as sacrosanct in the case of joint ventures. To be sure, foreign participants could not choose employees themselves but had to accept those offered to them – and for years this remained an obstacle and a source of irritation. To attract investors to the tourist industry, for example, the government allowed amortization over a period of four years, as well as repatriation of profits for one to ten years. Although a ceiling of 49 percent was initially set on foreign participation, permission could be given for this to be raised in individual cases. A legal amendment in 1995 even introduced a provision whereby foreign capital could acquire a 100 percent stake, although in practice this was rarely followed up. Castro himself gave it to be understood: "There are no rigid prescriptions. We are ready to consider any kind of proposition."[3]

Although, for reasons that are difficult to comprehend, the issue of private farmers' markets was still taboo in 1991, private pig-breeding had been allowed since the previous year. For, even if Cubans were willing to put up with more than one imagines possible in a modern industrial nation, they could not accept the idea that the national dish of pork with black beans and rice should no longer be available at certain public occasions or family parties. Shortly after the beginning of the "special period," Castro made one exception among the numerous restrictions he proposed to the National Assembly: "We've declared a general amnesty for pigs."[4] Within days, private households bought up 15,000 pigs from state cooperatives or the surviving private farms, and soon many a piglet was seen prospering on balconies, in back yards, small gardens or bathtubs.

At the beginning of the 1990s, more than 70,000 private farmers still operated on the island,[5] having successfully resisted decades of collectivization by insisting on the ownership rights given them for life during and after the revolution. Altogether, they owned roughly 650,000 hectares – that is, as much as 22 percent of land available for agriculture, and 34 percent of uncultivated land. They produced more than a half of all beans, tobacco, and vegetables, as well as just under 20 percent of citrus fruit. The state remained their only official customer, however, even if, with the worsening of the crisis, a growing share of their produce was illegally diverted to the black market.

The ending of Soviet oil deliveries caused the Cuban leadership ever greater concern, as the shortage of foreign currency meant that even desperate attempts to pay over the odds on the world market, bypassing the open US intervention, had become more and more difficult to sustain. Total imports had had to be reduced from a value of $8 billion to $2 billion in the three years since 1989. And the compulsory regression to earlier periods of agriculture and stock-breeding eventually led to a fall in the sugarcane harvest from 7 million tons to just over 4 million tons in 1993; the resulting loss of $500 million in foreign income was equivalent to all the receipts from tourism in the preceding year.

"We face the necessity . . . to search for foreign currency," Castro declared with an evident trace of despair.[6] The 26th of July 1993 of all days – the fortieth anniversary of the attack on the Moncada Barracks – witnessed a crucial capitulation, when the US currency (whose very possession had been a criminal offence) was permitted as a parallel currency. "Free circulation of the US dollar was simply an unavoidable necessity and not the result of an economic program," Castro maintained six years later. At the same time, he vaguely hinted at possible restrictions: "For the future, I think it will never again be necessary to prohibit possession of the US dollar or other foreign currencies, but free circulation of the US dollar in payment for many goods and services will exist only for the period in which the interests of the Revolution make this seem appropriate."[7]

One of the chief motives for legalization of the dollar was to bring secret hoards out from private pillows into the state's coffers, so that it could meet its external economic obligations. At that time, the size of the foreign-currency parallel economy was thought to be around 200 million dollars. The government went so far as to undermine its own official exchange-rate, by offering up to 25 pesos for a dollar. But, even so, the unofficial rate at first was 150 pesos to the dollar – roughly two-thirds of a worker's monthly income. A doctor or engineer might get as much as 2 dollars a month for their salary. Even if this served to divide society into two classes, those with dollars and those without, it still seemed the lesser evil. In any event, it was of more than symbolic significance that the enemy neighbor's "greenback" was driving out the banknotes with the iconic figure of Che Guevara, guerrilla leader and former president of the National Bank. It also marked the supreme leader's farewell to Guevara's dream of building a new man.

The lifting of controls on the dollar should also be seen – although that was not the official view – as a response to political pressure from the population inside the country. The measure was not sufficient, however, to prevent discontent from growing; people continued losing weight, because there was less and less to eat. Shortages were everywhere, and they were no longer bearable. After the National Assembly had convened on August 3 and 4, 1994, and adopted a new tax system, again failing to meet expectations of further market reforms or to make other concessions, a number of acts of violence broke out in Havana the following day. Several thousand people, most of them young, moved through the city throwing stones at the windows of hotels, dollar shops, and government buildings. For the first time anti-Castro slogans could be heard: "We've had enough! We want freedom! Down with Fidel!"[8] Some 300 policemen fired warning shots in the air and used their truncheons, until suddenly the Máximo Líder himself appeared on the scene with a large entourage and launched into discussion with the young people. The crowd immediately calmed down, listened to him, and dispersed. It is true that a sudden downpour helped him out.

This time, however, the leader's charisma did not for long take the edge off the hunger and the desire for greater permissiveness. When its effect subsided, the effervescence continued beneath

297

the surface. The government increased the police presence on the streets and squares, and suspected ringleaders were arrested. Meanwhile, in Miami, Radio Martí increased its number of frequencies to seven, doubled the power of its receivers, and beamed a daily total of 71 hours to Cuba to fan the flames of revolt 71 programs a day.

Soon afterwards, without asking the authorities, determined and desperate people once more chose the tried-and-tested Cuban path of civil disobedience: they opened the outlet to Florida. In their dozens, hundreds and thousands, they again marched to the seashore and set off in almost anything that floated – boats, rafts, or rubber tyres – mostly from the fishing village of Cojimar, near the capital. It was overwhelmingly young people who exposed themselves to the dangers of the crossing, although quite a few of them used violence to seize ferries or other ships in Havana Harbor. Within a month, the numbers leaving in this way had soared to around 35,000.

Those who wanted to leave could hardly be stopped. Many disappeared beneath the waves, and the scale of family tragedies was truly frightful. The worst had already happened in the middle of July, when a Cuban patrol boat rammed and (apparently after opening fire) sank a stolen vessel. The number who drowned was put at 41 by exile sources, and at 32 by Cuban officials. The incident caused revulsion around the world.

After a while, the United States resisted taking any more refugees; only those who made it to the US coast and set foot on shore would be allowed in. On August 11 President Bill Clinton declared that Cuban refugees would not be permitted to enter the United States. Thirteen ships from Cuba were immediately seized by the US coastguard, and those on board were held in a detention camp prior to being sent back. Castro let it be known that he could not guarantee protection of the US borders, and was evidently considering a second "Mariel." The White House chief then threatened a military blockade of Cuba, but his foreign minister, Warren Christopher, soon corrected him and pleaded for a peaceful solution. Former president Jimmy Carter recalls that, at the height of the conflict, Fidel Castro suddenly rang and asked him to intercede with President Clinton. In a televized speech, the Cuban leader gave assurances that he did not wish to offend Clinton or to cause electoral difficulties for him or the Democratic Party; in fact, he was prepared to put a stop to the exodus of the *balseros*, the "raft people."

At the end of August, the first talks took place between US government representatives, the Cuban parliamentary speaker, and Cuba's former foreign minister and UN ambassador, Ricardo Alarcón, and on October 12 an agreement came into effect whereby Cubans would again be allowed to travel to the United States. During the following year 26,000 entry visas were supposed to be issued, after which the annual total would be reduced to 20,000. The next few months saw a veritable run on the immigration permits. The *Neue Zürcher Zeitung* reported in the middle of 1998 that 435,000 people had applied for a visa at the office representing US interests in Havana – which would mean that one in 25 Cubans wanted to leave at that time.[9] As no rational selection could be made under these circumstances, the fate of the applicants was decided by a kind of computer lottery run by the US authorities, although the only ones with a chance of getting an entry visa were those who either had relatives in the USA, had suffered political or religious persecution in Cuba, or had at least a basic school-leaving certificate and several years of work experience.

The many thousands of boat refugees who had already been brought in, or fished out, by the US coastguard now had to reckon on being sent back to Cuba. At first they were held in camps at Guantánamo naval base or in Florida, Texas, military bases in Honduras, St Lucia, Dominica, and other islands, as well as in Panama. The US authorities obviously hoped that the often degrading conditions of their detention would be a powerful inducement for them to return to Cuba of their own free will. Yet fewer than a thousand actually made that decision, and instead there were revolts at the camps in Panama and Guantánamo. In the end, they were gradually allowed to enter the United States, after Cuban exile organizations had made representations on their behalf.

In the mid-nineties Cuban socialism seemed to have hit rock bottom, more or less finished but not dead as the whole world had expected. In retrospect, one can see that the *balsero* crisis marked the turning point. A few weeks later, Decree 191 and Resolution No. 423/91 gave the green light again for private farmers' markets, and on October 1, 1994, the first 120 of these long-awaited *mercados libres agropecuarios* opened for business around the country. By December there were already 200, and by May 1995 the figure had reached 250. According to *Granma*, the official paper of the Cuban Revolution, in its edition of October 2, 1994, the goals were "to stimulate agricultural production; to neutralize the negative effects of the black market; to make more accessible those products that cannot at present be distributed through state channels; and to strengthen the national currency."[10]

In September 1993, two months after legalization of the dollar and a year before the reintroduction of farmers' markets, private individuals were again authorized to provide services "on their own account." *Cuentapropistas* became the name for these small craftsmen, private family restaurants with a maximum of twelve places, private letters of rooms, and other private operators such as the rickshaw-owners offering a service for dollars in the old part of Havana. Altogether, there were some 130 permitted categories.

Soon the official figure for the number of "small businesses" had reached 208,000, although unofficially it was estimated to be closer to 600,000. From January 1, 1996, however, a *cuentapropista* licence was issued only to people who had a tax identification number and paid their taxes in due order. This was supposed to prune exorbitant profits and hence to keep the unavoidable social fall-out as low as possible.

The tax system was elaborated with considerable help from the former director of finances in Hamburg, Horst Gobrecht, who became a Cuban government adviser in 1995. On the basis of the tax reform law of 1994, this German Social Democrat and his team of initially 12 and later 60 young Cuban economists created the framework for a 30 to 35 percent tax on corporate profits, a graduated turnover tax for the self-employed, and a peso or dollar income tax for employees. In the case of dollar income, the tax rate was 10 percent up to a maximum of $2,400 a year, rising thereafter by stages to 50 percent on anything above $60,000. The turnover tax for produce sold on the farmers' markets was set at 5 percent in Havana, 10 percent in other towns, and 15 percent in the countryside. A newly created revenue service, with a staff of 2,000, was responsible for processing tax declarations. Standards were considered high, as 95 percent of persons with a fiscal liability filed their declarations and paid up on time.[11]

Although the privatization measures brought a temporary relief in political tensions, the "Jefe" of the revolution followed them with suspicion. But life in Cuba could no longer be imagined without these rudiments of a private sector, especially as most self-employed people were active in the tourist industry. A three-point joke did the rounds in which the Máximo Líder said: "The people don't want it, the Party doesn't want it, and I don't want it. But we've still got to do it."

The situation was similar with regard to joint ventures with foreign firms, which the state and Party leadership had authorized in 1986, more out of necessity than of its own free choice, in the rectification period following the Third Party Congress. Early in 1991, when the crisis hit Cuba in the wake of the Soviet collapse, there were already 55 joint ventures, with a total foreign stake of some $500 million. By the end of the decade, the figure was approaching 400, with foreign investment expected to rise above $2 billion.[12] Tourism has been the main sector for investment, with the result that between 1989 and 1993 the number of visitors doubled to approximately 550,000, and turnover soared 350 percent from $200 million to $750 million.

After the stimulus to joint ventures and the lifting of controls on the dollar, this sector continued to grow between 1993 and the end of the decade, achieving nearly two million visitors and gross income of $2 billion (the highest turnover in the Cuban economy). It has been estimated, however, that only 15 percent of this sum remained as net income, since the domestic economy was not in a position to produce most of the high-quality goods that tourists required and good foreign currency had to be spent on importing them. The main investors in the tourist industry came from countries with the highest number of Cuba-bound tourists: Spain, Italy, France, Canada, Germany, Sweden, Brazil, Mexico – countries, therefore, which clearly opposed the US pressure for an embargo. At first there was an emphasis on quantity, but the late nineties saw attempts to move away from cheap mass tourism toward city breaks and cultural trips, ecological and health tourism, and treatment at increasingly exclusive spas.

Joint ventures also proved attractive in heavy industry and the exploration and development of mineral resources. With the help of Canadian and European partners, the Cuban oil corporation Cubapetróleo managed to triple output in the space of a decade: from approximately 700,000 tons in 1989 to more than 2 million tons in 1999. Although Cuba still had to import a good three-quarters of its energy requirement, mostly from Mexico and Venezuela, it was producing by the end of the nineties more than 40 percent of its electricity from its own crude oil. Eventually, at the beginning of the year 2000, Cuba announced that it was opening up an area of 43,250 square miles of territorial waters in the Gulf of Mexico for deep-sea exploration of oil – and explicitly asked the US corporations expropriated 40 years before to develop the oil fields. "Our country," Castro admitted, "cannot tap and exploit the potential oil deposits . . . in the Gulf of Mexico without technology and capital from abroad."[13]

In another focus for the earning of foreign currency, the Cuban government built up the biotechnology sector to such a degree that by the early nineties Cuba was the world's largest exporter of such products, the demand being particularly high in the fields of skin regeneration and immunization against meningitis, hepatitis B, and other diseases. Although the pharmaceutical corporations of the USA, Europe, and Japan bitterly opposed it on international markets, Cuba was already making a profit by 1991 and aggressively competing as a supplier of low-priced products, especially to Third World countries. Nevertheless, this sector's share of total exports was no more than 3 to 5 percent, with a value estimated at less than $50 million. Cuba's competitiveness as a Third World country, in such a highly specialized area as biotechnology, was bound up with the high medical standards that had developed there over the decades. UN comparative statistics, on such crucial aspects as infant mortality and life expectancy (75.3 years in Cuba[14]), had for a long time placed it above countries in the First World, even the United States.

302

These standards were largely maintained even through the grave shortages of the special period. "In spite of budgetary restraint," noted the *Financial Times*, in a special report on Cuba in March 1999, "spending on health and education has been increased in real terms." UN social indicators showed that in 1997 Cuba was still at or near the top in Latin America, "with one of the lowest rates of poverty and illiteracy on the continent;"[15] in fact, the literacy rate was just under 97 percent at the end of the nineties.[16] The finance minister at the time, Manuel Millares, could claim: "We have tried to guarantee social fundamentals. Our people are in a better condition than the majority of Latin Americans."[17]

The free public health system also remained an essential feature of the Cuban Revolution, continuing to employ 340,000 staff and 64,000 doctors through the years of the special period – a ratio of one doctor per 193 inhabitants, compared with one per 313 in Germany.[18] For Castro, the negative example was the former Soviet Union: "They've published that the life expectancy in the part of the USSR which is Russia is now 56 years, 20 years less than in Cuba, 20 years!"[19] And he assured his audience: "We make sure that those medications which are vital, those which save lives, those which are essential are never lacking; we prioritize them."[20]

Yet, despite Castro's protestations, the population soon lacked the most basic medicines such as aspirin. At the beginning of the year 2000, the American Association for World Health (AAWH) reported that "more than 300 medicines and basic medical supplies are unavailable in Cuba, ... Surgery is performed only on selected cases, and there are limitations on ambulance services. . . . Also unavailable are several AIDS medications." A special cause for concern was the rising incidence of water-borne diseases such as typhoid fever and other intestinal infections, and viral hepatitis. The AAWH partly blamed the US embargo for this situation. In a report published in 1997, it stated: "A humanitarian catastrophe has been averted only because the Cuban government has maintained a high level of budgetary support for a health-care system designed to deliver primary and preventive health care to all of its citizens. Cuba still has an infant mortality rate half that of the city of Washington, D.C."[21]

The crash and new beginning also involved a reordering of economic priorities. Forty years after Batista and his American friends were driven out, tourism was again in first place. The second-largest source of foreign currency was the very *gusanos* or "worms" who drew Castro's scorn, the 1.25 million Cuban exiles in the United States, whose money transfers to poorer relatives were estimated in the late nineties to have reached $1.2 billion a year, a fifth of Cuba's total inflow of foreign currency. Sugar came only third in the economic statistics, although this was due more to necessity than to planning. Antiquated technology in the country's 156 sugar factories (more than a quarter of which had to stop running), plus the shortage of spare parts, fuel, and fertilizer, had brought down the sugar harvest from more than 8 million tons to the lowest level in 50 years: a mere 3.2 million tons.

The export of Cuban cigars, however, still among the best (and most expensive) in the world, was a thriving business. Between 1997 and the end of the millennium, efforts were made to double production to 200 million units and a turnover of $200 million – though even that was far from satisfying demand. Banned from the US market because of the embargo, Cuban cigars were greatly in demand there – at black-market prices.

The evolution of Cuba's balance of payments and state budget presented a "generally positive picture," admitted the *Financial Times* report of March 1999, and the government operated "a tight monetary programme which would have made any capitalist finance minister proud." At the beginning of 1999, the Cuban National Bank calculated the external debt in freely convertible currency at $11.2 billion;[22] this actually seemed rather modest in Third World terms, but it did not include the debt in non-transferable rubles to the former Comecon, the exact size of which was a matter of dispute because of wide differences over the rate of exchange that should be applied. In any event, the United Nations Economic Commission for Latin America (CEPAL) also praised Cuba's stabilization measures, especially the gearing of a "second economy" to market criteria.

CEPAL's comparative economic statistics suggest that in 1999 the Cuban Revolution reached the point at which it had been 40 years before, in 1959. New taxes and a 70 percent reduction in subsidies for unprofitable state enterprises (which now had to make a profit or shut down) had helped to bring the budget deficit down from 33 percent of GNP in previous years to just 3 percent. This had led to massive redundancies: in the sugar industry, for example, nearly 10,000 of the 90,000-strong workforce had been asked to look for work elsewhere.

A socialist society thus found itself facing what was, officially at least, an unprecedented phenomenon: unemployment. According to diplomatic sources, this was running in 1995 at 8 percent of the total labor force of 4 million. A plethora of countermeasures managed to reduce this over the next few years to 6 or 7 percent. But the IRELA institute in Madrid estimated in May 1999 that nearly a third of all Cuban workers were either jobless or underemployed.[23]

The architect of the new turn in economic policy, Carlos Lage, told the author in May 1999: "The collapse of the Communist system and the demise of the Soviet Union in the early nineties meant that we lost 85 percent of our external trade. So, between 1989 (or, to be more precise, 1991) and 1994, we had to swallow a 34 percent decline in our gross national product."[24] More than a third of this was recuperated in the years from 1995 to the end of the millennium; growth was running at a "yearly average of 3.5 percent." In 1999, according to CEPAL figures, the Cuban economy then surged by 6 percent to reach a GNP of $17.5 billion.[25] By that time, Lage said, "well over 50 percent of the Cuban population had access to dollars" – and the trend was continuing upward. The government hoped that the numbers would rapidly increase, so that the glaring inequalities between those with and those without dollars could be further narrowed.

Undoubtedly, dollarization did lead to a kind of two-class society: on one side, those who depended on a wage paid in pesos; on the other side, the self-employed and others working under privileged conditions, who received payment in dollars. "Dollarization has led to an inversion of the social pyramid," the Hamburg Institute of Latin American Studies put it in one of its analyses.[26] Whereas "the traditional supports of the regime – highly skilled income groups such as doctors, teachers and academics" had scarcely any access to dollars, "waiters, taxi drivers, prostitutes and domestic personnel . . . in the new economic milieu" were part of the country's "up-and-coming elite." What is more, many goods were no longer obtainable except on the black market, which was thought by experts still to account for 30 percent of all economic activity in the country.[27]

In the spring of 1999, Castro announced average pay rises of 5.7 percent for six out of ten employees, bringing the average wage to 223 pesos a month,[28] although for some occupational groups, such as doctors and teachers, it was raised by as much as 30 percent, to 530 pesos. (It should always be borne in mind, of course, that most social services, as well as housing, basic food, and local transport, cost next to nothing.) Many enterprises – above all, the joint ventures – had meanwhile gone over to paying a part of wages in dollars. But since the dollar was not an inter-changeable but a "parallel" currency, a "convertible peso" was introduced with its own notes and coins, which were also accepted in diplomats' shops (the so-called *diplotiendas*) and newly emerging shopping centers. In the tourist industry, it was no longer the case that all employees had to hand in tips given to them in foreign currency. With all these measures, the government hoped to have spread the ownership of dollars quickly enough for popular discontent to start waning again.

Experts doubted that a monetary reform could in the long term both end the problem of two currencies circulating alongside each other and "speed up the country's integration into the inter-national trade and finance system." The previously mentioned Hamburg study, for instance, pointed to experiences in other societies that had undergone transformation: "The monetary reform in Russia led in 1992 to a rate of inflation of 1600 percent; the associated losses of purchasing power have continued to destabilize the country more or less up to the present day."[29]

This example gave the Cuban leadership a degree of self-assurance. "We have done this by ourselves, with no support from any international financial organization," Castro's deputy, Lage, emphasized. "The blockade imposed by the USA means that we have no access to other finance markets and therefore to long-term loans. The World Bank and the International Monetary Fund are controlled by the USA." Cuba's annual financial requirement was estimated to be in the vicinity of $6.5 billion, but it could obtain loans only on the private capital market, at extortionate rates of interest that Lage put at "usually around 15 percent."

Representatives of German banks who accompanied the president of the German Confederation of Industry, Hans-Olaf Henkel, on his trip to Havana in spring 1999 held up Cuba's repayment standards as exemplary in comparison with other Latin American countries.[30] Surprisingly, Henkel was rather taken with his Cuban interlocutors: "It felt like meeting up with company colleagues and board members, rather than ministers and politicians." The Máximo Líder himself took Henkel prisoner for a four-hour talk, during which the German discovered – despite underlying ideological differences – such "an amazing number of areas of agreement"[31] that he made another (private) visit to Fidel Castro for the millennium celebrations. It was thanks to Henkel's pressure that the SPD-Green government of Gerhard Schröder restored the Hermes loan guarantee, which its predecessor had suspended in 1988 because of the lack of clarity surrounding Cuba's debt with the Soviet Union and other Comecon countries. Henkel was evidently concerned that the German economy was now falling behind.

The fact that "Castroism" not only outlasted Soviet Communism but was able to spare its people the neoliberal chaos which engulfed other Eastern bloc countries led many Western businessmen with a stake in the Cuban economy to make a (by no means politically correct) admission: "When you compare Cuba to Russia, they've done pretty well."[32] The other side of the coin was that no fundamental reform of Cuba's political system was likely in the near future. Yet Carlos Lage could also recognize: "We live in a globalized world, and globalization is not only irreversible but will actually grow deeper."

Despite these thoroughly unfamiliar tones coming out of Havana, there was no doubt about Lage's (and his master's) ultimate position. He told the author:

All past and future changes in our socialist system are designed to tie our economy closer and closer to the world economy, but

307

while maintaining the dominant role of state ownership. Even if we increasingly seek and permit the involvement of private foreign capital, we do not and will not have a privatization policy here. We don't believe in neoliberalism. We have not opened up in order to sell our country. I think that a firm's chances of holding its own in the world market depend not on the property relations but on its capacity to adapt its technology and management to world-market demands and to motivate its own workforce. Also, Cuba offers investors conditions that they will not find in other Third World countries: security, stability, and a population with high levels of health and education; an economy that has found its own way and achieved continuous growth; a country without corruption, without drugs and without organized crime.[33]

For a long time the "Cuban model" appeared to sketch out a third way between capitalism and Communism, and there is a lot to suggest that this impression was intended. But Carlos Lage, who is now seen as one of Castro's possible successors, emphatically rejects such an analysis. To admit it openly might only provoke further restrictions, both internally and externally.

The West does not like granting Castro his triumph over all opponents living and dead, especially as he is not prepared to accept economic reforms or a privatization of state firms comparable to the measures adopted by the Fifteenth Congress of the Chinese Communist Party. In this respect, the major industrial nations – at the instigation of the United States – do not allow Cubans the right of national self-determination, and any support from international organizations is subject to more rigorous conditions of regime change (in the direction of the neoliberal "new world order") than with regard to any other country. If Cuba integrated more into the international finance system and recovered on the basis of a "dollar economy," Castro would scarcely have any choice but to allow more and more political freedoms. But this also means that, the more the economy recovers against Washington's will, the more arguments there are for a further tightening of Castro's political system.

The Fifth Congress of the Communist Party of Cuba, held between October 8 and 10, 1997, marked the thirtieth anniversary of Che Guevara's death and put on a demonstration of unity with Fidel Castro and the Party and state leadership. Castro made his longest speech since 1960 – nearly seven hours in all. CIA director George Tenet told Congress in his extensive report on Cuba: "Fidel Castro appears healthy for a man of 70, and his political position seems secure."[34]

The 1,482 congress delegates did not, however, adopt any really new economic and political perspectives, apart from a reduction in the size of the Central Committee from 225 to 150 members. The most striking aspect was the strengthening of the role of the military, and therefore of the Party's orthodox wing, in the political apparatus; military men would in future comprise about a third of the Politbureau[35] and head six key ministries (defense and internal affairs, as well as communications, fisheries, transport, and sugar).[36] Castro seemed to regard the military as the institution which could ensure that the revolution moved in a disciplined manner into the new millennium. The Congress also made it clear that, far from showing readiness for a real political opening, the concessions to the market were intended only to maintain the state-run economy and to make it more efficient. It rejected a proposal to privatize at least small- and medium-sized state enterprises, and merely allowed people working on their own account to hire employees under certain circumstances.

Early in the year 2000, in a conversation with former UNESCO director Federico Mayor Zaragoza, Castro said:

> As a general principle, nothing will be privatized in Cuba that is suitable for, and can therefore be kept under, ownership by the nation or a workers' collective. Our ideology and our preference is that socialism should bear no resemblance to the egoism, the privileges and the inequalities of capitalist society. In our country, nothing ends up as the property of a high-ranking official, and nothing is given away to accomplices or friends. Nothing that can be used efficiently, and with greater profit for our society, will end up in the hands of private individuals, either Cubans or foreigners.[37]

The evident hardening of Castro's ideological positions had a lot to do with the fact that for ten years he had been able to watch the fate of his former friends in the Eastern bloc. Closer to home, in Latin America, where democratization and neoliberalism also seemed to have brought nothing to the mass of the population, he saw grim prospects in store that he did not wish Cuba to endure. He told Zaragoza:

> In many of these countries a third of the population can neither read nor write; millions of Latin Americans have no roof over their head. . . . The debt burden in Latin American countries is so high that many of them – regardless of the size of their gross national product – cannot provide most of their citizens with a dignified quality of life. . . . The weak Latin American currencies are unable to defend themselves from speculators. . . . Revenue from acts of privatization that have damaged the national heritage are . . . swallowed up. Latin America, like the rest of the Third World, is the victim of a world economic order imposed on it from outside. . . . Divided and balkanized, seduced by illusory visions of progress and development, . . . the Latin American countries run the risk of losing their independence for ever and being annexed by the United States.[38]

Cuba and the global policeman

On January 9 and 13, 1996, militant Cuban exiles from the *Hermanos al Rescate* ("Brothers to the Rescue") organization flew out from Florida in small civilian aircraft, entered Cuban air space and dropped thousands of anti-Castro leaflets on the streets of Havana. Nothing of the kind had happened since 1960. The defensive behavior of the Cuban air force encouraged the group to continue with its propaganda flights.

Originally, in 1991, the "Brothers to the Rescue" had been set up only to keep an aerial watch for refugees in the sea between Cuba and Florida, so that it could get the US coastguard to rescue them. Increasingly, however, it came to reinterpret its humanitarian goals as a political mission to arouse international attention by deliberately violating Cuban air space.

On February 24, 1996, three more sports planes belonging to this organization approached the Cuban coast, and at least one probably entered Cuban air space. But this time they did not get much further. Evidently on orders from above, the Cuban air force intercepted the three aircraft and shot two of them down.

As if to set an example, to deliver a clear lesson, the Cuban fighters opened fire without warning and without any attempt to force the intruders to land. The four people inside the two planes, all of them Cuban exiles (three with US citizenship), lost their lives. Two days later, at the request of the United States, the UN Security Council considered the incident and ruled that Havana had violated the principle according to which states should refrain from the use of weapons against civilian aircraft flying inside their air space.[39]

The provocative strategy of the anti-Castro forces in Miami had a macabre if dubious success, when overreaction by Havana's security apparatus triggered an immediate overreaction by Washington's political apparatus. On March 12, 1996, Democratic President Bill Clinton signed a law on "Cuban liberty and democratic solidarity" which, though passed by the Senate in October 1995, had been put on ice because of its explosive foreign-policy implications. Bearing the name of its two sponsors, Senator Jesse Helms and his fellow-Republican Dan Burton from the House of Representatives, the Helms-Burton Act soon entered the political vocabulary. It involved a dramatic sharpening of the 35-year-old Cuban economic embargo, at least as disproportionate as the shooting down of the exiles' aircraft and stretching well beyond other trade restrictions recently introduced by the United States. In the view of experts and politicians critical of Cuba, as well as of moderate Cuban exile circles, it was a bundle of political stupidity and short-sightedness.

The Helms-Burton Act was in some ways reminiscent of the Platt Amendment of 1901, whereby the United States had subjugated the Caribbean island after its long and bloody war of independence and forced it into a semi-colonial dependence. But, in extending sanctions to firms from third countries that had economic dealings with Cuba, the act represented a new claim to omnipotence that infringed the sovereignty of other states. The role once played by Platt's big stick of military intervention was now taken up by the cudgel of financial and economic sanctions, which were designed to hit not only the insubordinate Cubans but any firm or country that did not fall in with Washington's drive to isolate Cuba. Experts in all branches of politics and the law showed a rare unanimity in arguing that the Helms-Burton Act was an elementary violation of international law, because it placed US national law above all else and even encroached upon the democratic constitutions of friendly and allied states. It is true that similar sanctions had been imposed on other countries with which Washington had hostile relations at that time – in particular, Iran, Iraq, and Libya – but in those cases none of the legal provisions had been as draconian as the measures against Castro's Cuba.

Cuban exiles saw the new Act as a further step toward "ending the Castro tyranny." But, in Castro's eyes, it was much more than a blockade: "It's war, it's persecution, it's harassment," he declared.[40]

The four main clauses of the Helms-Burton Act left all earlier sanctions in the shade – even the list drawn up by Democratic congressman Robert Torricelli in October 1992 and signed by then-president George Bush. The provisions of previous embargoes, against both Cuba and other countries, had been a matter for executive orders rather than measures with the force of law; they had therefore left scope for foreign-policy considerations in the way in which they were handled. The Helms-Burton Act was a legislative measure that tied the hands of the executive; it could be amended or repealed only by Congress. The President himself therefore had very little leeway, even in areas where the Act conflicted with reasons of state and breached international law.

Title I of the Act – over and above the longstanding ban on direct or indirect dealings by US firms with Cuba – obliged the US government, in all international financial organizations such as the World Bank or the IMF, to block any loan or financial assistance to Cuba, or even its acceptance into the organization in question. In the event that a democratic majority in one of these institutions making up the international community should set aside the Helms-Burton Act as contrary to the law, Washington would be compelled by national legislation to violate its contractual obligations to that organization and the international community joined together within it, and to reduce its annual contribution by the amount of the sum granted to Cuba. At the same time, US firms were forbidden to import from third countries any products that contained material extracted and processed in Cuba, such as nickel, sugar, or citrus fruit. If the successor states to the Soviet Union continued to support Cuba by offering it more favorable conditions than those obtaining on the world market, an equivalent reduction of US financial assistance to those countries would be threatened. Title II ("Assistance to a Free and Independent Cuba") stipulated that there could be a question of lifting the embargo only when a "transition government" was in power in Cuba which corresponded to the values of the majority in the US Congress. One of its "requirements for determining a transition government" would be "that it is substantially moving toward a market-oriented economic system based on the right to own and enjoy property" and "has made demonstrable progress in returning to United States citizens (and entities which are 50 percent or more beneficially owned by United States citizens) property taken by the Cuban Government." Section 205A, paragraph 7 further specified that "a transition government is a government that . . . does not include Fidel Castro or Raul Castro."[41]

Even with Castro gone, however, the Helms-Burton Act explicitly ruled out that a democratic government in Cuba could ever endorse by parliamentary means the expropriations of the 1960s – as the *Alteigentümerverordnung* had done in reunified Germany, by ratifying all expropriation of landed estates over 100 hectares that the Soviet occupation authorities carried out after the war in Eastern Germany. For Cuba's future development, a return to the old property relations would be as catastrophic as an obligation to pay compensation at today's values.

Cuba expert Bert Hoffmann writes in his comprehensive analysis:

This second chapter of the act is fraught with political consequences. Should the kind of political change envisaged by the [US] hardliners actually come about in Cuba, the Helms-Burton Act already exists today as the undemocratic congenital defect of the new relations, much as the sinister "Platt Amendment" did in the case of Cuba's First Republic. Above all else, the Helms-Burton Act strengthens the rigidities of the Cuban system. All those among Cuba's leaders and officials who have limited enthusiasm for a political opening are shown only a deep precipice but no space in which to carry out a reform in dignity.[42]

The Helms-Burton Act is a blunt law for custodianship over a future Cuba: its aim is not democratization of the political system and its institutions, but reappropriation of the island by its neighbor to the north. A return of large chunks of the Cuban economy to private US corporations would not only mean restoring the (scarcely desirable) conditions existing before the revolution. The people of the island would still bear the burden of interest, and interest on interest, for generations to come, while the real beneficiaries would include the offspring of those Mafiosi who came into their possessions through violence and repression, corruption, theft, tax evasion, and the filing of dubious ownership claims. Nor does the Helms-Burton Act set any requirement for the return of at least the half a billion dollars plus interest that were stolen from the Cuban state coffers in the closing days of the Batista regime.

"The Helms-Burton Act," noted Bert Hoffmann, "therefore dictates the basic long-term political conditions in Cuba, far beyond the end of the Castro era. . . . Even many Cubans who resolutely oppose Castro find this too much to swallow."[43] For former US President Jimmy Carter, the Act was "one of the worst mistakes my country has ever made," because it severely hindered efforts to achieve democratization in Cuba.[44]

Furthermore, the Act infringes the sovereignty of all countries that have economic relations with the Caribbean island, especially the member-states of the European Union, Canada, and Mexico. Title III gives to US citizens and corporations which lost their property through the Cuban Revolution an explicit right to sue in US courts not only the Cuban state but also foreign companies doing business or operating joint ventures in any way connected with such former property. Title IV prohibits entry into the United States to directors, proprietors, or majority shareholders of any

314

foreign company that is in breach of the Act and has had transactions with any former US possessions expropriated by the Cuban state. This provision applies even to members of such persons' families.

The right to seek redress before US courts for any property confiscated in Cuba was specifically extended to all Cuban exiles who had subsequently acquired US citizenship. In the view of legal experts, this violated the principle of international law whereby such suits could be filed only before a court in the plaintiff's country of origin. It also contradicted the ruling three decades before by the US Foreign Claims Settlement Commission, which held that, according to international law, claims for compensation required American citizenship to have been present at the time of the loss.[45] The effect was dramatically to increase the potential number of lawsuits for the return of confiscated property. Instead of the 300 or so previously thought likely, the US State Department estimated in the late nineties that the figure would be between 75,000 and 200,000;[46] while other experts considered this too low and spoke of as many as 400,000 claims.[47]

The list of those entitled to file a lawsuit therefore included not only owners of US firms such as General Electric, American Sugar, or Standard Oil, but also, for example, US-domiciled inheritors of Cuban firms such as the Bacardi rum company, formerly based in Havana, who now had the right to take action against French or Spanish drinks corporations, insofar as these had business relations with Cuban state enterprises that had taken over former Bacardi property. In fact, Bacardi did manage to get a New York court to ban the registration of a Cuban rum brand "Havana Club," which was being produced in a joint venture with the French company Pernod Ricard. And relatives of the gangsters Santos Trafficante and Meyer Lansky, being US citizens, might well file collection claims in US courts against tourist companies in Germany, Spain, or Italy, on the grounds that they accommodate package tourists in the Mafia's old "Capri" and "Riviera" hotels.

At the beginning of the millennium, the American justice system was handling just 5,900 such cases; claims totalled $6 billion (including interest), going back to the early sixties, not only for property-related matters but also for allegedly unexplained deaths. But the number of suits is growing. In 1999, a US court awarded the astronomical sum of $186.7 million in compensation to relatives of the three "Brothers to the Rescue" members shot down in February 1996 – more than $60 million for each family member. (Relatives of the fourth man went short only because they did not have US citizenship.) So that the money could be collected without delay, a confiscation order was made – against the will of the US State Department – for $19 million due to the Cuban telephone company ETECSA for communications between the two countries. Cuba reacted to this by closing down 85 percent of the telephone lines to the United States.

Meanwhile, Havana had replied to Washington's demands with its own set of figures. In a "Report to the Secretary-General of the United Nations" in 1999, the Castro government stated that "scientific estimates" had put at $67 billion the total damages caused to Cuba by the US blockade up to 1998. To this was to be added for each subsequent year roughly 1.5 percent of Cuba's GNP. The government in Washington seemed quite unperturbed by the condemnations of the US blockade that the UN General Assembly had for years been passing with an overwhelming majority. In the year 2000, for example, 166 of the 189 member-states voted with Cuba against the embargo; only Israel and the Marshall Islands actually cast a positive vote alongside the United States.

The rival estimates of damages entered a new round in May 1999, when the People of Cuba filed a suit with a Havana court for compensation against the Government of the United States of America. It made detailed claims that, over the previous 40 years, US secret agents had been responsible for the death of 3,478 Cubans and the disabling of 2,099 more Cuban citizens.[48] The list of US-based actions stretched from Eisenhower's presidential order of March 17, 1960, for a "program of covert operations against the Castro regime," through the Bay of Pigs invasion, "Operation Mongoose" (begun in 1961) and the release of pests to destroy the sugar harvest, to the operations of the Cuban terrorist organizations "Alpha 66" and "Omega 7," such as the bomb attack that killed 73 people on a Cuban DC-8 from

Barbados to Havana on October 6, 1976. The statement submitted to the court also accused the US government of biological warfare against Cuba: that is, US agents were alleged to have released in May 1981 a type of dengue fever virus, which led to an almost simultaneous epidemic affecting some 350,000 people in various regions between Havana and the east of the island. It was only thanks to prompt and comprehensive vaccinations and other countermeasures that no more than 158 people, including 101 children, died as a result.

Interesting in this connection is an extract from the minutes of talks between Castro and GDR leader Erich Honecker, during the latter's visit to Cuba in late May 1980. Castro complained behind closed doors:

> We have had some very strange plagues appearing here recently. It is our view that the three major plagues have been acts of sabotage. One of these was a fungus on the tobacco plantations, which destroyed 90 percent of this year's tobacco production and forced us to import tobacco. . . . It involved blue mold. We also had a very serious plague on the sugar plantations. . . . It caused a loss of roughly a million tonnes of sugar. . . . Then we had the African swine fever. . . . We now have this swine fever virtually under control.

Less than two weeks before, an aircraft had flown over the island "dropping a gelatine-like substance with a highly refined fungus in microscopically small capsules," over an area 15 miles wide. "It is all very disturbing," Castro thought, "because these can be signs of bacteriological warfare." Investigations had shown that the substances in question did not come "from one small group of counter-revolutionaries" but were part of "a highly developed industry."[49]

The statement submitted to the court in Havana also spoke of numerous "plans to assassinate the leader of the Cuban Revolution," Fidel Castro. Since December 11, 1959, when the CIA head of operations in the Western hemisphere, Colonel J. C. King, wrote a memorandum suggesting Castro's overthrow, "Cuban state security [had] disclosed, investigated, uncovered or neutralized . . . 637 attempts on the life of Commander-in-Chief Fidel Castro."[50]

On November 2, 1999, the people's court in Havana handed down a judgment that it will scarcely be possible ever to follow up: namely, that the government of the United States should pay $181 billion in damages and compensation to the Cuban people.[51] "You must not forget that the government of the United States already owes the Cuban people more than 300 billion dollars for human damages caused by its mercenary invasion at the Bay of Pigs, its dirty war and many other crimes, as well as for the effects of the blockade on the national economy," Castro told a rally at Pinar del Río in July 2000.[52]

One who boasted of "drafting a large part of the Helms-Burton Act," and of actually being "responsible" for its aggravation of the embargo, was none other than congressman Lincoln Díaz-Balart from Florida. In fact, he was Castro's nephew, born in 1954 in Havana when Castro was in prison for the attack on the Moncada Barracks. His father, then, was Castro's brother-in-law, Rafael Díaz-Balart, his close friend, political comrade, and speechwriter from university days, whose sister Mirta had been Castro's wife at the time. The family link and the political friendship both fell apart after Batista's seizure of power and the attack on the Moncada Barracks, when Castro considered that the Díaz-Balarts, as close followers of the dictator, were giving cover to the brutal repression and even shared some of the responsibility for it. Thus, Castro's former father-in-law was Batista's public prosecutor, as well as mayor of Batista's native town of Banes and a member of his cabinet; and Rafael Díaz-Balart, his son of the same name, was serving as deputy minister of the interior at the time of Castro's imprisonment. After the victory of the revolution, the erstwhile friend was regarded as a traitor and had to flee the island.

The past ties of Rafael and then Lincoln Díaz-Balart with the man now in Havana's Palace of the Revolution gave the struggle over Cuba some of the characteristics of bitter family warfare, which assumed even more bizarre dimensions in 1999 when the young refugee Elián González was washed up on the coast of Florida.

Since the Helms-Burton Act came into force, Washington had been trying to impose its worldwide implementation. One day in late 1999 this author himself felt its absurd complications, when he applied for a Cuban visa and used the United Parcel Service to send his passport from Hamburg to the Cuban embassy in Berlin, only to receive the package back three days later without having achieved anything. The company refused to deliver the article in question and would give no explanation for the three days' delay. But a UPS employee had clearly indicated the reason by writing the word "Embargo!" on the envelope, complete with an exclamation mark. To the objection that the American embargo had no validity or legal force in the Federal Republic of Germany, the person at the other end of the telephone line tersely replied that that did not interest him: UPS was a US company and followed the business policy laid down at headquarters. Incidentally, it was also on the list of "top contributors" to Lincoln Díaz-Balart's election campaign in 1996.

In October 1996, half a year after the Helms-Burton Act came into force, the EU's Council of Europe adopted regulations which forbade European companies and their subsidiaries to respect the terms of the Act. The EU Commission in Brussels opened a kind of bureau to which Europe's ever more frequent experiences with the US embargo could be reported. Companies that were prosecuted in the USA had the right to bring a counter-claim in Europe, if the US plaintiff had a branch on this side of the Atlantic. Mexico and Canada introduced similar procedures.

At first, in view of the unanimously negative reaction around the world, it seemed that the USA had gone too far with the Helms-Burton Act. After all, the President was able to extract the agreement of Congress that certain provisions of the Act could be "suspended" for periods of six months – and from the very first day he used this leeway in connection with sanctions against foreign companies doing business with Cuba. In reality, however, this "suspension" was not a climbdown but a threatening gesture. What it said was that, if Europe in future did not give adequate support to US policy in Cuba, the full force of sanctions would be brought to bear against third countries.

The threat proved effective. Talks begun in 1995 to explore the possibility of a EU cooperation agreement with Cuba were broken off for the time being, and the expansion of economic assistance to Cuba was explicitly tied to visible progress on human rights issues and political freedoms. Spain's new conservative premier, José María Aznar, in contrast to his Socialist predecessor, Felipe González, adopted a particularly negative attitude to Castro's Cuba, ending economic assistance and coming down so hard on human rights that a crisis and a three-year break in diplomatic relations ensued between the old colonial power and its former overseas possession. Meanwhile, the uproar in various European governments was dismissed in Washington as mere rhetoric. After the Clinton administration promised to suspend extra-territorial action under the Helms-Burton Act until the end of his term in 2001, the EU made concessions of its own at the World Trade Organization by withdrawing its complaint against the United States for violation of the international freedom of trade; it also ordered European companies to refrain from making use of expropriated property anywhere in the world, not only in Cuba.

But there were still companies which ignored the Helms-Burton Act. Mercedes-Benz, for example, a German-American firm belonging to Daimler-Chrysler, traded in Cuba as neither German nor American but as Egyptian, in the form of a Cairo-registered joint venture with the Cubans in which the Egyptian partner was one of the few to which the Cuban government had allowed a stake of 51 percent. At the end of the millennium, its annual turnover was estimated to be over $50 million. Its business consisted of supplying and assembling buses and small trucks, and providing Mercedes limousines for the Cuban government and engines for Cuban agriculture, evidently paid for out of the proceeds of sugar sales on the international market.

Mercedes-Benz, trading in this case as "MCV – Manufacturing of Commercial Vehicles," did not choose Cuba only as a local market with good prospects for the future; it also saw the island as an ideal springboard for business in the Caribbean. Nowhere in the region was "the social climate as healthy as in Cuba," enthused Günther Roller, then commercial director of the company on loan from Stuttgart, who had good connections with the

Comandante and his economics chief Carlos Lage. Nowhere else in the region was the potential workforce so well educated, so capable, so creative and so highly motivated.[53]

Cuba's political system and security apparatus provided its main advantages as a business location: the ubiquitous police presence ensured public safety and order; millions did not vegetate in slum areas as in other countries of South and Central America (including nearby Haiti or Jamaica); and crime and corruption were scarcely a problem, in sharp contrast to the rest of the Caribbean and Latin America. This apparatus, which had the positive effect of preserving law and order, was the same as the one which represented the darker side of the system by restricting personal and political freedoms. But, for the "Egyptians" and for others attracted for the same reasons, the involvement in Cuba was of strategic significance: "First," Günther Roller stated, "Cuba with its population of eleven million is the largest market in the Caribbean. Second, it offers a huge potential for expansion in the Caribbean and the countries bordering on it."

When Fidel Castro, as in the old days, attended the UN millennium summit in New York in September 2000 to uphold the complaints of the Third World against the industrial nations, Cuba had diplomatic relations with a total of 170 countries, nearly every one in the world. Thus, by the end of the twentieth century, Cuba had quietly made further advances in breaking the international isolation promoted by the United States. Castro's new non-military "internationalism," defined in opposition to the globalization of politics and economics, was meant to establish his profile once more as a spokesman for the Third World. As he said at the millennium summit, he had "the privilege of being able to speak absolutely freely, since we are dependent neither on the World Bank nor on the Monetary Fund, and we have resisted for ten years the double blockade [by the US and also by the countries of the former Eastern bloc]."[54]

Once again, as 40 years before, he knew how to take the stage as a media star. This time he did not put up in a Harlem hotel, but he did visit the black district of New York, and his opponents again served as useful supernumeraries by drawing attention to him with their vociferous insults. At the UN General Assembly he did not, as then, speak for four and a half hours, but kept to the time limit of five minutes that everyone was expected to observe. Fully aware of his enduring charisma, he took the opportunity to put on a little show to frighten his audience – not with a thermos flask, this time, but with a white handkerchief that he used to cover the red light at the rostrum, in allusion to his reputation as a marathon speaker. To the photographers, he offered a welcome opportunity to take a snapshot that relieved the tedium of the usual UN poses. The picture in question, which grateful editors all around the world immediately published, made his appearance the most widely noted event of the summit.

The audience at the plenary session listened to a man who expressed himself slowly and deliberately, in well-chosen words and fleshed-out sentences. Nothing seemed to have changed in this respect, except that his voice had become slightly more brittle. But even when he sounded a little fossil-like, he never lost the thread. He presented his case in a more forthcoming manner, ostensibly with greater wisdom and maturity, than on previous occasions when he had adopted a more combative style. A fighting spirit anyway comes to him more readily when he is at home, among his fellow-countrymen, capable of speaking for hours in the wettest or sultriest weather, unimpressed by the fact that young and old members of the audience meanwhile feel faint and have to be carried away by paramedics.

Despite its ideological handicap, or maybe because of it, Cuba had meanwhile escaped wider public notice as it had grown into a leading political and economic role among the countries and islands of the Caribbean. Since 1993 it had had a cooperation agreement with the CARICOM economic community; it had observer status at meetings of the Caribbean Forum; it joined in December 2000 the 78-member group of African, Caribbean and Pacific states (ACP); and it was a founding member of the Association of Caribbean States (ACS). Havana wanted to develop the island as a hub for the entire region, which was not in good shape either economically or politically. Colombia was paralyzed by the gang terror of drug barons, leftist guerrillas, and rightist paramilitary death squads. Venezuela was stuck in a deep economic crisis, as were Central America and the Caribbean.

322

And, particularly in Central America, the US-nurtured promises of a better life after the civil war had not been fulfilled.

At the end of 1999, a strategic alliance between Cuba and Venezuela seemed to be taking shape within Latin America, much to Washington's chagrin. Venezuela's unpredictable populist head of state, Hugo Chávez, who in 1992 had staged an abortive coup against the regime of Carlos Andrés Pérez and ended up in jail, was a self-professed admirer of Fidel Castro. And the hothead was of interest to the Cuban leader, not so much because of his flattery as because his country was endowed with great oil wealth. After the Ibero–American summit in Havana in 1999, Chávez stayed on for a state visit lasting several days; he shared a baseball match with Castro, signed an economic and military cooperation agreement, and received the highest Cuban decoration. Shortly after his departure, the Cubans were able to prove their usefulness in an especially vital sphere, when Castro's secret service claimed to have uncovered an attempt by exile circles to assassinate the Venezuelan leader. And, when his country was struck by a natural disaster, Cuba sent doctors and other relief workers to help with the reconstruction.

Castro had mounted a similar aid operation after Hurricane Mitch left a trail of destruction in Central America. Another extremely clever move, which also raised Castro's and Cuba's prestige in Latin America, was the official opening of an Escuela Latinoamericana de Medicina during the Ibero–American summit in Havana – a center for the training of doctors and medical personnel that had no parallel elsewhere in Latin America. Quite consciously, Cuba was here drawing political capital from its international reputation in the field of medical research and training.

In late October 2000, Castro strengthened the ties with Venezuela by paying a four-day official visit to his friend Chávez, who was emulating him with a not yet clearly defined "Bolivarian revolution." Castro came back with a five-year agreement for economic and technical cooperation, the most important point of which was an undertaking by Venezuela to supply 53,000 tons daily of oil or oil derivatives on preferential terms – an invaluable gesture at a time when OPEC, the organization of oil-exporting countries, was conducting a high-price policy. Cuba did not even have to pay for this oil in hard currency, but undertook to supply in return medicine, sugar, and other goods, as well as technical support services in agriculture, tourism, medicine, education, and sport – for example, 3,000 sports trainers and specialists to instruct Venezuelan hotel staff.[55] Admittedly the Venezuelan medical profession, conscious of the threat to its social standing, loudly protested at the idea of swapping oil for humanitarian aid in the form of Cuban doctors. (But a general strike aimed at ousting Chávez in 2003 brought the oil supplies to Cuba temporarily to a halt.)

The Cubans' growing self-assurance was somewhat clouded by a bureaucracy which – as Western firms such as MCV complained – "hampered the orderly conduct of business." At the same time, there was a marked "tendency to huge and spectacular projects," as well as weaknesses in the decision-making process attributable to the fact that Castro still wanted to decide too much himself. A country that had been written off politically and economically just a few years before was now seen as being "in great need of development, but also with a great capacity for development." MCV was not the only Western firm to consider a "first-rate scandal" the ideologically motivated refusal of organizations such as the World Bank (where US influence was strong) to provide Cuba with development capital. "As soon as the blockade comes down," Mercedes-Benz/MCV-Cuba wanted to export "small 25- to 30-seater buses from Cuba to Florida" – unless, of course, the embargo was replaced with a protectionist barrier.

The MCV example makes it clear that, after the collapse of the Communist system in the Eastern bloc, Europe rediscovered, captured, and divided up the relatively small Cuban market much more quickly than anyone in Washington had thought possible. However cautiously European politicians proceeded, European business soon found the ways and means to get round the considerable obstacles placed in its way by the Helms-Burton Act. When King Juan Carlos, 500 years after Christopher Columbus and 40 years after the revolution of 1959, became the first Spanish monarch ever to set foot on Cuban soil and jointly presided with

Fidel Castro over the ninth summit of Ibero–American heads of state and government, the old colonial power was already Cuba's most important economic partner in Europe – even if next year's newspapers reported that tourists from Japan had pushed Spain into second place in the holiday statistics.[56]

Castro took advantage of the favorable situation in the middle of 1999 and had the euro introduced as a second convertible currency for trade with the EU. But, although the EU had appeared in the place of the defunct Eastern bloc, Russia was coming back into the picture: a decade after the end of the Soviet Union, it was already receiving 25 percent of all Cuban exports,[57] and the two-way trade was running at a little under $900 million. In December 2000, to Washington's horror, President Vladimir Putin and a large entourage were due to make a three-day trip to Havana, the first high-ranking visit by a Russian leader since the end of the Soviet Union, which demonstrated that Cuba was again a significant partner in Russian foreign policy. The old power wanted to put out fresh feelers in Latin America – still with the help of its listening station at Lourdes near Havana (which nevertheless was closed down in 2002).

Putin may have picked up the "signal for help" that Castro sent out at the end of a speech lasting several hours at the end of a cultural congress in 1999, in which he praised Cuba's own experience.

It is my conviction . . . that Russia can save itself and does not necessarily have to depend on loans from the West. Sooner or later its leading figures will grasp this, even if today they still unquestionably depend on the loans. . . . We have neither the huge Siberian forests and gas and oil deposits nor major steel and machine-building industries. If we had nothing else than the raw materials, the economy of this country – with the experience we have today, . . . for we must learn to be much more efficient and make better use of resources – would perhaps grow by 12 percent or 14 percent."[58]

Such trends caused anxiety in the US that it might arrive on the scene too late. For a long time there had been an awareness that the embargo had failed in its purpose of protecting American economic interests in Cuba and reserving its market for US firms. The response was now a kind of twin-track strategy: on the one hand, politicians hoped that the embargo would hasten the collapse of the Castro regime; on the other hand, US economic interests did everything behind the scenes to prepare starting-blocks that they could use when Day X dawned on the island. Of the 120,000 US citizens who annually got round the travel ban in the late nineties, a good half were businessmen and politicians holding special permits, who mostly flew direct to Havana in chartered aircraft or private jets from Miami, Los Angeles, New York, or other US cities. In order to meet the sudden surge in demand for aircraft seats theoretically excluded under the Helms-Burton Act, the US government even gave the go-ahead for more frequent flights and an expansion of the route network. As American entrepreneurs, managers, and high-ranking politicians came and went in a steady stream to the ministries and offices of the Cuban nomenklatura, right up to Fidel Castro himself, they sent a clear signal that large sections of US business (especially the Mid West's powerful farming lobby) were in favor of ending the embargo.

A report in the US-based *Cuban Studies* estimated:

> There is probably another $8–10 billion of profitable investment available to foreign capital in Cuba in the coming years. According to some sources, twenty-five of the sixty largest US claimants have indicated an interest in doing business with Cuba without first settling their claims. Once the US embargo is lifted, within five years US exports to Cuba could reach around $6–7 billion and generate some 70,000–100,000 jobs in the United States. On the Cuban side, some estimates have suggested that even a partial lifting of the US embargo on Cuba would result in a doubling of import capacity and a 25 percent increase in Cuban national income.[59]

In 1998 the Clinton administration began to see which way the wind was blowing and cancelled a number of restrictions. A Pentagon study, produced together with the CIA and the army secret service, helped the government out by arguing: "At present Cuba does not represent a major danger either for the USA or

326

for other countries in the region."[60] US defense experts assessed the strength of Castro's army at no more than 65,000 men, with training and equipment considerably weakened by lack of resources. An army with a high level of activity in the Third World had turned into a stationary force with a minimal conventional fighting power. The navy was no longer capable of operating outside Cuban waters, and the air force had only a couple of dozen airworthy MIGs from Soviet times. On the other hand, Cuba had one of the most broadly developed biotechnological industries in the Third World, and was in a position to develop biological warfare agents. The report suited Castro's opponents because it tended to present their arch-enemy as a paper tiger, but they did not at all like its political direction and tried to ensure, through their lobby in Congress, that it was sent back for reworking.

Clearly, however, Washington was by this time no longer interested in a violent overthrow of the aging Castro. On October 27, 1997, when US coastguards west of Puerto Rico seized a Miami-registered yacht with damaged engines, they found in a secret compartment two .50 calibre telescopic-sight rifles with a range of nearly 1 mile. All four men on board the *Esperanza* (Spanish for "hope") were Cuban exiles, on their way to Venezuela. One of them confessed that they had been planning to shoot Castro on the island of Margarita, during the seventh summit meeting of Ibero–American leaders. The FBI immediately took over the investigation, and its agents discovered that the guns had been acquired by a Bay of Pigs veteran and none other than the managing director of the Cuban American National Foundation (CANF), Francisco Hernández. The person who sold them was also a Bay of Pigs veteran, while the owner of the boat proved to be a member of the CANF's 28-member executive committee. Further enquiries revealed that a total of seven people had been involved in the plot. The four in the yacht were taken to Miami and later charged with attempted murder.

In late November 1997, not long after the failure of this assassination attempt, the CANF had to report the surprise death of its chairman and Hernández's superior, Jorge Mas Canosa. The autocratic leader of the militant Cuban exile association, described by the *Miami Herald* as a "dictator in waiting," died at the age of 58 of bone cancer. And so, the fact that Castro had outlived yet another of his powerful opponents increased the level of bitterness among the 55,000 CANF members. The organization now began to lose power and influence, as Mas Canosa – rather like Castro – had not groomed a strong successor during his lifetime.

In the autumn of 1999, Cuba saw the highest-ranking visit from the United States since the revolution, when the Republican governor of Illinois, George Ryan, arrived on a five-day trip with an entourage of 500 politicians, businessmen, religious leaders, and journalists. The guest from Chicago, whose state was one of the main exporters of grain and other farming produce, was a declared opponent of the Helms-Burton Act; his meeting with Fidel Castro went on for seven hours. One of the members of the delegation was the president of the US Chamber of Commerce, and in a demonstrative gesture the guests brought with them an aid package of goods worth a million dollars.

The Cuban exile community in Florida was stunned. But there too the front gradually started to break up, after surveys showed that more than two-thirds of the US population were opposed to the embargo. Finally, in October 2000, Congress took a historic vote that might spell the beginning of the end of the embargo. After the House of Representatives, the Senate voted 86 to 8 for a lifting of the ban on the export of food and medicine to Cuba. On the other hand, although in July both Houses had originally voted on a first reading to restore the right of US citizens to travel to Cuba, the constitutionally dubious restrictions on this freedom were in the end not only maintained but further tightened. Whereas it had previously been possible at any time for the President to issue an order setting these restrictions aside, they were now enshrined in a law which, like the Helms-Burton Act, could be amended by Congress alone. Only politicians, journalists, and others holding special permits could travel with impunity to Cuba, as well as individuals invited by Cuban organizations that agreed to bear the costs (a category which foreign-currency shortages kept virtually empty).

The changing attitude of Congress was due to pressure from American business and farming associations, which had been having to sit and watch as this largest, and increasingly lucrative, Caribbean market was gradually lost to the European and Canadian competition. Even now, though, US farmers and other businessmen did not obtain a major relaxation of trade, for there were built-in conditions that greatly limited the positive effect. Thus, exports of food and medicine to Cuba could not be financed by public loans from the USA, nor could they be delivered to government institutions. Yet Cuba depended on credit financing for 80 percent of its food imports, and the state was the commercial partner at nearly every level of transactions (apart from Church organizations such as Caritas, which were not given an easy time by the state). To be sure, money might be available from the big European banks, which would be glad to do business with Cuba at high rates of interest.

The group which most often boasted of watering down the draft legislation in the run-up to the US presidential elections of 2001 was the "Cuban-American Lobby" in Congress, and, in particular, the politicians Helms, Burton, and Lincoln Díaz-Balart. Scarcely had the law been passed when the latter's uncle, Fidel Castro, mobilized a vast crowd of 800,000 in Havana and marched off with them waving little flags to the US representation of interests on the Malecón, where they protested against the constant "humiliation" of their country. Immediately afterwards, he ordered a 10 percent increase in the taxes chargeable to US telephone companies for communications between the USA and Cuba.[61] The Republican-dominated farmers' lobby in the United States was certainly not happy with the new legislation, but it felt reassured that it again had a foot in the door for doing business with Cuba – and that was rather more important to it. A lobby spokesman promptly announced that the door now needed to be opened wider, so that not only wheat, rice, beans, and dairy produce but also fruit, vegetables, and meat could pass through.

On September 6, 2000, when Cuban state and Party leader Fidel Castro was on his way in a dark suit to join 160 colleagues for a photo opportunity at the UN millennium summit in New York, he suddenly found himself facing Bill Clinton. Out of "simple good manners," as he later put it, he stretched out his hand to the American president, who did "exactly the same."

The two men then exchanged a few words. Over four decades, eight successive US presidents had given Castro a very wide berth, but now all that was supposed to be over. Now, 60 years after Castro's childhood letter to Roosevelt, and 40 years after the victory of the Cuban Revolution, a US president was for the first time talking to the Máximo Líder – and the whole world soon heard the news. In Miami militant Cuban exiles shouted "treason," because Clinton had not simply given their arch-enemy the brush-off; Clinton's spokesman followed up the "handshake" with a lame denial that no one believed; and Fidel Castro felt "content with his respectful and civilized behavior towards the president of the country hosting the summit."[62] The political earthquake lasted less than 20 seconds: for many it was the collapse of a whole world, for others the beginning of a new historical phase.

The wary normalization of US–Cuban relations was due in part to a little Cuban boy called Elián González, who in late November 1999 lost his mother in a sunken ship full of refugees before being washed ashore on the coast of Florida. A great-uncle living in Miami and the militant Cuban exile movement immediately took him under their wing and, in the guise of loving care, used the traumatized child as a political weapon against Castro's Communist regime. Havana, for its part, mobilized hundreds of thousands of people to demonstrate over a period of months outside the US representation, demanding the child's return to his Cuban father and grandparents. On December 6, when Elián celebrated his sixth birthday in his great-uncle's house, relatives took a picture of him in a fighting pose, with a helmet on his head, surrounded with weapons and wrapped in the Stars and Stripes. "In other words," wrote Gabriel García Márquez in the *New York Times*, "the real shipwreck of Elián did not take place on the high seas, but when he set foot in America."[63] In the end, after six months had gone by, the child had to be forcibly released by a special unit of the immigration authorities acting on the instructions of the US Supreme Court; only then could he be returned to his real father.

The person who excelled himself in the unworthy game over the little Cuban boy was once again Castro's nephew, Republican Congressman Lincoln Díaz-Balart. In doing so, he was evidently working off a family trauma of the Díaz-Balart clan, associated with Fidel's and Mirta's son Fidelito. For, in its ideological faultlines, the drama over young Elián did indeed recall the fate of Fidel Castro Jr after his parents' divorce early in 1955, when Castro was in prison for the Moncada Barracks attack and Mirta moved with their six-year-old son to New York, where the family of her future second husband lived. She apparently had the blessing of the family court, especially as Castro, up until the Moncada incident, had not particularly distinguished himself as a caring father. Fidel Castro saw what happened as a "kidnapping" and was beside himself with rage. "I don't like to think that my son will sleep even one night under the same roof with my worst enemies and be kissed on his innocent cheek by those evil Judases. . . . Only over my dead body will they take that child away from me," he wrote in late November 1954, in a letter from prison to his half-sister Lidia.[64] The next year, when the budding revolutionary was allowed to receive a visit from Fidelito in his Mexican exile, Castro simply kept the child and entrusted him to the care of a Mexican couple he had befriended and two of his sisters who were also living there. Then the Díaz-Balart family hired three agents, who kidnapped the boy while he was out walking with Castro's sisters in Chapultepec Park, in the center of Mexico City, and handed him over to his mother who had meanwhile hurried down from New York. With the victory of the revolution, the ten-year-old Fidelito went back to Cuba and remained with his father, apparently with his mother's agreement.

The reason for this arrangement was probably that, during the revolution, Mirta had married the son of the former Cuban ambassador to the United Nations, Emilio Núñez Portuondo, whom Batista had made his prime minister in 1958. Later she moved to Madrid, while Fidelito attended school in Cuba and eventually went on to study nuclear physics and to graduate from, among others, Moscow's Lomonosov University; he then became head of the Cuban program for the peaceful use of nuclear energy. After 1992, when he was removed from that post because the nuclear power station at Juragua was still incomplete after years of construction work, the younger Fidel dropped out of public view. This also put an end to the (perhaps not unjustified) suspicions that his father had wanted to be eventually succeeded as head of state by the son who, though strikingly reserved in manner, outwardly resembled him so much. In 1997, at the age of 48, Fidelito published a book on the prospects for nuclear energy in the twenty-first century.[65]

At the time of the Elián drama, Fidelito's cousin, Lincoln Díaz-Balart, did not spell out all the facts when he claimed on CNN News that it was very strange "to hear Castro saying he had a small child's interests at heart, when he even kidnapped his own son;" nor did he notice the conflict between this condemnation of Castro and his own battle for the US courts to place little Elián in the care of his elderly great-uncle, instead of returning him to his legal father in Cuba.[66] In the end, Díaz-Balart argued, Elián would be going back to "a dictator who has reiterated he would 'reprogram,' in other words destroy emotionally and psychologically, this defenseless boy."[67] When Díaz-Balart visited the completely shaken Elián in the great-uncle's house, penetrated day and night by media floodlights, he praised the numerous demonstrators who had been keeping watch to ensure that the boy did not escape the political captivity of his "welfare worker." He brought the boy a black Labrador puppy as a plaything. This elicited a commentary in the *International Herald Tribune* to the effect that nothing the boy had experienced since being washed ashore had been "as bad as Congressman Díaz-Balart" and his cuddly toy. "Elián has lost his mother. He needs his father and his grandparents, not a Labrador puppy."[68]

In cynically playing with the fate of little Elián, the Cuban exiles lost sympathy and influence not only in the world at large, but among the especially important American public and political class. The Clinton government used this to expand its room for maneuver in relation to Cuba, although the Helms-Burton Act was not going to disappear overnight and there was hardly any imminent danger for the exile organizations. Even if the two sides did not say as much, the anachronistic system of regulations had over the years been a politically stabilizing factor that suited their respective plans. Alejandro Álvaro Bremer from the

University of Miami wrote in the *Journal of Latin American Affairs*:

> Paradoxical though it may appear, Fidel Castro represents for the United States political and social stability in this phase of upheaval. The embargo, even if sharper still, offers greater security for a progressive transformation on the island. A lifting of the embargo would most likely trigger a genuine revolution as well as the hoped-for change in internal policy. . . . Radical change in Cuba [,however,] will move outside the simulations of the administration. . . . Let us consider why this is so. On the Cuban stage, there is no political force capable of replacing Fidel Castro, and the political groups in exile are all completely rootless.[69]

Castro, God, and the Pope

Does Fidel Castro, the Jesuit boarder and professed Marxist-Leninist, believe in God? One could not help asking this question when it became certain that Pope John Paul II would visit Cuba between January 21 and 25, 1998. But the answer is known only to the Comandante himself – perhaps also to the Pope, since the audience he granted Castro at the Vatican in November 1996, and possibly to the Brazilian Dominican Frei Betto. After Castro's godfather and lifesaver, Bishop Enrique Pérez Serantes, turned away in disappointment from the revolution in the early sixties, Betto seems to have become in the seventies (when the two first met) the priest in whom the Cuban leader had the greatest confidence. He is the only person to whom Castro has spoken in detail about questions concerning belief and religion, state and Church under socialism, and to whom he has afforded deep insight into his private and political world of belief and lived experience.

Even in his talks with Frei Betto, however, Castro avoided a direct answer to the direct question of whether he believed in

God. He has told journalists that he does not wish to make any public statement on the issue.

> These are personal matters about which I do not speak in public. Besides, if I say now that I don't believe, I will upset those Cubans who do believe in God; if I answer that I do believe, I will become a preacher for religion that I am not. I respect believers and non-believers; I have respect for any religious conviction. That is the duty of a politician.[70]

He has also said that not even the Pope put the question to him.[71]

Everyone will have to work out the answer for themselves – with the help of a "set of clues" that Castro provided in his 1985 conversations with Frei Betto. It must certainly mean something that, when he went beyond day-to-day matters to discuss his philosophical (and sometimes very private) thoughts about politics and religion, faith and conviction, he confided not in a Communist author but in a member of a Catholic order who was identified with the socially militant Liberation Theology. What emerged was an autobiographical statement of a kind of spiritual affinity between Communist ideology and Christian faith, a belief in the need for partnership between Communism and the Church in the struggle to overcome social inequalities. The conversations with Betto were indeed a unique document for the Communist world at that time, which must have fueled, and must continue to fuel, doubts about the reliability in Marxist-Leninist terms of a man who was able to cut across ideological boundaries in that way.

Even many of Castro's opponents admit that, in his political activity, he has also been driven by high moral demands on himself. He told Betto:

> My ethical values were created at school, by the teachers, and even at home, by the members of my family. I was told very early in life that I shouldn't lie. I was undoubtedly taught ethical values. . . . They weren't Marxist, and they didn't stem from an ethical philosophy. They were based on a religious ethic. I was

taught what is right and wrong, things that should and should not be done. In our society, the first notion children got of an ethical principle may have been based on religion. In the prevailing religious environment, people absorbed a number of ethical values as a matter of tradition, even though there were some irrational beliefs, such as thinking that the flight and screeching of an owl or the crowing of a rooster could foretell disaster. . . . Undoubtedly, my teachers, my Jesuit teachers – especially the Spanish Jesuits, who inculcated a strong sense of personal dignity, regardless of their political ideas – influenced me. Most Spaniards are endowed with a sense of personal honor, and it's very strong in the Jesuits. They valued character, rectitude, honesty, courage and the ability to make sacrifices. . . . The Jesuits clearly influenced me with their strict organization, their discipline and their values. They contributed to my development and influenced my sense of justice.[72]

In Castro's view, the affinity between Christianity and socialism was located not at the institutional level of the official Church and Party, but in the readiness to make sacrifices for an idea. "I'm sure that the same pillars that sustain the sacrifices a revolutionary makes today sustained the sacrifices made in the past by a martyr who died for his religious faith. I think that religious martyrs were generous, selfless men; they were made of the same stuff of which revolutionary heroes are made."[73] He still clearly remembered that during his school years "one of the things the Church felt most proud of . . . was the martyrology of the early years."[74] And his further remarks showed how much his revolutionary motivation was derived from the faith instilled in him as a child. His examination of early Church history strikes one as much more emotional and fundamental than his more calculated statement that he was already influenced by Marxism before the attack on the Moncada Barracks.

There is no doubt . . . that Christianity was the religion of the slaves, of the oppressed and of the poor, who lived in the catacombs . . . and were subjected to all kinds of persecution and repression for centuries. The Roman Empire considered that doctrine to be revolutionary. . . . I always related [that], later on,

335

to the history of the Communists. . . . The great historic truth is that the Communist movement also has its martyrology in its struggles to change an unfair social system. . . . If there was ever a name that the reactionaries hated more than "Communist," it was "Christian," in another time.[75]

Castro agreed that "throughout the Church's history its martyrs must have been motivated by something more inspiring than fear or punishment." That was "much easier to understand" for people with a revolutionary background than for those whose only concern was to obtain material possessions, and to preserve their life rather than to sacrifice it. Like the Church before it, the revolution "called for self-sacrifice and, at times, for martyrdom, heroism and death." It could not be appreciated too highly when someone chose to "give his life for a revolutionary idea and to fight, knowing he may die, . . . even though he knows there is nothing after death."[76] Castro himself had set an example of this in the way he lived his life, never showing fear in his student years or in the Sierra Maestra, or again when facing assassins in the pay of secret services or the US-backed mercenaries at the Bay of Pigs. All the time his great model was José Martí, the man whom Cuban revolutionaries and nationalists think of as the "apostle," even though (or precisely because) the Catholic Church excommunicated him as a freemason and agnostic.

However much Castro has avoided a self-relating personality cult as in China during Mao's lifetime or the Soviet Union during Stalin's, he has deliberately allowed a martyr cult to grow up around such dead heroes as Camilo Cienfuegos (who disappeared in his light aircraft a few weeks after the victory of the revolution) and, above all, Che Guevara. Just a few months before the Pope's visit to Cuba, on the thirtieth anniversary of Che's death, Castro arranged with a great flurry of propaganda for the recently redis-covered remains of his former comrade to be brought from Bolivia to Cuba and buried in a relatively modest mausoleum in Santa Clara, where in late 1958 he had won the decisive vic-tory for the revolution. From then on, images of the national hero transfigured into a revolutionary martyr followed everyone around in their daily lives. In the museums dotted around the

Sierra Maestra and at Playa Girón, as well as in the Museum of the Revolution in Havana, the personal objects of fallen heroes – even their bullet-riddled, bloodstained clothing – were put on display as so many priceless relics.

This individual way of honoring heroes marked the limits of Castro's identification with the basic beliefs of the institutional Church. He told Betto:

> If someone were to ask me when I held religious beliefs, I'd have to say, "Never, really." I never really held a religious belief or had religious faith. At school, nobody ever managed to instill those values in me. Later on, I had other values: a political belief, a political faith, which I forged on my own, as a result of my experience, analysis and feelings. . . . Political ideas are worthless if they aren't inspired by noble, selfless feelings. Likewise, noble feelings are worthless if they aren't based on correct, fair ideas.[77]

Castro therefore accepted that his teachers had sown the seeds of his later political development. What kept him from becoming a convinced follower of the Church was the lack of rationality in the Christian faith. Whereas Castro, with his sharp mind, learned to question everything and to take nothing as given, the Jesuits had to give him pat answers to elementary philosophical questions of human existence.

> Looking back, . . . I think that, in some respects, it wasn't positive; everything was very dogmatic – "This is so because it has to be so." You had to believe it, even if you didn't understand it. If you didn't, it was a fault, a sin, something worthy of punishment. Reasoning and feelings weren't developed. It seems to me that religious faith, like political belief, should be based on reasoning, on the development of thought and feelings. . . . If you have to accept things because you're told they are a certain way, you can't argue or reason them out. Moreover, if the main argument used is reward or punishment – punishment more than reward – then it's impossible to develop the reasoning and feelings that could be the basis of a sincere religious belief.[78]

To demonstrate his unreceptiveness to the doctrine of his Jesuit teachers, Castro gives the example of their spiritual exercises.

I remember long sermons for meditation on hell – its heat and the suffering, anguish and desperation it caused. I don't know how such a cruel hell as the one described to us could have been invented, because such severity is inconceivable, no matter how great a person's sins may have been. . . . I'd describe it as a form of mental terrorism; sometimes those explanations turned into mental terrorism.[79]

Yet the moral rigor confronted Castro as a challenge.

If you mix ethical values with a spirit of rebellion and rejection of injustice, you begin to appreciate and place a high value on a number of things that other people don't value at all. A sense of personal dignity, honor and duty form the main foundation that enables people to acquire political awareness. This was especially so in my case, since I didn't acquire it by having poor, proletarian or farm origins – that is, through social circumstance. I gained my political awareness through reasoning, thinking, by developing feelings and deep conviction. I think that what I was telling you about faith – the ability to reason, think, analyse, meditate and develop feelings – is what makes it possible to acquire revolutionary ideas. In my case, there was a special circumstance: nobody taught me political ideas.[80]

Castro's remarks on the dogmatic character of religious instruction naturally provoke some consideration of his own dogmatic shortcomings in the field of politics. In particular, critics of his system will find food for thought there about the prevailing socialist doctrine, as he used it in his assessment of Christian doctrine. Many of his close comrades, especially in the "26th of July Movement," went through a dialectical process in relation to ideology that was similar to the one he described in relation to the Christian faith: that is, their "ability to reason, think, analyse, meditate and develop feelings" eventually kindled in them a desire for democracy. The consequences of such sins were and are incomparably harsher: the socialist "Inquisition" has usually given no pardon; "excommunication" has followed quickly and definitively.

Nevertheless, the Bible has always been one of Castro's favorite books. "I always liked biblical history, because its content was fascinating," he told Betto; "few [stories] are as fascinating as the ones in the Old Testament."[81] This corresponds to the picture that, not least because of the petty-bourgeois and farmer-based structure of the 26th of July Movement, the Christian faith still played quite a large role for the Sierra Maestra revolutionaries, larger in any event that that of the *Communist Manifesto*, even if Castro later tried to give the opposite impression. (To Frei Betto, he insisted that he had had "not only a revolutionary attitude but also a Marxist-Leninist, Socialist concept of political struggle several years before 1951," as had "a handful of those of us who organized the 26th of July Movement."[82]) In the mountains, and later during his march to victory, Castro even wore around his neck a holy image that a little girl in Santiago de Cuba had given him. Crucifixes and pictures of the Virgin Mary are said to have hung in his headquarters in the Sierra, and also in the early days in his office in Havana.

Right from the beginning, the revolution had many friends among the lower clergy and lay people in the countryside; eight priests actually joined Castro in the Sierra Maestra, the best-known being Father Guillermo Sardiñas, who had the encouragement of Bishop Pérez Serantes in Santiago de Cuba. "He joined us not as a soldier but as a priest. He was there with the troops, living with us, sharing our daily lives. He had everything he needed to carry out his duties; he could even celebrate Mass." Castro added that Sardiñas had performed "mainly religious, not political work," especially administering baptism, which "was very important to the farmers." "Father Sardiñas baptized scores of children there. . . . Families went to see him. They took their children and asked me to be their godfather, which in Cuba is like being a second father. I have a lot of godchildren in the Sierra Maestra."[83]

Until the victory of the revolution in 1959, the hierarchy had made an effort to remain neutral, once Cardinal Arteaga's peace plan had been rejected by both sides. But then the revolutionary Fidel Castro came into serious conflict with his Church. To Frei Betto he insisted that there had not been "any problems with Catholic beliefs;" "the problems that arose concerned Catholic institutions."[84] And he explained:

The Church in Cuba wasn't popular; it wasn't a Church of the people, the workers, the farmers, the low-income sectors of the population. . . . In our country, where 70 percent of the people lived in the countryside, there weren't any rural churches, . . . not a single priest in the countryside! . . . Allegedly, it was a Catholic society, and it was customary to baptize children, . . . but there was no real religious education or religious practice. Religion in Cuba was disseminated, propagated, mainly through private schools – that is, schools run by religious orders – which were attended by the children of the wealthiest families in the country, the members of the old aristocracy, . . . the children of the upper middle class and part of the middle class in general. . . . besides, a large part of the clergy was of foreign origin, [mostly] Spaniards who held reactionary, right-wing, Spanish-Nationalist – even pro-Franco – ideas.[85]

Often the richest families paid the priest's income and the costs of running the parish.

In 1960, according to Church sources, between 70 percent and 75 percent of Cubans were nominally Catholic – the lowest proportion anywhere in Latin America. Of those, 5 to 8 percent were considered to be practicing Catholics, who attended Mass at least four times a year.[86] The number of priests was also low in Latin American terms: only one per 7,500 of the population.

And yet, at the First National Catholic Congress on November 28, 1959, the bishops put a million people back on their feet in Revolution Square in Havana. In the rainy night, hundreds of thousands of candles greeted the arrival of a procession that had accompanied an image of the Merciful Virgin of Cobre through-out its journey of more than 600 miles from Santiago de Cuba at the other end of the island. The Church leaders wanted to show that the charismatic leader of the revolution (who himself attended the final Mass) was not the only one capable of mobilizing the masses.

The greeting from Pope John XXIII to the Catholic Congress, and his appeal for it to seek mutual respect, forgiveness and reconciliation, was drowned out by a declaration of war from the leader of the lay Catholic university organization, José Ignacio

Lasaga. While the crowd chanted *"Cuba sí, comunismo no!"*, he declaimed:

> Liberal capitalism allows there to be a few proprietors in the face of a multitude of dispossessed. Communism, and in general all totalitarian socialist regimes, converts all persons into the dispossessed, since there exists only one proprietor, that is, the State. An ideal social order would be one that permits all persons, in one or another form, to feel as if they were proprietors, in the fullest sense of the word.[87]

But the Church did not succeed in marshaling the faithful behind it; its basis of trust in the countryside was too weak.

The revolution met no resistance as it took up the needs of the rural population and enlisted rapidly growing support for its political goals. In the countryside, unlike in the cities, one often came across the attitude: "If Fidel's a Communist, then I'm a Communist too."

Meanwhile, the estrangement between Church and people grew ever more pronounced, as the clergy maintained its identification with the old bourgeoisie and several top ecclesiastics allowed themselves to be used against the revolutionary government. The executive secretary of the Conference of Cuban Bishops, Monsignor Carlos Manuel de Céspedes, declared in 1970: "Many priests actively supported the counter-revolutionary movement that arose, especially after the summer of 1960, and that culminated in the Bay of Pigs invasion in April 1961."[88] Many leading figures in the Church even organized some counter-revolutionary groups. Manuel Artimé, for instance, from the influential Agrupación Católica, eventually founded a Movimiento de Recuperación Revolucionario (MRR), which recruited mainly from Catholic student and youth organizations. The MRR worked closely with the CIA and played a considerable role in organizing the Bay of Pigs invasion, and after nearly two years in a Cuban prison Artimé left for Florida to join the inner circle of exiles and CIA agents who plotted in the sixties to assassinate Castro. His name later cropped up again in the circle of acquaintances of Kennedy's presumed assassin, Lee Harvey Oswald, as well as in connection with the break-in at the Democratic Party's Watergate headquarters in Washington.

On both sides of the Florida Strait, then, leading Church figures were involved in the most cynical operations to undermine the moral authority of the revolutionary government. Castro told Betto:

> For instance, as part of the campaign to promote the exodus, a completely false decree was invented one day – it was said that somebody had taken the decree out of a ministry. It was alleged to be a decree to deprive families of legal authority over their children. . . . Another rumor was that the children were going to be sent to the Soviet Union.[89]

The director of the Catholic Service Bureau in Miami, Monsignor Walsh, claimed that he had himself hatched and launched this operation together with people from the State Department and the CIA, with the support of a Church leader in Cuba. According to Walsh, rumors alone led to the flight of 15,000 children from Cuba between December 1960 and October 1962, as their parents feared their sons and daughters would otherwise be shipped off to Siberia. Instead they landed in US reception camps, where politicians briefly came to visit them as living testimony to the foulness of the Castro regime, and gave them candy and toys before lining them up to be photographed. Many of the children did not see their parents again for a long time – some never did at all.[90] The whole thing was named Operation Peter Pan, after the little boy in James Barrie's tale who did not want to grow up and led a lost band of children from Never-Never Land. Here, "Peter Pan" was the CIA.

Tensions between the revolutionary government and the Church leadership sharpened in May 1960, when Castro's long-time "resident priest" and supporter, Archbishop Pérez Serantes, came out openly against the revolution following the establishment of diplomatic relations with the USSR. In a pastoral letter he announced that the frontiers between the Church and its enemies were now clearly defined: "We cannot say that communism is at our doors for in reality it is within our walls, speaking out as if it were at home;"[91] any cooperation with Communism was out of the question. Margaret Crahan, a US researcher on religion, described the situation as so tense that, even though the government had not issued any anti-religious laws, many Catholic dignitaries took refuge in a veritable laager mentality.[92]

Revolutionary militias searched numerous Catholic schools for weapons during the Bay of Pigs invasion in 1961, and after its collapse the government closed down all private Church schools and banned Artimé's "Agrupación Católica." On September 12, 132 Spanish priests found guilty of counter-revolutionary activity were expelled from the country on board the *Covadonga*. Two years later, in 1963, 70 percent of the 723 Catholic priests and 90 percent of the 2,225 members of religious orders had been compelled to leave the island.[93] Their duties were taken over, if at all, by lay persons.

Whereas, at the beginning of the revolution, measures were taken only against top people in the Church, pressure came to be exerted against ordinary members. Under the growing influence of the PSP, Party officials disrupted Masses, harassed people attending Bible classes, and pilloried religious children at school before their teachers and classmates. Any commitment to the Church was regarded as suspicious, because the counter-revolutionary groups operating in the Escambray Mountains also included some religiously motivated associations. Castro told Betto: "There were also cases of complicity with serious counter-revolutionary activities, which could have led to trial and such severe punishment as execution. In no case was this applied, however. . . . Regardless of the circumstances, we didn't want to . . . present the image of the Revolution executing a priest."[94]

The US sociologist Juan Clark from Miami-Dade Community College, an expert in Cuban religious affairs, has confirmed that there was no bloody persecution of Christians in Cuba as there had been in the revolutions in China, Mexico, and Spain.[95] Church officials in Havana reported in the late nineties that "there had been a very harsh but bloodless repression, with the full force and efficiency of a totalitarian system; control through fear, not terror, crippled people."[96] Young Christians who refused to do compulsory military service were treated as "troublemakers" or

343

"social parasites" and confined in labor camps – the so-called "military units for the support of production" (UMAPs) – along with homosexuals, male prostitutes, and common criminals. Even Jaime Ortega, the later cardinal, who in 1998 would join Castro in welcoming the Pope to Cuba, served ten months in such a camp in 1965.

The general discrimination and marginalization directed at the Church and its active members put an end to virtually any public religious practice, as even a profession of belief in the Church was enough to arouse the suspicion of the authorities. Since the Communist Party of Cuba – contrary to Castro's idea of an affinity between Christian social doctrine and Communism – excluded self-avowed Christians from membership, Church people were unable to involve themselves in processes of social development until the end of the 1990s. "We weren't exactly demanding that the person had to be an atheist," Castro said by way of justification; "we weren't inspired by antireligious ideas. What we were demanding was complete adherence to Marxism-Leninism." This could be achieved only because "the great masses of the people . . . weren't active Catholics." "If . . . the great masses of workers, farmers and university students had been active Christians, we couldn't have formed a revolutionary party based on those premises." In other words, in a devoutly Catholic country a Communist-style revolution would scarcely have had a chance. "But, since most of the active Catholics were well-to-do, supported the counter-revolution and left the country, we could – and had to – establish a severe, orthodox rule."[97]

The irreconcilability of Christians and materialists was connected not only with political radicalization and the gravitation of "Castroism" toward the Soviet system, but also with the reactionary encrustation and political inflexibility of the Church leadership. The main opponent of the revolution was Cardinal Arteaga, who in 1952 had given the seal of approval to Batista's coup d'état, and who continued to embody the old ecclesiastical order until his death in March 1963.

Only toward the end of the sixties, when a new generation of priests, in the wake of the Second Vatican Council (1962–5), pushed the Cuban clergy into internal reforms and a greater openness to political realities, did a gradual change begin in relations with the government. The decisive signal came with the publication of two pastoral letters in the spring and summer of 1969, which condemned the US embargo and called on Catholics to support the government's program for education and health. In November 1971, during his weeks traveling through Chile under Salvador Allende, Castro surprised a Church audience by suddenly announcing that in his view "there are ten thousand times more coincidences between Christianity and communism than between Christianity and capitalism."[98] Despite repeated setbacks, the Party and government took a crucial step forward in the mid-seventies, when they guaranteed the freedom of religion in the basic program of the Communist Party as well as Article 54 of the new Constitution. Finally, in October 1977 Castro declared that there were "no contradictions between the aims of religion and the aims of socialism."[99] Yet it remained no more than lip service. Discrimination continued against people who practiced their religion.

It took another 15 years before a constitutional amendment of July 12, 1992, prohibited social discrimination against believers, and the fourth Congress of the CPC allowed Church members to join the Party. Castro had already pointed towards this in his 1985 discussions with Frei Betto, but had said that more time would be needed: "This must be explained to all the Party members and analyzed with all of them. It isn't our policy to say 'This is so' from the top."[100] Castro had even hinted that he had a guilty conscience for what had happened over the years on this matter: "In principle, I can't agree with any kind of discrimination. I say this very openly. If I were asked if any subtle discrimination existed against Christians, I'd say 'Yes.' It's something we haven't overcome as yet."[101] Even so, it was only six years later that the decision was taken that no one should suffer at work or in political life because of their religious beliefs.

In January 1985 the first meeting took place between Castro and the Cuban bishops. Later that year a bureau for religious affairs was established within the Central Committee – at a time when hardly any pastoral workers were left on the island. There was then just one priest for each 53,000 Cubans, compared with seven in 1959. This meant that the Catholic Church in Cuba was by far the weakest in Latin America.[102] But change seemed to be in the air when a delegation from the US Bishops' Conference, led by Bishop James W. Malone, visited the island. In September 1985 and September 1987, Cuban bishops made return visits to the United States and spoke in favor of lifting the embargo. In 1988 Cardinal John O'Connor from New York went to Havana for three hours of talks with Fidel Castro.

Nor did the Vatican hesitate to grasp Castro's outstretched hand. Beginning in the mid-eighties, Church officials traveled from Rome to Havana to normalize relations with the Cuban state and Communist Party, and to give life to the declarations of intent on both sides.

The new public leeway for the Church became evident when it issued an expression of concern in September 1993 about the political and economic conditions prevailing in the "special period:"

> Things are not good: this is a matter of public discussion. There is discontent, insecurity and hopelessness among the people. Official statements, media reports and newspaper articles allow certain aspects to show through. But the situation is worsening apace, and the only solution on offer seems to be to put up with everything, without any idea of how long it will last.[103]

In these difficult times, and despite the Church's critical attitude to the political system, the state and Party leadership began to realize that no one outside the Church could play the role of reducing tensions among the population, while also credibly representing the national component and supporting the government in its search for a solution. The turn toward the Christian faith, which more and more people made in the years of hardship, stood both the Church and the state in good stead. Gradually the Church evolved from its stance of adversary to one of partner with a leader who was still well versed in the Bible.

This opening to the government enabled the Church, so long dependent upon the pre-revolutionary order, to develop for the first time a national identity. It thereby signaled to the militant exile organizations in Florida and their friends in Washington that it was prepared to seek a reconciliation between the two camps, laying the basis for non-violent reform of the system as soon as this came up for debate.

In this connection, it was important that the Church leaders openly took up position against the US economic embargo. But, also in his Third World policy and his demands for a new world economic order, Castro now received the support of "his" Church.

The gradual rapprochement between Communism and the clergy eventually led to the Pope's visit to Cuba in January 1998, just under 20 years after Castro first invited John Paul II to stop off in Cuba on his way from an Episcopal conference in Puebla, Mexico. On that previous occasion, following immediate protests from Cuban exiles and an alternative invitation to Miami, the supreme pontiff had avoided a squabble by flying back via the (mainly Protestant) former British colony of Bahamas. By 1985, Castro was telling Frei Betto that John Paul II would certainly "be interested in having contacts with our revolutionary people," and that he was "sure a visit by the Pope would be useful and positive for the Church and for Cuba," as well as "for the Third World in general."[104] But the fact that the project took many more years to finalize indicates the mountain of difficulties that both sides had to overcome. First came Castro's humble trek to Rome in the autumn of 1996, when he received a papal audience wearing a muted suit and tie instead of his olive-green battledress. Afterwards he described his meeting with the Holy Father as little short of a "miracle."

Soon the miracle was shared with the Cuban people. As the "messenger of truth and hope," the Cuban bishops' conference announced on November 1, 1997, that God's deputy on earth would visit the island "in one of the most difficult moments of our history." "The political, social and economic situation in recent years," it went on, "will be reflected in the qualities of the papal visit, and in the future work of the Catholic Church in Cuba."[105] The head of the ten dioceses took the opportunity to call for a widening of its still tightly circumscribed sphere of public activity.

The regime made hesitant steps to accommodate the Church. "On this Holy Night we should not sleep, we have a duty to celebrate," Cardinal Jaime Ortega told a thousand faithful on December 25, 1997, in Havana Cathedral, where they had gathered for Christmas for the first time in nearly 30 years.[106] The Pope had wanted the great Christian festival to be restored, and the Máximo Líder had given his permission as a gesture of good will. "We shall do all we can for the [Pope's] visit to be a success," he promised at the National Assembly. "It should also be a success for the Revolution. We would like the Pope to return to Rome feeling he has had the best trip ever to another country."[107] "The old is finished, the new has begun," the pontiff proclaimed, alluding to the Apostle Paul, in the first papal message to the Cuban people for 38 years. And he left no doubt that he expected that, after his visit, "the Church . . . will continue to have the necessary freedom to fulfill its mission."[108]

All the churches in Cuba were full that Christmas night. In view of recent economic growth, the "special period" administrators exceptionally provided all that was needed for a merry Christmas in the true sense of the word. There was enough pork, rice, and black beans for Cuba's national dish; it was even possible to buy, for dollars, Christmas flowers made of plastic (as usual in the Caribbean), Father Christmases, dolls, toys, and other modest gifts. Castro wanted it to be clear that the restoration of Christmas, for the first time since 1969, was a "special exception." But people understood this in a very Cuban way: "An exception! Okay, fine. One exception for today, one exception for tomorrow . . . At least there is one. And, from one exception to the next, everything will get better."[109] And that is how it worked. The "exception" became the rule in following years.

On Wednesday, January 21, 1998, the Holy Father finally landed at José Martí international airport and received the red carpet treatment from Fidel Castro. Again, instead of his olive-green uniform, the state and Party leader was wearing a dark two-piece suit, with a white shirt and cufflinks, and a fashionable, decently spotted tie. The Pope's visit to Cuba was a historic event. He had already been to more than 120 countries around the world, and this was the last one on the list in Latin America.

John Paul II spent his five days traveling around the island, whose population had meanwhile risen above 11 million, and which had a social system unparalleled in the Third World but virtually no political let alone religious freedoms. He found a Church that had more or less been lost to the faithful over the past few decades, with only some 40 percent of Cubans baptized in the Catholic faith. What had been flourishing, with varying degrees of state toleration, was syncretism. Significantly, one of the most important Masses during the preparations for the papal visit had been celebrated by Cardinal Jaime Ortega before tens of thousands of people, at the St Lazarus pilgrimage site in El Rincón near Havana. This is a religious center that mingles together Catholicism and Afro-Cuban cults, where Lazarus (under the name of Babalú-Ayé) is venerated as one of the highest gods of the *santería* religion, and where there is also an Aids clinic. The Pope himself stopped off there on the fourth day of his trip and presented his credentials.

On the day after his arrival, however, the first thing he did was say Mass in Santa Clara, the town associated with the most important "saint" of the Cuban Revolution, Ernesto Che Guevara. Later stopping places included Camagüey and Santiago de Cuba, in the far east of the island. Each evening he returned to Havana, and it was there, on Sunday, January 25, that he said the final Mass before hundreds of thousands on the Plaza de la Revolución, 38 years after the Catholic conference of 1959 at which a message had been read from Pope John XXIII.

This Pope seemed to be a stroke of good fortune for Cuba and Castro, as he already indicated at the arrival ceremony. His opening words of greeting to the Cuban people dressed up his criticism of the lack of pluralism and of the US embargo in a wish that "Cuba, with all its wonderful opportunities, may open up to the world, and the world open up to Cuba"[110] – and, in the course of his visit, he made himself even clearer. At the same time, he avoided anything that might be seen as open incitement of the faithful. It was left to the many thousands of foreign reporters to read between the lines and to produce commentaries of every kind – often evidently overdrawn and owing more to their own wishful thinking than to anything the Pope had actually said. The "danger" that Cubans might pay attention to such reports was anyway rather slight, in view of the continuing constraints on the freedom of information. All they managed to hear was the Pope's original tone of voice. At least an advance guard of Vatican diplomats and the Cuban clergy had with difficulty won agreement that all his Masses should be broadcast on nationwide television.

Many political prisoners and their families had written to Rome for help, but when the Pope tackled the delicate issue and appealed for a large number of them to be released, he did so not on a public occasion but at a private talk in Castro's wing on the second floor of the Palace of the Revolution, amid the decorative jungle plants from the Sierra Maestra. The meeting behind closed doors with the head of the Cuban state and Party lasted one hour. Then the Pope also met Castro's brothers Raúl and Ramón, as well as his sisters Ángela and Augustina, in a private audience. On the way into his offices, the Cuban leader slowed his pace out of respect for the frail visitor, who had to support himself with a stick. "You see what it's like for us over-seventies," the 77-year-old Pope said to the 71-year-old Comandante, who looked positively sprightly by comparison.

The Pope's most important service, in the Plaza de la Revolución in Havana, was kept until the last day of his trip. Interrupted no fewer than 38 times by loud cheers, shouts and applause, he pressed some moral truths home not only for the host standing beside him but also for the supporters of unfettered capitalism.

> The ideological and economic systems succeeding one another in the last two centuries have often encouraged conflict as a method, since their programs contained the seeds of opposition and disunity. This fact profoundly affected their understanding of man and of his relations with others. Some of these systems also presumed to relegate religion to the merely private sphere, stripping it of any social influence or importance. In this regard, it is helpful to recall that a modern state cannot make atheism or religion one of its political ordinances. The state, while distancing itself from all extremes of fanaticism or secularism, should encourage a harmonious social climate and suitable legislation which enables every person and every religious group to live its faith freely. . . . On the other hand, some places are witnessing the resurgence of a certain

capitalist neoliberalism which subordinates the human person to blind market forces, and conditions the development of peoples on those forces. From its centers of power, such neoliberalism often places unbearable burdens upon less favored countries. Hence, at times, unsustainable economic programs are imposed on nations as a condition for further assistance. In the international community, we thus see a small number of countries growing exceedingly rich at the cost of the growing impoverishment of a great number of other countries; as a result the wealthy grow ever wealthier, while the poor grow ever poorer.[111]

The Pope's central message, however, delivered to cheering from the crowd, contained unmistakable words of advice to the Cuban nomenklatura: "Freedom cannot be reduced to its social and political aspects alone, but acquires its fully developed form only in the exercise of the freedom of belief, the basis of all other human rights."[112]

In his farewell address at Havana airport, the Pope strongly urged both Castro and Washington to reconsider their existing policies: "In our day, no nation can live in isolation. The Cuban people therefore cannot be denied the contacts with other peoples necessary for economic, social and cultural development, especially when the imposed isolation strikes the population indiscriminately, making it ever more difficult for the weakest to enjoy the bare essentials of decent living." In order to overcome the suffering of the people, it was necessary to end the "oppressive economic measures – unjust and ethically unacceptable – imposed from outside the country."[113]

For Castro, the papal visit was undoubtedly a great triumph of internal and external policy. But the Vatican also seems to have gained from it, if only because, nearly four decades after the revolution, Castro had recognized the Church before the whole world as a moral authority alongside the Communist Party. Some 300 prisoners were freed as a result, the Church was allowed greater space in which to hold Masses and other events, and it was able to add to the 900 men and women (including 300 priests) who made up its personnel on the eve of the papal visit. Cardinal Ortega received permission to publish the Church paper *Aquí la Iglesia* ("Here is the Church") and the periodical *Nueva Palabra*

("New Word"). Most important of all, the Catholic Church engaged in a "Christianization drive" in 1998, when the number of baptisms shot up from 10,000 to 45,000 in the year. Its welfare organization, Caritas, drew on some 5,000 volunteers to carry out humanitarian work, especially in caring for young and old people hard hit by the problems in the economy.

It was as if a circle in Castro's life closed with the Holy Father's visit, and at times it seemed more to answer a need on Castro's part than to meet a necessity for the Party and state leadership. For years there had been persistent rumors that Castro was receiving treatment from Swiss doctors for a heart condition or Parkinson's disease or loss of cerebral function or cancer. Visitors repeatedly said that he looked physically shrunken, exhausted and debilitated, although he was fully alert during conversations. Deep down, perhaps, Castro was also making his own highly personal peace with the Church. "The Pope told me that when he prayed he would also pray for me. I thanked him for that," Castro gave away shortly before the pontiff's arrival in Cuba.[114]

Freedom or "socialismo tropical"

The news item was terse, its language matter-of-fact: "Following the Pope's visit, suppression of political dissent continued, but was generally less severe than the previous year." The four pages on Cuba in the Amnesty International report covering the year 1998 went on to state that, after John Paul II's five-day visit, approximately 300 prisoners, including at least 120 political prisoners, were released, but that "at least 350 others remained imprisoned, including some 100 prisoners of conscience."[115] Already in May 1998 the human rights organization had spoken in an interim report of 500 to 3,000 political prisoners in Cuba, but acknowledged that no one knew the exact number, because relatives did not dare report cases of detention to aid agencies for fear of reprisals. "Often political dissidents were jailed on the pretext of a non-political offence."[116] One favorite variant was "short-term detention" for the purposes of intimidation, when people were arrested for hours or a few days without being allowed to contact their family or a lawyer, and often without knowing whether it might last for years.

Foreign correspondents' reports spoke of a "sense of disappointment and emptiness following the papal visit," and criticized the fact that "the Castro regime could not bring itself to introduce any decisive reforms." In the view of the *Neue Zürcher Zeitung,* it was on "a zig-zag course between reform and dogged persistence."[117] *The Economist* reported that, after the papal aircraft left Havana on the evening of January 25, "the regime moved fast to show who [was] in charge." Within hours "large groups of 'special brigade' police were on every street corner. Young people strolling in Havana's parks and squares [were] being constantly harassed by police." Elizardo Sánchez from the Cuban Commission for Human Rights and National Reconciliation, which by the late nineties had become the most important organization of its kind in Cuba, commented: "The Pope's demands will not prompt any radical changes because the government . . . does not respect any of the civil and political rights recognized in international law."[118]

In February 1999, a special two-day session of the Cuban National Assembly passed a series of measures that tightened existing penal legislation, including the death penalty for serious drugs-related crimes and longer prison sentences for robbery with violence. A new "Law for the Protection of the National Independence and Economy of Cuba" (Law No. 88) threatened up to 20 years' imprisonment against anyone "providing information to the US government; owning, distributing or reproducing material produced by the US government or any other foreign entity; and collaborating, by any means, with foreign radio, television, press or other foreign media, with the purpose of destabilizing the country and destroying the socialist state."[119] That this was directed against political dissidents, Amnesty International learned from opponents of the regime who had been warned against a continuation of their activities. But a particularly important target was Cuban journalists who had asserted some independence and were using reports from 15 press agencies abroad.

At first sight it is difficult to comprehend why, after more than 40 years, Castro still uses repressive machinery which harasses critics of the system for the slightest reason. After all, the fact that hundreds of thousands of Cubans have been driven into exile means that there is only weak political opposition to his rule inside the country. It is true that not everyone can just up and go without permission, and only the privileged can get a passport to travel abroad. But unlike in the Soviet Union, the GDR, and other Eastern bloc countries, Castro has not really prevented his opponents from leaving the country if they so wish – indeed, he has encouraged this when it seemed a useful way of relieving political pressure. He has even consistently put up with the emigration of well-educated academics and skilled workers, despite the great damage this does to the national economy.

In the last decade of the twentieth century, many factors lay behind the growing alienation of part of the population from the institutions of the Cuban state. No amount of propaganda could offset that loss of faith in the future of the Marxist-Leninist social order which came with the end of Communism in Eastern Europe, and doubts about the viability of the system only increased as a result of the catastrophic economic effects of the Soviet collapse. From the mid-nineties on, the cautious opening by necessity to foreign investment, the boosting of tourism, and the introduction of market niches within the state-run economy created ever greater space for new impressions, influences, and thinking. Suddenly small circles of oppositionists sprang up all over the country. In October 1995, 140 of these came together to form a "Cuban Council" (*Concilio Cubano*), but a few months later, in February 1996, its meetings were forbidden and some of its leading members arrested.

New thinking was supposed to be expressed only behind closed doors, in the leadership bodies of the Party and state; at all other levels of society, increased vigilance was the order of the day. "In the nineties," noted Jorge Domínguez, a Cuba expert at Harvard University, "a new centralization of power may be observed in the hands of Fidel Castro."[120] In Cuba, after 20 years during which Castro had been prepared to delegate a large part of his administrative powers, the decade that saw the end of the Cold War, democratization in Latin America, and the spread of globalization was marked by a return to the authoritarianism of the sixties.

Although an estimated 100 to 200 small groups of dissidents exist on the island, the number of "genuinely" active dissidents is probably no higher than 500,[121] and only a few of these manage to gain such a reputation abroad that they cause the government any real political difficulties. One case that did make the world's headlines was that of René Gómez, Félix Bonne, Martha Roque, and Vladimiro Roca (son of the legendary Communist leader Blas Roca), who were arrested in July 1997 and, 19 months later, sentenced at a closed trial to terms of three and a half to five years' imprisonment; several EU countries responded by freezing their development aid to Cuba, and the King of Spain canceled a trip to Cuba that had been planned for the spring of 1999. Canada, too, whose prime minister Jean Chrétien had paid a friendly visit to Castro a few months before, suspended cooperation with Havana and announced that it would no longer support Cuba's entry into the Organization of American States. Yet Castro did not budge during the period from the papal visit in January 1998 through to the Ibero–American summit in autumn 1999 (which did, in the end, take place in the presence of the Spanish monarch). Not even condemnation by the UN Human Rights Commission in Geneva was capable of making him change his mind, and it was only in the summer of 2000 that three of the group of four dissidents were released. Vladimiro Roca had to serve out the whole of his sentence.

In autumn 1997 the four had distributed a 34-page pamphlet at the Fifth Congress of the CPC, attacking the claim of the Party and the ruling nomenklatura to be the nation's sole legitimate representative and demanding a new economic and political opening. In this connection, they called for a boycott of the upcoming elections to the people's assemblies. What made the Cuban leadership act so intransigently against them was ostensible evidence that they had been closely collaborating with the CANF and other militant exile organizations in Miami, as well as with people in or around the CIA, and representatives of US interests in Havana. They were alleged to have coordinated the distribution of leaflets, the holding of press conferences, and the organization of interviews for dozens of broadcasts by the US-funded propaganda station Radio Martí.

Obvious interference from abroad, or collaboration by internal opposition groups with the "class enemy," makes more difficult the work of those who go their own serious way and do not wish to be suspected of being the playthings of Miami or anonymous forces in Washington. Those who come under this category are Elizardo Sánchez, head of the Cuban Commission for Human Rights and National Reconciliation (CCDHRN); Gustavo Arcos, executive secretary of the Cuban Committee for Human Rights (CCPHD); Héctor Palacios from the Center for Social Studies (CES), and a number of others. These all refuse any collaboration with forces abroad that support or promote the US embargo. Instead, they look hopefully to dialogue with the government, in the medium to long term, convinced that only this can achieve a peaceful and orderly transition to democracy which preserves the social security and other good aspects of the revolution. In this, they have the backing of the Miami-based Cuban Committee for Democracy and Eloy Gutiérrez Menoyo's *Cambio Cubano* (Cuban Change), both of which are led by former active fighters against Castro. Thus, the lawyer Alfredo Durán took part in the abortive Bay of Pigs invasion in 1961 and spent nearly two years in a Cuban prison; he then left for Florida, where for a long time he held high the banner of the militant veterans' association, "Brigade 2506." He has since renounced the aim of toppling Castro by force: "We cannot either overthrow Castro or govern Cuba. Castro himself must lead the country to reconciliation, if he wants to save his legacy."[122]

Gutiérrez Menoyo's views are similar. At the Ibero–American summit held in Havana in November 1999, he appealed to the heads of state and government to make Washington "end its conspiracy with elements . . . that profit from a lucrative business: the 'anti-Castro industry'." With the authority of a man who spent 22 long and bitter years in a Cuban jail, he claimed in his open letter that "certain circles in Washington" were seeking to block the request of the Cuban opposition and to prevent an improvement of relations with Havana. "In the guise of peaceful means," they were continually trying to revive the "old stances and formulas of confrontation" from the days of the Cold War.[123]

In 1994 and 1995, Castro invited to Havana representatives of Cuban exile organizations that were open to dialogue, and even laid on an official reception for them, while Miami hardliners, particularly from the CANF, angrily denounced what they saw as an attempt to divide the opposition to his regime. In June 1995, Castro also had a long discussion with Gutiérrez Menoyo, who afterwards wrote in the German weekly *Die Zeit*, with an eye on his diehard compatriots in Miami:

> As a revolutionary and an opponent of Castro . . . , I have better credentials than most of the others. I certainly have more reason than they to hate. But I don't live in the past. . . . Rather, it is time to leave hate and the past behind us. I have long been convinced that we will better help people in Cuba through dialogue with the government than by confronting the Castro regime head-on and isolating it.[124]

Another center of the anti-Castro movement is the Spanish capital, Madrid. It was there in November 1999, just before the Ibero–American summit in Havana, that the billionaire former president of the Telepizza fast-food chain, Leopoldo Fernández Pujals, set up the Elena Mederos Foundation and confidently presented himself more or less overnight as a personal alternative to Fidel Castro. Having grown up in Miami, he sought to fill the vacuum left in the Cuban exile community by the death of CANF chairman Mas Canosa;[125] the only question was whether the others would accept him. This underlined the greatest lack in the anti-Castro opposition: a charismatic leader with a convincing political project for a democratic Cuba.

Drawing upon his experience of democratization processes in other Latin American countries, the former director of the Madrid-based Institute for European–Latin American Relations (IRELA), Wolf Grabendorff, has stressed "the indispensability of agreement among internal and external actors about the goals and stages of the transition [in Cuba];" rival political objectives among oppositional forces would be counterproductive. As an example, he mentions the support of part of the Cuban diaspora for the Helms-Burton Act. But so long as there are no serious forces inside the country able to resist the demands for power and representation coming from outside, there seems little point in looking for models elsewhere in Latin America that might be applied to a transition in Cuba. Experiences in Chile and Nicaragua, in particular, have shown that at the decisive stage of the transition it is the opposition existing inside the country – and not exiles returning from abroad – who shape the change of government.[126] Conversely, so long as the opposition on the spot is dominated and debilitated by its friends in exile, a process of democratic change is unthinkable on the island itself.

The cautious approach taken by opposition forces inside Cuba has been of little use to them. Castro has closed his ears, dismissing them as lackeys of imperialism to be taken no more seriously than their "friends" in Miami, while disunity in the opposition, and its lack of a leader to match Castro, have allowed him to run rings round them. The anachronistic and disproportionate bunker mentality of the Castro system toward opponents who represent no real threat can be explained only on the assumption that, within his own apparatus, there may be considerable frictions and a greater degree of discontent than one can detect from outside.

Referring to an unnamed director of a state economic institute, the *Neue Zürcher Zeitung* wrote in a background report that we should not imagine the top political levels in Cuba to be as rock-solid as they appear. Away from the limelight, "hardliners" and "heretics" within the ruling apparatus fight out bitter struggles with each other, and the rebels include a growing group of technocrats who have no chance of making a career for themselves under the revolution.[127]

One sign of ongoing struggles over power and orientation has been the changes in the 25-member Politbureau. Whereas this supreme political authority operated as a monolith in the years from 1965 to 1980 and scarcely ever brought on fresh blood, the Fourth Party Congress in 1991 left in place no more than five men from the time of the victory of the revolution: Fidel and Raúl Castro, Juan Almeida, José Machado, and Carlos Rafael Rodríguez. Many other former mainstays of the revolution disappeared from public life, at the latest at this Fourth Congress. "The new faces in the government were generally much younger," Domínguez noted. "The rejuvenation of the regime's political leadership marked its willingness to accept new ideas and to adopt a new style of politics." This was connected with a certain widening of the room for political maneuver – but only within a framework stamped with the personal authority of Fidel Castro.[128]

This became especially apparent in 1996, during the conflict between the ruling apparatus and a large number of intellectuals over the fate of the political research institutes founded by the Party's Central Committee in 1976: the Centro de Estudios sobre Europa (European Studies Center) and the Centro de Estudios sobre América (American Studies Center). The publication of a series of books in the first half of the nineties, which were critical of the country's economic and political development, led to a massive reaction by the Party leadership, because the constructively posed demands for further liberalization contradicted the prevailing Party doctrine. Another reason why the two centers were in the firing line was that their funding came not only from the Party but also from foreign sources, and they operated academic exchanges with colleagues from political and scientific foundations in Europe and North America. They were accused of collaborating with "Cubanologists" in the service of Washington, of adopting their theses and half-truth, and even of constituting a fifth column in the service of imperialism.[129]

It was a clear signal when the Central Committee and Politbureau put a military man, Defense Minister Raúl Castro, in charge of publicly disciplining the academics on March 23, 1996, and when he subsequently engineered a "restructuring" of the two institutions and the dissolution of the CEA management. Castro had previously stressed that, in the "new ideological battle," socialism remained the irreversible dogma of Cuban politics. According to the IRELA institute in Madrid, many of the academics involved in the conflict now limited themselves to "gazing outward from the Malecón [the Havana waterfront]."[130] Others went into internal exile, changed their job, or left the country.

Another problem group for the regime were the children of the revolution. IRELA reported in 1999 that 63 percent of the population belonged to the post-revolutionary generation; at most they had an emotional link via their parents and grandparents to the struggles of the 1950s, from which the Castro generation derived the legitimacy of its rule.

> For many young Cubans the political system appears in many ways less attractive. Economically, because of the continuing special period, rising unemployment and lower wages, . . . they have less and less interest in attending university, but find it much more appealing to work in jobs that require fewer qualifications or none at all. Politically, there is limited scope for involvement and renewal, and the disenchantment, social dissatisfaction and a certain political apathy make it clear that large numbers of young people in Cuba no longer consider themselves represented by a system that appears to many as a "legacy from the past" offering little in the way of visions for the future.

The IRELA analysis concludes that this may lead in the long term to a "revolution with no heirs."[131]

Castro, who is well read and by no means closed to the world, is certainly aware that for these reasons too he cannot halt the long-term trend toward greater openness. Nevertheless, he still seems to be trying to slow the process down – in line with his longstanding political principle of moving in pilgrim-like stages. In the case of the Pope, for instance, the first step was to go to Rome and bow to the Holy Father, and the second step was to get him to visit Cuba. In this way, he boosted his reputation on the international political stage, brought the Church over to his side as part of the nation, defined its future scope for action, and kept it so well under control that it would not really be able to move without him and the Party. The next step was therefore backwards. Suddenly the limits were no longer where people thought they had pushed them, but were being redrawn by a new round of repression. This is the method he has used for decades, especially against intellectuals, artists, or poets, until it is almost possible to say: "Every good Cuban writer is an exiled writer."

Pope John Paul II, of course, did not gladly put up with Castro's political maneuvers: he felt he was having the wool pulled over his eyes, and he said as much. Nearly two years after the papal visit, when a new Cuban ambassador, Isidoro Gómez Santos, presented his credentials at the Vatican, the Spanish daily *El País* reported that "during the normally humdrum ceremony he received a sound diplomatic ticking-off," and that "John Paul II vigorously demanded greater efforts 'to create an atmosphere of detente and trust' in which the basic rights of each individual, whether a believer or not, would be guaranteed." By adopting a more direct and critical tone than in his meetings with Fidel Castro, the head of the Church was seeking "to re-establish genuine credibility on the international arena," which might then permit "a broad and effective opening of the world to Cuba, and of Cuba to the world." Everything would be "much simpler if Cuba allowed its people new space for freedom and participation."[132]

The lack of democracy and human rights has become an especially sore point as civilized countries (a category to which Castro would like Cuba to belong) have insisted on these principles of human coexistence in society. Castro's shortcomings in this respect have become more clearly recognized since the dictatorships of the Eastern bloc and Latin America passed into history. The fate of a Honecker, Ceauşescu, Pinochet, Fujimori, or Milošević, but also of the Institutional Revolutionary Party (PRI) in Mexico, or even the opening of China's economy by its Communist rulers, confirm how much the peoples of the world have emancipated themselves or are today shaking off ideological constraints. This process will develop in Cuba too.

But Castro has no time for criticisms of the human rights situation in Cuba. In his conversation in 1992 with the Nicaraguan writer and former interior minister, Tomás Borge, he expressed himself as follows:

> I am firmly convinced that no country in the world has done more than Cuba to protect human rights. No children in Cuba have to beg or go homeless; no children have to scrounge for a living. . . . In our country, everyone knows how to read and write. Hundreds of millions of children in the world don't have access to medical treatment, but in Cuba every child has a school to go to and has access to medical care.[133]

He further emphasized that Cuba had one of the lowest infant mortality rates and one of the highest life expectancies in the world.

> In many countries, there are millions of beggars, women who have been forced into prostitution and adolescents and citizens in general who take drugs. . . . [In Cuba] those irritating differences between millionaires and beggars have disappeared; no one has to beg here now. People need more than bread: they need honor, dignity, respect and to be treated like human beings. . . . With the Revolution and with socialism, we have created a sense of solidarity and fraternity. . . . We don't have any gross inequality. . . . Here, our citizens feel that they count; they are a part of society; they feel they have a national dignity and a homeland – something that is very rare and inaccessible to the vast majority of the people in today's world. . . . Our Revolution has a characteristic . . . that very few revolutions have had in all of history: our people have been taught to hate crime, to hate torture, to hate the use of physical violence against individuals, to hate abuses of power.[134]

Castro traced these ethical standards of the revolution back to the years of struggle. "Since the triumph of the Revolution," he claimed in a spirit of idealism, "nobody has been assassinated, no prisoners have been tortured and no physical violence has been used against prisoners; . . . since the triumph of the Revolution, Cuba hasn't had any death squads or any victims of those illegal methods of imposing order. No people have disappeared in Cuba."[135]

In his conversations with Borge, Castro also spelled out his understanding of democracy, as something with quite different origins and a different dialectic from the political system of the Western democracies that expected Cuba to follow their example.

> People used to cite Greek democracy as an example, democracy from the classical age of Greek antiquity, which was the prototype of democracy, had 40,000 citizens – men, women and children – and 90,000 slaves. . . . I think of [José] Martí – Martí never conceived of that form of democracy. I think of Bolívar – Bolívar never conceived of that form of democracy for the Latin American

countries. To the contrary, he criticized attempts to imitate the forms of political organization of France or the United States. Those great thinkers of Our America never identified themselves with the kind of democracy that the imperialists wanted to impose or had imposed or are trying to impose on us – and with which they have weakened our societies, breaking them up into a thousand pieces, so they can't solve problems. There is no real participation by the people in that kind of democracy, because opinions are manipulated to a great extent by the mass media. People's criteria and decisions are almost completely influenced by advertising, propaganda and what are called "scientific" methods for influencing how people think.[136]

Castro explained the world of difference between his basic philosophical understanding of democracy and that of his opponents. His position was cogent in that he applied it to himself:

I don't believe it's really necessary to have more than one party, either. For our countries, and especially for a country such as Cuba, one of the most important things is unity . . . which has made it possible for us to stand firm against all of the United States' threats and acts of aggression. How could our country have stood firm if it had been split up into ten pieces? What is usually called democracy is a mechanism that serves as a tool; it's a system that includes not only the political but also the economic and social ideas of imperialism. . . . I think that our system is incomparably more democratic than the system in the United States. . . . I think that the exploitation of one human by another must disappear before you can have real democracy.[137]

True democracy, then, could not exist amid social inequality. "Democracy can exist only in socialism. The highest form of democracy will be communism, but we haven't reached that yet.[138]

Castro's political view of the world is based not on parliamentary democracy, but on Lenin's democratic centralism in which the Party represents the majority of the population, the working class, and makes all decisions in its interests. As Sheldon Liss put it: "As the leader of the party and elected government, Castro, in Rousseauean fashion, believes that he interprets the will of the people, . . . when society is guided by the dictatorship of the proletariat."[139] Castro therefore denies to the United States the right to sit in judgment, because it uses capitalist ideas and methods to analyze the political situation in Cuba. No one can look at democratic centralism from a liberal-democratic viewpoint and come to an objective evaluation.

If, especially since the end of the Cold War in 1989–90, Castro has acclaimed the observance of human rights as one of the pillars of his "democratic centralism," the annual reports of Amnesty International and other human rights organizations suggest otherwise. In 2000, for instance, Amnesty International reported that:

> dissidents, who included journalists, political opponents and human rights defenders, suffered severe harassment during the [preceding] year. Freedom of expression, association and assembly continued to be severely limited in law and in practice. Those who attempted to organize meetings, express views or form organizations that conflicted with government policy were subjected to punitive measures and harassment. These included short-term detention, interrogation, threats, intimidation, eviction, loss of employment, restrictions on travel, house searches, house arrests, phone bugging and physical and verbal acts of aggression carried out by government supporters.[140]

The report estimated at "several hundred" the number of people imprisoned for "political offences;" "some trials of prisoners of conscience took place which did not conform to international standards;" there were "at least 13 executions" for criminal offences, and at least nine prisoners were still in death cells. Amnesty was especially critical of "the absence of any official data on the prison population," and of "the difficulties imposed by the authorities on access to the country for independent human rights monitoring." The Human Rights Information Bureau in Havana estimated that in the autumn of 1999 at least 110,000 persons – roughly 1 percent of the total population, with a disproportionate number of blacks – were serving sentences either in prison or in labor camps.[141]

The actions of the Cuban state against moderate dissidents caused a stir at the summit meeting of Ibero–American heads of state and government, held in November 1999 in Havana. Amnesty International estimated that, shortly before the arrival of delegations from abroad, between 200 and 300 dissidents were temporarily detained or placed under house arrest, and that others were beaten or physically intimidated by the security forces, or prevented from gathering together. When oppositionists tried to hold meetings in the run-up to the summit, or to gain a world-wide audience by contacting foreign embassies, Fidel Castro dealt with the subject for the first time in the presence of the international press, in a television broadcast lasting several hours. By himself mentioning dissidents such as Elizardo Sánchez by name, the Cuban head of state finally recognized before the Cuban public that an opposition existed inside the country. "They were planning a summit of their own," he said angrily, as justification for the measures against the "counter-revolutionaries." But his attempt to isolate them misfired. Several heads of government – some discreetly, others more openly – had meetings with an anti-Castro delegation led by Sánchez and Palacios. Spain's prime minister, Aznar, met critics of the regime in the Spanish embassy in Havana, which was besieged for the occasion by a large number of journalists. And, at the banquet table for the summit guests, King Juan Carlos I also urged a new approach, despite his sympathies with the host sitting next to him: "It is our firm belief that our nations can meet the challenges of the twenty-first century . . . only with genuine democracy, comprehensively guaranteed freedoms and a deep respect for human rights."[142]

But this made no impression on Castro. Whenever anyone accused him of violating human rights and jailing dissidents, he countered by pointing to the social achievements of the revolution. Presumably, therefore, so long as he lived and remained the Máximo Líder, there would be no freedom of opinion, no free elections, and no full economic freedom, such as existed in Western countries. For foreign observers who asked whether there was any chance that other political parties would be permitted, Castro had only one answer: "Parties, different ideologies and objectives? . . . No, I can't do that. If it became absolutely necessary, my successor would have to do it."[143]

10

Don Quixote and History

★

He always considered death an unavoidable professional hazard.
He had fought all his wars in the front lines, without suffering a
scratch. . . . He had emerged unharmed from every assassination
attempt against him, and on several occasions his life had been saved
because he was not sleeping in his own bed. . . . His disinterest
was not lack of awareness or fatalism, but rather the melancholy
certainty that he would die in his bed, poor and naked and without
the consolation of public gratitude.[1]

These lines are from Gabriel García Márquez's *The General in
His Labyrinth*, a novel dealing with the last days of South America's
great liberator from Spanish rule, Simon Bolívar (1783–1830). It
is a melancholy reflection on the collapse of a great idea. More
than once, especially when it draws out resemblances or parallels
in the lives of the two figures, the reader cannot help but feel that
its author also saw his friend Fidel Castro in the person of Bolívar.
García Márquez is one of only a few people who can really
claim to know Castro well and to be familiar with details of his
personal life. He tells us: "Many times I have seen him arrive at
my house late at night, still trailing the last scraps of a limitless
day." The Colombian novelist is also one of the few remaining
friends with whom Castro feels at ease and is able to behave as a
private individual, although one can never quite think of Castro
as anything other than a public, political person. It is true that,
with García Márquez, he has occasionally wallowed in memories
of his childhood on the family farm in Birán, but he always
prefers to return to his political dreams. "Spain, the land of his

ancestors, is an obsession with him," García Márquez writes. "His vision of Latin America in the future is the same as that of Bolívar and Martí: an integral and autonomous community capable of influencing the destiny of the world."[2]

Fidel Castro always wanted to go down in history – first only as an heir of the Cuban freedom-fighter José Martí, then as a legitimate successor of Bolívar and a renewer of Latin America. Cuba was meant to be just the beginning. Nor was he the only one to feel in himself the makings of a historical figure: his charisma impressed his enemies as much as it did his teachers and companions. We should remember that no less a person than John F. Kennedy, writing in 1960 before his election as US president, was convinced that "Fidel Castro [was] part of the legacy of Bolívar, who led his men over the Andes Mountains, vowing 'war to the death' against Spanish rule."[3] Kennedy also then thought that the latter-day Cuban Bolívar would help to make the US dominant in Latin America, if he was not prevented from doing so.

Kennedy was certainly the only one who might have been able to steer Castro and his revolution in a different direction, but in November 1963 the assassin's bullets in Dallas removed that possibility. It is clear that, for all their antagonism, the two men were fascinated by each other. After the missile crisis, there were discreet feelers between Havana and Washington and behind-the-scenes attempts to bring about a rapprochement – and we now know that, on the eve of Kennedy's murder, they were already so far advanced that a public uproar was likely to break out sooner rather than later.[4] There have always been suspicions and clues suggesting that this was the real motive for the assassination. An agreement between the ostensible arch-enemies Castro and Kennedy would not only have shattered the picture of the world underlying the unholy alliance of Cuban exiles, CIA, Mafia, and Pentagon reactionaries, who blamed and hated Kennedy for the Bay of Pigs fiasco. It would also have removed any basis for their holy war against the revolutionaries in Havana.

Castro's efforts to maintain secret contacts with Kennedy's successor were unsuccessful. As recently declassified US documents show, Lyndon B. Johnson put an end to talks with Havana and robbed the continent of a political perspective that might have broken down Cold War patterns of thinking. García Márquez recalls how, at one of Castro's meetings with the US politicians who still frequented Havana even in the darkest days of ideological confrontation, the most conservative among them suddenly said he was sure that no one could better play the role of mediator between Latin America and the United States than Fidel Castro.[5]

Kennedy, who competed with Castro for the favor of young people around the world, knew the power of attraction that the Cuban held for the Latin American left and Third World liberation movements – and not only for them. The Cuban Revolution (whose legitimacy Kennedy recognized because of the exploitative Cuba policy of his predecessors) and the high moral purpose with which Castro and his comrades overturned the political conditions on their island also found an enthusiastic response among the rebellious post-war generation of the First World. Weary of the two-faced political morality of their parents and grandparents, young people saw in Che Guevara and Fidel Castro the harbingers of a purer, juster, less materialistic world, and the basis for a new socialist International that many thought should be oriented more toward Mao than Marx. In their eyes, Marx stood for Moscow and the old order of things, for the Cold War and – especially after the missile crisis – the status quo of non-intervention and so-called peaceful coexistence; whereas Mao stood for a new ideological departure and the export of revolution to the Third World, for a "second, third Vietnam." That was the path down which Guevara strayed, and for a time Castro allowed his foreign and economic policy to be led in the same direction, believing as he did that Guevara was ideologically more developed than himself. But whereas his comrade left Cuba and eventually met his death in the Bolivian jungle, Castro returned to the marriage of convenience with the Soviet Union.

Any export of revolution now took place only with Moscow's agreement. Logical and ideological support was given only where the major powers were fighting surrogate wars or conflicts – as in Africa or Central America. Thus, Cuban soldiers hastened the end of colonialism and apartheid in South Africa and Namibia, and threatened the US sphere of influence in the Horn of Africa by intervening in Ethiopia; and Castro hoped that aid to the Sandinistas in Nicaragua and the guerrilla forces in Guatemala would help to bring about another Cuba. But the decade or more of war in Angola, where at one point as many as 40,000 Cuban soldiers were engaged, overstretched Cuba's economic capacities to such an extent that Castro had to be careful that it did not end up becoming his Vietnam. When the war game grew too risky and costly, and when the late eighties and early nineties brought peace agreements, democratization, and the collapse of the Soviet empire, the modern Bolívar had to withdraw into his Cuban preserve. He now sent only doctors instead of soldiers to the Third World, and carved out an image of himself as spokesman for the debt-ridden developing countries. Nevertheless, despite the economic catastrophe that hit Cuba when its East European allies pulled out, he achieved the miracle of protecting the revolution from widely expected collapse and carrying it into the new millennium without any outside support.

Like his model Bolívar, Castro appears in a way to have arrived in his twilight years at the point from which he started; his life has come full circle. Yet it has certainly been one of the most fascinating and controversial political biographies of the last century. If he has become a myth in his own time, this is largely thanks to the United States and – as he once said in an interview – "to the failure of its countless attempts to put an end to my life." Naturally he will remain a myth after his life is over. Or, as he added with a mixture of self-assurance and delicate mockery: "Should the merit of having fought for so many years against such a mighty empire be treated lightly?"[6] Perhaps more than Bolívar, however, Castro has had to assume that he will end his life "without the consolation of public gratitude," or, if he is lucky enough to receive some, that it will be kept within very narrow limits – the limits of Cuba. There, at least, he has made more progress than his model José Martí. But any such gratitude will not mainly stem from his achievement in leaving behind education and health systems without equal in the Third World, for a population that has doubled since the time he launched his political struggle in the middle of the twentieth century. Nor will it count for much that the mass of Cubans, despite economic hardship and shortages, are better off than 50 years ago – better, or anyway hardly worse off, than most people in large parts of Central and Southern America, not to speak of elsewhere in the Third World. For the fact is that nearly two-thirds of today's Cubans were born after the revolution, and many of them consider that the achievements have been bought at too high a price. Discontent continues to result from lack of political and material freedoms, uncertain prospects at work and in private life, uncertain political conditions, and consumer temptations that cannot be satisfied within the system.

What does count, and what Cubans are grateful to Castro for, is their liberation from colonial dependence and their ability to lead a civilized life in dignity. That was not there before the revolution. Cubans are a proud people, not at all broken by the hardship that both the US government and, to a large extent, Castro expect them to put up with. Anyone who travels there can see that for themselves. Identification with the revolution is still high among ordinary people, including many young people, and it will outlive the Máximo Líder. One thing Cubans certainly do not want is to return to the old dependence on the great neighbor to the north. The early introduction of the euro as a convertible currency alongside the dollar was, in this respect, also an appeal for help that many European politicians did not understand.

"History will absolve me!" Castro declared in his final address to the court, before he was sentenced to 15 years' imprisonment for his failed attack on the Moncada Barracks in Santiago de Cuba. It was during the two years which he eventually served in prison that he planned the overthrow of the dictator Fulgencio Batista. Former *New York Times* journalist Tad Szulc wrote in his mid-eighties biography of Castro: "Batista's rule was so widely hated that it brought more unity to Cubans than any event since the Machado dictatorship twenty years earlier, unity which Batista himself failed to understand and which would serve as the main trigger for the revolution." "As directed and inspired by Fidel Castro," the Cuban struggle had two objectives: the "tactical objective of ousting Batista," and the "strategic objective of all-embracing social revolution."[7]

The belief and the hope that history would absolve him became a kind of obsession. But history does not actually acquit anyone: each revolutionary, liberator, or statesman is guilty. And since the court's verdict is handed down by others who also want to make history, and who therefore are themselves "guilty" of bias, it falls at best to the appeal courts of later generations to pass a more lenient judgment. Are the history books not filled with admiration or sober respect for "undemocratic" rulers, for despots from antiquity down to modern times, in comparison with whom the revolutionary Fidel Castro from the Caribbean appears as rather a small fish? No more than other politicians could he count on receiving a suspended sentence. If it was to be granted him, it would have to be as a bonus of political office. And mercy is something else that history does not know.

There are, however, extenuating circumstances: perhaps, in Castro's case, the US embargo dating back to the early sixties, the longest, most uncompromising, and politically most senseless economic blockade that a large country has ever inflicted on a smaller one, and which has had the opposite of the intended effect. It did not weaken but strengthened Castro in his politics and his basic principles: "They [the Americans] will see," he said as long ago as 1980, "that they will never bring us to our knees, that we can resist for one, ten or as many years as necessary, even if we have to live like the Indians that Christopher Columbus found here when he landed 500 years ago."[8] He would be proved right. In the 1990s, when the Soviet Union disappeared and the United States tightened the embargo still further, Cubans were indeed forced to live almost as the Indians had done before them. And they pulled through.

One of the main replies that Castro's opponents make to his plea for historical absolution is also one of their main accusations against his regime: namely, that he has imposed his will on the people like a patriarch. He has withheld virtually all the individual freedoms characteristic of a progressive society, because he has always believed that he alone knows what is best for his people. "We are working out our own Cuban system, to meet our problems and satisfy our people," he said in 1967. People had to be guaranteed a decent existence, in which money no longer played a role and the state looked after them, while in return their work would be their "contribution to the good of all people and the State." That was "true Marxism-Leninism, as we see it, . . . not Communism as it is practised in Russia, Eastern Europe or China."[9] Again and again, he infuriated orthodox comrades with this kind of revolutionary individualism.

Yet, just as scarcely anyone can refrain from openly or secretly admiring the fact that, despite numerous plots to murder him, he has been able to maintain himself for half a century at the head of a revolution-turned-state, so does everyone also realize that such a degree of autocracy cannot be good for a country. What will happen when the power accumulated over decades in the hands of a single person suddenly disappears, through either abdication or death? It may lead to a rude awakening. For, when the debits and credits are weighed up, it will certainly be apparent that Cuba – despite its much-praised social system – has lagged behind technologically and economically to a depressing degree. And these aspects, so crucial for the country's future, are capable of developing only in an open society.

When Castro has been asked about what will come after him, his replies have always been vague. Once, in 1998, he told North American journalists: "Nothing will happen, and maybe things will get better."[10] In the early nineties, when Tomás Borge suggested that politicians ought to resign when they reached 60, Castro countered by citing Plato's view that no one should assume public office before the age of 55 – and, given the advance in life expectancy, he noted with a touch of self-irony that the equivalent age today would be 80.

Such questions are relative, he said by way of justification; they ultimately depend upon the individual's state of health and whether he or she is still able to perform public functions. For himself, he carried them out with pleasure and a sense of duty. But, he added, "I don't have the energy I had when we were in the mountains or in the early years after the triumph of the Revolution." He felt strong enough to go on struggling for a long time to come, "as long as my comrades believe that I'm needed in that battle." There had been many statesmen in the modern world who had remained active well past the age he had already reached. "My problem isn't age so much as my forgetting that I'm not 30 any more; that's my problem. My mind is adapted to being 30, and I'm not 30."[11]

To Federico Mayor Zaragoza, former director of the United Nations Educational, Scientific and Cultural Organization (UNESCO), he said in the year 2000, when he was 74:

> I know well enough that man is mortal; and the key to my life has always been never to think about that. When my rebellious character became caught up in the risky career of a revolutionary fighter, without anyone forcing me into it, I also knew that I was unlikely to have a long life. I was not a head of state but a quite ordinary person. I have not inherited any office and I am not a king; therefore I have no need to prepare any successor, certainly not to spare the country the trauma of a chaotic transition.

He repeated the assurance:

> There will be no trauma, and no transition will be necessary. The transition from one social system to another has been taking place [in Cuba] for more than forty years. The important thing is not the replacement of one man by another. Once a genuine revolution has consolidated itself and the seeds of ideas and consciousness are bearing fruit, no individual is indispensable, however important his personal contribution may have been.[12]

To emphasize that others were equally suited to lead the revolution, that he was but one among many, Castro pointed out that there was "no personality cult" around him: "No streets, parks or schools bear the name of living leaders. You won't even come across official photos." But then there is no need for them: everyone knows that he is Cuba. The revolution was and is Fidel Castro, and he will continue to be everywhere even after his death. In his lifetime, any public floating of the name of a future successor is purest speculation, and for the person concerned it carries the risk that he will sink into oblivion. That has actually happened to many potential candidates whose names have been mentioned at various times.

For decades the outside world seems to have been waiting impatiently for news of his passing away. The gauge of when this might come has always been his external appearance: whether his latest speech was long or short, whether the pauses seemed to last forever, whether he read from a text or just used notes, whether he was wearing glasses or not, whether he spoke slowly or hesitantly, whether he managed to pick up the thread after a particularly long sentence or intricate idea, whether his voice was firm or brittle, whether his hands trembled, whether his face was gaunt and waxen, whether his complexion was healthy or pallid, whether his eyes still gleamed or looked dull and weary, whether his hair was thin and tousled, his beard strawy and translucent, whether he walked upright or shuffled along, whether his handshake was firm or limp. Stomach cancer, lung cancer, a brain tumor, Parkinson's, a heart attack: his condition has been diagnosed by a succession of screen doctors, as well as by Castrologists in the diplomatic corps and the press offices. It has been going on for 10 or 15 years, and in the meantime Castro really has been growing old. Whatever the immediate cause of death may one day be, he will certainly have succumbed to exhaustion. "I nearly always live and work at every hour, day and night. Can you lose any time when you are past seventy?" he asked in his conversation with Federico Mayor Zaragoza. "As for my speeches, I have come to the conclusion, perhaps too late, that they should be kept short." But that does not mean that, when some new infirmity is rumored, he will not again stand up and torture his audience for four, five, or six hours at a time. Things are not going to change, until he draws his final breath.

And when he is no longer there, everyone will miss him – even his opponents. No one really knows what should happen then. Future names are one problem, future policies another. Officially, his brother Raúl, five years younger than himself, has always been considered the candidate for the succession. But even in Cuba no one wants or is able to imagine him in the role of single ruler; he is not much loved and he knows it. He has always been in the shadow of his bigger, and indeed physically larger, brother. Since Fidel had the luck to be the elder of the two, though not the firstborn in the family, the order of precedence did not pose any problems for a Latin American farmer's son. (The eldest son, Ramón, like Fidel's son Fidelito, never succeeded in politics and is said to live a secluded farmer's life somewhere in Cuba, though both he and his sister Juana are also said to have toyed with the idea of leaving the country because of their powerful brother's oppressive presence.)

A collective leadership is the most likely in the period after Castro, as he himself indicated a couple of times to Federico Mayor Zaragoza: "The succession . . . has not only been planned in advance, but has already been functioning for some time. . . . The country's life will be in the hands of a large group of experienced young people, plus a smaller group of revolutionary veterans with whom they deeply identify."[13] First among the "experienced young people" are Carlos Lage, the deputy head of government and architect of the economic turn following the collapse of the Soviet Union; Ricardo Alarcón, the parliamentary speaker, former foreign minister and Castro's chief emissary in matters concerning Cuban–US relations; and Felipe Pérez Roque, the youngest of the three, foreign minister and formerly Castro's right-hand man. Of the few remaining old hands, the most prominent apart from Raúl Castro are Juan Almeida, Fidel's comrade-in-arms from Moncada days, and General Abelardo Colomé Ibarra, an Angola veteran and, since the execution of General Ochoa, interior minister and a close associate of the Castro brothers. But Castro also has ready a number of other leaders in the Party's periodically rejuvenated ideological reserve department, in the Politbureau.

If Raúl Castro outlives his brother, he will certainly be part of the new leadership. For the security apparatus comes under his responsibility, and in a period of transition it will be especially important if the country is not to risk sliding into anarchy. Its future cohesion seems to have been assured both by privileged treatment from the Castro brothers and by the activities of militant Cuban exiles in Miami, whose dire threats, constantly issued over Radio Martí, have welded the police and military more firmly together inside Cuba. There are also many in the population at large who have something to lose, however little, in the sphere of social security. Castro may have failed to shape a "new man" in

Cuba, but he has built a new Cuban who, though wishing to live better than or as well as family relatives in Florida, has no desire to give up his personal or national identity.

We shall be able to tell from personnel trends which way things are moving politically in a post-Castro Cuba. The options are: either everything continues as before, or there is a further cautious opening under the sole rule of the Communist Party, perhaps similar to the one in China. "We must and shall continue bringing our economic structures into line with changes and prevailing trends in the world economy. We live in a globalized world, and globalization is not only irreversible but will grow deeper still," Castro's political foster-son Carlos Lage told the author in 1999, though he left no doubt that the adjustment would occur within the framework of the existing system. "We are not planning any third way, because we are Communists."[14] Castro himself has defined the framework for the changes that he and his colleagues wish to pursue:

> We have not committed the follies and stupidities there have been in other countries, which have accepted the advice of European and US experts as if they were biblical prophets. . . . The madness of privatization did not have us in its grip, much less the folly of confiscating goods from the state and handing them over to relatives or friends.[15]

Every effort will be made to prevent a neoliberal opening in the manner of Eastern Europe and a return of the all too well-known phenomenon of *gangsterismo*. Even if the political right in the USA and sections of Cuban exiles in Miami dream of a collapse in Cuba, it should not be wished on anyone. Whether post-Castro Cuba heads into chaos, or toward a transitional model, will ultimately depend upon the degree of rationality and willingness to negotiate in Havana, Washington, Miami, and various European capitals.

In any event, it should be expected that the security apparatus will exert stronger pressure for an indeterminate period. Already in the late nineties, the regime was visibly pursuing an "increasingly belligerent course against all internal and external enemies of the Revolution." Susanne Gratius, from the Hamburg Institute for Iberoamerican Studies, evaluated this in spring 1999 as "a dependable barometer of rising tensions in the internal political situation"[16] – as if the country was already in a process of transition. The government evidently thought it was "exposed to a growing threat from within" and feared that it might "lose control of the situation." The "half-hearted" opening to the market that began in the early nineties had already "shaken Cuban socialism to its foundations" and undermined the legitimacy of the political elite.

> The political spectrum in Cuba has widened, as new space for the Catholic Church and many smaller non-governmental organizations has developed alongside the Communist Party. At the same time, the distance between government and intellectuals is growing larger. . . . Greater freedom of opinion and a degree of pluralism are emerging even within the country's political elite. Although there are undoubtedly reform forces inside the Communist Party, they have not up to now managed to assert themselves against the hardliners.

The last Party congress makes it clear, however, that "the united party is by no means a monolithic bloc, and that there is certainly disagreement between renovators and traditionalists concerning the content and implementation of the reform process."[17]

Jorge Domínguez also notes: "Cuba has changed, not because the Party and government leadership wanted change, but because it was no longer able to forbid it." Never before in the country's history, and scarcely ever elsewhere in Latin America, has a state concentrated so much power as Cuba under Castro. But, for all its efforts, that state is no longer in the same position as before to watch over the lives of its citizens. "What has been declining," Domínguez argues, "is not the state's need to repress, but fear of the state and its efficiency."[18] Beneath the surface, things appear to be breaking up – and this is not to the liking of the Party apparatus. "The death of a regime," writes American sociologist Irving L. Horowitz, "is sometimes made evident by dramatic events: mass uprisings from below or regicide from above. But . . . , in the case of Fidel, it is made evident by the exhaustion of ideology."[19]

Has everything been in vain, then? At the beginning of the nineties, just before the Soviet Union vanished from the political map, Castro told Tomás Borge with a touch of self-doubt: "I really wish that, with today's experience, I still had the youth of the early revolutionary years. In these difficult times, which require such great efforts, I wish above all else that I still had that youth." His ego did not permit that someone else should take over; the thought of it tormented him and kept him going. The American writer Gene Vier has written that, in common with other charismatic figures, Castro believes that "no single person represents an absolute value." "They are always seeking the universal, which implies a detachment from the particular." Hence, the charismatic leader cannot have a wife, cannot look after others or even his own children, and cannot give himself to another person. "The true charismatic leader is a vehicle, a human sieve, . . . a 'purifying agent' through which the soul and spirit of his people presses."[20]

Unlike other leaders, Castro never seems to have been driven by material motives. Not only those who claim to know him personally, but also his various opponents, think that he is one of the few absolute rulers who have not enriched themselves in office and salted away millions in Switzerland.

Castro has repeatedly said that his favorite literary hero is Cervantes's Don Quixote, as if he wants to ensure the indulgence of world history when it comes to pass judgment on his time. Unable to stop himself, he will go on jousting at windmills until the bitter end. "If I had it to do over again, I'd take the same revolutionary path. I can't feel entirely satisfied with what I've done; I will always feel I could have done better." And, as if to console himself: "Martí also said that today's dreams are tomorrow's reality."[21]

But now it is too late. The last words that Gabriel García Márquez makes his dying hero, the Liberator Bolívar, dictate to posterity are also free of any self-deception. "The man who serves a revolution ploughs a sea," the general in his labyrinth dryly states. And since he knows what people are like, he sarcastically and without any pathos ventures to look into the future destiny of his life's work – a destiny that one evidently cannot wish for Castro's: "This nation will fall inevitably into the hands of the unruly mob and then will pass into the hands of almost indistinguishable petty tyrants of every color and race."[22]

Notes

Preface to the English Edition

1 All quotations from *www.abcNEWS.com*, May 15, 2002.
2 Ibid.
3 Ibid.

Chapter 1   The Heroic Myth

1 Gabriel García Márquez, "A Personal Portrait of Fidel," in Fidel Castro, *My Early Years*, p. 18.
2 Ibid., p. 24.
3 Ibid., p. 15.
4 Ibid., p. 25.
5 Ibid., p. 17.
6 Peter G. Bourne, *Castro: A Biography of Fidel Castro*, p. 20.

Chapter 2   The Young Fidel

1 Letter from Fidel Castro, as a young student, to President Franklin D. Roosevelt, National Archives and Records Administration, Washington; cf. Robert E. Quirk, *Fidel Castro*, p. 14; and Geoffrey Leslie Simons, *Cuba: From Conquistador to Castro*, pp. 265ff.
2 According to the author's copy of the letter of November 6, 1940, to President Roosevelt, made available by the National Archives

and Records Administration of the State Department, Fidel Castro came into the world in 1928.

3 Carlos Franqui, *Diary of the Cuban Revolution* (hereafter *Diary*), pp. 1–2.

4 According to Ramón Castro, his brother was born a year later, in 1927, and his date of birth was moved back a year so that he could go to school earlier. The official date given by the Cuban Council of State is August 13, 1926. Cf. Lionel Martin, *The Early Fidel: Roots of Castro's Communism*, pp. 5 and 235; Bourne, *Castro*, p. 21.

5 Frei Betto, *Fidel and Religion: Castro Talks on Revolution and Religion with Frei Betto* (hereafter Betto), p. 100.

6 Ibid., pp. 101, 104.

7 Ibid., p. 105.

8 Ibid., p. 106.

9 See Bourne, *Castro*, p. 21; Tad Szulc, *Fidel: A Critical Portrait*, pp. 101ff.

10 Hugh Thomas, *The Cuban Revolution*, p. 18.

11 *Süddeutsche Zeitung*, March 26, 1991; *Die Zeit*, July 7, 1995.

12 Betto, pp. 99, 101.

13 Ibid., p. 101.

14 Ibid., pp. 127–8.

15 Thomas, *The Cuban Revolution*, p. 18.

16 Betto, p. 94.

17 Ibid., p. 110.

18 Betto (German edn, *Nachtgespräche mit Fidel*), p. 101.

19 Betto, *Fidel and Religion*, p. 114.

20 Franqui, *Diary*, pp. 4–5.

21 Betto, p. 111.

22 Ibid., pp. 111–12.

23 Ibid., pp. 115–16.

24 Ibid., pp. 102–13.

25 Ibid., pp. 245ff.

26 Szulc, *Fidel*, p. 115.

27 Franqui, *Diary*, p. 6.

28 Ibid., p. 7.

29 Ibid., p. 8.

30 Ibid.

31 Szulc, *Fidel*, pp. 128ff.

32 Bourne, *Castro*, p. 7.

33 *Die Zeit*, February 19, 1998.

34 Simons, *Cuba*, pp. 354ff.
35 Under this doctrine, promulgated by President James Monroe in the middle of the nineteenth century, the United States reserved for itself a kind of police function in its political sphere of influence in Central and South America.
36 Simons, *Cuba*, p. 219.
37 Jan Suter, "Politische Partizipation und Repräsentation in Kuba, 1902–1958," in Harald Barrios and Jan Suter (eds), *Politische Partizipation und Repräsentation in der Karibik. Kuba, Haiti, Dominikanische Republik im 19. und 20. Jahrhundert*, Opladen, 1996, pp. 17ff.
38 Szulc, *Fidel*, p. 120.
39 Betto, p. 136.
40 Ibid., p. 140.
41 Ibid., p. 122.
42 Szulc, *Fidel*, pp. 133ff.
43 *Revolución*, April 10, 1961.
44 Kitty Kelley, *His Way: The Unauthorized Biography of Frank Sinatra*, London, 1987, p. 123.
45 Franqui, *Diary*, p. 1.
46 Martin, *The Early Fidel*, p. 21.
47 Ibid., p. 27.
48 Thomas, *The Cuban Revolution*, p. 25, quoting remarks to Gloria Gaitán de Valencia, in *América Libre* (Bogotá), May 22–8, 1961.
49 Franqui, *Diary*, p. 9.
50 Thomas G. Paterson, *Contesting Castro: The United States and the Triumph of the Cuban Revolution*, Oxford, 1994, p. 50.
51 Simons, *Cuba*, p. 267.
52 See Georgie Anne Geyer, *Guerrilla Prince: The Untold Story of Fidel Castro*, Boston, 1991, pp. 54ff.; Bourne, *Castro*, pp. 45ff.; Szulc, *Fidel*, pp. 166ff., 182; Thomas, *The Cuban Revolution*, pp. 26ff.
53 Geyer, *Guerrilla Prince*, pp. 54ff.
54 Bourne, *Castro*, p. 36.
55 Szulc, *Fidel*, pp. 166ff.
56 Thomas, *The Cuban Revolution*, p. 27.
57 Szulc, *Fidel*, p. 182.
58 Martin, *The Early Fidel*, p. 19.
59 Castro, *My Early Years*, p. 72.
60 Martin, *The Early Fidel*, p. 126.
61 Castro, *My Early Years*, pp. 112ff.
62 Ibid., p. 123.

63 Franqui, *Diary*, p. 19.
64 Castro, *My Early Years*, p. 123.
65 Szulc, *Fidel*, p. 203.
66 Castro, *My Early Years*, p. 75.
67 Szulc, *Fidel*, p. 205.
68 Ibid., p. 144.
69 Simons, *Cuba*, p. 263.

Chapter 3   The Young Revolutionary

1 "Report of Sir Adrian Holman on the Conclusion of His Tour of Duty as Ambassador at Havana," cited in Paterson, *Contesting Castro*, p. 26.
2 Betto, p. 177.
3 Franqui, *Diary*, p. 43.
4 Szulc, *Fidel*, p. 223.
5 Martin, *The Early Fidel*, p. 101.
6 Betto, p. 152.
7 Castro, *My Early Years*, p. 124.
8 Szulc, *Fidel*, p. 227.
9 Carlos Franqui, *The Twelve*, p. 27.
10 Franqui, *Diary*, pp. 58–9.
11 Betto, p. 163.
12 Sarría was subsequently arrested and tried by a military court, which ordered his demotion and sentenced him to a long term in prison for disobedience; he was released only shortly before the fall of Batista. After the victory of the revolution, Castro promoted him and decorated him with the (rare) title of Hero of the Revolution. He became adjutant to the President of Cuba and died of cancer in 1972. Castro gave the graveside speech at his funeral in Havana, and recalled how he had once saved his life.
13 "History Will Absolve Me," in *Revolutionary Struggle, 1947–1958*, vol. 1 of *The Selected Works of Fidel Castro*, Cambridge, Mass, 1972, p. 221.
14 Franqui, *Diary*, p. 76.
15 Ibid., p. 77.
16 The Madrid paper *ABC* published six letters from Fidel Castro to Natalia Revuelta (made available by their daughter Alina Fernández) in a supplement in early 1997.

17 Alina Fernández, *Ich, Alina. Mein Leben als Fidel Castros Tochter,* pp. 103ff.
18 Franqui, *Diary,* p. 82.
19 Ibid., p. 81; Szulc, *Fidel,* p. 241.
20 Simons, *Cuba,* p. 274.
21 Martin, *The Early Fidel,* p. 160.
22 Fernández, *Ich, Alina,* pp. 19–28.
23 Martin, *The Early Fidel,* p. 162.
24 Thomas, *Cuban Revolution,* p. 81.
25 Franqui, *Diary,* p. 90.
26 Szulc, *Fidel,* pp. 325ff.
27 Jon Lee Anderson, *Che: Che Guevara, a Revolutionary Life,* p. 175.
28 Jorge G. Castañeda, *Compañero. The Life and Death of Che Guevara,* p. 84.
29 Ernesto "Che" Guevara, *Back on the Road,* London, 2001, p. 99.
30 Interview given to Jorge Masetti, in *Granma,* October 16, 1967.
31 Szulc, *Fidel,* pp. 330ff.
32 Franqui, *Diary,* pp. 91, 94; Matthews, p. 77.
33 Szulc, *Fidel,* p. 340.
34 Paterson, *Contesting Castro,* pp. 20ff.
35 Ibid., p. 15.
36 Gregorio Selser, *La Revolución Cubana,* Buenos Aires, 1966, pp. 102–18.
37 "Enough Lies!," in *Selected Works,* p. 323; "Basta ya de mentiras!," *Bohemia,* July 15, 1956.
38 Geyer, *Guerrilla Prince,* pp. 148–9.
39 Szulc, *Fidel,* pp. 362ff.
40 Geyer, *Guerrilla Prince,* p. 150.
41 Ibid. (translation slightly modified).
42 Szulc, *Fidel,* p. 362.
43 Warren Hinckle/William Turner, *Deadly Secrets: The CIA–MAFIA War against Castro and the Assassination of J.F.K,* p. lxii.
44 Castañeda, *Compañero,* p. 99.
45 Paterson, *Contesting Castro,* p. 33.
46 Oficina de Publicaciones del Consejo de Estado, *La Epoya del Granma,* Havana, 1986, pp. 7ff.
47 Franqui, *Diary,* p. 124.
48 Ibid., p. 111.
49 Ibid., p. 129.
50 Szulc, *Fidel,* pp. 33ff.

51 Franqui, *The Twelve*, p. 63.
52 Franqui, *Diary*, p. 126.
53 Franqui, *Diary*, pp. 139–40.
54 Ibid., p. 140.
55 Geyer, *Guerrilla Prince*, pp. 182, 251.
56 Matthews, *Castro: A Political Biography*, London, 1969, p. 94.
57 Franqui, *The Twelve*, p. 78.
58 Matthews, *Castro: A Political Biography*, p. 95.
59 Ibid.
60 Ibid., p. 97.
61 Batista y Zaldívar, *Cuba Betrayed*, p. 52.
62 Paterson, *Contesting Castro*, pp. 96ff, 103.
63 Anderson, *Che*, p. 261.
64 Ibid., p. 219.
65 Ibid., p. 237.
66 Ibid.
67 Szulc, *Fidel*, p. 424.
68 Ibid.
69 Frank País, Letters to Alejandro (Fidel Castro's cover name in the Sierra Maestra), July 5 and July 7, 1957; quoted in Franqui, *Diary*, pp. 196–9, 202–5.
70 Letter to Frank País, undated, in ibid., pp. 195ff.
71 Letter of December 14, 1957, in ibid., pp. 265–7.
72 Thomas, *The Cuban Revolution*, p. 192.
73 Franqui, *Diary*, p. 301.
74 Szulc, *Fidel*, p. 448.
75 Franqui, *Diary*, pp. 324–5.
76 Ibid., p. 351.
77 Ibid., p. 370.
78 Ibid., p. 362.
79 Ibid., p. 363.
80 Ibid., pp. 392, 394.
81 Szulc, *Fidel*, p. 448.
82 Thomas, *The Cuban Revolution*, p. 216.
83 Sebastian Balfour, *Castro*, p. 49.
84 Paterson, *Contesting Castro*, p. 65.
85 Ibid., p. 63.
86 Ibid., pp. 35ff.
87 Ibid., pp. 64, 105ff.
88 Szulc, *Fidel*, p. 429.
89 Paterson, *Contesting Castro*, p. 235.

90 See "Declaración de la Asamblea Nacional del Poder Popular," Havana, September 13, 1999, p. 2.
91 Paterson, *Contesting Castro*, pp. 222ff.
92 Franqui, *Diary*, p. 488.
93 Balfour, *Castro*, pp. 59ff.
94 Szulc, *Fidel*, p. 456.
95 Balfour, *Castro*, pp. 59ff.

Chapter 4   The Young Victor

1 Carlos Franqui, *Family Portrait with Fidel*, p. 3.
2 Franqui, *Diary*, pp. 489ff.
3 Paterson, *Contesting Castro*, pp. 200, 305.
4 *Bohemia*, January 11, 1959; Thomas, p. 262.
5 Paterson, *Contesting Castro*, p. 233.
6 Thomas, *The Cuban Revolution*, p. 251.
7 Bourne, *Castro*, pp. 161–2.
8 Franqui, *Diary*, p. 461.
9 Szulc, *Fidel*, p. 464.
10 Thomas, *The Cuban Revolution*, p. 256.
11 Franqui, *Diary*, p. 76.
12 *Bohemia*, January 11, 1959, p. 95.
13 Franqui, *Family Portrait with Fidel*, pp. 21ff.
14 Ibid., p. 24, 22.
15 Ibid., pp. 5ff.
16 Szulc, *Fidel*, pp. 471ff.
17 Thomas, *The Cuban Revolution*, p. 441.
18 Szulc, *Fidel*, p. 503.
19 Betto, pp. 172–3.
20 Philip W. Bonsal, *Cuba, Castro and the United States*, p. 36.
21 Ibid.
22 Szulc, *Fidel*, p. 483.
23 Thomas, *The Cuban Revolution*, p. 431.
24 Quirk, *Fidel Castro*, p. 227.
25 In James G. Blight/Peter Kornbluh, *The Politics of Illusion: The Bay of Pigs Invasion Reexamined*, p. 32.
26 Franqui, *Family Portrait with Fidel*, p. 18.
27 Paterson, *Contesting Castro*, p. 255.
28 Betto, p. 197.

s A. Pérez, Jr, *Cuba between Reform and Revolution*, p. 319.

rson, *Contesting Castro*, p. 41.

Lopez-Fresquet, *My 14 Months with Castro*, p. 10.

., p. 10.

33 Franqui, *Family Portrait with Fidel*, p. 42.

34 Betto, pp. 174ff.

35 Núñez Jiménez, Antonio, *En marcha con Fidel*, Havana, 1998, p. 308.

36 Ibid.

37 Jules R. Benjamin, *The United States and the Origins of the Cuban Revolution*, pp. 181ff.

38 "Probleme der innen- und wirtschaftspolitischen Lage Kubas," secret report of the intelligence department of the GDR ministry for foreign affairs, November 23, 1960, SAPMO-Barch, DY 30/3647, Bl. 5–15.

39 Franqui, *Family Portrait with Fidel*, p. 54.

40 Quirk, *Fidel Castro*, pp. 252ff.

41 Pérez Jr, *Between Reform and Revolution*, p. 330.

42 Ibid., p. 324.

43 "Information über eine Aussprache mit dem Generalsekretär der SVP Kubas, Blas Roca, am 13. Juni 1961 in Havanna," SAPMO-Barch, DY 30/3647, Bl. 43–50.

44 "Vertrauliche Aktennotiz an Walter Ulbricht," December 17, 1958, SAPMO-Barch, DY 30/3647, Bl. 1.

45 Thomas, *Cuban Revolution*, p. 495.

46 "Fragmentos de documentos por los obispos cubanos durante las últimas cuatro décadas en relación con la situación nacional," *El Nuevo Herald* (Miami), December 21, 1997.

47 Szulc, *Fidel*, p. 529.

Chapter 5   Old Enemies, New Friends

1 Franqui, *Diary*, p. 338.

2 Paterson, *Contesting Castro*, p. 251.

3 Ibid., p. 258.

4 Benjamin, *The United States*, p. 203.

5 Paterson, *Contesting Castro*, p. 257.

6 Peter Kornbluh, *Bay of Pigs Declassified – The Secret CIA Report on the Invasion of Cuba*, p. 7.

7 Bourne, *Castro*, p. 166.

8 Fidel Castro and Che Guevara, *To Speak the Truth: Why Washington's Cold War against Cuba Doesn't End*, New York, 1992, p. 72.
9 John F. Kennedy, *The Strategy of Peace*, p. 132.
10 Szulc, *Fidel*, p. 480.
11 Lopez-Fresquet, *My 14 Months with Castro*, p. 83.
12 Szulc, *Fidel*, p. 519.
13 Ibid., p. 518.
14 Ibid.
15 Simons, *Cuba*, p. 304.
16 Pérez Jr, *Between Reform and Revolution*, p. 335.
17 Hans Ulrich Kempski, "Protest-Ouvertüren für das große Welttheater," *Süddeutsche Zeitung*, September 19, 1960.
18 Ibid.
19 Hans Ulrich Kempski, "Hohnrufe und nasse Füße am Pier 73," *Süddeutsche Zeitung*, September 21, 1960.
20 Ibid.
21 Hans Ulrich Kempski, "Castros Auftritt mit der Thermosflasche," *Süddeutsche Zeitung*, September 28, 1960.
22 Quoted in Bonsal, *Castro and the United States*, p. 291.
23 Szulc, *Fidel*, p. 480.
24 Kornbluh, *Bay of Pigs Declassified*, p. 7.
25 Blight/Kornbluh, *The Politics of Illusion*, p. 84.
26 Szulc, *Fidel*, p. 530.
27 Kornbluh, *Bay of Pigs Declassified*, p. 9.
28 Colonel Jack Hawkins, "Secret Memorandum for the Record. Actions against the Castro Government of Cuba," May 5, 1961, National Security Archive, George Washington University, Washington.
29 Blight/Kornbluh, *The Politics of Illusion*, p. 86.
30 Ibid.
31 Szulc, *Fidel*, p. 523.
32 Ibid., p. 524.
33 Simons, *Cuba*, p. 306.
34 Blight/Kornbluh, *The Politics of Illusion*, p. 86.
35 Simons, *Cuba*, p. 306.
36 Marita Lorenz, *Marita: One Woman's Extraordinary Tale of Love and Espionage from Castro to Kennedy*, pp. 59ff.
37 Gabriele Wojtiniak, "Alemanita mia!," *Freitag* (Berlin), July 14, 2000.
38 In *Lieber Fidel – Maritas Geschichte*, a film by Wilfried Huismann, Sur Films Bremen, October 2000.

39 Lorenz, *One Woman's Extraordinary Tale*, pp. 62, 65ff., 80ff.
40 Wojtiniak, "Alemanita mia!," op. cit.
41 Claudia Furiati, *ZR Rifle – The Plot to Kill Kennedy and Castro. Cuba Opens Secret Files*, pp. 48ff.
42 Blight/Kornbluh, *The Politics of Illusion*, p. 88.
43 Kornbluh, *Bay of Pigs Declassified*, p. 2.
44 *News Conference No. 9, April 12, 1961*, John F. Kennedy Library.
45 Betto, pp. 208–9.
46 Ibid.
47 Szulc, *Fidel*, p. 545.
48 Hawkins, "Secret Memorandum for the Record," p. 25.
49 Hinckle/Turner, *Deadly Secrets*, p. 93.
50 Kornbluh, *Bay of Pigs Declassified*, p. 309.
51 Ibid., p. 311.
52 Franqui, *Family Portrait with Fidel*, p. 123.
53 Hawkins, "Secret Memorandum for the Record," p. 39.
54 *The People of Cuba vs. The Government of the United States of America for Human Damages. Demand Submitted to the Civil and Administrative Court of Law at the Provincial People's Court in Havana, 31 May 1999*, p. 24.
55 Kornbluh, *Bay of Pigs Declassified*, p. 2.
56 Hans Magnus Enzensberger, *Das Verhör von Havanna*, pp. 25ff.
57 Blight/Kornbluh, *The Politics of Illusion*, p. 169.
58 Ibid., pp. 65ff.
59 Ibid., pp. 266ff.
60 Arthur M. Schlesinger Jr, *A Thousand Days: John F. Kennedy in the White House*, p. 293.
61 "The Inspector General's Survey of the Cuban Operation," in Kornbluh, *Bay of Pigs Declassified*, pp. 23–132.
62 Blight/Kornbluh, *The Politics of Illusion*, p. 169.
63 Aleksandr Fursenko/Timothy Naftali, *One Hell of a Gamble. The Secret History of the Cuban Missile Crisis, Khrushchev, Castro, and Kennedy 1958–1964*, p. 144.
64 Hawkins, "Secret Memorandum for the Record," pp. 7ff.
65 Quirk, *Fidel Castro*, pp. 328ff.
66 Hinckle/Turner, *Deadly Secrets*, pp. 75ff.
67 Blight/Kornbluh, *The Politics of Illusion*, pp. 183ff.
68 Franqui, *Family Portrait with Fidel*, p. 124.
69 Betto, pp. 209–10.
70 Pérez Jr, *Between Reform and Revolution*, p. 331.
71 Betto, p. 205.

72 Ibid.
73 Franqui, *Family Portrait with Fidel*, pp. 124, 126–7, 128.
74 Ibid., p. 140.
75 Szulc, *Fidel*, p. 547.
76 Fursenko/Naftali, *One Hell of a Gamble*, p. 135.
77 Ibid., pp. 136ff.
78 Franqui, *Family Portrait with Fidel*, p. 233.
79 Lee Lockwood, *Castro's Cuba, Cuba's Fidel. An American Journalist's Inside Look at Today's Cuba – in Text and Picture*, pp. 160ff.
80 Ibid., p. 162.
81 "Information über eine Aussprache mit dem Generalsekretär der SVP Kubas, Blas Roca, am 13. Juni in Havanna," SAPMO-Barch, DY 30/3647, Bl. 43–50.
82 Ibid.
83 Betto, p. 143.
84 Nikita Khrushchev, *Khrushchev Remembers*, p. 492.
85 Quoted in Fursenko/Naftali, *One Hell of a Gamble*, p. 161.
86 "1. Erweiterte Konzeption zur gegenwärtigen Lage und Entwicklung in den ORI," April 5, 1962, PAAA, Bestand MfAA, A 3371/3, Bl. 198–206.
87 Quirk, *Fidel Castro*, p. 366.
88 "Informationsbericht des ADN-Korrespondenten in Havanna," PAAA, Bestand MfAA, A 3151, Bl. 359.
89 Theodore Draper, *Castroism: Theory and Practice*, p. 152.
90 Quoted from Franqui, *Family Portrait with Fidel*, pp. 234ff.
91 "Einige bemerkenswerte Gedanken aus einem Gespräch mit Blas Roca am 29. Oktober 1963," secret report, November 7, 1963, PAAA, Bestand MfAA, A 3363/Az.: 9211.
92 "Einschätzung zur Entwicklung und zum gegenwärtigen Entwicklungsstand der Einheitspartei der Sozialistischen Revolution (PURS)," August 24, 1964, PAAA, Bestand MfAA, A 3363/Az.: 9211.
93 Fursenko/Naftali, *One Hell of a Gamble*, p. 150.
94 Ibid.
95 Ibid., pp. 144ff.
96 Ibid., p. 147.
97 Simons, *Cuba*, pp. 306ff.
98 Ronald Steel, *In Love with Night. The American Romance with Robert Kennedy*, pp. 79ff.
99 Hinckle/Turner, *Deadly Secrets*, p. 140.
100 Fursenko/Naftali, *One Hell of a Gamble*, pp. 152ff.
101 Ibid., pp. 150ff.

102 Jane Franklin, *Cuba and the United States – A Chronological History*, p. 50.
103 Robert McNamara, "Foreword," in Chang/Kornbluh, *The Cuban Missile Crisis*, p. xii.
104 Khrushchev, *Khrushchev Remembers*, p. 493.
105 Fursenko/Naftali, *One Hell of a Gamble*, p. 171.
106 Khrushchev, *Khrushchev Remembers*, p. 494.
107 Mark J. White, *Missiles in Cuba: Kennedy, Khrushchev, Castro and the 1962 Crisis*, p. 35.
108 Fursenko/Naftali, *One Hell of a Gamble*, p. 179.
109 Foreign Broadcast Information Service, "Transcript of Fidel Castro's Remarks at the Havana Conference on the Cuban Missile Crisis, 11 January 1992," in Chang/Kornbluh, *The Cuban Missile Crisis*, p. 346.
110 Fidel Castro, CNN television interview, September 13, 1998.
111 McNamara, "Foreword," p. xi.
112 Fursenko/Naftali, *One Hell of a Gamble*, pp. 188ff.; Yuri I. Pavlov, *Soviet–Cuban Alliance 1959–1991*, pp. 40ff.; and Ernest R. May/Philip D. Zelikow, *The Kennedy Tapes: Inside the White House during the Cuban Missile Crisis*, pp. 676ff.
113 Fursenko/Naftali, *One Hell of a Gamble*, p. 294.
114 Chang/Kornbluh, *The Cuban Missile Crisis*, p. 350.
115 Fursenko/Naftali, *One Hell of a Gamble*, p. 196.
116 White, *Missiles in Cuba*, p. 62.
117 May/Selikow, *The Kennedy Tapes*, p. 678.
118 White, *Missiles in Cuba*, p. 49.
119 Fursenko/Naftali, *One Hell of a Gamble*, p. 218.
120 White, *Missiles in Cuba*, p. 63; Fursenko/Naftali, *One Hell of a Gamble*, p. 219.
121 Fursenko/Naftali, *One Hell of a Gamble*, p. 219.
122 Robert Kennedy, *Thirteen Days. A Memoir of the Cuban Missile Crisis*, pp. 22ff.
123 Ibid., p. 13.
124 May/Zelikow, *The Kennedy Tapes*, p. 169.
125 Robert Kennedy, *Thirteen Days*, pp. 48ff.
126 Ibid., p. 36.
127 Ibid., pp. 131–9.
128 Chang/Kornbluh, *The Cuban Missile Crisis*, p. 351.
129 *Con la razón historica y la moral de baragua. 1962 Crisis de Octubre*, p. 6.
130 Ibid., pp. 14ff.
131 Fursenko/Naftali, *One Hell of a Gamble*, p. 273.

132 *Con la razón histórica y la moral de baragua. 1962 Crisis de Octubre,* pp. 20ff.
133 Ibid., pp. 25ff.
134 Pavlov, *Soviet–Cuban Alliance 1959–1991,* p. 45.
135 Fursenko/Naftali, *One Hell of a Gamble,* p. 263.
136 Ibid., p. 275.
137 Robert Kennedy, *Thirteen Days,* pp. 173–9.
138 May/Zelikow, *The Kennedy Tapes,* p. 635.
139 *Con la razón histórica y la moral de baragua. 1962 Crisis de Octubre,* pp. 16ff.
140 Ibid., pp. 18ff.
141 Franqui, *Family Portrait with Fidel,* p. 194.
142 May/Zelikow, *The Kennedy Tapes,* p. 664.
143 White, *Missiles in Cuba,* p. 147.
144 Robert Kennedy, *Thirteen Days,* pp. 184ff.
145 Fursenko/Naftali, *One Hell of a Gamble,* p. 312.
146 Ibid., p. 296.
147 Ibid., pp. 305–6.
148 Ibid., p. 306.
149 Ibid., p. 307.
150 Ibid., p. 326.
151 Khrushchev, *Khrushchev Remembers,* pp. 494–500.
152 Henry A. Kissinger, *The White House Years,* p. 633.
153 Ibid., p. 634.
154 May/Zelikow, *The Kennedy Tapes,* p. 193.
155 Szulc, *Fidel,* pp. 559ff.
156 White, *Missiles in Cuba,* p. 150.
157 See Peter Kornbluh (ed.), *Kennedy and Castro: The Secret Quest for Accommodation,* George Washington University/National Security Archive (NSA), Electronic Briefing Book No. 17, Documents 1–11, Washington 1999, http://www.gwu.edu/~nsarchiv; and Peter Kornbluh, "JFK & Castro: The Secret Quest for Accommodation," *Cigar Aficionado,* September/October 1999.
158 "The Cuban Problem," option paper drafted by McGeorge Bundy, George Washington University/National Security Archive (NSA), Electronic Briefing Book No. 17, Document 2, Washington 1999, http://www.gwu.edu/~nsarchiv.
159 "William Attwood's Report to National Security Adviser McGeorge Bundy (8 November 1963, secret)," quoted in Castañeda, *Compañero : The Life and Death of Che Guevara,* pp. 242–3.
160 Geyer, *Guerrilla Prince,* p. 299.

161 Tomás Borge, *Face to Face with Fidel Castro*, p. 85.

162 Ibid., p. 84.

163 Lorenz, *Marita: One Woman's Extraordinary Tale of Love and Espionage from Castro to Kennedy*, pp. 126–38.

164 Hinckle/Turner, *Deadly Secrets*, p. lii.

165 Geyer, *Guerrilla Prince*, p. 301.

166 Paterson, *Contesting Castro*, pp. 261ff.

167 Furiati, *ZR Rifle*, pp. 70ff.

168 Carol Oglesby, "The Conspiracy That Won't Go Away," *Playboy* magazine, February 1992, p. 149.

169 "To: President Lyndon B. Johnson, From: Prime Minister Fidel Castro; Verbal message given to Miss Lisa Howard of ABC News on February 12, 1965 in Havana , Cuba," Lyndon Johnson Library/Peter Kornbluh, ed., "Kennedy and Castro: The Secret Quest for Accommodation," George Washington University/ National Security Archive (NSA), Electronic Briefing Book No. 17, Document 10, Washington 1999, http://www.gwu.edu/~nsarchiv.

Chapter 6 The Long March with Che

1 Chang/Kornbluh, *The Cuban Missile Crisis*, p. 356.

2 Ibid.

3 See Pavlov, *Soviet–Cuban Alliance 1959–1991*, p. 56.

4 Chang/Kornbluh, *The Cuban Missile Crisis*, p. 357.

5 Sheldon B. Liss, *Fidel! Castro's Political and Social Thought*, p. 36.

6 Lockwood, *Castro's Cuba, Cuba's Fidel*, p. 162.

7 Ibid., p. 163.

8 "Communists Take Over 90 Miles from U.S.", *US News and World Report*, June 1960.

9 *Che en la memoria de Fidel Castro*, ed. David Deutschmann and with an introduction by Jesús Montané, Melbourne, 1998, p. 23.

10 Liss, *Fidel!*, p. 38.

11 Ibid., pp. 38–9.

12 "Man and Socialism in Cuba," in *Venceremos: Speeches and Writings of Che Guevara*, ed. John Gerassi, London, 1969, p. 539.

13 "On Party Militancy," in *Venceremos*, p. 348.

14 *Brandstiftung oder Neuer Friede?*, p. 18.

15 "On Sacrifice and Dedication," in *Venceremos*, p. 148.

16 Quoted in *Granma Weekly Review*, December 13, 1987.

17 "On Sacrifice and Dedication," pp. 164, 165–6.
18 "On Party Militancy," pp. 343–4.
19 "Man and Socialism in Cuba," p. 541.
20 "On the Budgetary System of Financing," in *Venceremos*, p. 418.
21 See Hans-Jürgen Burckhardt, *Kuba. Der lange Abschied von einem Mythos*, p. 16.
22 Quoted in Matthews, *Fidel Castro*, p. 131.
23 Szulc, *Fidel*, pp. 597ff.
24 Castañeda, *Compañero*, p. 258.
25 "Einschätzung zur Entwicklung und zum gegenwärtigen Entwicklungsstand der Einheitspartei der Sozialistischen Revolution (PURS)," August 24, 1964, PAAA, Bestand MfAA, A 3363/Az.: 9211.
26 Guevara, "Freedom of competition or 'A free fox among free chickens'?," Address to the Geneva Trade and Development Conference, March 25, 1964, in Fidel Castro/Che Guevara, *To Speak the Truth*, pp. 99ff.
27 Guevara, "Colonialism Is Doomed," Address to the General Assembly of the United Nations, December 11, 1964, in *Venceremos*, pp. 521ff.
28 Guevara, "Speech to the Second Economic Seminar of Afro-American Solidarity," February 1965, in *Che: Selected Works of Che Guevara*, eds Rolando E. Bonachea and Nelson P. Valdes, Cambridge, Mass, 1969, pp. 351–2.
29 Castañeda, *Compañero*, p. 297.
30 "Alles dreht sich um die 'Zafra'," Informationsbericht des ADN-Korrespondenten in Havanna, May 10, 1965, PAAA, Bestand MfAA 3363/3, Bl. 248–55.
31 Ibid.
32 Elmar May, *Che Guevara*, p. 79.
33 "Brief des DDR-Botschafters Jone in Havanna an den stellvertretenden DDR-Aussenminister Stibi," October 12, 1965, PAAA, Bestand MfAA 3363/1, Bl. 144.
34 "Einschätzung zum Brief Ernesto Guevaras an die Wochenzeitschrift 'Marcha' (Uruguay)," Botschaft der DDR in der Republik Kuba, October 26, 1965, Bl. 133–8.
35 "Brief des DDR-Botschafters Jone in Havanna an den stellvertretenden DDR-Aussenminister Stibi," October 12, 1965, PAAA, Bestand MfAA 3363/1, Bl. 143.
36 Quoted from Ernesto "Che" Guevara, *The African Dream*, London, 2000, p. xii.
37 Castañeda, *Compañero*, p. 319.

38 See *Manual de los Partidos Políticos de América Latina*, pp. 168ff.
39 May, *Che Guevara*, pp. 82ff.
40 Ibid.
41 Bonachea/Valdes, *Che: Selected Works of Che Guevara*, pp. 313–28.
42 Daniel James, *Che Guevara: A Biography*, pp. 319ff., 382, 389. Cf. *"Tania"*. *La guerrillera inolvidable*, Havana, 1970, pp. 321ff.
43 Castañeda, *Compañero*, p. 388.
44 Ibid., p. 275.

Chapter 7 Bad Times, Good Times

1 *Granma*, January 13, 1968, quoted in Balfour, *Castro*, p. 90.
2 Szulc, *Fidel*, p. 610.
3 "2. Einschätzung zu den Ereignissen in Verbindung mit den Reden des Genossen Fidel Castro vom 19. April und 1. Mai 1964," Vertrauliche Verschlussache B 7/27–10/64, May 16, 1964, PAAA, Bestand MfAA, A 3363, AZ:2001.
4 "Stand und Perspektive der ökonomischen Beziehungen zwischen der DDR und Kuba," n.d., SAPMO-BArch, NY 4182/1242, Bl. 152.
5 "Aktenvermerk über eine Besprechung mit dem Stellvertreter des sowjetischen Botschafters, Ministro Consejero N.A. Belous, am 23. Dezember 1964," Vertrauliche Verschlussache, 4. Januar 1965, PAAA, Bestand MfAA, A 3363, AZ: 900.
6 "Aktenvermerk über ein Gespräch mit dem sowjetischen Botschafter in der Republik Kuba, Genossen Alexejew, am 3. Juni 1964," Vertrauliche Verschlussache B7/27–14/64, PAAA, Bestand MfAA, A 3363, AZ: 9211.
7 "Brief der DDR-Botschaft in Havanna an das MfAA," Vertrauliche Verschlussache, 5 September 1966, PAAA, Bestand MfAA, A3363/1, Bl. 6–14.
8 Szulc, *Fidel*, p. 604.
9 "Informationsbericht des ADN-Korrespondenten in Havanna," May 11, 1966, Vertraulich, PAAA, Bestand MfAA, A3363/1, Bl. 49–51.
10 The available sources indicate that Che never actually used the legendary words: "Create two, three, many Vietnams!," which seem to have been a freely rendered variant of the title given to the "Message" in the Feltrinelli collection *Lateinamerika – Ein zweites Vietnam* (Reinbek, 1968, pp. 99ff.): "Let us create two, three, many Vietnams!" In fact, even this formulation is inexact. For the original

text on page 106 of that volume reads: "America . . . will have a task of greater significance: the creation of a second, third Vietnam in the world."

11 "Brief der DDR-Botschaft in Havanna an das MfAA," Vertrauliche Dienstsache, 8, August 1966, PAAA, Bestand MfAA, A3363/1, Bl. 17–21.

12 "Antwort der Kommunistischen Partei Venezuelas," March 13, 1967, in Feltrinelli, *Lateinamerika – Ein zweites Vietnam*, pp. 285ff.

13 Castro, "Antwort auf die Stellungnahme der Kommunistischen Partei Venezuelas zu seiner Rede vom 13. März 1967," in ibid., p. 297.

14 "Vermerk über ein Gespräch mit dem Vertreter der KP Honduras, Genossen Logino Becerra," Botschaft der DDR in Havana, October 2, 1966, PAAA, Bestand MfAA, A 3363/1, Bl. 1–5.

15 "Stellungnahme zu den Veröffentlichungen über die Tagung des Zentralkommitees der Kommunistischen Partei Kubas. Abteilung Internationale Verbindungen des ZK," Berlin, January 31, 1968, SAPMO-BArch, NY 4182/1241, Bl. 182ff.

16 Szulc, *Fidel*, p. 609.

17 "Brief von DDR-Aussenminister Otto Winzer an Staats- und Parteichef Walter Ulbricht," July 11, 1968, SAPMO-BArch, NY 4182/1241, Bl. 185ff.

18 Quoted in Balfour, *Castro*, p. 95.

19 Quoted in Pavlov, *Soviet–Cuban Alliance*, p. 90.

20 Balfour, *Castro*, pp. 95ff.

21 Szulc, *Fidel*, p. 621.

22 *Granma Weekly Review*, October 26, 1969.

23 Quoted in Mauricio Vincent, "Navidades rojas," *El País* (Madrid), December 22, 1997.

24 Balfour, *Castro*, pp. 98ff.; Szulc, *Fidel*, p. 622.

25 Quoted in Balfour, *Castro*, p. 105.

26 Ibid., p. 106.

27 Ibid., p. 108.

28 Thomas M. Leonard, *Castro and the Cuban Revolution*, p. 99.

29 Wayne S. Smith, *The Closest of Enemies – A Personal and Diplomatic History of the Castro Years*, p. 93.

30 See Pavlov, *Soviet–Cuban Alliance*, pp. 95ff.

31 "Unkorrigierte stenographische Niederschrift der Verhandlungen der Partei- und Regierungsdelegation der DDR und der Republik Kuba am 21. und 26. Februar 1974 in Havanna," SAPMO-BArch, DY 30/J IV2/201–1157, Bl. 89–96.

32 Che Guevara, *Guerrilla Warfare*, Lincoln: University of Nebraska Press, 1985.
33 Balfour, *Castro*, p. 124.
34 Ibid., p. 126.
35 Szulc, *Fidel*, p. 627.
36 Balfour, *Castro*, pp. 125ff.
37 "Unkorrigierte stenographische Niederschrift der Verhandlungen der Partei- und Regierungsdelegation der DDR und der Republik Kuba am 21. und 26. Februar 1974 in Havanna," SAPMO-BArch, DY 30/ J IV2/201–1157, Bl. 81–86.
38 Paterson, *Contesting Castro*, p. 39.
39 "Unkorrigierte stenographische Niederschrift der Verhandlungen der Partei- und Regierungsdelegation der DDR und der Republik Kuba am 21. und 26. Februar 1974 in Havanna," SAPMO-BArch, DY 30/J IV2/201–1157, Bl. 81–86.
40 Ibid.
41 Smith, *The Closest of Enemies*, p. 95.
42 "Geheimvermerk für DDR-Staats- und Parteichef Honecker über ein Gespräch des DDR-Politbüromitglieds Hermann Axen mit dem kubanischen Staats- und Parteichef Fidel Castro, 27. Juli 1984," SAPMO-BArch, DY 30/IV 2/2.035, Bl. 2–11.
43 Szulc, *Fidel*, p. 639.
44 Ibid.
45 Ibid.
46 Carlos Moore, *Castro, the Blacks, and Africa*, p. 328.
47 Liss, *Fidel!*, p. 92.
48 Moore, *Castro, the Blacks, and Africa*, p. 329.
49 Ibid., p. 328.
50 Balfour, *Castro*, p. 121.
51 Ibid., p. 135.
52 *Fidel Castro Speeches: Cuba's Internationalist Foreign Policy 1975–80*, p. 167.
53 Ibid., p. 200.
54 "Instructions for Joining a New Society," in Heberto Padilla, *A Fountain, A House of Stone: Poems*, New York: Farrar, Straus and Giroux, 1991, p. 27.
55 Quoted from Quirk, *Fidel Castro*, pp. 662ff.
56 See Friedl Zapata, *Geschichten aus der Geschichte Kubas*, pp. 11ff.
57 Quirk, *Fidel Castro*, pp. 668ff.
58 Ibid., pp. 671ff.
59 Szulc, *Fidel*, p. 625.

60 Ibid.
61 Haubrich, "Mumifizierte Revolution," *Frankfurter Allgemeine Zeitung*, January 8, 1999.
62 Franqui, *Family Portrait with Fidel*, p. 129.
63 Ibid.
64 Ibid.
65 Castro, *Palabras a los intelectuales*, pp. 11ff.
66 Ibid., pp. 20ff.
67 PAAA, Bestand MfAA, A 3153, Bl. 35.
68 "Zur Lage der politischen Kräfte in Kuba. Mission der DDR in der Republik Kuba," January 10, 1963, PAAA, Bestand MfAA, A16378/1, Bl. 15–19.
69 Liss, *Fidel!*, pp. 141, 146.
70 Hausbrich, "Schützende Hände," *Frankfurter Allgemeine Zeitung*, January 26, 1998.
71 Hausbrich, "Grüsse aus dem Fegefeuer," *Frankfurter Allgemeine Zeitung*, February 20, 1996.
72 Borge, *Face to Face with Fidel Castro*, pp. 164ff.
73 Ibid., pp. 156ff.
74 Ibid., p. 166.

Chapter 8   Alone against All

1 Smith, *The Closest of Enemies*, p. 209.
2 Ibid., p. 211.
3 *Fidel Castro Speeches: Cuba's Internationalist Foreign Policy 1975–80*, p. 276.
4 Ibid., p. 278.
5 Jorge I. Dominguez, "Cooperating with the Enemy? U.S. Immigration Policies toward Cuba," in Mitchell, *Western Hemisphere Immigration and United States Foreign Policy*, p. 34.
6 Ibid., p. 41.
7 "Vertraulicher Informationsbericht des ADN-Korrespondenten in Havanna," May 11, 1966, PAAA, Bestand MfAA, A3363/1, Bl. 53–64.
8 "Vertraulicher Informationsbericht des ADN-Korrespondenten in Havanna," May 11, 1966, PAAA, Bestand MfAA, A3363/1, Bl. 49–52.
9 "Brief des DDR-Botschafters in Havanna, Johne, an das Ministerium für Auswärtige Angelegenheiten," October 12, 1965, PAAA, Bestand MfAA, A3363/1, Bl. 139–49.

10 "Brief des DDR-Botschafters in Havanna, Johne, an das Ministerium für Auswärtige Angelegenheiten," October 12, 1965, PAAA, Bestand MfAA, A3363/1, Bl. 126–32.

11 "Vertraulicher Informationsbericht des ADN-Korrespondenten in Havanna," May 11, 1966, PAAA, Bestand MfAA, A3363/2, Bl. 119–22.

12 Leonard, *Castro and the Cuban Revolution*, p. 70.

13 "Informationen zu bekannt gewordenen exilkubanischen Terrororganisationen," Ministerium für Staatssicherheit der DDR, July 22, 1980, BstU, MfS-HAXXII Nr. 17 843, Bl. 78–89.

14 "Sachstandsbericht zur konterrevolutionären antikubanischen Terrorszene," Ministerium für Staatssicherheit der DDR, May 27, 1982, BstU, MfS-HAXXII Nr. 17 843, Bl. 112–18.

15 Bourne, *Castro*, p. 180.

16 Ibid.

17 Borge, *Face to Face with Fidel Castro*, p. 169.

18 Betto, pp. 49ff.

19 "A Conversation with Fidel," *Cigar Aficionado*, Summer, 1994.

20 Franqui, *Diary*, p. 320.

21 Balfour, *Castro*, p. 138.

22 Fidel Castro, *War & Crisis in the Americas. Speeches 1984–1985*, p. 110.

23 Julio Carranza Valdés, "Die Krise – Eine Bestandaufnahme," in Hoffmann, *Wirtschaftsreformen in Kuba*, pp. 16ff.

24 Susan Eva Eckstein, *Back from the Future: Cuba under Castro*, p. 72.

25 Julio Carranza Valdés, "Die Krise – Eine Bestandaufnahme," in Hoffmann, *Wirtschaftsreformen in Kuba*, pp. 16ff.

26 Betto, p. 301.

27 Balfour, *Castro*, p. 139.

28 Betto, pp. 299ff.

29 Ibid., pp. 300ff.

30 Balfour, *Castro*, pp. 148ff.

31 *Granma Weekly Review*, December 13, 1987, p. 10; cf. Eckstein, *Back from the Future*, p. 62.

32 Carollee Bengelsdorff, *The Problem of Democracy in Cuba: Between Vision and Reality*, p. 135.

33 Ibid., p. 141.

34 Ibid., p. 134.

35 Ibid., p. 201.

36 Julie Marie Bunck, *Fidel Castro and the Quest for a Revolutionary Culture in Cuba*, p. 18.

37 "Telegramm der Botschaft der DDR in Havanna an das ZK der SED, Abteilung Internationale Beziehungen, Kopie aus der Politbüroakte Erich Honecker," July 27, 1987, SAPMO-Barch, DY 30/2359, Bl. 432–3.

38 Liss, *Fidel!*, p. 154.

39 Eckstein, *Back from the Future*, p. 65.

40 Balfour, *Castro*, p. 150.

41 Quoted in Liss, *Fidel!*, p. 155.

42 Eckstein, *Back from the Future*, p. 71.

43 Ibid.

44 "Telegramm der Botschaft der DDR in Havanna an das ZK der SED, Abteilung Internationale Beziehungen, Kopie aus der Politbüroakte Erich Honecker," July 27, 1987, SAPMO-Barch, DY 30/2359, Bl. 432–3.

45 Fidel Castro, *In Defense of Socialism. Four Speeches on the 30th Anniversary of the Cuban Revolution*, p. v.

46 Balfour, *Castro*, p. 153.

47 Ibid.

48 Fidel Castro, *In Defense of Socialism. Four Speeches on the 30th Anniversary of the Cuban Revolution*, pp. 100ff.

49 Andres Oppenheimer, *Castro's Final Hour: The Secret Story behind the Coming Downfall of Communist Cuba*, p. 101.

50 Pavlov, *Soviet–Cuban Alliance*, p. 111.

51 "Brief des sowjetischen Staats- und Parteichefs Michail Gorbatschow an DDR-Staats- und Parteichef Erich Honecker," SAPMO-BArch, DY 30/2359, Bl. 1–2.

52 "Niederschrift über das Treffen der führenden Repräsentanten der Bruderparteien sozialistischer Länder des RGW am 10. und 11. November 1986 in Moskau," SAPMO-BArch, DY 30/2358, Bl. 1–2.

53 Ibid., Bl. 72–8.

54 Pavlov, *Soviet–Cuban Alliance*, p. 132.

55 Bengelsdorff, *The Problem of Democracy in Cuba*, p. 139.

56 Quoted in Pavlov, *Soviet–Cuban Alliance*, pp. 133ff.

57 Borge, *Face to Face with Fidel Castro*, p. 108.

58 "Vermerk über das Gespräch des Genossen Erich Honecker, Generalsekretär des ZK der SED und Vorsitzender des Staatrates der DDR, mit Genossen Jorge Risquet, Mitglied des Politbüros und Sekretär des ZK der KP Kubas, am 17. April 1989," Abteilung Internationale Verbindungen des Zentralkommittees der SED, SAPMO-BArch, DY 30/2359, Bl. 439–40.

59 "Vermerk über das Gespräch des Genossen Hermann Axen, Mitglied des Politbüros und Sekretär des ZK der SED, mit Genossen Jorge Risquet, Mitglied des Politbüros und Sekretär des ZK der KP Kubas, am 17. April 1989," Abteilung Internationale Verbindungen des Zentralkommittees der SED, SAPMO-BArch, DY 30/IV 2/2035, Bl. 12–21.

60 Ibid.

61 "Rede des Genossen Fidel Castro am 26. Juli 1989," Abteilung Internationale Verbindungen des Zentralkommittees der SED, SAPMO-BArchiv, DY 30/IV 2/2035, Bl. 29–32.

62 "Vermerk über das Gespräch des Genossen Hermann Axen, Mitglied des Politbüros und Sekretär des ZK der SED, mit Genossen Raúl Castro Ruz, 2. Sekretär des ZK der KP Kubas und 1. Stellvertreter des Staats- und Ministerrats der Republik Kubas am 3. September 1989 in Berlin," SAPMO-BArch, DY 30/IV 2/2035, Bl. 38–40.

63 Estervino Montesino Segui, "The Cuban Perspective on Cuban–Soviet Relations," in Wayne S. Smith, *The Russians Aren't Coming: New Soviet Policy in Latin America*, p. 141.

64 Quoted in ibid., pp. 140ff.

65 Quoted in ibid., p. 143.

66 Hoffmann, *Wirtschaftsreformen in Kuba*, p. 45.

67 Ibid., pp. 46ff.

68 Ibid., p. 47.

69 Ibid., p. 53.

70 Ibid., pp. 45ff.

71 Mikoyan, "The Future of the Soviet–Cuban Relationship," in Smith, *The Russians Aren't Coming*, pp. 119ff.; Eckstein, *Back from the Future*, p. 92.

72 Bengelsdorff, *The Problem of Democracy in Cuba*, p. 149.

73 Quoted in Estervino Montesino Segui, "The Cuban Perspective on Cuban–Soviet Relations," in Smith, *The Russians Aren't Coming*, p. 144.

74 Eckstein, *Back from the Future*, p. 93.

75 Ibid.

76 Ibid.

77 Pavlov, *Soviet–Cuban Alliance*, p. 234.

78 Ibid., p. 264.

79 Oppenheimer, *Castro's Final Hour*, p. 127.

80 Fidel Castro, *War & Crisis in the Americas. Speeches 1984–1985*, pp. 141ff.

81 Millett, *From Triumph to Survival*, p. 140.
82 *El Nuevo Herald*, Miami, 1998; in *Cuba News/Noticias – CubaNet News*.
83 Richard L. Millett, "From Triumph to Survival: Cuba's Armed Forces in an Era of Transition," in Millett et al., *Beyond Praetorianism*, p. 135.
84 Phillys Green Walker, "Cuba's Revolutionary Armed Forces: Adapting in the New Environment," *Cuban Studies*, 26 (Pittsburgh, 1989), 69.
85 Phyllis Green Walker, "Challenges Facing the Cuban Military," *Cuban Briefing Papers Series*, 12, Washington DC: Georgetown University, October 1996, p. 3.
86 Bengelsdorff, *The Problem of Democracy in Cuba*, p. 143.
87 Phyllis Green Walker, "Challenges Facing the Cuban Military," *Cuban Briefing Papers Series*, 12, Washington DC: Georgetown University, October 1996, p. 4.
88 "Die Krise – Eine Bestandsaufnahme," in Hoffmann, *Wirtschaftsreformen in Kuba*, p. 19.
89 Quoted in ibid., p. 59.
90 *Süddeutsche Zeitung*, October 12–13, 1991, p. 7.
91 Bengelsdorff, *The Problem of Democracy in Cuba*, p. 138.
92 Fidel Castro, "Conversation with Federico Mayor Zaragoza," ex-director of the United Nations Educational, Scientific and Cultural Organization (UNESCO), January 24–28, 2000, Consejo de Estado. E-mail to the author.
93 *Süddeutsche Zeitung*, March 19, 1991.
94 Fidel Castro, "Conversation with Federico Mayor Zaragoza."
95 Eckstein, *Back from the Future*, p. 124.
96 Ibid., p. 96.
97 Ibid., p. 98.
98 Ibid., p. 110.
99 Ibid., p. 115.
100 *Süddeutsche Zeitung*, October 16, 1991.

Chapter 9   The Eternal Revolutionary

1 Eckstein, *Back from the Future*, p. 102.
2 Bengelsdorff, *The Problem of Democracy in Cuba*, p. 168.
3 Ibid., p. 169.

4 Eckstein, *Back from the Future*, p. 109.

5 Liss, *Fidel!*, p. 61.

6 Fidel Castro, "'Einige dieser Massnahmen sind uns zuwider' – Dokumentation der Rede zur Legalisierung des US-Dollars," in Hoffmann, *Wirtschaftsreformen in Kuba*, pp. 47ff.

7 Fidel Castro: "Conversation with Federico Mayor Zaragoza."

8 Carmelo Mesa-Lago, "Cuba's Raft Exodus of 1994: Causes, Settlement, Effects, and Future," *The North–South Agenda* (Miami), April 12, 1995, pp. 4ff.

9 *Neue Zürcher Zeitung*, June 23, 1998.

10 Jennifer Abbassi, "The Role of the 1990s Food Markets in the Decentralization of Cuban Agriculture," *Cuban Studies*, 27 (Pittsburgh, 1998), 32.

11 Volker Skierka, "Brave Zahler – Ein Deutscher entwickelte das kubanische Steuersystem," *Die Zeit*, January 22, 1998.

12 *Süddeutsche Zeitung*, July 17, 2000. The article gives the number of joint ventures as 370, and estimates total direct investment up to 1998 at $1.8 billion (citing the Institute for European Latin American Relations). The likelihood that this figure would reach at least $2 billion by the end of the millennium came from, among other things, the report in late 1999 that the Spanish Altadis group had bought into the Havanos S.A. tobacco company to the tune of some $500 million. The Cuban side, however, has not issued exact figures.

13 Fidel Castro, "Conversation with Federico Mayor Zaragoza."

14 Instituto de Relaciones Europeos-Latinoamericanas (IRELA), *Dossier 68: 40 años de revolución en Cuba: transición hacia donde?*, Madrid, 1999, p. 24.

15 *Financial Times*, March 24, 1999.

16 Institut für Iberoamerikakunde, *Lateinamerika Jahrbuch 1999*, Hamburg, 1999, p. 287.

17 *Financial Times*, March 24, 1999.

18 IRELA *Dossier*, 68 (see n. 14), 24.

19 *Granma International*, December 14, 1997, p. 6.

20 Ibid., p. 9.

21 César Chelala, "Provide a Health Boost for Cubans," *International Herald Tribune*, February 8, 2000.

22 Carlos Lage, in conversation with the author, in *Die Zeit*, July 22, 1999.

23 IRELA *Dossier*, 68 (see note 14), 23.

24 Carlos Lage, in conversation with the author, in *Die Zeit*, July 22, 1999.

25 *Süddeutsche Zeitung*, July 17, 2000.

26 Susanne Gratius, "Kuba 1999: Zwischen Repression und Agonie," *Brennpunkt Lateinamerikas*, 10 (May 28, 1999), 79.

27 IRELA *Dossier*, 68 (see note 14), 26.

28 *Süddeutsche Zeitung*, July 17, 2000.

29 Gratius, "Kuba 1999: Zwischen Repression und Agonie," *Brennpunkt Lateinamerikas*, 10 (May 28, 1999), 79.

30 *Die Zeit*, May 20, 1999.

31 Ibid.

32 *Financial Times*, March 24, 1999.

33 *Die Zeit*, July 22, 1999.

34 "Castro Healthy, Firmly In Power, CIA Chief Says," *Miami Herald*, December 6, 1997.

35 IRELA *Dossier*, 68 (see note 14), 10ff.

36 "Cuba after the V. Party Congress: An Irela Briefing," Instituto de Relaciones Europe–Latinoamericanas, BRF-97/8-CUB, November 5, 1997; IRELA *Dossier*, 68, 10ff.

37 Castro, "Conversation with Federico Mayor Zaragoza," op. cit.

38 Ibid.

39 Jorge I. Dominguez, "U.S.–Cuban Relations: From the Cold War to the Colder War," *Journal of Interamerican Studies & World Affairs*, 39(3) (Miami, 1997), 63.

40 *Granma International*, December 14, 1997, p. 12.

41 US Department of State International Information Programs (online), *Cuban Liberty and Democratic Solidarity (Libertad) Act of 1996*.

42 Bert Hoffmann, "Helms-Burton und kein Ende?," p. 41.

43 Ibid., p. 40.

44 John M. Kirk, *The Effectiveness of Helms-Burton, 1996–97: A Canadian Perspective*, Dalhouse University, Halifax, February 1997, p. 1.

45 Hoffmann, "Helms-Burton und kein Ende?," p. 41.

46 Robert L. Muse, *Is the Helms-Burton Act Legal as a Matter of International Law?*, Washington, 1997, p. 3.

47 Joaquin Roy, "The Helms-Burton Law: Development, Consequences, and Legacy for Inter-American and European–US Relations," *Journal of Interamerican Studies & World Affairs* (Miami), 39(5), 83.

48 "The People of Cuba vs. The Government of the United States of America for Human Damages. Demand submitted to the Civil and Administrative Court of Law at the Provincial People's Court in Havana," May 31, 1999.

49 "Stenografische Niederschrift der offiziellen Gespräche des DDR-Staats-und Parteichefs Erich Honecker mit Fidel Castro in Havanna, 28. Mai 1980," SAPMO-BArch, DY 30/2359, Bl. 55–6.

50 "The People of Cuba vs. The Government of the United States of America for Human Damages," op. cit., pp. 36ff.

51 "Expediente Civil No. 88/99. Sentencia Número Ciento Diez (110)," Havana, November 2, 1999, in *Condenado El Gobierno de Estados Unidos. Sentencia del Tribunal Provincial Popular de Ciudad de La Habana en el proceso por la Demanda del Pueblo de Cuba contra el gobierno de Estados Unidos por daños humanos*, Havana, 1999, pp. 88ff.

52 Fidel Castro, "Speech on the occasion of the 47th anniversary celebrations of the attack on the Moncada barracks on 26 July 1953, on the Plaza Provisional de la Revolución in Pinar del Río," Consejo del Estado, Havana, August 5, 2000.

53 Volker Skierka, "Karle und die Manager – Auf Umwegen zieht auf Kuba der Kapitalismus ein," *Die Zeit*, September 9, 1999; and Günther Roller, Commercial Director, MCV Cairo, in conversation with the author.

54 "Contribution by Cuban state and Party leader Fidel Castro to Round Table No. 3 at the United Nations summit of 7 September 2000 in New York," Consejo del Estado, Havana, e-mail to the author.

55 *Neue Zürcher Zeitung*, November 1, 2000.

56 "Cuban Beaches Lure Japanese," *International Herald Tribune*, September 5, 2000.

57 Central Intelligence Agency, *The World Factbook 2000*, http://www.odci.gov/cia/publications/factbook/index.html

58 Fidel Castro, Closing speech at the First International Congress on Culture and Development, June 11, 1999, Palacio de las Convenciones, Havana, recorded by the Stenographic Service of the Council of State. Consejo del Estado, Havana, June 1999, pp. 75 and 39.

59 Manuel Pastor Jr and Andrew Zimbalist, "Has Cuba Turned the Corner? Macroeconomic Stabilization and Reform in Contemporary Cuba," *Cuban Studies* (Pittsburgh), 27, 1998, p. 15.

60 Retranslated from "Bericht des Pentagons über Kubas Streitkräfte," *Neue Zürcher Zeitung*, May 9–10, 1998.

61 *Neue Zürcher Zeitung*, October 31, 2000.

62 Fidel Castro, "El saludo a Clinton," Consejo del Estado/Embajada de Cuba, *Info über Kuba/Millenniumsgipfel*, e-mail to the author, September 12, 2000.

63 Gabriel García Márquez, "Rescued at Sea, Elián Was Shipwrecked on Land," *International Herald Tribune*, March 30, 2000.
64 Conte Agüero, *Cartas del Presidio*, Havana, 1959, pp. 65ff.
65 Fidel Castro Díaz-Balart, *Energia Nuclear. Peligro ambiental o solución para el siglo XXI?*, Havana-Turin, 1997.
66 Associated Press/CBC News, *The Canadian Press*, Internet download.
67 "Congressman Visits Elian's Home," April 18, 2000: http://www.herald.com.
68 "Elián Needs His Father, Not a Labrador Puppy," *International Herald Tribune*, January 20, 2000.
69 Alejandro Álvaro Bremer, "El Embargo a Cuba: Un nudo gordiano," *Journal of Latin American Affairs* (Miami), 4(1), (Spring/Summer, 1996), 5.
70 Walter Haubrich, "Glaubt Fidel Castro an Gott? Seltsame Dinge geschehen dieser Tage im atheistischen Kuba," *Frankfurter Allgemeine Zeitung*, January 17, 1998.
71 Volker Skierka, "Die Versöhnung der heiligen Väter," *Die Zeit*, January 22, 1998.
72 Betto, pp. 139ff.
73 Ibid., p. 141.
74 Ibid., p. 271.
75 Ibid., pp. 271ff.
76 Ibid., pp. 124ff.
77 Ibid., p. 141.
78 Ibid., p. 123.
79 Ibid., p. 136.
80 Ibid., p. 140.
81 Ibid., pp. 137ff.
82 Ibid., p. 196.
83 Ibid., p. 169.
84 Ibid., p. 186.
85 Ibid., 181ff.
86 Margaret E. Crahan, "Fidel Castro, the Catholic Church and Revolution in Cuba," in Dermat Keogh, *Church and Politics in Latin America*, p. 268.
87 Ibid., p. 253.
88 Ibid., p. 259.
89 Betto, pp. 206ff.
90 Furiati, *ZR Rifle*, pp. 37, 43.

91 Crahan, "Fidel Castro, the Catholic Church and Revolution in Cuba," p. 268.
92 Ibid.
93 Ibid.
94 Betto, p. 194.
95 "Sufrida Iglesia aguarda al Papa," *El Nuevo Herald*, December 21, 1997.
96 Ibid.
97 Betto, pp. 210ff.
98 Ibid., p. 33.
99 Crahan, "Fidel Castro, the Catholic Church and Revolution in Cuba," p. 263.
100 Betto, p. 214.
101 Ibid.
102 Liss, *Fidel!*, p. 171.
103 "Fragmentos de documentos por los obispos cubanos durante las últimas cuatro décadas, en relación con la situación nacional," *El Nuevo Herald* (Miami), December 21, 1997.
104 Betto, pp. 265ff.
105 Obispos Católicos de Cuba, *Démonos fraternalmente la paz*, http://www.nacub.org., Havana, November 1, 1997.
106 Elaine De Valle, "Cubanos tuvieron Nochebuena," *El Nuevo Herald*, December 26, 1997.
107 "Visita papal será éxito," *El Nuevo Herald* (Miami), December 17, 1997.
108 "Mensaje del Papa Juan Pablo II al pueblo cubano ante la proximidad de su visita y con ocasión de la fiesta de Navidas," http://www.nacub.org., Vatican City, December 20, 1997.
109 Volker Skierka, "Die Versöhnung der heiligen Väter," *Die Zeit*, January 22, 1998.
110 "Discurso en la Ceremonía de Llegada al Aeropuerto Internacional José Martí," in http://www.nacub.org., *La iglesia católica de Cuba/Visita Santo Padre/Discursos y Homilías de Su Santidad Juan Pablo II*, Havana, January 21, 1998.
111 "Homilía pronunciada en la Celebración Eucarística en la Arquidiócesis de La Habana," in http://www.nacub.org., *La iglesia católica de Cuba/Visita Santo Padre/Discursos y Homilías de Su Santidad Juan Pablo II*, Havana, January 25, 1998; quoted in English from Reynaldo González, "A Pope in the Land of the *Orishas*," www.cubaupdate.org/art12.

112 "Homilía pronunciada en la Celebración Eucarística en la Arquidiócesis de La Habana," in http://www.nacub.org., *La iglesia católica de Cuba/Visita Santo Padre/Discursos y Homilías de Su Santidad Juan Pablo II*, Havana, January 25, 1998.

113 "Palabras en la Ceremonía de despedida," in http://www.nacub.org., *La iglesia católica de Cuba/Visita Santo Padre/Discursos y Homilías de Su Santidad Juan Pablo II*, Havana, January 25, 1998.

114 Volker Skierka, "Die Versöhnung der heilgen Väter," *Die Zeit*, January 22, 1998.

115 *Amnesty International Report 1999*, http://www.amnesty.org.

116 Amnesty International, *ai-Journal*, May 1998, http://www.amnesty.de.

117 "Kuba zwischen Reformieren und Verharren," *Neue Zürcher Zeitung*, June 23, 1998.

118 "One Small Chink in Cuba's Prison Doors," *The Economist*, February 21, 1998.

119 *Amnesty International Report 1999*, http://www.amnesty.org.

120 Jorge I. Domínguez, "Comienza una transición hacia el autoritarismo en Cuba?," *encuentro* 6/7 (Madrid, 1997), 12.

121 Karen DeYoung, "For Dissidents in Cuba, a Lonely Crusade," *International Herald Tribune*, July 18, 2000.

122 Leo Wieland, "Zaghafte Annäherungsversuche zwischen verhärteten Fronten: Castro und die Exilkubaner," *Frankfurter Allgemeine Zeitung*, July 8, 1995.

123 "Exile Leader Asks U.S. to Sever Ties with 'Anti-Castro Industry,'" *Miami Herald*, November 11, 1997.

124 Eloy Gutiérrez Menoyo, "Alter Feind, neue Hoffnung," *Die Zeit*, July 7, 1995.

125 Susanne Gratius, "'Fin de siglo' in Havanna – Kuba und das 9. Iberoamerikanische Gipfeltreffen," *Brennpunkt Lateinamerika*, 22 (Hamburg, 1999), 24.

126 Wolf Grabendorff, "Algunas transiciones hacia la democracia en América Latina: elementos comparativos y tímidas lecciones," *encuentro* 6/7 (Madrid, 1997), 63.

127 "Kuba zwischen Reformieren und Verharren," *Neue Zürcher Zeitung*, June 23, 1998.

128 Jorge I. Domínguez, "Comienza una transición hacia el autoritarismo en Cuba?," *encuentro* 6/7 (Madrid, 1997), 12.

129 Walter Haubrich, "Am Sozialismus wird nicht gerührt," *Frankfurter Allgemeine Zeitung*, May 4, 1996.

130 IRELA *Dossier*, 68 (see ch. 9, n. 14), 13.

131 Ibid., pp. 13ff.

132 Lola Galán, "El Papa reprende duramente a Castro por la falta de libertades," *El País*, December 3, 1999.

133 Borge, *Face to Face with Fidel Castro*, p. 129.

134 Ibid., pp. 130ff.

135 Ibid., pp. 133ff.

136 Ibid., pp. 64ff.

137 Ibid., pp. 65ff.

138 Ibid., p. 69.

139 Liss, *Fidel!*, p. 131.

140 *Amnesty International Report 2000*, http://www.amnesty.org.

141 Alfred Herzka, "Cuba's Prisons and Their Prisoners," *Neue Zürcher Zeitung* (*NZZ Online English Window*), October 11, 1999.

142 Juan Carlos I at the ninth Ibero–American Summit, author's tape-recording, Havana, November 15–16, 1999.

143 Walter Haubrich, "Don Quijote der Geschichte," *Frankfurter Allgemeine Zeitung*, January 29, 2000.

Chapter 10   Don Quixote and History

1 Gabriel García Márquez, *The General in His Labyrinth*, London: Penguin, 1991, p. 8.

2 Márquez, "A Personal Portrait of Fidel," in Fidel Castro, *My Early Years*, p. 21.

3 John F. Kennedy, *The Strategy of Peace*, p. 132.

4 See Peter Kornbluh (ed.), *Kennedy and Castro: The Secret Quest for Accommodation*, George Washington University/National Security Archive (NSA), Electronic Briefing Book No. 17, Washington, August 16, 1999, Digital National Security Archive: *The Cuban Missile Crisis*, http://38.202.78.21/introx.htm.

5 Márquez, "A Personal Portrait of Fidel," in Fidel Castro, *My Early Years*, p. 22.

6 "Conversation with Federico Mayor Zaragoza," p. 22 (see ch. 8, n. 92 above).

7 Szulc, *Fidel*, p. 149.

8 Pérez Jr, *Between Reform and Revolution*, p. 381.

9 Eric Williams, *From Columbus to Castro: The History of the Caribbean 1492–1969*, London, 1970, p. 486.

10 *El Mercurio* (Santiago de Chile), October 26, 1998.

11 Borge, *Face to Face with Fidel Castro*, pp. 170ff.

12 "Conversation with Federico Mayor Zaragoza," p. 22 (see ch. 8, n. 92 above).

13 Ibid.

14 Carlos Lage in conversation with the author, *Die Zeit*, July 22, 1999.

15 "Conversation with Federico Mayor Zaragoza," p. 4 (see ch. 8, n. 92 above).

16 Susanne Gratius, "Kuba 1999: Zwischen Repression und Agonie," *Brennpunkt Lateinamerikas* 10 (May 28, 1999), 77.

17 Ibid., pp. 77ff.

18 Domínguez, "Comienza una transición hacia el autoritarismo en Cuba?," *encuentro*, 6–7 (Madrid, 1997), 7ff.

19 Irving Louis Horowitz, "Castro and the End of Ideology," *North–South* (Miami), December 1993/January 1994, p. 8.

20 Geyer, *Guerrilla Prince*, pp. 77ff.

21 Borge, *Face to Face with Fidel Castro*, p. 178.

22 García Márquez, *The General in His Labyrinth*, p. 257.

Bibliography

1 Bibliographies, reference works, general literature on the history and contemporary reality of Cuba

Amnesty International Annual Report, London, 1990 – ongoing.

Brennpunkt Lateinamerika. Politik, Wirtschaft, Gesellschaft, Hamburg: Institut für Iberoamerika-Kunde.

Creutzmann, Sven, and Henky Hentschel, *Salsa einer Revolution. Eine Liebeserklärung an Cuba zum 40. Geburtstag*, Hamburg, 1999.

Cuba, la perla de las Antillas. Actas de las I Jornadas sobre "Cuba y su historia", (eds) Consuelo Naranjo Orovio and Tomás Mallo Gutiérrez, Madrid, 1994.

Herzka, Alfred, *Kuba. Abschied vom Kommandanten?* Frankfurt/Main, 1998.

Hoffmann, Bert, *Kuba*, Munich, 2000.

Humboldt, Alexander von, *Cuba-Werk*, ed. and commentary by Hanno Beck, Darmstadt, 1992.

Kuba, Merian, 11/2000, Hamburg, 2000.

Lateinamerika Jahrbuch, Frankfurt/Main: Institut für Iberoamerika-Kunde (Hamburg), 1992.

La economía cubana. Reformas estructurales y desempeño en los noventa, Mexico City: Comisión Económica para América Latina y el Caribe, 1997.

Las Casas, Bartolomé de, *The Devastation of the Indies: A Brief Account*, Baltimore, MD: Johns Hopkins University Press, 1992.

Manual de los partidos políticos de Américas Latina, Madrid: IRELA, 1997.

2 Fidel Castro

a) Works

Political, Economic and Social Thought of Fidel Castro, Havana, 1959.
Playa Girón: A Victory of the People, Havana, 1961.
Fanal Kuba. Reden und Schriften 1960–1962, with a preface by Blas Roca, Berlin, 1963.
La Historia me absolverá, Havana, 1967; *History Will Absolve Me: The Moncada Trial Defence Speech, Santiago de Cuba October 16th 1953,* London, 1968.
Revolutionary Struggle 1947–1958. Selected Works of Fidel Castro, Roland E. Bonachea and Nelson P. Valdés (eds), Cambridge, Mass., 1972.
Fidel en Chile. Textos completos de su diálogo con el pueblo, Santiago de Chile, 1972.
Informe del Comité Central del Partido Comunista Cubano al Primer Congreso, Havana, 1975.
La Revolución de Octubre y la Revolución Cubana, Havana, 1977.
El Pensamiento de Fidel Castro, 2 vols, Havana, 1983.
My Early Years, Melbourne/New York, 1998.

b) Speeches

Cuba's Internationalist Foreign Policy. Speeches 1975–1980, New York, 1981.
"Discurso sobre Ernesto Guevara (18 de octubre de 1967)," Santa Clara: *Islas* 10(1), 1968, 5–18.
En la trinchera de la revolución: selección de discursos 7 de diciembre de 1989 a 7 de marzo de 1990, Havana, 1990.
El pueblo gobierna: discursos y comparencia en televisión; 6, 11 y 20 de febrero, 1 y 15 de marzo de 1993, Havana, 1993.
Esta tiene que ser la guerra económica de todo el pueblo: discurso, Período Ordinario de Sesiones de la Asamblea Nacional del Poder Popular, 7, La Habana, 28/12/1984, Havana, 1985; *This Must Be an Economic War of all the People: Speech, December 28, 1984,* Havana, 1985.
Fidel en Brasil: selección de intervenciones 14 al 19 de marzo de 1990, Havana, 1990.
"Fidel habla del Che" (several contributions), *Bohemia* 62(41), 1970.

Bibliography

Fidel in Chile: A Symbolic Meeting between Two Historical Processes. Selected Speeches of Fidel Castro during His Visit to Chile, November 1971, New York, 1972.

In Defense of Socialism. Four Speeches on the 30th Anniversary of the Cuban Revolution, New York, 1989.

Kuba verteidigt entschlossen seine Revolution: Rede anlässlich des 30. Jahrestages des Sturms auf die Moncadakaserne, Berlin, 1983.

Nacimos para Vencer. Discurso en la clausura del VI congreso de la Federación de estudiantes de la Enseñanza Media, Havana, 1984; *We Are Born to Overcome, Not To Be Overrum!* [sic]: *Close of 6th Congress of the Federation of Students Intermediate Education (FEEM)*, Havana, 1984.

Nuestro poder es el del pueblo trabajador. Acto de Constitución de la Asamblea Nacional del Poder Popular de la República de Cuba, La Habana, 2.12.1976, Havana, 1976.

Palabras a los intelectuales, Havana, 1961.

Período Ordinario de Sesiones de la Asamblea Nacional del Poder Popular, 2, La Habana, 28/12/1977, Havana, 1978.

"Rede Fidel Castros beim Trauerakt zu Ehren der in Grenada gefallenen Kubaner" (extracts), in *Generalprobe Grenada: Augenzeugenberichte und Analysen*, Werner Heiner et al. (eds), Hamburg, 1984, pp. 169–77.

So arbeitet und kämpft Kuba: Rede zum 28. Jahrestag des Sturms auf die Moncada-Kaserne, Berlin, 1981; *28th An[n]iversary of the Attack on the Moncada Garrison: Las Tunas, 26th of July 1981: Speech*, Havana, 1981.

To Speak the Truth. Why Washington's "Cold War" against Cuba Doesn't End (with Che Guevara), New York, 1992.

Una batalla por nuestra dignidad y soberanía. Multitudinaria Concentración Conmemorativa por el Primero de Mayo, La Habana, 1.5.1980, Havana, 1980.

"Unsere Revolution kann sich weder verkaufen, noch sich ergeben," in *19. Bundesdelegiertenkonferenz 19.–21. November 1993: Reader, Teil 1.*, Freundschaftsgesellschaft BRD-Kuba, Köln, Cologne, 1993, pp. 1–12.

War & Crisis in the Americas. Speeches 1984–1985, New York, 1985.

3 Personal Testimony

Betto, Frei, *Fidel and Religion: Castro Talks on Revolution and Religion with Frei Betto*, New York, 1987.

Castro, Fidel, Interview with the US news channel CNN, broadcast on September 13, 1998.

413

Bibliography

Conte Agüero, Luis, *Cartas del Presidio*, Havana, 1959.

Díaz, Regino, "The Unpayable Debt: An Interview with Fidel Castro," in Susanne Jonas and Nancy Stein, eds, *Democracy in Latin America: Visions and Realities*, New York, 1990, pp. 117–43.

García Márquez, Gabriel, "A Personal Portrait of Fidel" (1987), in Fidel Castro, *My Early Years*, Melbourne/New York, 1998, pp. 13–25.

Interview für die mexikanische Zeitung Excelsior *am 21. März 1985*, Berlin, 1985.

López-Fresquet, Rufo, *My 14 Months with Fidel Castro*, New York, 1966.

"Materialien zur Revolution," in *Reden, Aufsätzen, Briefen von Fidel Castro, Che Guevara, Régis Debray*, Darmstadt, 1968.

Miná, Gianni, *Un encuentro con Fidel. Entrevista realizada por Gianni Miná*, Havana, 1987; *An Encounter with Fidel: An Interview*, Melbourne/New York, 1991.

4 On Fidel Castro

a) Monographs

Balfour, Sebastian, *Castro*, "Profiles in Power" series, London/New York, 1990.

Borge, Tomás, *Face to Face with Fidel Castro*, Melbourne, 1993.

Bourne, Peter G., *Castro: A Biography of Fidel Castro*, New York, 1986.

Casuso, Teresa, *Cuba und Castro*, Cologne, 1962.

Conte Agüero, Luis, *Fidel Castro: Vida y obra*, Havana, 1959.

Edwards, Jorge, *Persona Non Grata: An Envoy in Castro's Cuba*, London, 1977.

Escalona, Roberto Luque, *The Tiger and the Children: Fidel Castro and the Judgement of History*, New Brunswick, 1992.

Fernández, Alina, *Ich, Alina. Mein Leben als Fidel Castros Tochter*, Reinbek, 1998.

Franqui, Carlos, *The Twelve*, New York, 1968.

Franqui, Carlos, *Diary of the Cuban Revolution*, New York, 1984.

Franqui, Carlos, *Family Portrait with Fidel*, New York, 1994.

Geyer, Georgie Anne, *Guerrilla Prince: The Untold Story of Fidel Castro*, Boston, 1991.

Huhn, Klaus, *Compañero Castro: Auf Kubas steinigem Weg*, with a preface by Eberhard Panitz, Berlin, 1996.

Bibliography

Liss, Sheldon B., *Fidel! Castro's Political and Social Thought*, Latin American Perspectives series, Boulder, CO, 1994.

Lockwood, Lee, *Castro's Cuba, Cuba's Fidel. An American Journalist's Inside Look at Today's Cuba – in Text and Picture*, New York, 1969.

Lorenz, Marita, *Marita: One Woman's Extraordinary Tale of Love and Espionage from Castro to Kennedy* (with Ted Schwarz), New York, 1993.

Martin, Lionel, *The Early Fidel: Roots of Castro's Communism*, Secaucus, NJ, 1978.

Matthews, Herbert L., *Fidel Castro: A Political Biography*, London and New York, 1969.

Meneses, Enrique, *Fidel Castro*, London, 1968.

Oppenheimer, Andres, *Castro's Final Hour: The Secret Story behind the Coming Downfall of Communist Cuba*, New York, 1993.

Pardo Llada, José, *Fidel: de los jesuitas a la Moncada*, Bogota, 1976.

Quirk, Robert E., *Fidel Castro*, New York, 1993.

Szulc, Tad, *Fidel: A Critical Portrait*, New York, 1986.

Thomas, Hugh, *The Cuban Revolution*, New York, 1977.

Timerman, Jacobo, *Cuba: A Journey*, New York, 1990.

b) Articles

Castro, Juana, "Mi hermano Fidel es un tirano," *Life en español*, August 28, 1964.

Valdés, Nelson P., "Fidel Castro y la política estudiantil de 1947 a 1952," *Aportes* 22 (Paris, 1971), 23–40.

5 On Ernesto Che Guevara

a) Monographs

Anderson, Jon Lee, *Che: Che Guevara, a Revolutionary Life*, New York, 1997.

Castañeda, Jorge G., *Compañero. The Life and Death of Che Guevara*, New York, 1997.

Deutschmann, David (ed.), *Che en la memoria de Fidel Castro*, with a preface by Jesús Montané, Melbourne, 1998.

James, Daniel, *Che Guevara: A Biography*, New York, 1969.

May, Elmar, *Che Guevara*, Reinbek, 1978.

Schnibben, Cordt, *Ché und andere Helden*, Hamburg, 1997.

b) Articles

Tablada, Carlos, "The Creativity of Che's Economic Thought," in Centro de estudios sobre América (Havana), (ed.), *The Cuban Revolution into the 1990s: Cuban Perspectives*, Boulder, CO, 1992, pp. 87–102.
Weiss, Peter, "Che Guevara," *Anales de la Universidad de Chile* (Santiago de Chile), 126 (1968), pp. 5–11.

6 On the Cuban Revolution

a) Monographs and collections

Agüero, Conte, *Cartas del Presidio*, Havana, 1959.
Alarcón Ramirez, Dariel (Benigno), *Memorias de un soldado cubano. Vida y muerte de la Revolución*, Barcelona, 1997.
Batista y Zaldivar, Fulgencio, *Cuba Betrayed*, New York, 1962.
Debray, Régis, and Castro, Fidel [et al.], *Der lange Marsch. Wege der Revolution in Lateinamerika*, Munich, 1968.
Dirección Nacional del PURSC, Comisión de Orientación Revolucionaria (ed.), *Relatos del asalto al Moncada*, Havana, 1964.
Draper, Theodore, *Castroism: Theory and Practice*, New York, 1965.
Feltrinelli, Giangiacomo, ed., *Lateinamerika – Ein zweites Vietnam? Mit texten von Douglas Bravo, Fidel Castro, Régis Debray, Ernesto Che Guevara et al.*, Reinbek, 1968.
Guevara de la Serna, Ernesto, interview with Jorge Masetti, "Che en Guatemala," *Granma*, October 16, 1967.
Guevara, Ernesto Che, *Venceremos! Wir werden siegen*, Frankfurt/Main, 1968.
Guevara, Ernesto Che, *Guerrilla. Theorie und Methode. Sämtliche Schriften zur Guerrillamethode, zur revolutionären Strategie und zur Figur des Guerilleros*, ed. Horst Kurnitzky, Berlin, 1968.
Guevara, Ernesto Che, *Brandstiftung oder Neuer Friede? Reden und Aufsätze*, ed. and with a new afterword by Sven G. Papcke, Reinbek, 1969.
Guevara, Ernesto Che, *Ausgewählte Werke in Einzelausgaben*, ed. Horst-Eckart Gross, Bonn, 1992.
Guevara, Ernesto Che, *The Complete Bolivian Diaries of Che Guevara*, ed. and with an introduction by Daniel James, London, 1968.

Bibliography

Guevara, Ernesto Che, *Back on the Road*, London, 2001.

Guevara, Ernesto Che, and Raúl Castro, *Die Eroberung der Hoffnung. Tagebücher aus der kubanischen Guerilla Dezember 1956 bis Februar 1957*, Bad Honnef, 1997.

Leonard, Thomas M., *Castro and the Cuban Revolution*, Westport, 1999.

Martí, José, *Un drama terrible*, Havana, 1987.

Martí, José, *Diarios*, with a preface by Guillermo Cabrera Infante, Barcelona, 1997.

Martí, José, *Reader: Writings on the Americas*, Melbourne, 1999.

Matthews, Herbert L., *Revolution in Cuba*, New York, 1975.

Núñez Jiménez, Antonio, *En marcha con Fidel*, Havana, 1998.

Oficina de Publicaciones del Consejo de Estado, *La Epoya del Granma*, Havana, 1986.

Paterson, Thomas G., *Contesting Castro: The United States and the Triumph of the Cuban Revolution*, Oxford, 1994.

Selser, Gregorio, *La Revolución Cubana*, Buenos Aires, 1966.

The Second Declaration of Havana. With the First Declaration of Havana, New York, 1994.

b) Articles

Becali, Ramón, "Las Cartas de Camilo [Cienfuegos]," *Bohemia* (Havana) 62(44), 1970.

Cárdenas, Roberto de, "La Muerte de Camilo Cienfuegos," *Reconstruir. Revista libertaria* (Buenos Aires) 15, 1961, 19–27.

Debray, Régis, "Revolución en la revolución?," *Cuadernos de la revista Casa de las Américas* (Havana) 1, 1967; *Revolution in the Revolution?* New York, 1967.

Guevara, Ernesto, "Camilo Cienfuegos," *Vida universitaria* (Havana). 19(213), 1968, 45–7.

7 On the Political Situation

a) Monographs and collections

Alleman, Fritz René, *Die Revolution der Bärte*, Hamburg, 1961.

Ayers, Bradley Earl, *The War That Never Was: An Insider's Account of CIA Operations against Cuba*, Indianapolis, 1976.

Bibliography

Bender, Lynn Darrell, *The Politics of Hostility: Castro's Revolution and United States Policy*, Hato Rey, 1975.

Bengelsdorff, Carollee, *The Problem of Democracy in Cuba: Between Vision and Reality*, Oxford, 1994.

Benjamin, Jules R., *The United States and the Origins of the Cuban Revolution*, Princeton, 1990.

Bonsal, Philip W., *Cuba, Castro and the United States*, Pittsburgh, 1971.

Bunck, Julie Marie, *Fidel Castro and the Quest for a Revolutionary Culture in Cuba*, University Park, Pennsylvania, 1994.

Burckhardt, Hans-Jürgen, *Kuba: Der lange Abschied von einem Mythos*, Stuttgart, 1996.

Case 1/1989. End of the Cuban Connection [official summary and account of the Ochoa case], Havana, 1989.

Centro de Estudios sobre América (ed.), *The Cuban Revolution into the 1990s: Cuban Perspectives*, Latin American Perspectives, 10, Boulder, CO, 1992.

Crooks, Robert, "Fidel Castro und die revolutionäre Tradition Cubas. Studien zur revolutionären Tradition Cubas, 1868–1959," dissertation, Munich, 1972.

Cuba Despierta. Seminario "Cuba y la Unión Europea," ed. Manuel Soriano, Madrid, 1996.

Cuban American National Foundation, *Castro's "Special Period in a Time of Peace": Proceedings from a Conference Sponsored by the Cuban American National Foundation*, Washington, DC, 1991.

Domínguez, Jorge, *Cuba: Order and Revolution*, Cambridge, 1978.

Eckstein, Susan Eva, *Back from the Future: Cuba under Castro*, Princeton, 1994.

Fermoselle, Rafael, *Cuban Leadership after Castro: Biographies of Cuba's Top Commanders*, 2nd edn, Coral Gables, 1992.

Franklin, Jane, *Cuba and the United States – A Chronological History*, Melbourne/New York, 1997.

Friedl Zapata, José-Antonio (ed.), *Geschichten aus der Geschichte Kubas*, Frankfurt/Main, 1990.

García, María Cristina, *Havana USA: Cuban Exiles and Cuban Americans in South Florida, 1959–1994*, Berkeley, 1996.

Halebsky, Sandor et al., *Cuba in Transition: Crisis and Transformation. Conference "Thirty Years of the Cuban Revolution: An Assessment", Halifax, November 1989*, Latin American Perspectives, 9, Boulder, CO, 1992.

Hoffmann, Bert (ed.), *Wirtschaftsreformen in Kuba: Konturen einer Debatte*, 2nd enlarged edn (No. 38 of a series published by the Institut für Iberoamerika-Kunde, Hamburg), Frankfurt/Main, 1996.

Bibliography

Horowitz, Irving Louis, *The Conscience of Worms and the Cowardice of Lions: Cuban Politics and Culture in an American Context*, Coral Gables: University of Miami (North-South Center), 1993.

Instituto Cubano de Geodesía y Cartografía, *Atlas de Cuba: XX aniversario del triunfo de la revolución cubana*, Havana, 1978.

Instituto Cubano del Libro (ed.), *El más alto ejemplo de heroísmo. Acto Conmemorativo del XIII Aniversario de la creación de los Comités de Defensa de la Revolución, La Habana, 28.9.1973*, Havana, 1973.

Jorge, Antonio, *A Reconstruction Strategy for Post-Castro Cuba: A Preliminary Outline of the Strategies for Reconstruction and Development in the Process of Decollectivization and Desocialization*, Coral Gables: Research Institute for Cuba, 1991.

Kissinger, Henry A., *The White House Years*, London, 1979.

Kuba: Materialien zur Landeskunde, ed. and commentary by Martin Franzbach, 2nd enlarged edn, Frankfurt/Main, 1988.

Leiner, Marvin, *Sexual Politics in Cuba: Machismo, Homosexuality, and AIDS* (series: Political Economy and Economic Development in Latin America), Boulder, CO, 1994.

Mesa-Lago, Carmelo, ed., *Cuba after the Cold War. Conference "Cuba in the Post Cold War Era", Pittsburgh, April 1992* (Pitt Latin American series), Pittsburgh, 1993.

Moore, Carlos, *Castro, the Blacks, and Africa*, 3rd edn, Los Angeles: Center for Afro-American Studies, University of California, 1991.

Naranjo Orovio, Consuelo, and Gutiérrez Tomás Mallo (eds), *Cuba: la perla de las Antillas. Actas de la I Jornadas sobre "Cuba y su Historia,"* Madrid, 1994.

Pavlov, Yuri, *Soviet–Cuban Alliance 1959–1991*, Miami, 1994.

Pérez Jr, Louis A., *Cuba and the United States: Ties of Singular Intimacy*, 2nd edn, Athens, Georgia, 1997.

Pérez Jr, Louis A., *Cuba between Reform and Revolution*, Oxford, 1988.

Pérez Jr, Louis A., *Cuba under the Platt Amendment, 1902–1934* (Pitt Latin American series), Pittsburgh, 1991.

Pérez López, Jorge F., *The Economics of Cuban Sugar* (Pitt Latin American series), Pittsburgh, 1991.

Pérez López, Jorge F., *Cuba's Second Economy: From Behind the Scenes to Center Stage*, New Brunswick, 1995.

Ratliff, William E., *The Selling of Fidel Castro. The Media and the Cuban Revolution*, New Brunswick, 1987.

Simons, Geoffrey Leslie, *Cuba: From Conquistador to Castro*, New York, 1996.

Smith, Wayne S., *The Closest of Enemies – A Personal and Diplomatic History of the Castro Years*, New York/London, 1987.

419

Smith, Wayne S. (ed.), *The Russians Aren't Coming: New Soviet Policy in Latin America*, Boulder, CO, 1992.

US Congress, *Cuban Liberty and Democratic Solidarity (LIBERTAD) Act of 1996* (the "Helms-Burton Act" tightening US sanctions against Cuba), Washington, DC, 1996.

Vollmann, Anna, and Zahn, Werner, *Kuba. Vom "Modell" zurück zum "Hinterhof"?* (Beiträge zur politischen Bildung, 28), Heilbronn, 1996.

Williams, Eric, *From Columbus to Castro: The History of the Caribbean 1492–1969*, London, 1970.

b) Articles

Chaffee Jr, Wilber Albert, "Poder Popular and the Buro Político: Political Control in Cuba," in Wilber Albert Chaffee Jr and Gary Prevost (eds), *Cuba: A Different America*, Lanham, 1992, pp. 19–35.

Crahan, Margaret E., "Fidel Castro, the Catholic Church and Revolution in Cuba," in Dermot Keogh (ed.), *Church and Politics in Latin America*, New York, 1990, pp. 253–71.

Domínguez, Jorge I., "The Cuban Armed Forces, the Party and Society in Wartime and during Rectification (1986–88)," in Richard Gillespie (ed.), *Cuba after Thirty Years: Rectification and the Revolution*, London, 1990, pp. 45–62.

Domínguez, Jorge I., "Cooperating with the Enemy? U.S. Immigration Policies toward Cuba," in Christopher Mitchell (ed.), *Western Hemisphere Immigration and United States Foreign Policy*, Pennsylvania: University Park, 1992, pp. 31–88.

Domínguez, Jorge I., "U.S. Policy toward Cuba in the 1980s and 1990s," in Anthony P. Maingot (ed.), *Trends in U.S.–Caribbean Relations*, Thousand Oaks, Philadelphia: American Academy of Political and Social Science, 1994, pp. 165–76.

Domínguez, Jorge I., "Cuba in a New World," in Abraham F. Lowenthal and Gregory F. Treverton (eds), *Latin America in a New World*, Boulder, CO, 1994, pp. 203–16.

Grabendorff, Wolf, "El perfil de las relaciones entre la Unión Europea y Cuba. Taller de trabajo 'Cuba en los Años 90: Su Reinserción en la Economía Internacional y el Papel de Europa,' La Habana 6–9.12.1993," in Instituto de Relaciones Europeo-Latinoamericanas (IRELA), *Cuba: Apertura económica y relaciones con Europa*, Madrid, 1994, pp. 175–205.

Bibliography

Hennessy, Alistair, "The Cuban Revolution: A Wider View," in Richard Gillespie (ed.), *Cuba after Thirty Years: Rectification and the Revolution*, London, 1990, pp. 3–16.

Hoffmann, Bert, "Kuba: von der Schwierigkeit, das Trojanische Pferd zu füttern, ohne von ihm gefressen zu werden," in Dietmar Dirmoser et al. (eds), *Markt in den Köpfen*, Bad Honnef, 1993, pp. 217–27.

Hoffmann, Bert, "Helms-Burton und kein Ende? Auswirkungen und Perspektiven für Kuba, die USA und Europa," in *Lateinamerika. Analysen, Daten, Dokumentation*, 33, Hamburg, 1997.

Machín, Ana Núñez et al., "Angel Santana Suárez: Cuban Sugar Worker," in Judith Ewell and William Beezley (eds), *The Human Tradition in Latin America: The Twentieth Century*, Wilmington, 1994, pp. 75–88.

Martín, Juan Luis, "Youth and the Cuban Revolution," in Centro de Estudios sobre América (Havana) (ed.), *The Cuban Revolution into the 1990s: Cuban Perspectives*, Boulder, CO, 1992, pp. 141–6.

Millett, Richard L., "From Triumph to Survival: Cuba's Armed Forces in an Era of Transition," in Richard L. Millett et al., *Beyond Praetorianism*, Miami, 1996, pp. 133–56.

Rodríguez, Ernesto, "La migración hacia los Estados Unidos," in Centro de Estudios sobre América (ed.), *Cuba en las Américas: una perspectiva sobre Cuba y los problemas hemisféricos*, Havana, 1995, pp. 58–66.

Rosenberg, J. C., "Health Care and Medicine in Cuba," in Wilber Albert Chaffee Jr and Gary Prevost (eds), *Cuba: A Different America*, Lanham, 1992, pp. 116–28.

Salwen, Michael B., "The Dark Side of Cuban Journalism: Press Freedom and Corruption before Castro," in Richard R. Cole (ed.), *Communication in Latin America: Journalism, Mass Media, and Society*, Wilmington, 1996, pp. 139–54.

Shearman, Peter, "Gorbachev and the Restructuring of Soviet–Cuban Relations," in Richard Gillespie (ed.), *Cuba after Thirty Years: Rectification and the Revolution*, London, 1990, pp. 63–83.

Stahl, Karin, "Politische Institutionalisierung und Partizipation im postrevolutionären Kuba," in Harald Barrios et al. (eds), *Politische Repräsentation und Partizipation in der Karibik*, Opladen, 1996, pp. 71–97.

Suter, Jan, "Politische Partizipation und Repräsentation in Kuba, 1902–1958," in Harald Barrios et al. (eds), *Politische Repräsentation und Partizipation in der Karibik*, Opladen, 1996, pp. 11–70.

Walker III, O. William (ed.), "Castro's Cuba and Illicit Drug Traffic, 1959," in *Drugs in the Western Hemisphere*, Wilmington, 1996, pp. 170–2.

8 On the Bay of Pigs Invasion

Bissell Jr, Richard M., *Reflexions of a Cold Warrior* (with Jonathan E. Lewis and Frances T. Pudlo), New Haven, 1996.

Blight, James G., and Kornbluh Peter (eds), *The Politics of Illusion: The Bay of Pigs Invasion Reexamined*, Boulder, CO, 1998.

Elliston, Jon, *Psy War on Cuba. The Declassified History of U.S. Anti-Castro Propaganda*, Melbourne, 1999.

Enzensberger, Hans Magnus, *Das Verhör von Havanna*, Frankfurt/Main, 1970.

Kornbluh, Peter (ed.), *Bay of Pigs Declassified – The Secret CIA Report on the Invasion of Cuba*, New York, 1998.

Lynch, Gayston L., *Decision for Disaster. Betrayal at the Bay of Pigs*, Dulles, 1998.

9 On the 1962 Missile Crisis, Castro and John F. Kennedy

Buckley Jr, William F., *Mongoose R.I.P.*, Nashville, 1987.

Chang, Laurence, and Kornbluh Peter (eds), *The Cuban Missile Crisis. A National Security Archive Documents Reader*, New York, 1998.

Foreign Broadcast Information Service, "Transcript of Fidel Castro's Remarks at the Havana Conference on the Cuban Missile Crisis, January 11, 1992," in Laurence Chang and Kornbluh Peter (eds), *The Cuban Missile Crisis. A National Security Archive Documents Reader*, New York, 1998.

CIA Targets Fidel. The Secret Assassination Report, Melbourne, 1996.

Con la razón histórica y la moral de baragua. 1962 Crisis de Octubre (correspondence between Fidel Castro and Nikita Khrushchev during the missile crisis), Havana, 1990.

Furiati, Claudia, *ZR Rifle – The Plot to Kill Kennedy and Castro. Cuba Opens Secret Files*, Melbourne, 1994.

Bibliography

Fursenko, Aleksandr, and Naftali, Timothy, *One Hell of a Gamble. The Secret History of the Cuban Missile Crisis. Khrushchev, Castro, and Kennedy, 1958–1964*, New York/London, 1997.

Garthoff, Raymond L., *Reflections on the Cuban Missile Crisis*, revsd edn, Washington DC: Brookings Institution, 1989.

Hawkins, Col. Jack, "Secret Memorandum for the Record: Actions against the Castro Government, 5 May 1961," Washington DC: National Security Archive, George Washington University.

Hersh, Seymour M., *The Dark Side of Camelot*, New York, 1997.

Hilsman, Roger, "The Cuba Crisis: How Close We Were to War," *Look*, August 25, 1964.

Hinckle, Warren, and Turner, William, *Deadly Secrets. The CIA-Mafia War against Castro and the Assassination of J.F.K.*, New York, 1993.

Kennedy, John F., *The Strategy of Peace*, New York, 1960.

Kennedy, Robert, *Thirteen Days. A Memoir of the Cuban Missile Crisis*, with introductions by Robert S. McNamara and Harold Macmillan, New York, 1969.

Khrushchev, Nikita, *Khruschev Remembers*, Boston, 1970.

McNamara, Robert, "Foreword," in Laurence Chang and Peter Kornbluh (eds), *The Cuban Missile Crisis. A National Security Archive Documents Reader*, New York, 1998.

May, Ernest R., and Zelikow, Philip D. (eds), *The Kennedy Tapes: Inside the White House during the Cuban Missile Crisis*, Cambridge/London, 1997.

Oglesby, Carol, "The Conspiracy That Won't Go Away," *Playboy Magazine*, February 1992.

Pavlov, Yuri I., *Soviet–Cuban Alliance, 1959–1991*, 2nd revsd edn, Coral Gables, 1996.

Posener, Alan, *John F. Kennedy*, Reinbek, 1991.

Schlesinger Jr, Arthur M., *A Thousand Days: John F. Kennedy in the White House*, Boston, 1965.

Steel, Ronald, *In Love with Night. The American Romance with Robert Kennedy*, New York, 2000.

The Warren Commission Report. Report of the President's Commission on the Assassination of President John F. Kennedy, New York/Washington, 1964.

White, Mark J., *Missiles in Cuba: Kennedy, Khrushchev, Castro and the 1962 Crisis*, Chicago, 1997.

10 CD-Roms

Todo de Cuba/All about Cuba (official information about the country), Havana, 1997.
Che. Hasta la victoria – siempre. Edición Multimedia del Diario del Che en Bolivia, Havana, 1997.

11 Internet

http://www.cubaweb.cu	Official homepage of the Republic of Cuba
http://www.cinecubano.cu/	Homepage of the Cuban film institute, ICAIC
http://www.cult.cu/casa/	Homepage of Casa de las Americas
http://www.granma.cubaweb.cu	Homepage of *Granma*, central organ of the Central Committee of the Communist Party of Cuba
http://afrocubaweb.com/acoutacw.htm	
	Website on Afro-Cuban culture
http://www.nacub.org/	Homepage of Cuba's Catholic Church
http://www.amnesty.org/	Amnesty International
http://www.cubanet.org/	Reports by dissident journalists and international agencies
http://www.herald.com/	Homepage of the *Miami Herald*
http://cubainfo.de/	Cuban Tourist Office, Frankfurt
http://www.lanic.utexas.edu/la/cb/cuba	
	Current web link for the Latin America Information Center of the University of Texas
http://www.state.gov/www/regions/wha/cuba/index.html	
	Cuba page of the US State Department
http://www.odci.gov/cia/publications/factbook/geos/cu.html	
	World factbook of the Central Intelligence Agency, Cuba section

http://www.latinworld.com/caribe/index.html
                                      Latin America search engine for Caribbean

http://www.carilat.de   German-based information and news about the Caribbean and Latin America

http://www.rrz.uni-hamburg.de/IIK/
                                        Institut für Iberoamerika-Kunde, Hamburg

http://www.fu-berlin.de/lai/   Latin America Institute of the Free University, Berlin

http://www.irela.org/es/index.asp Instituto de Relaciones Europeos Latinoamericanas

12 Author's website and e-mail address

http://www.skierka.de
castro@skierka.de

Index

Note: FC denotes Fidel Castro

Index

Index

Index

Index

Index

Index

Index

437

Index

Index